Multicultural Students with Special Language Needs

Practical Strategies for Assessment and Intervention

Second Edition

Celeste Roseberry-McKibbin, Ph.D., C.C.C.
Department of Speech Pathology
California State University, Sacramento

with a contribution by Lisa Domyancic, M.S.

Academic Communication Associates, Inc.

P. O. Box 4279
Oceanside, CA 92052-4279

Dedication

To Mike
for always being there

About the Author

Dr. Celeste Roseberry-McKibbin is currently an Associate Professor in the Department of Speech Pathology at California State University, Sacramento. In addition to teaching at the university level, she continues to work on a part-time basis as a speech-language pathologist in the schools.

Dr. Roseberry-McKibbin lived in the Philippines for much of her childhood and came to live in the United States permanently at 17 years of age. She has lectured and given workshops nationwide on issues relating to multicultural assessment and intervention. Her previous publications include textbooks, assessment instruments, and professional journal articles.

Academic Communication Associates, Inc.

P.O Box 4279
Oceanside, CA 92052-4279
WEB: http://www.acadcom.com
E-Mail: acom@acadcom.com
Telephone Order Line: (888) 758-9558
Fax: (760) 722-1625
Printed in the United States of America
International Standard Book Number: 978-1-57503-091-3

ACKNOWLEDGEMENTS

There are so many people to thank any time a book is published. A book is truly a community effort. I want to acknowledge Dr. Larry Mattes and the staff at Academic Communication Associates, for all their help in making this second edition possible. I could never complete a project like this without the love and support of my husband, Mike McKibbin—Honey, thanks for shoving food under the study door during the many long days I spent working on this book. My precious son Mark is always an inspiration to do my best to serve those who read my work; he continuously reminds me of what is truly important in life.

My students at California State University, Sacramento, were instrumental in helping me revise and improve chapters in the second edition of this book. I am grateful for their insight, humor, and specific suggestions. Phyllis Carlburg spent many hours editing; Phyllis, thank you for squeezing this job into your already full schedule! I also want to thank other CSUS students for spending time helping with edits on this second edition: Stephanie Baum, Denise Dove, Shelley Dunn, Laura Enos, Kelly Gorman, Dorrita Hansen, Jenny Noma, Aaron Reese, Kara Schweitz, and Brodi Wetherbee. Thanks, you guys. I'll never forget Dollars and Doughnuts!

Mostly, I acknowledge and thank from the bottom of my heart the families and children who have taught me so much over the years. It is a privilege to be a part of their lives. As I tell my university students, I will always be a student myself; I never stop learning new things that make me a more humble, knowledgeable, and, I hope, better professional and human being.

PREFACE

Many challenges are faced by educational professionals in their efforts to provide appropriate instructional programs for linguistically and culturally diverse (LCD) students. Many of these students find themselves in vulnerable situations when they enter our schools, especially if classroom instruction is provided in a language that they do not speak. These students are likely to become frustrated easily when they do not understand what is expected of them. They may also have difficulty following the "social rules" of the classroom.

When these students do not perform as expected in the classroom, they are often referred to speech-language pathologists and other special education personnel for testing. Sometimes the problems observed result from disabilities that affect the student's functioning in the classroom setting. Students, however, may also experience failure because the classroom instruction is culturally and/or linguistically inappropriate for their needs. Schools need to provide culturally and linguistically appropriate programs to promote academic development, language development, and, ultimately, empowerment.

This book is written to help school professionals develop a better understanding of linguistically and culturally diverse students so that they can work effectively with children who have special learning needs. The book is based on research from a number of disciplines, including anthropology, linguistics, second language acquisition, health care, sociology, communicative disorders, bilingual/multicultural education, and special education. The goal is to provide a multidisciplinary, well-rounded, and comprehensive view of LCD students.

A special challenge faced by educators in the schools is the appropriate, accurate identification of linguistically and culturally diverse students with special education needs. When an LCD student struggles academically, there are many questions that need to be considered.

❑ Is the student a "typical" second language learner who is struggling because of limited proficiency in the language of instruction?

❑ What linguistic and/or sociocultural variables are playing a role in the student's performance?

❑ Is the student's performance in the first language similar to that observed among other students who have had similar cultural and linguistic experiences?

❑ Does the student have a disability that affects his/her ability to acquire language skills?

❑ What service delivery model is most appropriate for the needs of the student?

These questions are of great importance, for they determine the focus of assessment and, ultimately, the direction of the services provided to the student.

A major issue of concern for special education professionals is that research relating specifically to multicultural students with special learning needs is limited. Strategies for meeting the needs of multicultural student populations are evolving as educational professionals learn more about other cultures and their languages. What is needed is a cohesive, empirically and theoretically sound body of research on which to base practice. Much can also be learned by interacting with professionals who have had extensive experience working with students from diverse cultural and linguistic backgrounds. When reading this book, it is important to remember that there are no easy solutions to many of the problems that confront special education professionals when they work with linguistically and culturally diverse populations.

Many educators in both regular and special education programs have had little or no training relating specifically to issues in the education of linguistically and culturally diverse students in the schools (Rosa-Lugo & Fradd, 2000; Roseberry-McKibbin & Eicholtz, 1994). There is a great dearth of bilingual, bicultural professionals who are competent to work with the heterogeneous populations in U.S. schools.

Since the first edition of this book was published, many changes have occurred in our schools. The use of bilingual speech-language pathology assistants, for example, has made it possible for a greater number of students to receive services. The increased availability of collaborative service delivery programs is also making it possible to meet the needs of a greater number of students. Issues relating to the education of children from multicultural backgrounds have become the focus of many workshops and training programs throughout the country.

Although changes are occurring, it is clear that much needs to be done if schools are to meet the needs of the growing number of LCD students. The second edition of *Multicultural Students with Special Language Needs* includes a discussion of current practices in serving special needs students who come from diverse cultural and linguistic backgrounds. It is my hope that this book will provide speech-language pathologists, special education specialists, and other educational professionals with strategies that they can use to develop high-quality, culturally relevant programs for linguistically and culturally diverse students who are experiencing various types of learning difficulties.

TABLE OF CONTENTS

INTRODUCTION

The world is changing rapidly and these changes are having a profound effect on how we think, behave, and interact with others. Our schools have become increasingly "multicultural" and educational professionals often have difficulty adapting to the increasing cultural and linguistic diversity that exists within their classrooms.

In addition to adapting instructional programs to meet the needs of linguistically and culturally diverse (LCD) students, our schools must teach students to appreciate cultural differences so that they can interact effectively with others who have different customs, values, and beliefs. Although progress is being made, cultural "misunderstandings" often lead to conflicts in our schools and communities.

Unfortunately, negative attitudes toward people who are "different" continue to exist in our country and throughout the world. As our economy becomes more global, it is critical that individuals from diverse cultural backgrounds learn to understand and respect one another. The terrorist attacks that took place on September 11, 2001 in the United States shocked millions of Americans and caused many to ask, "How can Americans be perceived so differently from the way we perceive ourselves?"

Within our own country, differences in how situations are perceived and interpreted have a profound effect on behavior in the classroom and in our communities. It is important for school professionals to develop the cultural competencies necessary to provide appropriate instructional programs for LCD students and to facilitate the development of positive social relationships within the learning environment (Roseberry-McKibbin, 2002).

Providing culturally and linguistically appropriate programs for LCD students becomes most difficult if the child has a disability that affects learning. The materials that are available for special education students who speak a language other than English are limited. Moreover, there are few special education professionals who are able to speak a second language fluently. What should a school do if a child who speaks only Vietnamese needs special education services? How does one determine if a child's learning problems can be attributed to limited proficiency in English or to a "disorder" that is affecting his or her ability to acquire language skills? These are important questions that do not have easy answers.

The demand for special education services designed to meet the needs of students from diverse cultural and linguistic backgrounds has been increasing every year. The U.S. Bureau of the Census (2000) reported that racial and ethnic minorities accounted for up to 80% of the nation's population growth in the 1990s. In the year 2000, there were nearly 87 million persons from minority backgrounds living in the U.S., up 43% from 1990 (in the 1980s, the growth rate was 33%). Over the past 20 years, the population of individuals in the U.S. from racial minorities grew by over 90%, while the non-Hispanic White population grew by 7.6%. Population growth among specific segments of the U.S. population during the 1990s was as follows:

1. The Hispanic population increased by 58%.
2. The Asian population increased by 48%.
3. The Native American and Alaska Native[1] population increased by 26%.
4. The African American Population increased by 16%.
5. The Pacific Islander and Alaska Native population increased by 9%.

[1]The "Alaska Native" category is often reported in combination with both the "Native American" and Pacific Islander categories.

Demographers believe that by the year 2020, one out of every three persons in the United States will be from what is now referred to as a "minority" group (Sobol, 1990). The National Center for Education Statistics (1997) predicted that by the year 2010, there will be an increase of 50% or more in the numbers of Asian, Hispanic, Pacific Islander, American Indian, and Alaskan Native students attending public schools. During this same period of time, the White, monolingual-English speaking population is expected to decrease by more than 10%.

Although experts acknowledge the great potential resource that multilingual, multicultural students present to United States society, these students have often become academic underachievers with consequent limited vocational and economic opportunities (Garcia, 1992). Sobol (1990) stated:

> We are not always dealing well with this diversity. In our schools, the rate of failure is higher among people of color than among whites. In our economy, we are developing a seemingly permanent underclass, skewed by race... A society dedicated to liberty and justice for all its people cannot deny justice to some without betraying its ideals. Nor can our economy thrive with a permanently alienated underclass: we must help all young people to acquire the skills and knowledge they need to function effectively in the workplace. (p. 28)

When professionals take a look at the "big picture," it is clear that culturally and linguistically fair, appropriate, and success-promoting materials, pedagogy, and placement options are needed for linguistically and culturally diverse students. A major barrier to achieving this goal is that many professionals who work with these students lack the appropriate academic and experiential preparation (Rosa-Lugo & Fradd, 2000). Although college and university courses are beginning to include subject matter relevant to serving these students, many practicing professionals have had no such training. In a national survey of 1,145 speech-language pathologists, Roseberry-McKibbin & Eicholtz (1994) found that 90% of them did not speak a second language fluently enough to provide services in that language; 76% of them had no coursework addressing the needs of multicultural children. It was also shown in one study that more than 85% of classroom teachers believed that they were not prepared to assess or instruct students who were learning English as a second language (National Center for Education Statistics, 1999). Universities and school districts must place a greater emphasis on educating professionals to meet the needs of these students.

A second major barrier to the provision of appropriate services is the limited availability of bilingual-bicultural professionals in the schools. In Los Angeles county, for example, over 90 different languages are spoken by school children. Other regions of the United States are experiencing a great influx of students from many language backgrounds. Often, there are no professionals who are of the same ethnic-linguistic background as these students. As one of its focused initiatives, the American Speech-Language-Hearing Association (see ASHA, 2001) is working to increase the numbers of racial/ethnic minority members of ASHA as well as giving all ASHA members access to resources developed to facilitate the acquisition of cultural competency. It is hoped that these efforts will increase and improve service delivery to members of multicultural populations.

A third barrier to the provision of appropriate services is the limited availability of the empirical research necessary to develop appropriate assessment and treatment services. There is much research in the fields of second language acquisition and bilingualism, but this research generally focuses on individuals who do not have disabilities. In the fields of speech-language pathology and special education, there are few empirical studies that provide scientifically sound information on which to base nonbiased assessment and treatment practices.

A fourth barrier to the provision of appropriate services is the time frame typically allotted for assessments. Many practitioners have found that the assessment of linguistically and culturally diverse students takes much longer than the assessment of monolingual, English-speaking students. Langdon (1992) estimated that assessment of a monolingual child, on the average, takes 3.5 hours. Assessment of a bilingual child, however, takes approximately six hours. In the author's experience, assessment may take longer than six hours, especially when the child has a complex case history.

The fifth barrier to provision of appropriate services is the limited availability of appropriate materials (Roseberry-McKibbin, 2001). Although there is a plethora of materials for working with ESL children, there are few published materials for special education professionals to use when assessing and treating culturally and linguistically diverse children. The lack of appropriate assessment materials and methods is particularly acute (Goldstein, 2000; Wyatt, 2002).

All of these barriers operate together and, thus, make it challenging for professionals to provide appropriate services for linguistically and culturally diverse students. This book was written with these issues in mind. Each section begins with an explanatory narrative of the topics to be covered. The goal of each narrative is to provide a theoretical context and rationale for the practical suggestions that follow. Readers will find many references for further reading and more in-depth study of the topics covered. Practical "tips" and suggestions for working with linguistically and culturally diverse children are included.

The second edition of this book differs in numerous respects from the first edition. The research has been updated and new material has been added to make the information relevant to the changes that are occurring within school programs. Since the first edition of this book was published, many schools have become actively involved in helping teachers develop the cultural competence that they need to work with students who come from diverse cultural and linguistic backgrounds. Among the other changes contained in the second edition are the following:

1. Internet resources are included for readers who wish to learn more about certain topic areas by accessing the world wide web.

2. A chapter relating to the language and culture of immigrants and refugees from the former Union of Soviet Socialist Republics (USSR) is included in the second edition. Since the first edition of this book was published, thousands of immigrants and refugees from the former USSR have settled in the United States, and thus the second edition includes information to help professionals who serve members of this growing population.

3. Maps have been added to the book to show many of the countries that are the "homeland" for students entering our schools as second language learners.

4. There are new pedagogical aids to make the book more interactive, especially for university students who use the book as a course text. The case studies and thinking questions (i.e., "reflections") in each chapter are included to help students reflect actively on what they are reading. Test questions at the end of each chapter help students evaluate their own learning as they progress through the book.

5. Topics relating to assessment are now covered in two separate chapters, with updated information on assessment. Additional information has been included relating to the biases inherent in the standardized tests used with LCD students.

6. The chapters relating to intervention have been expanded to include a wider range of topics relating to the development of language and literacy skills that are critical for academic success. Strategies are described, for example, that can be used to promote phonological awareness in LCD students with language-learning disabilities.

GOALS FOR THE READER

This book was written to help readers achieve the following goals:

❑ The reader will be able to give a basic definition of culture.

❑ The reader will demonstrate cultural competence and awareness of factors that often affect communication between students, families, and professionals.

❑ The reader will demonstrate awareness of general cultural and linguistic characteristics, including cross-cultural differences in communication styles.

❑ The reader will be able to describe normal second language acquisition and bilingual development in children.

❑ The reader will demonstrate familiarity with laws and public policies that affect service to students from multicultural backgrounds.

❑ The reader will demonstrate an understanding of the information that needs to be obtained to differentiate between communication differences and communication disorders in linguistically and culturally diverse populations.

❑ The reader will demonstrate an understanding of potential limitations of standardized testing and issues related to the use of alternative, nonstandardized methods for nonbiased assessment.

❑ The reader will demonstrate familiarity with procedures for using a team-oriented, multidisciplinary approach to identification, assessment, and intervention.

❑ The reader will demonstrate familiarity with educational program planning and the various options that are available for serving multicultural students.

❑ The reader will demonstrate familiarity with effective intervention techniques/strategies and the materials available for use with multicultural students.

❑ The reader will demonstrate the ability to write instructional goals that reflect a collaborative, holistic, communicative competence approach to language learning.

❑ The reader will acquire knowledge that will facilitate effective interactions with families of students from diverse backgrounds.

It is my hope that readers of this second edition will receive valuable, practical information that will increase their overall cultural competence and give them many hands-on, "Monday-morning" strategies for increasing and improving service delivery to the many LCD students in our schools. It is also my hope that readers will be able to use the information to help students in their instructional programs become more accepting of students who have different customs, beliefs, and values so that they can interact with one another harmoniously and learn from one another.

PART 1

CULTURAL AND LINGUISTIC VARIABLES AFFECTING SERVICE DELIVERY

Chapter 1

LEARNING ABOUT CULTURAL DIVERSITY

Outline

Professionals working with students from diverse cultural populations must have an understanding of cultural characteristics and the impact that these characteristics have on students' performance in the classroom learning environment. Cultural behaviors affect how students interact with one another and how they respond to the learning experiences made available to them. An awareness of cultural differences is essential to ensure that students from multicultural backgrounds are provided with appropriate educational programs. It is also important for professionals to be aware of the impact that immigrant/refugee status can have on students and their families.

Information about a variety of cultural groups is presented in this book to show the diversity that exists in our schools and to help professionals understand general trends within various cultural groups. The references cited can be used by professionals who need additional information about specific cultural groups. Learning about other cultures helps professionals to develop a better understanding of behaviors observed in the school setting. By becoming "culturally competent," professionals will be able to adapt their instructional programs to meet the needs of students from diverse cultural and linguistic backgrounds.

The understanding of basic issues relating to culture, race and ethnicity is critical in the discussion of cultural competence. These terms are defined below.

KEY TERMS

• **Culture** (defined in more detail later) is the shared beliefs, traditions, and values of a group of people.

• **Race** is a classification that distinguishes groups of people from one another based on physical characteristics such as skin color.

• **Ethnicity**, a term sometimes confused with race, is the social definition of groups of people based on various cultural similarities. Ethnicity includes race and also factors such as customs, nationality, language, and heritage (Coleman & McCabe-Smith, 2000).

LEGAL CONSIDERATIONS

The development of appropriate educational programs for students is challenging when students come from diverse cultural backgrounds. When students from linguistically and culturally diverse backgrounds do not succeed in schools, the "problems" observed are often incorrectly viewed as evidence of a disability (Moore-Brown & Montgomery, 2001; Roseberry-McKibbin & Eicholtz, 1994). Assessment measures that are culturally and linguistically inappropriate have often been used to assess and place these students in special education programs. But legally, when students are assessed because of learning problems in the classroom, nondiscriminatory assessment procedures must be used.

The Individuals with Disabilities Education Act (IDEA, 1997) includes provisions relating specifically to the assessment of culturally and linguistically diverse students. Legal mandates included are as follows:

❏ Testing procedures and the materials used in assessment must not be racially or culturally discriminatory.

❏ Assessment instruments must be administered so that the results obtained reflect performance ability in the specific area tested rather than the individual's level of proficiency in English.

In order to understand what constitutes a communication disorder, one must understand basic normal, developmental features of the student's primary language. One must also be able to identify "errors" commonly produced in English that result from the influence of the primary language. These "errors" are not signs of a disorder, but of language differences. Students are not eligible for remediation in a special education program if their "problems" can be attributed to limited experience in using the English language; one must demonstrate a disability that will impact performance in any language spoken by the student. In addition, professionals must recognize cultural influences that impact students' communication behaviors (Brice, 2002). Professionals who do not recognize the effect of cultural influences on students' communication are in danger of violating legal mandates that require schools to provide all students with culturally and linguistically appropriate assessment and instruction. Therefore, before making decisions regarding a student's need for special education services, professionals must know what "normal" behavior is for the student's community and culture.

UNDERSTANDING CULTURAL DIVERSITY

Culture has been described by Cheng (1991) as a dynamic, multi-faceted phenomenon:

> Culture is dynamic, never fixed or static; it is learned and shared by a people; is creative and meaningful to the lives of individuals . . . . it has value and belief systems that guide people in their thinking, feeling, and acting . . . in short, culture is the total way of life of people in a society. (p. 4)

Culture can be viewed as a framework through which actions are filtered as individuals go about the business of daily living (Hanson & Hynch, 1998). Values are at the heart of culture; thus, when we study other cultures, it is important to examine their basic values.

One of the dangers inherent in the study of any cultural group and its values is that stereotyping and overgeneralizing may occur. Stereotypes can be viewed as a means of categorizing others based upon perceptions that are incomplete (Penfield, 1990).

Payne (1986) stated that:

> Stereotyping exists when an uncritical judgment is made about an entire group based on the actions of a few members. Sometimes stereotyping is the result of a misinterpretation or an exaggeration of an actual cultural behavior, either intentionally or unintentionally . . . generalizations about cultures or ethnic groups are valid only when influences of class and personality can be factored out or when historical evidence is unquestionable. (p. 24)

Part of being a culturally competent professional is the ability to recognize that each person in any cultural group must be viewed first and foremost as an individual. If we view people in some sense as "representative" of a culture, then we presume a "homogeneous and fixed presence" that can be adequately represented by those whom we serve (Greene, 1993). When learning about other cultures, it is important to understand that not all members of a culture have the same beliefs, values, or customs; much variation occurs within any cultural group. Professionals should keep in mind the great heterogeneity that exists within cultural groups (Langdon & Cheng, 2002). Although cultural norms tend to influence behavior, each individual and each family has unique experiences that influence beliefs, attitudes, and behavior.

A student who comes from a specific cultural group can be viewed through various "lenses." Professionals sometimes view students solely through the lens of their personal knowledge, experience, and biases. Many people have selective perception—what they look for, they find. This practice often leads to subjective and incorrect decisions regarding service delivery to students from multicultural backgrounds. Hanson (1998a) recommended that professionals take a transactional and situational approach wherein individual students and their families are recognized as having unique needs, characteristics, and strengths.

It is the author's profound hope that readers will not be led to form stereotypes of other cultures as they read about cultural "tendencies" in this book. The values, behaviors, and customs described for a specific culture are not necessarily observed among the majority of people within that culture.

The statement that "Americans watch a lot of baseball," for example, does not mean that most Americans enjoy baseball or that they spend a considerable amount of time watching the game. Americans do, however, have a tendency to enjoy baseball, although some have no interest in the sport. Much diversity exists within the "American culture" and within virtually every other cultural group. It is important for professionals to realize that individuals adapt to cultural expectations in different ways. By increasing one's understanding of tendencies within various cultural groups, it will be easier for professionals to view students as individuals within the general framework of their community and culture.

✐REFLECTION✐

Define **culture**. Why is it important to understand cultural tendencies of various groups with whom we work as professionals?

_____

_____

_____

_____

_____

CULTURAL VARIABLES INFLUENCING BEHAVIOR

Many variables influence the behavior of individuals within a culture. The manner in which services are provided may be influenced by general cultural practices in combination with variables unique to the individual. Thus, professionals must understand not only general characteristics of various cultural groups, but also the variables that interact to make each student and family unique within that cultural group. An understanding of these variables can be enhanced by interacting with family members and asking questions. Many families appreciate the opportunity to share their stories and appreciate being viewed as unique. The following variables are important to consider:

❑ Educational level

❑ Languages spoken

❑ Length of residence in an area

❑ Country of birth (immigrant vs. native born)

❑ Urban vs. rural background

❑ Individual choice within the intrapersonal realm (e.g., idiosyncratic behavior)

❑ Socioeconomic status/upward class mobility

❑ Age and gender

❑ Religious beliefs and their impact on daily life activities

❑ Neighborhood of residence and peer group

❑ Degree of acculturation into mainstream American life

❑ Generational membership (first, second, third generation)

If the family immigrated to the United States, reasons for this immigration should be considered. It is also important to find out about generational patterns of immigration. To what extent are other relatives living in close proximity? To what extent are members of a cultural group marrying those from different ethnic backgrounds? These questions and all the above factors need to be considered when professionals provide services to students and families from various cultural backgrounds.

WORKING WITH IMMIGRANTS AND REFUGEES

Many professionals in the schools work with large numbers of students who are immigrants or refugees. The term *immigrant* is used to describe an individual who enters a country with the intention of becoming a permanent resident. The term *refugee* is used to describe an individual who flees to another country because of fear of persecution. Religion, nationality, race, political opinion, or an affiliation with a particular social group may account for the individual's departure from the homeland (Asian American Handbook, 1991). An awareness of the effects that immigrant/refugee status has on students, their families, and the delivery of instructional services is a critical component in cultural competence.

For the purposes of efficiency in this section, immigrants and refugees are often referred to as "immigrants/refugees." It is important to remember that not all immigrants are refugees, and not all refugees are immigrants. Professionals should keep the above definitions and distinctions in mind when reading this section.

GENERAL BACKGROUND INFORMATION

Unless otherwise indicated, the statistics reported below are from the U.S. Center for Immigrant Studies, as summarized by Steven Camarota (2001):

❑ In 1900, there were 10.3 million immigrants to the United States. In 2000, there were 28.4 million immigrants to this country. The growth rate of the foreign-born population since 1970 is higher than at any previous time in history.

❑ On November 29, 1990, President George Bush Sr. signed the Immigration Act of 1990. This reform increased annual immigration in the United States to 700,000.

❑ The 11.2 million legal immigrants who arrived in the United States in the 1990s represented 43.8% of the country's population growth in that decade.

❑ More than 1.2 million legal and illegal immigrants combined now settle in the United States each year.

❑ The number of immigrants living in the United States has more than tripled, from 9.6 million in 1970 to 28.4 million in 2000. In terms of percentage of the U.S. population, immigrants have more than doubled from 4.7% in 1970 to 10.4% in 2000.

❑ According to the Hudson Institute's Workforce 2000, it is projected that 800,000 legal and illegal immigrants will enter the United States annually throughout the rest of this century (Holliday, 2001).

❑ Mexico has the highest rate of immigration and accounts for 27.7% of all immigrants worldwide, with 7.9 million of these immigrants living in the United States.

❑ There is enormous diversity among immigrants/refugees. They represent every echelon of society from wealth, privilege and education to poverty and illiteracy; they speak varying degrees of English.

Profile

Thuy, a 12-year-old Vietnamese boy, was referred for a speech-language evaluation. He was making poor academic progress in comparison to other Vietnamese students, and an underlying language-learning disability was suspected. Thuy was the youngest of eight children and had spent the great majority of his life in Southeast Asian refugee camps. Apparently he had been placed in school at one point, but the family moved so frequently that he received a very fragmented education. He had minimal literacy in Vietnamese. The speech-language pathologist's challenge was to determine the extent to which Thuy's limited formal education was contributing to his lack of academic progress. Was Thuy truly language-learning disabled, or was he struggling because of lack of educational opportunities in his home country?

❑ Over 70% of immigrants to the United States live in only five states. The percentage of immigrants that settle in each of these states is shown below:

1. California (8.8 million, or 30.9% of the nation's total immigrant population)
2. New York (12.8%)
3. Florida (9.8%)
4. Texas (8.6%)
5. Illinois (4.1%)

❑ In the year 2000, there were 8.6 million school-aged children from immigrant families in the United States. Immigration accounts for most of the increase in public school enrollment over the past decades.

GENERAL CHARACTERISTICS OF IMMIGRANTS AND REFUGEES

Due to the great diversity among immigrants/refugees, it is impossible to construct a paradigm into which they will all neatly fit. The following characteristics are true of **SOME, but not all** immigrants/refugees. Students and families must be evaluated and served based on an understanding of their unique characteristics, backgrounds, and needs. They should not be stereotyped.

❑ Persons who wish to immigrate to the United States legally must meet the requirements of United States immigration laws. Medical screenings, for example, are required of immigrants.

❑ Many immigrants/refugees are educated, financially successful individuals who come to the United States because of a desire for greater freedom and increased economic opportunity.

❑ Some immigrant/refugee students come to the United States with good literacy skills; others are illiterate and have had minimal education.

❑ Many refugees have spent time in camps in "countries of second asylum," during a period of transition while preparing for resettlement. Some refugees have even lived in countries of third asylum. For example, refugees from Vietnam might have lived in Cambodia and then in the Philippines before finally coming to the United States to settle permanently. Consequently, children may have had little or no formal education before coming to the United States.

❑ Historically, immigrants/refugees were encouraged to adopt American values and to speak English rather than their native language. The importance of respecting cultural differences is now recognized.

❑ There are some common ways in which refugees/immigrants adapt to United States culture (Cheng & Butler, 1993). Professionals should attempt to discover how each individual student and family have chosen to adapt:

1. **Reaffirmation** - making an effort to revive native cultural traditions. The individual may reject the majority culture.

2. **Synthesis** - a selective combination of cultural aspects of various groups.

3. **Withdrawal** - a rejection of both cultures because of areas of conflict. The individual doesn't commit to either culture.

4. **Compensatory adaptation** - an attempt to blend completely into the new culture and avoid identifying with the home culture.

5. **Biculturalism** - full involvement with both cultures; the individual learns to adapt to each culture during various types of social interactions.

6. **Constructive marginality** - a tentative acceptance of the two cultures. The individual fails to become integrated completely into either culture.

ACCULTURATION

The term **acculturation** refers to "the degree to which people from a particular cultural group display behavior which is like the more pervasive American norms of behavior" (Randall-David, 1989, p. 3).

It is important for professionals to determine the degree of acculturation experienced by students and their families. Generally, immigrants/refugees who experience a high level of acculturation tend to have smoother transitions and experience greater success in the mainstream society. Factors that may result in a higher level of acculturation include:

❑ a relatively high level of formal education

❑ high socioeconomic status

❑ being born into a family that has lived in the United States for at least a few years

❑ immigration to the United States at an early age

❑ limited migration back and forth to the country of origin

❑ previous residence in an urban environment

❑ extensive contact with people outside the family and/or ethnic network

DIFFICULTIES COMMONLY EXPERIENCED BY IMMIGRANTS/REFUGEES

Unless otherwise indicated, the statistics reported below are from the U.S. Center for Immigrant Studies, as summarized by Steven Camarota (2001).

❑ Undocumented immigrants/refugees may be quite fearful of forced repatriation. If they must return to the homeland, consequences can be quite severe. For example, some Chinese repatriated refugees have been sentenced to forced labor camps.

❑ Undocumented immigrants/refugee workers may be treated poorly by their employers and paid less than the minimum wage.

❑ Many refugees have witnessed and/or endured oppressive and traumatic experiences such as disease, persecution, death, atrocities, forced labor, separation from family members, starvation, and being uprooted. Such experiences can result in post-traumatic stress disorders, health problems, and many other negative consequences.

❑ Many refugees/immigrants have been separated from their families due, in part, to situations in which some family members come to the United States while others remain in their homeland. It may be years before family members are reunited.

❑ Students may experience problems adjusting to schools in the United States that have rules and expectations different from those experienced in the homeland.

❑ Some immigrants/refugees from rural areas may have experienced difficulty adjusting to the technological emphasis in the urban work environment.

❏ Many immigrants/refugees experience substantial poverty in the United States, even if they are from middle-upper class socioeconomic backgrounds.

❏ In comparison to U.S. natives, who represent 28.8% of the population that is living in or near the poverty level, 41.4% of immigrants live in or near poverty. Among children of immigrants (under age 21), 53% live in or near poverty. ("Near poverty" is defined as income that is below 200% of the poverty threshold.)

❏ The annual median income of immigrants is approximately 76% that of U.S. natives; for the most recent immigrants, median income is only 58% of that earned by U.S. natives.

❏ The proportion of immigrant households that receive welfare benefits is 30-50% higher than that of native households.

❏ One third of immigrants have no health insurance. Immigrants who arrived after 1989 and their U.S.-born children account for a 60% increase in the size of the uninsured population in the United States.

❏ Highly-trained immigrants often encounter barriers in the United States because their professional training is viewed as inadequate. They may need to "jump through the hoops" by completing additional schooling, additional credentialing, etc. For example, an individual who was a heart surgeon in his homeland may end up working as a dishwasher in this country.

❏ Older immigrants who have moderate or heavy accents in English may encounter vocational and social barriers because of these accents.

✐ REFLECTION ✐

Describe two difficulties commonly experienced by immigrant/refugee students and their families. How might we as professionals help these students and their families to deal with these difficulties?

_____

_____

_____

_____

_____

POSSIBLE FAMILY CONCERNS

Many researchers have documented the existence of intergenerational tensions in families as they immigrate to the United States and experience changes in almost every area of life (Chan, 1998a; Rick & Forward, 1998; Sharifzadeh, 1998). Some of the sources of tension are as follows:

❏ Young people often want to become Americanized, but they are expected to maintain traditional customs by their elders.

❑ Children often learn English more quickly than their elders, and thus become spokespersons for their families; this may usurp the elders' traditional role as authority figures. This author knows of numerous young children who pay electric bills, negotiate at the bank, and carry out other adult responsibilities because they speak English and their parents do not.

❑ Some family members (e.g., parents) must work long hours in order to survive financially and may not be available to their children for much of the day.

❑ Children may want to marry Americans instead of persons from their home culture; elders may greatly disapprove of this practice.

❑ The harmonious nature of marital relationships may be disrupted if women who have stayed at home and obeyed their husbands begin working outside the home to earn income for the family.

❑ Many families have traditionally been interdependent; the American social emphasis on independence may cause upheaval in families with members who rely on one another.

❑ Families from middle-upper class socioeconomic backgrounds may experience poverty in the United States.

PUBLIC PERCEPTIONS ABOUT IMMIGRANTS/REFUGEES

As the number of immigrants/refugees to the United States increases, it is important to look not only at the facts and numbers, but also at the attitudes of Americans toward immigrants/refugees. Beliefs about immigrants/refugees help determine public policy, including educational and financial provisions and services. These provisions and services impact the availability of school resources that serve immigrant students. The attitudes of professionals toward immigrants/refugees also impact service delivery to these students and their families.

The United States is a nation of immigrants and descendants of immigrants. Some immigrants came voluntarily, others involuntarily. Immigrants/refugees bring many positive qualities to the United States. Many immigrants/refugees are diverse, young, and dynamic persons who have great potential to contribute positively to American society.

Many people living in the United States have negative feelings about individuals who immigrate to this country. These perceptions are reflected in increased legislation to stem the flow of immigrants into the United States. Many believe that these immigrants cause social and economic problems. Professionals who work directly with immigrants/refugees must make certain that they personally do not hold biases that could negatively impact the effectiveness of service delivery.

IMPLICATIONS FOR PROFESSIONALS

❑ How students need to adapt to function effectively in the United States is influenced by age. Children entering adolescence, for example, must face the changes of adolescence as well as problems commonly encountered when adjusting to a new country.

❑ Degree of acculturation of students and families may impact the way that services are viewed and received. A highly-educated immigrant/refugee family might be more responsive to special education, for example, than a family with limited educational experiences.

❏ Students from undocumented immigrant/refugee families may suddenly "disappear" from the school; this may be due to forced repatriation.

❏ Emotional problems that affect school performance may be experienced by students who have encountered great trauma. Help may need to be provided for these problems. Professionals can help students express feelings through art and writing.

❏ When professionals collect case histories from members of immigrant/refugee families, they should remember that past experiences may be painful for some families, making it difficult for them to talk about the past in detail. This is especially true if family members and/or their loved ones have encountered traumatic experiences.

❏ Professionals can facilitate mutual enrichment for immigrant/refugee and mainstream students by asking immigrant/refugee students to provide information about their home language, culture, and experiences living in various countries and situations.

❏ One of the best forms of assistance is to help families connect with local support networks consisting of persons from their own culture who can provide needed information and resources (Roseberry-McKibbin, 2002). In the area near Sacramento, California where this author lives, for example, Russian immigrants have been provided with assistance in a variety of areas by Russian churches.

❏ Many refugees in our schools have experienced poor health care and/or medical conditions that may affect learning. In addition, pregnant female refugees who are malnourished may deliver babies with health problems or specific disabilities.

❏ Some families do not know the exact birth dates of their children; for example, refugees who are fleeing for their lives may not attach great importance to birth certificates and other records.

❏ Professionals should stress that their concern is to help the family. Some families "suffer the daily torment of never knowing when and how they may be discovered and subjected to deportation." (Zuniga, 1998).

❏ Some families may have difficulty planning for the future because they have spent so much effort trying to survive from one day to the next. Thus, it may be hard for them to understand the long-term goals often emphasized in special education programs.

❏ Many immigrant/refugee students need to acquire the practical, functional skills necessary to read bus schedules, use telephone directories, etc.

❏ School in the United States is compulsory for immigrant students who arrive in their teens. However, in some cultures, school is not required at this age. Attending school may cause a conflict between American law and family traditions and values. (In one dramatic instance in California, the mother of a teenage Vietnamese boy wanted her son to drop out of school so that he could help run her beauty parlor. After dropping out against his wishes, the boy ended up participating in criminal activities with his peers.)

❏ Some students may have had family servants in the native country. These students may be unaccustomed to caring for themselves and functioning independently and, therefore, may be viewed as "too dependent" by teachers and other school professionals.

CONCLUSION

American society has been enriched by immigration. Providing services to students and families from immigrant/refugee backgrounds can be challenging and very rewarding. As professionals work with culturally and linguistically diverse student groups, they expand their knowledge, become more flexible, and expand their expertise in service delivery.

Profile

Jose was a 13-year-old, monolingual Spanish-speaking student from Mexico. He experienced a head injury after being struck by a car and received language and cognitive rehabilitation at the local facility. Jose's family was very supportive of the services offered by the speech-language pathologist and often expressed gratitude for the services that were being provided.

After 34 weeks of treatment, Jose suddenly stopped coming to therapy. A somewhat incomprehensible phone message was left on the facility's answering machine. After numerous phone calls, it was learned that Jose's family returned to Mexico after being identified as "illegal aliens." The family left the country without any written documentation about the intervention program that had been provided.

SUGGESTIONS FOR INCREASING CULTURAL COMPETENCE

1   Team up with persons from the local cultural community who can act as informants and interpreters. Utilizing the knowledge and skills of these individuals is generally the best way to obtain the information necessary to serve multicultural students and their families.

2   Read as much as possible about the family's culture and language. Such information may be gathered from local community libraries, university libraries, and individuals in the community from that cultural group. In addition, references cited in this text (e.g., Battle, 2002; Brice, 2002; Cheng, 1991; Brigham Young University, 1992; Goldstein, 2000; Lynch & Hanson, 1998) include excellent information about specific cultural groups.

3   Visit students' homes. Ascertain that the family is willing to be visited, and choose times that are convenient for these visits.

4   Evaluate your own assumptions and values. Consider how your own assumptions and values influence your way of communicating information about students' achievements, instructional needs, and goals for school success.

5   Consider the student's needs in the larger context of the family and community. If you want the student to receive additional services above and beyond those available in the regular classroom, examine the student's needs within the context of the family as a whole. Be sure to include family members in the decision-making process.

6   Consider the value system of the family when setting goals. For example, educational professionals often stress the importance of helping physically disabled students to become as independent as possible. However, in a particular child's culture, independence may not be emphasized or considered important; family members may be expected to care for all of the student's needs. Intervention plans will not succeed unless the family's values and style of living are considered.

7 **Be aware that verbal and nonverbal communication can impact a family's attitudes toward the school and toward professionals who are working with the student.** Professionals need to show that they are truly interested in the family.

8 **Talk with individuals from a variety of cultural backgrounds.** Participate in social interactions with people whose cultural, ethnic, and linguistic origins are different from yours. This can be accomplished by attending holiday celebrations, community functions, etc.

9 **Ask students to share important aspects of their culture with you and other students.** Some students may not be comfortable talking about their cultural/language background. However, when students are willing to share, everyone benefits from this exchange.

10 **Learn some basic communication skills (e.g., vocabulary, simple phrases) in the student's language.** Many American professionals are monolingual English speakers. When these professionals begin learning a second language, their empathy for ESL students may increase greatly! In addition, multicultural families appreciate professionals' efforts to relate to them, even if they speak only a few simple phrases of the family's home language.

11 **Be aware that students from different cultural backgrounds may begin school with different cultural assumptions about human relations and about the world.** These assumptions may cause conflict for the student initially. Professionals need to be sensitive to this possibility, especially for students who enter the country as immigrants or refugees.

STUDY QUESTIONS

1. Teachers are referring a large number of multicultural students to you for assessment. You decide to conduct an inservice to help teachers identify students who are appropriate referrals. What will you tell the teachers about laws governing assessment and placement of multicultural students in special education?

2. Describe three ways in which professionals can increase their cultural competence.

3. Describe four specific ways that professionals can help immigrant/refugee students and their families.

TRUE-FALSE

Circle the number beside each statement that is true.

4. Multicultural students in public schools are eligible for special education if their primary problem is limited proficiency in the English language.

5. A good way to increase one's cultural competence is to attend social events sponsored by various cultural groups.

6. Immigrant families from middle- and upper-class backgrounds in their home countries generally experience a similar or higher level of success in the U.S.

7. In immigrant/refugee families, older persons who do not speak English are very grateful that their children speak English and are able to take care of tasks such as paying the utility bills.

8. Highly trained immigrants generally are able to find jobs in the U.S. that are comparable to jobs they had in their home countries.

9. Some families may find it painful to discuss the past when efforts are made by professionals to obtain case histories.

10. *Compensatory adaptation* occurs when the individual attempts to blend completely into the new culture and avoids identifying with the home culture.

MULTIPLE CHOICE

Circle the letter beside each correct response. More than one correct response is possible.

11. Factors that tend to impact a family's acculturation into U.S. life include:

A. Urban vs. rural background
B. Educational level
C. Neighborhood of residence and peer group
D. Length of residence in an area
E. Number of times church is attended each week

12. Which of the following is/are false statements about acculturation?
    A. In *reaffirmation*, efforts are made to revive native cultural traditions. The individual may reject the majority culture.
    B. In *synthesis*, there is a selective combination of cultural aspects of various groups.
    C. In *biculturalism*, there is a tentative acceptance of the two cultures; the individual does not fully integrate into either culture.
    D. In *withdrawal*, there is a rejection of both cultures because of areas of conflict; the individual doesn't commit to either culture.

13. Difficulties commonly experienced by immigrants and refugees include the following:
    A. Forced repatriation is feared.
    B. Students who have had servants in their native countries are often considered "immature" and "dependent" by American teachers.
    C. Separation from family members causes various difficulties functioning in society.

14. When working with immigrant/refugee students and families, it is helpful for professionals to do the following:
    A. Ask immigrant/refugee students to provide information about their home language, culture, and experiences living in various countries and situations.
    B. Help families connect with local support networks consisting of persons from their own culture who can provide needed information and resources.
    C. Assure families that even though professionals may report their illegal status to the INS, services will still be continued if the families remain in the U.S.
    D. Encourage use of English in all social situations.

15. Which one of the following statements is FALSE?
    A. The 11.2 million immigrants who arrived in the U.S. in the 1990s account for 43.8% of the U.S. population growth during that decade.
    B. On November 29, 1990, President George Bush Sr. signed the Immigration Act of 1990. This reform restricted annual immigration in the United States to 500,000.
    C. More than 1.2 million legal and illegal immigrants combined now settle in the U.S. each year.
    D. California has 8.8 million immigrants or 30.9% of the nation's total immigrant population.
    E. The Hudson Institute's Workforce 2000 reported projections that 800,000 legal and illegal immigrants will enter the U.S. annually throughout the rest of this century.

ANSWERS TO STUDY QUESTIONS

    4. False
    5. True
    6. False
    7. False
    8. False
    9. True
    10. True
    11. A , B, C ,and D
    12. C
    13. A, B, and C
    14. A and B
    15. B

Chapter 2

THE IMPACT OF
RELIGIOUS DIFFERENCES

Outline

Most Americans from traditional backgrounds have at least a nodding acquaintance with the basic tenets of Judeo-Christian religious practices. As ethnic diversity increases in the United States, religious diversity also increases. It is important for the professional who works with ethnically diverse students and their families to understand their religious beliefs because these beliefs influence behavior and attitudes towards school services (Roseberry-McKibbin & Hegde, 2000). Three of the major religions now represented in the United States are described briefly here. It is impossible to provide an in-depth description and analysis of each religion; the purpose of this section is to give the professional a general overview of each religion's basic tenets. These ideas and tendencies are described as generalities, not absolutes. Each religion has great variety within it and, therefore, each family and student must be considered individually. The information presented should help professionals to better understand how various beliefs impact service delivery. Moreover, the information should help professionals to become more sensitive to family dynamics that might be influenced by religion.

ISLAM

KEY TERMS

- **Islam** is the religion; it is a monotheistic (one God) faith.

- **Allah** is the term used for "God" in Arabic.

- **Muhammed** is the prophet (also spelled Mohammed). He was born in 570 A.D. in Mecca, and his teachings began around 612 A.D.

- A **Muslim** is a follower of Islam (also spelled Moslem). Some Muslims may believe the term Mohammeden is an insulting misnomer (Mansuri, 1993) because according to Islamic teaching, the prophet Muhammed was not the founder of a new religion. Islam was the first religion of humanity (Kozlowski, 1991, p. 68).

- The **Quran** (also spelled **Koran**) is the sacred book of Islam. It has 30 parts containing 114 chapters.

- **Mecca** is the principal holy city for Muslims. Most Muslims try, at least once in their lives, to complete the Hajj or pilgrimage to Mecca.

❑ Islam has existed for over 13 centuries. It is the world's second largest religion, with more than one billion followers worldwide.

❑ The world's largest Muslim community is in Indonesia. Large Muslim populations can be found in areas of Asia, India, and much of Africa (Omar Nydell, 1996).

❑ Islam is the fastest growing religion in the United States and in the world; there are at least four million followers in the United States.

❏ Muslims believe that Allah revealed through the Angel Gabriel to the Prophet Muhammed the rules that govern society and that Allah gave mores for the conduct of the members of society. These mores are presented in the Quran.

❏ Muslims are not a homogeneous group; they represent a variety of ethnic and cultural backgrounds.

❏ Two major Muslim sects are the Sunnis (Majority) and the Shi'ites (Minority). There have been some schisms between Sunni and Shi'ite Muslims. Shi'ite Muslims are frequently regarded as "radical" by other religious groups.

❏ Muslims pray at five specific times during the day, turning toward Mecca and reciting a prescribed prayer.

❏ Obligatory practices for Muslims include fasting during the month of Ramadan (no food or drink from sunrise to sundown) and pilgrimage to Mecca. Ramadan falls at different times each year depending upon the lunar calendar.

❏ Muslims are not supposed to drink alcohol or eat pork.

❏ Education is very important to Muslims. Many Muslim children and youth learn Arabic.

❏ Family ties are extremely important to Muslims, and extended families are common.

❏ The Islam religion strongly endorses procreation. For many Muslims, not having children is a cause for great unhappiness (Sharifzadeh, 1998).

❏ In some areas, patriarchal hierarchies allow the father/senior male of the household almost complete authority over the rest of the family (Sharabi, 1985; Sharifzadeh, 1998). However, this is not true everywhere.

❏ Some Muslim marriages are arranged; the bride and groom may not meet until the wedding day. Many Muslim parents prefer that their children marry other Muslims.

❏ Among Muslim Arabs, especially in nomadic and rural communities, families prefer that first and second cousins marry each other. This within-family marriage helps ensure that people marry a "known quantity" and also that money and possessions remain in the family (Omar Nydell, 1996).

❏ Many Muslims greatly frown upon divorce.

❏ Muslims are permitted to practice polygamy in some countries. For example, polygamy is outlawed in Iraq and Tunisia, but the practice is allowed in Yemen, Jordan, Syria, and Iraq. In some cases, court approval is required for such marriages to occur.

❏ The role of Muslim women has traditionally been viewed by other cultures as being very repressive. However, the role of Muslim women varies depending upon the country in which they reside.

❏ Some Muslim women cover themselves from head to toe with clothing. Women are valued as mothers and guardians of the family, and modest dress for women is regarded as symbolic of this value. Theoretically, dressing modestly and wearing a veil preserves women's respect, dignity, and virginity as well as protecting women from abuse and harassment by men.

❑ Women's roles and consequent rules for dress differ from country to country. For instance, the former Taliban regime of Afghanistan incited a mob to beat a woman to death for accidentally exposing her arm when she was driving a car. Issues regarding the Taliban's strict rules of conduct and acts of terrorism caused concern throughout the world, especially since the terrorist attacks against the United States that occurred on September 11, 2001. In late 2001, the Taliban was overthrown. In contrast to Afghanistan, attitudes regarding women's dress in Iran have liberalized; women are now being encouraged to wear brightly-colored head scarves instead of black veils.

❑ Among some Muslim groups, sexual activity outside of marriage is considered to be so wrong that it is punishable by flagellation, imprisonment, or even death (Sasson, 1992). Forms of punishment, however, vary greatly from area to area.

✐ REFLECTION ✐

List and describe three Muslim values/practices that differ from those of mainstream Americans. Why is it important for professionals to be aware of these values/practices?

_____

_____

_____

_____

_____

_____

BUDDHISM

> ### KEY TERMS
>
> • The term **Buddha** refers, literally, to a Supremely Enlightened person; the present Buddha is Siddhartha Gautama, an Indian prince, who lived from approximately 584-563 B.C. Buddha is not considered to be a god, but rather a man and a teacher.
>
> • **Karma** means that a person's fate or destiny in this life is determined by what happened in a previous life. Karma also embodies the principle that those who do good receive good and those who do evil receive evil.
>
> • **Reincarnation** is the repeated cycle of being born into the world as we know it.
>
> • **Nirvana** is a divine state that allows one to end the cycle of reincarnation. It represents separation from pain, escape from misery and trouble, and is the highest state of spiritual bliss that one can achieve.

❏ Buddhism originated in India (560-480 B.C.)

❏ Many Asians practice Buddhism. It is the primary religion in Laos, Vietnam, and Cambodia. Shintoism, a religion based on the worship of ancestors and ancient heroes, is practiced widely in Japan.

❏ There are various forms of Buddhism. The two primary types are Theravata Buddhism (found predominantly in Sri Lanka, Burma, Laos, Thailand, and Cambodia), and Mahayana Buddhism, commonly practiced in Vietnam, China, Korea, Japan, Mongolia, and Tibet (Chan, 1998a).

❏ Although an individual undergoes a cycle of reincarnations, the average layperson has little hope of achieving Nirvana (Ebihara, 1966).

❏ One's chances of a better life in the next rebirth are determined largely by the number of good deeds accomplished in the present lifetime. Buddhists are encouraged to avoid evil and to achieve merit. Buddhism emphasizes supreme human effort.

❏ Buddhism stresses the importance of four major principles (see Chan, 1998a):

1. All of life is suffering and is inevitably sorrowful.

2. People suffer because they experience craving, are attached to the world, and are not content with what they have.

3. One must eliminate desire to extinguish suffering and attachment.

4. One can eliminate desire by living a virtuous life of carefully disciplined and moral conduct. This involves the eight-fold path of enlightenment, which stresses the right view, intent, speech, conduct, means of livelihood, endeavor, mindfulness, and meditation.

❏ To live a virtuous life requires the avoidance of lying, theft, immoral sexual conduct, excessive alcohol consumption, and various "frivolous" activities such as dancing.

❏ The individual's responsibility for actions taken is an important value among many practitioners of Buddhism.

❏ Some forms of Buddhism emphasize asceticism.

❏ Buddhists may visit a Buddhist temple when ill, in order to facilitate the healing process.

❏ Buddhist temples in some areas of the United States have provided support for refugees.

❏ Buddhists regard a child's third, fifth, and seventh birthdays as extremely important. Families go to shrines on these birthdays and pray for the child's development (Nellum-Davis, Gentry & Hubbard-Wiley, 2002).

❏ Most Buddhists are vegetarians.

> ## Profile
>
> A speech-language pathologist worked at San Quentin prison with Phuong, an 18-year-old Laotian Buddhist. Phuong was in prison because he had shot and killed eight people in a drive-by shooting. The speech-language pathologist tried to help Phuong with his spoken and written English skills, as these skills were extremely low. Phuong said that he did not expect to improve because he had a "bad spirit." Efforts to improve his language skills were unsuccessful at first.
>
> The speech-language pathologist talked to some Buddhist members of the community and, based on their recommendations, implemented a novel strategy to help Phuong. She tied a new white string around his left wrist. Many Buddhists believe that a white string represents "salvation." After Phuong started wearing this string, he told the speech-language pathologist that the bad spirit had left him and a good spirit had entered him. Phuong suddenly began to make progress in developing oral and written language skills.

CONFUCIANISM

❑ Confucianism was established by Confucius, a Chinese philosopher who lived from 551-479 B.C.

❑ In pure Confucian philosophy, the terms "God" and "Heaven" are synonymous and imply a supreme spiritual state or being.

❑ Confucius did not discuss the question of life after death.

❑ The goal of Confucius was not religious salvation, but rather full realization in the present life of human potential for virtue and wisdom.

❑ According to Confucius, Heaven's will cannot be changed by human prayers.

❑ The teachings of Confucius had a profound impact on China's history.

❑ Confucianism is practiced by Asians from a number of countries. The religion has been especially influential in Japanese, Chinese, and Vietnamese cultures.

❑ Confucius stressed two primary virtues from which all others spring: *li* (rules of proper conduct) and *ren* (benevolent love).

❑ Major tenets of Confucianism are righteousness, morality, appropriate conduct, benevolence, humanism, and loyalty.

❑ The most important moral qualities one can have are believed to be compassion, wisdom, and courage.

❑ Major goals for followers of Confucianism are contentment, enjoyment, and the absence of pain.

❏ Followers of Confucianism believe that the universe is characterized by order, regularity, and harmonious integration of its parts; a person's highest calling is to devote himself to the accumulation of knowledge of this order.

❏ Confucianism also emphasizes harmony in human society. This harmony is achieved by each person accepting a social role and contributing to social order through proper behavior.

❏ Followers of Confucianism believe that hierarchy is natural. Almost all social interaction is defined by relative status differences. Common distinctions that guide interaction are gender, age/seniority, educational attainment, and place of employment (Long, 1992). Each person is to act in accordance with his status to create a harmoniously-functioning society and to ensure loyalty to the state.

❏ The family's welfare and continuity are more important than the individual interests of any family member. Individuals are considered members not only of the living family but of a long line of ancestors and future descendants.

❏ Confucianism strongly emphasizes filial piety. Children are expected to revere ancestors and give parents unquestioning obedience and loyalty (Cheng, 1991).

❏ Monarchical absolutism, filial piety, the subordinate role of women, and the family system are viewed as integral to the functioning of society.

❏ Confucian norms emphasize acceptance of authority and delineate five basic relationships: subordination of subject to ruler, son to father, wife to husband, younger brother to elder brother, and mutual respect between friends.

❏ It is important for wives to produce male heirs to carry on the family line. If there is no male heir, a husband may divorce to marry someone else.

✐REFLECTION✐

You provide special education programs for students in a school district that has just had an influx of families that practice Confucianism. When you provide service delivery to children from these families, what are two important things that you will keep in mind?

_____

_____

_____

_____

_____

_____

IMPLICATIONS FOR PROFESSIONALS

When professionals are aware of a family's religious background and basic beliefs, they can relate to the family in ways that are more sensitive and culturally appropriate. Some of the following implications may apply in various situations when working with families from diverse religious backgrounds:

❑ In some families (especially those from Muslim backgrounds), a specific family member such as the father may be the spokesperson (Nellum-Davis et. al, 2002). It is considered inappropriate for professionals to address questions to the wrong family member during meetings relating to the needs of a student.

❑ If the family believes in seniority and authority based on age, the grandparents might have the final say in any decisions that are made relating to assessment and intervention.

❑ It might be considered inappropriate for a female professional to make any kind of physical contact with a male in the family (e.g., shaking hands).

❑ Many Buddhist and Muslim families prefer that professionals not work with family members who are of the opposite sex. Therefore, they believe that female professionals should not be allowed to work with male clients and vice versa.

❑ Muslims often have negative views of female professionals who wear "immodest" clothing. These female professionals should consider dressing conservatively when interacting with traditional Muslim families.

❑ Families of Muslim children may not want home-based services because they view the home as a private place (Campbell, 2001).

❑ Students from Muslim backgrounds, after age 8 or 9, might not be allowed to eat during the day in the month of Ramadan. Professionals should try to avoid serving snacks during this period or offering food or drink to family members during meetings.

❑ Some Muslims discourage anthropomorphism. Thus, stories that use talking animals would be viewed as inappropriate if used in the instructional curriculum (Nellum-Davis et al., 2002).

❑ Families from various religious backgrounds may believe that disabilities (e.g., stuttering, cleft palate, etc.) are caused by the actions of God or by fate. Thus, attitudes toward the student's disability may appear fatalistic.

❑ If the family believes that a child was born handicapped because of fate or because of actions that God has taken, intervention may be viewed as inappropriate or undesirable. For example, some Muslims believe that stuttering is an affliction from Allah that tests the stuttering individual and his family's faith. Individuals who stutter are thus not provided with treatment.

❑ Parents may feel personally responsible for a child's disabling condition. In some religious belief systems, the actions of parents are viewed as the cause of disabilities. Professionals must be especially sensitive to emotional issues surrounding the student's disability and must work in a supportive manner with families who hold these beliefs.

❑ Some families may resist intervention efforts that are in conflict with their belief systems about life and death. Buddhist families, for example, often believe that disabled children will be reincarnated into a more whole form.

❑ The family may balk at medical practices suggested by professionals (e.g., pressure equalizing tubes to drain middle ear fluid, braces, surgery to correct a physical defect) if the treatment procedures differ from those used within the culture.

❑ In some religions and cultures, girls are expected to marry at a young age. Their primary duties after marriage are to raise children and to be faithful wives. Education for girls may be viewed as less important than education for boys. Professionals might become frustrated if a female student has poor school attendance, or by the fact that girls drop out of school early to get married.

Profile

Nadia, a 10-year-old child, was from a religiously conservative Eastern European family with 13 children. She was absent from school frequently and experienced repeated academic failure. Her poor school attendance was an important factor to consider in determining her need for special education services.

Nadia's parents believed that a girl's role in life is to grow up, marry, and raise children. Nadia and the other girls in her family were expected to take care of their younger siblings. If her younger siblings were ill, Nadia was expected to stay home and care for them. The family believed that education was unimportant for Nadia because she would not need a formal education for her future role as a mother.

❑ Professionals want to be careful about scheduling major events on religious holidays. For example, planning a school party on the last day of Ramadan might be viewed as insensitive by some Muslims.

❑ Students may come from religious backgrounds that do not permit the celebration of holidays commonly commemorated in U.S. schools.

❑ Parents may pull their children out of school in order to celebrate or observe religious holidays or activities.

❑ Many public schools offer family life (sex education) activities for students. Some religious groups may object to this type of education.

❑ Some students who are fasting for religious reasons may not be able to take part in certain school activities.

Profile

Pablo, an 11-year-old male, generally participated actively in instructional activities in the classroom. When crossword puzzles relating to the Easter holiday were presented, however, he showed signs of disinterest. When asked to explain what was the matter, he said that his father disapproved of activities relating to the celebration of Easter. Pablo felt that doing the crossword puzzle activity was a violation of his father's wishes.

CONCLUSION

It is critical for professionals working with multicultural students to be sensitive to the religious beliefs of their families. Not every family will fit neatly into a religious category. Many people practice a combination of religions. When religious beliefs impact service delivery, professionals must be sensitive to the concerns of the family.

Often, a professional can achieve the best results by working with an interpreter from the family's culture who understands both the family's religious viewpoint and the value of intervention. If this person can build trust and rapport with the family, chances of providing appropriate treatment to students will be greatly increased.

STUDY QUESTIONS

1. Describe the major tenets of Buddhism.

2. List six values that are important to Muslims.

3. How might some Buddhist families regard suggestions for intervention? What might their attitude be when a professional recommends placement in a special education program?

TRUE-FALSE

Circle the number beside each statement that is true.

4. Followers of Confucius believe that a child's third, fifth, and seventh birthdays are extremely important.

5. The religious group that often discourages anthropomorphism is the Muslims.

6. When professionals meet with Muslim families, questions should be addressed primarily to the mother because she is the family caretaker.

7. Confucianism has been especially influential in Japanese, Chinese, and Vietnamese cultures.

8. Buddhist families may resist intervention efforts because they believe that a disabled child will be reincarnated into a whole form in the next life.

9. Shi'ite Muslims are the minority in the Muslim world and are often regarded as "radical" by outsiders.

10. Followers of Confucianism believe that hierarchy is natural, and that it is very important in governing human relationships.

MULTIPLE CHOICE

Unless otherwise indicated, circle the letter beside each choice that is correct.

11. The philosophy underlying the belief that a person's fate or destiny in this life is determined by what happened in a previous life is called:
    A. Nirvana
    B. Ramadan
    C. Karma
    D. Hajj
    E. Asceticism

12. Shintoism is a religion that is practiced widely in:
    A. Vietnam
    B. Japan
    C. China
    D. Laos
    E. Cambodia

13. When working with Muslim families, it is important to remember the following:
    A. Women dress modestly because theoretically, this modest dress symbolizes their role as mothers and guardians of the family.
    B. Most Muslims are eager for home-based services because they appreciate the convenience of having a professional come to them.
    C. Family ties are extremely important, and extended families are common.
    D. Female teachers are likely to be trusted more than male teachers.

14. Which one of the following is FALSE regarding general principles professionals should remember when serving students from various religious groups?
    A. Girls are strongly encouraged to get an education, so school attendance and any necessary intervention are extremely important to families.
    B. Family members may believe that disabilities are caused by the actions of the child's parents.
    C. Female professionals may not be allowed to work with male clients and vice versa.
    D. Celebration of traditional U.S. holidays may be viewed as offensive.
    E. Parents may pull their children out of school to celebrate religious holidays.

15. Yousef, a Muslim 12-year-old male, has been diagnosed as having a language-learning disability. Which of the following may NOT be appropriate in his situation?
    A. Addressing primarily his father during the meeting.
    B. Shaking the father's hand warmly upon meeting him.
    C. Believing that Yousef's family will view intervention as the will of Allah.
    D. Telling the family that he will receive intervention from a female speech-language pathologist in a one-to-one situation.
    E. Showing the family potential therapy materials that include books with interesting animal characters such as Donald Duck.

ANSWERS TO STUDY QUESTIONS

  4. False
  5. True
  6. False
  7. True
  8. True
  9. True
10. True
11. C
12. B
13. A and C
14. A
15. B, C, D, E

Chapter 3

FAMILIES FROM ANGLO EUROPEAN BACKGROUNDS

Outline

Anglo European monolingual English-speaking Americans continue to be the dominant cultural group in the United States, although demographics are changing rapidly. Many Anglo European Americans raised in traditional, middle-class, mainstream, monolingual English-speaking households have not had the opportunity to view their culture through the eyes of people from different cultures and/or other countries. Lynch (1998b) stated that mainstream Anglo European Americans often have a limited awareness of the influence that their cultural background has on their behavior and interactions. The "melting pot" theory heavily influenced how the dominant culture expected immigrants to interact and behave during the early waves of immigration. Persons from "other" cultural backgrounds were encouraged to disavow their cultural and linguistic roots so that they could take on American customs and values.

Thus, the purpose of this section is to help professionals from mainstream American backgrounds develop a heightened awareness of unconsciously-held assumptions and values that influence their interactions with others. This knowledge will help professionals become more sensitive to cultural differences and how they might affect service delivery to students and families from various cultural groups. Most people tend to be less judgmental and more open-minded when they realize what assumptions they themselves hold (Roseberry-McKibbin, 2000a).

GENERAL BACKGROUND INFORMATION

❑ The United States is the third largest country in the world (following China and India), with a population exceeding 280 million.

❑ The United States is slightly over 200 years old, making it one of the youngest countries in the world.

❑ The original inhabitants were indigenous peoples, primarily Native American Indians, who were displaced by European settlers beginning in the 17th century.

❑ The United States, which has been composed primarily of people of Anglo European descent, is rapidly changing in ethnic composition.

❑ In the 2000 census, Americans were given the option of selecting more than one racial category. In response, 97.6% of Americans chose one race category, and 2.4% chose two or more race categories.

❑ Racial and ethnic minorities accounted for approximately 80% of the U.S. population growth in the 1990s. In 1990, 43 million residents of the U.S. were minorities; in 2000, nearly 87 million residents were minorities (U.S. Bureau of the Census, 2000).

❑ Racial minorities and Hispanics now comprise approximately one-third of the U.S. population, and in the past 20 years have increased by more than 90%. In contrast, the white non-Hispanic population has increased 7.6%. The growth rate was found to be at least 48% among Asians, 26% among Native Americans and Alaska Natives, 16% among African Americans, and 9% among Native Hawaiians and Pacific Islanders (U.S. Bureau of the Census, 2000).

❑ The United States was founded on Judeo-Christian principles and values. Most Anglo European Americans are Protestants or Catholics. Approximately 90% of Americans identify with a religion (Brigham Young University, 1992).

❏ Historically, the United States was regarded as a melting pot in which members of various ethnic groups disavowed their original identities as they blended together to form an American culture. Many ethnic groups, however, have continued to maintain their customs and way of life. The United States is, in reality, a culturally pluralistic nation with many cultures, languages, and life styles.

❏ The United States has prided itself on guaranteeing freedom and equal rights for all. White male Americans, however, have traditionally had greater access to these liberties than women and persons of color. White male Americans also have the highest median income of any group (Sleeter, 1994).

❏ White males make up 35% of the adult population in the United States. They comprise 80% of tenured professors, 80% of the House of Representatives, 90% of the U.S. Senate, 92% of the Fortune 500, 97% of school superintendents, 65% of physicians, and 71% of lawyers (James, 1999).

ANGLO EUROPEAN AMERICAN FAMILY LIFE

❏ Although the American family has been considered the basic unit of society, it has undergone substantial changes in the past few decades.

❏ Many American homes have been comprised of "nuclear families" that include the father, mother, and children. There has been a shift toward other family structures.

❏ In 1950, 22% of all householders were unmarried; in 2000, 48% of all householders were unmarried. In 1970, 40% of householders had children; in 2000, 24% of householders had children. Between the years 1990 and 2000, the number of families headed by single mothers increased 25% to more than 7.5 million households (U.S. Bureau of the Census, 2000).

❏ In 1970, 90% of White children, 58% of Black children, and 78% of Hispanic children lived in households with both their mother and father. In 1998, those numbers had decreased to 74% of White children, 36% of Black children, and 64% of Hispanic children living in two-parent households (U.S. Bureau of the Census, 2000).

❏ A major and pressing need for many modern American families is accessibility to high quality, affordable child care. Many American children are placed in child care programs and spend most of the day with caregivers other than their parents.

❏ American adults often feel uncomfortable living under the same roof as their parents. Elderly parents also often desire their own dwellings, preferring not to live with their children and grandchildren.

It is common for Anglo European Americans to hold these beliefs:

1. Children should be encouraged to be independent as soon as possible. Families have high expectations for children to develop self-help and self-reliance skills. For example, only 26% of American mothers breast-feed children who have reached six months of age; at that age, children are expected to drink from a cup. However, in many countries, children are routinely nursed until they are between 3 and 4 years old.

2. It is natural for families to be mobile and to move from place to place.

3. After marriage, the husband and wife should no longer live with other family members. They should seek a home of their own.

4. There are specific places and personnel outside of the home to care for children and the elderly (e.g., day care centers, skilled nursing facilities).

✐ *REFLECTION* ✐

Matthew, a 3-year-old male, was brought to a speech-language pathologist by his parents. Both parents had doctorates. The father, who was born and raised in the Midwestern U.S., had concerns that his son might be "slow" because of several factors in the child's history. First, it was difficult to wean him from breast-feeding prior to 2 years of age. At age 3, Matthew was still not dressing himself and had only recently been potty-trained. The father was concerned because Matthew did not want to attend preschool and preferred to stay home with his mother. In addition, he was very quiet around other children, although he reportedly talked freely and in complete sentences at home. Matthew's mother was raised in the Philippines as the daughter of Baptist missionaries. She was not concerned about Matthew's development because his behavior seemed typical of that observed among many Filipino children. The father, however, insisted that the child be evaluated and, if necessary, seen for intervention.

What would you as a professional say to these parents? Does Matthew have a delay, or is the concern a by-product of the father's cultural values as an American born and raised in the U.S?

EDUCATION AND LITERACY

❑ Education in the United States is compulsory for students from 5 to 16 years of age.

❑ Americans view education as a major determinant of professional and social opportunity.

❑ In American schools, the freedom allowed to students is greater than that allowed in many other countries. Parents educated in other countries may be shocked when they learn about the degree of freedom and informality available to American students. For example, in Hong Kong, it would be unthinkable for students not to rise and bow when a teacher enters the classroom.

❑ Many American children are expected to attend college, regardless of their innate capacity to succeed in the academic curriculum. Parents, especially those from middle- and upper-socioeconomic backgrounds, generally expect that their children will complete college with a Bachelor's degree.

CULTURAL CUSTOMS, COURTESIES, AND BELIEFS

Many Anglo European Americans hold the following beliefs:

❑ Independence is extremely important; each individual's goal is to be as independent as possible.

❑ Individualism and autonomy are to be encouraged (as opposed to conformity). Many Americans believe in the importance of "looking out for number one." Group effort is not as important as individual effort and performance.

❑ Hard work is a virtue. The harder people work, the more industrious and valuable they are to their employers and to society in general.

❑ Time is of utmost importance. Promptness and punctuality are necessary in social and work settings.

❑ Financial independence and material prosperity are hallmarks of success and of "making it" in life.

❑ Privacy for individuals is highly valued.

❑ Youth and beauty are highly desirable. Growing old is often viewed negatively because physical attractiveness, strength, and ability supposedly diminish with age.

❑ It is each individual's right to challenge authority when injustice is experienced.

❑ Individuals have a great deal of control over their own destinies. It is believed that "God helps those who help themselves."

❑ It is appropriate for members of the opposite sex to show physical affection in public.

❑ If someone does a good job on a task, offering praise through public accolades is one of the most effective rewards.

❑ Men and women should have the same rights and should be treated equally. Ideally, women should be allowed to have the same work opportunities as men and should be given equal pay for their work. However, this opportunity is still not available in many work settings. American women tend to earn less than American men who hold similar jobs.

❑ Speed and efficiency are extremely important when completing any task. The rapid completion of tasks is valued.

❑ People must plan for the future. Progress and change are high priorities.

❑ Competition is a way of life, and it is healthy for children to learn to compete at an early age.

❑ Cleanliness is of utmost importance; natural odors should be covered by using perfume or deodorant.

> ## *Profile*
>
> Meghan K. was a 16-year-old girl from an Anglo English-speaking home. Her father was a high school physical education instructor, and her mother had full-time employment inside the home caring for Meghan and her younger brother. The family came from a middle-class neighborhood. When Meghan was born, the umbilical cord was wrapped tightly around her neck, resulting in fetal anoxia. Meghan was slow in reaching developmental milestones, and she had been in special education settings since kindergarten. The speech-language pathologist at Meghan's high school was asked to carry out a comprehensive speech and language assessment so that Meghan could be placed in the most appropriate setting. The results indicated that Meghan was functioning approximately seven years below her chronological age. Assessment data obtained by the school psychologist indicated that she had a full-scale IQ of 70, a score that is considerably below normal.
>
> The assessment team recommended that Meghan continue in special education and that she participate in a vocational training program designed specifically for students with special learning needs. Meghan's parents were incensed, and the meeting lasted for 3 hours. The parents felt outraged that a "vocational track" was recommended for their daughter. They shared that she was going to go to college, and they were determined to see that she attended the best college available. The parents were not interested in special education for their child in her high school years.

HEALTH CARE AND DISABLING CONDITIONS

❏ Traditional American health care has focused on cures for illness rather than prevention, although this may be changing in some areas. Many insurance companies cover few, if any, costs for preventative care.

❏ American medical practitioners tend to separate illnesses of the body and mind, in contrast to other cultures in which the body and mind are seen holistically as being inseparable.

❏ American medicine relies greatly on technology. American medical technology has made it possible for many disabled and elderly individuals to maintain "life" that relies almost exclusively on expensive, highly technological mechanical support.

❏ Most Americans believe that disabilities can be caused by variables such as genetics, trauma, disease, and teratogens (e.g., toxins).

❏ The two greatest causes of adult health problems in the United States are risky physical behavior and sedentary lifestyles (Brigham Young University, 1992).

❏ In recent decades, the American legal system has mandated that persons with disabilities be given equal access to education and jobs.

Profile

A Hmong child was hospitalized after undergoing surgery for a cleft palate. The American speech-language pathologist smelled smoke one afternoon when walking past the child's room. After calling for fire extinguishers, she entered the room to discover that the family had made a small fire under the child's hospital bed. The family believed that the smoke from the fire would drive out the evil spirits that had caused the cleft palate. The speech-language pathologist made an appointment with the hospital's Hmong interpreter to discuss how they might best approach the family to discuss their perspective regarding communication disorders and their treatment.

ANGLO EUROPEAN AMERICAN COMMUNICATION STYLES

❑ It is generally considered impolite to ask personal questions of others. For instance, asking someone to reveal information about salary is considered inappropriate in most contexts. It is also considered rude to ask people to reveal their age.

❑ Americans tend to be friendly and to make informality a goal in interactions. This may seem discourteous and "uncultured" to people from other cultural groups.

❑ When two Americans converse, they generally stand about two feet apart.

❑ Americans tend to be outspoken and frank; they appreciate these same qualities in others.

❑ In professional situations such as meetings, most Americans get to the point immediately with little preamble or small talk.

❑ Most Americans rely more on verbal than nonverbal messages; this can be termed "low-context" communication (Westby & Rouse, 1985).

❑ When talking to others, Americans generally consider it important to make direct eye contact and to maintain an open yet assertive physical stance.

❑ Americans believe that directness and assertiveness are critical in interactions with other people. For example, if one is angry at another person, this feeling may be expressed directly. Candidness is valued.

❑ In the U.S., people believe that good listeners make eye contact, ask questions, clarify when they don't understand something, nod occasionally, and make facial expressions that indicate empathy with and interest in their conversational partners.

ANGLO EUROPEAN AMERICAN LANGUAGE CONSIDERATIONS

❑ Many citizens of the United States speak Mainstream American English.

❑ Americans from different areas of the United States speak different dialects (e.g., Appalachian English) but are still able to understand one another.

❑ Many languages are spoken in the United States by various ethnic groups; the most common minority language is Spanish.

✐*REFLECTION*✐

List four qualities of "good" communicators from an Anglo European American perspective. How might these qualities conflict with the communication expectations and practices of students and families from other cultural backgrounds?

_____

_____

_____

_____

_____

IMPLICATIONS FOR PROFESSIONALS

It is important to remember that people from different backgrounds often have cultural assumptions that differ from those of "mainstream" Americans. Again, it is crucial not to make judgments about which cultural attitudes are right or wrong. Much can be learned by interacting with others who have beliefs, ideas, and styles of living different from one's own.

The following guidelines for interaction should help professionals to reduce the negative impact of mainstream U.S. assumptions during interactions with individuals from other cultural groups.

❑ Professionals should use titles when addressing adults from other cultures. Addressing others by the first name, a common practice among American professionals, may be viewed as offensively over-familiar to some families. It is probably best to err on the side of being too formal when working with persons from different cultures.

❑ Persons from some cultures (e.g., Filipino) may ask personal questions such as "Are you married?" or "Why don't you have any children?" (Roseberry-McKibbin, 1997b). Professionals need to be aware that questions such as these are considered appropriate within some cultural groups.

❑ Professionals need to be patient and open. Because many Americans believe in their personal ability to shape and control their own future, they may be less tolerant of those who believe in fate or outside forces that they cannot control.

❑ Professionals should take time to engage in preliminary courtesies. American professionals must remember that it is considered rude in some cultures (e.g., Hispanic, Arab) to delve immediately into business without small talk and some conversational preamble (Brice, 2002).

❑ American professionals must remember that most cultures value the family unit highly. Professionals must work with students and their families, rather than working only with students.

☐ In many cultures (e.g., Asian, Middle Eastern), elderly family members are highly valued and respected; their opinions carry more weight than those of younger family members. Thus, professionals should defer to the oldest family members present in an interaction.

☐ Upon conducting home visits, American professionals may be shocked to find large numbers of people sharing a single apartment. However, this is the norm in many countries. For example, in the Arab culture, there is no word for "privacy;" individuals long for and expect a great degree of closeness and physical proximity to one another (Omar Nydell, 1996).

☐ Some American professionals may experience frustration when they discover that nontraditional forms of healing are being used by the family to help a child. Although school professionals may not feel that these treatment practices are appropriate, the beliefs of the family should be respected. School professionals should work in tandem with health practitioners that the family trusts. For example, some Hispanic families might be more open to accepting educational recommendations made by a priest than to accepting recommendations made by a special education teacher.

☐ Professionals must exercise caution in using terms such as "dependent," "immature," etc. because early independence may not be considered to be an important goal within the child's family. American parents foster independence in children at an early age. Other cultures, however, have different beliefs about early independence (Roseberry-McKibbin, 2000a).

☐ In the American culture, it is considered acceptable for females to ask direct questions to males. In some cultures, this practice is often considered highly offensive. For example, in some Muslim countries, only males ask direct questions of one another.

☐ Because Americans are generally accustomed to equality between men and women, female professionals may be shocked and chagrined to discover that due to their gender, men from some cultural groups do not respect them and will not listen to their opinions and statements (Roseberry-McKibbin, 2000a). It is important to be willing to allow a male professional to speak with these men, remembering that the most important goal of any interaction is ultimately the welfare of the child.

☐ American professionals may discover that certain adolescent immigrant students do not regularly use deodorant or bathe daily. It is important to gently and sensitively advise these students and their families about mainstream U.S. expectations, and to diplomatically discuss the social consequences of allowing one's natural body odors not to be covered.

☐ American professionals may find multicultural students and their families to be quite "slow" in completing tasks or in responding to messages. Although speed and efficiency are highly valued in the U.S., American professionals need to realize that "speed" and "deadlines" are less important in other cultures. Families should not be made to feel inadequate if they are not as quick in meeting deadlines as might be expected.

☐ Professionals who work with Anglo American families can expect that these families may be angered when informed that a child with special needs may not have the skills required to attend or graduate from college. Families may remain in denial until their children graduate from high school.

✐REFLECTION✐

You are a female speech-language pathologist or special education teacher in a school where a 5th grade boy from the Middle East has been identified as being in need of special education services. The father has indicated that he will not speak with you about the child's needs because you are a woman. The custodian at the school is from the Middle East, and he has volunteered to serve as a "cultural broker" or go-between in this situation. What will you do? Will you work with the custodian, or will you expect the father to listen to what you have to say? Why?

_____

_____

_____

_____

_____

ASSUMPTIONS ABOUT AMERICANS

Commonly held beliefs about Americans have been described by a number of authors (see Omar Nydell, 1996; Penfield, 1990; Sasson, 1992). Many were also encountered by this author while growing up in the Philippines. These include:

❏ Americans are talkative and friendly.

❏ Americans are honest and frank.

❏ Americans are loud and shout a lot.

❏ Americans are materialistic and think only about money.

❏ Americans are rich.

❏ Americans do not have the ability to enjoy the present; they are always rushing toward the future.

❏ Americans do not frown on premarital sex and are highly immoral.

❏ Americans are rude. They always rush into business without engaging in any preliminary social amenities.

❏ Americans have superficial relationships.

❏ Americans do not value their families. They are more concerned about success and "getting ahead" than about the happiness of family members.

❏ When Americans travel to other countries, they drink a lot of alcohol.

❏ Americans eat hot dogs and wear cowboy boots.

❏ Americans are very aggressive.

❏ Americans are much too permissive with their children, and do not demand that they respect and obey their elders.

❏ Americans want to control the world.

Some readers may find these assumptions and stereotypes offensive because no one wants to be "categorized" and "stereotyped" without consideration of individual differences. Most Americans would not want to be described in this way. Yet some people from other cultures hold these stereotypes about Americans as a group.

Whenever members of a cultural group hold stereotypes about members of other cultural groups, the potential for misunderstanding and conflict is great. By realizing how Americans are stereotyped by members of other cultures, one can better understand how members of other cultural groups feel when they are stereotyped. It is important to look inward at one's own cultural beliefs and assumptions. Professionals must be honest with themselves if they are to develop the sensitivity necessary to serve others without bias. As previously stated, a major part of cultural competence is contained in the statement "know thyself."

STUDY QUESTIONS

1. Choose three mainstream U.S. values that you consider important to maintain (e.g., the belief that men and women should have equal rights). Why are these values important to you?

2. Describe three stereotypes about mainstream Americans that you find particularly offensive. Why do these stereotypes offend you?

3. Describe four mainstream Anglo American communication behaviors that might be viewed as inappropriate by individuals from other cultural backgrounds. Why might these behaviors be viewed negatively?

TRUE-FALSE

Circle the number beside each statement that is true.

4. Members of most cultural groups appreciate the fact that Americans are informal and address others using their first name.

5. In the U.S., the two greatest causes of health problems are a sedentary lifestyle and risky behavior.

6. Anglo European Americans generally believe that the extended family should care for children and elderly parents; they would be dismayed at the thought of sending family members to convalescent homes or day care settings.

7. Anglo European Americans tend to value being indirect, diplomatic, and subtle in interactions with others.

8. Americans are often stereotyped as having weak family values.

9. Anglo European American professionals appreciate the fact that multicultural clients usually carry out intervention recommendations with speed and efficiency.

10. American females who work as professionals might be angered if not accepted as professionals by men from other cultural groups.

MULTIPLE CHOICE

Circle the letter beside each of the choices that is correct.

11. Which of the following statements about Anglo European Americans are FALSE?
    A. Most are Protestants or Catholics.
    B. They believe that "children should be children" and allowed to develop at a relaxed pace.
    C. They value directness and assertiveness in communication.
    D. Men and women have equal rights and receive equal pay for equal work.
    E. They believe in privacy for the individual.

12. Which statements about health care are TRUE?
    A. Anglo European American medical practitioners tend to separate illnesses of the body and mind.
    B. American medicine relies greatly on technology.
    C. Most Anglo European Americans believe that factors such as genetics, trauma, disease, and teratogens (e.g., toxins) can cause disabilities.
    D. Most disabilities affecting learning can be treated using medication.

13. Which of the following statements is/are often made to "stereotype" Americans?
    A. Americans are rich.
    B. Americans are morally decadent.
    C. Americans are too strict with their children and need to allow their children much more freedom.
    D. Americans are superficial.
    E. Americans love soccer.

14. Which of the following communication behaviors do most Anglo Europeans view as being acceptable?
    A. Asking others personal questions about their age, salary, and marital status
    B. Standing approximately two feet apart during conversations
    C. Maintaining a manner of openness, friendliness, and informality during interactions
    D. Beginning a meeting or business interaction with lengthy, personal chit-chat to help all parties feel comfortable before business is addressed
    E. Making eye contact and asking questions to indicate interest during interactions

15. An Anglo European American mother has brought her 26-month-old son to you for an assessment. She stays at home and cares for him, and he is her only child. He does not go to preschool. Her son says no words yet, and he appears not to comprehend even simple requests and questions. Which of the following would be APPROPRIATE in your interaction with this mother?
    A. Being quite indirect and suggesting that time might automatically take care of the problem
    B. Telling her that the communication problem may persist into adulthood and that, in the future, the child should be trained for a vocation that does not require a college education
    C. Recommending a preschool for several hours a day to increase his speech and language skills
    D. Telling her to spend several hours a day drilling him on new vocabulary words

ANSWERS TO STUDY QUESTIONS

    4. False
    5. True
    6. False
    7. False
    8. True
    9. False
    10. True
    11. B and D
    12. A, B, and C
    13. A, B, and D
    14. B, C, and E
    15. C

Chapter 4

FAMILIES FROM AFRICAN AMERICAN BACKGROUNDS

Outline

General Background Information

African American Family Life

Education and Literacy

Health Care and Disabling Conditions

African American Communication Styles

African American English Considerations

Misconceptions About African American English

Bias in Assessment Measures

Factors to Consider in Assessment

Implications for Professionals

GENERAL BACKGROUND INFORMATION

❏ African Americans are unique in their history of immigration (Willis, 1998). Historically, some chose to enter the United States. However, most were forcibly taken from African villages (either by White slave traders or by Africans from other villages) and sold into slavery in the southern United States. Today, Black immigrants enter the United States each year from such areas as South and Central America, Africa, and the Caribbean.

❏ In 1990, there were 29,986,060 Blacks or African Americans in the U.S. (12.1% of the total U.S. population). In 2000, there were 34,658,190 Blacks or African Americans (race alone) in the U.S. (U.S. Bureau of the Census, 2000).

❏ When the figures were obtained for race alone and race in combination (e.g., a person indicated that he was from both African American and Hispanic backgrounds), there were 36,419,434 Blacks or African Americans in the United States (U.S. Bureau of the Census, 2000). Blacks or African Americans experienced a much slower growth rate than Hispanics and Asians.

❏ In early African religions, ancestors and spirits of nature were worshiped. Religion has traditionally played an important role in African American communities in the United States and it is integral to the lives of many African Americans today. They often come from traditional Christian backgrounds including Baptist, Methodist, and Episcopal denominations (Willis, 1998).

❏ At the time of the Civil War, the vast majority of the country's African Americans lived in the south.

❏ The Emancipation Proclamation (1863) resulted in freedom from slavery. Many African Americans moved to the northern United States to find better opportunities. Prejudice, however, was widespread. In recent years, there has been a "reverse migration" of African Americans back to southern states (Cole, 1989).

❏ "By 1901, laws dealing with 'Jim Crow,' a term that had become synonymous with African Americans, had become the fabric of how the races would relate to one another based on skin color and myths of genetic superiority for whites and inferiority for African Americans" (Willis, 1998).

❏ Historically there was much discrimination against African Americans, including widespread segregation and the absence of voting rights. Such deprivation denied them true assimilation into mainstream society.

❏ Historical turning points for African Americans included:

1. the 1954 Brown v. Board of Education decision, and its effect in eliminating segregated schools.
2. the Civil Rights Movement with its leader, Dr. Martin Luther King.
3. the implementation of the Economic Opportunity Act and the Civil Rights Act of 1964.
4. the implementation of the Voting Rights Act of 1965.

❏ Unfortunately, even today "African Americans remain only partially assimilated. . .Their path to full assimilation appears to be blocked by the lack of opportunities for mobility upward and out of the predominantly Black enclaves where African American language flourishes" (van Keulen, Weddington, & DeBose, 1998, p. xxii).

❑ The experiences of slavery, institutional racism, and continued economic oppression in the U.S. have caused many African Americans to experience distrust and anger toward European Americans (Terrell, Battle, & Grantham, 1998; van Keulen et al., 1998).

❑ Middle class African Americans may feel more anger than low income African Americans because they work hard, are educated, and have been exposed to the rewards the system offers. Yet because they are black in skin color, they have not had equal access to these rewards and have not been equally remunerated (Terrell & Terrell, 1996).

❑ Poverty is widespread for African Americans as a group. According to U.S. Census Bureau figures over the years (1986, 1987, 1990), one out of every two African American children lived in poverty; 28% of African Americans had incomes below poverty level.

❑ Forty percent of native-born African Americans work in low-paying occupations that employ high percentages of immigrants compared to 22.9% of Anglos who work in these jobs (Center for Immigration Studies, 2001).

❑ Fortunately, there has been a slight reversal in this trend, with African Americans in the U.S. gaining increased financial stability and equity (Hodgkinson, 2001).

❑ Graham (2000, p. ix) challenged the widespread stereotypes of African Americans in the U.S.: "The stereotype of the working-class black or impoverished black is one that whites, as well as blacks, have come to embrace and accept as an accurate and complete account of the black American experience." He discussed in detail the "black elite," a highly-educated and financially successful segment of the African American population in the U.S., and encouraged Americans of all ethnic backgrounds to remember the great heterogeneity that exists within all ethnic groups.

✐REFLECTION✐

Takesha, an 8-year-old African American girl on your caseload, tells you that she has not been receiving invitations to any of her classmates' birthday parties. Also, despite the fact that there are eight Girl Scout troops represented at the school, none of them has a space for Takesha. She seems depressed because of this. How will you handle this situation? Will you talk with Takesha about it? How can you assist her in this situation?

_____

_____

_____

_____

_____

AFRICAN AMERICAN FAMILY LIFE

❑ Families from African American backgrounds may include blood relatives and others who are not blood relatives but have special caring relationships.

❑ Many African Americans place high value on developing children's knowledge of who their immediate and extended family members are (Willis, 1998). These families emphasize knowledge of African American heritage, a sense of pride, and knowledge of cultural uniqueness.

❑ Although many African American households are designated "female single head of household" status, this designation does not take into account extended relationships and support systems available to many families (Willis, 1998). African American families generally provide more help for one another across generations than White families.

❑ Rather than emphasizing the importance of individual effort and gain, many families emphasize group effort for the common interest and expect that those who succeed will share with the larger community. These families view collective responsibility, interdependence, and cooperation as important values.

❑ Most families value obedience to parents, older siblings, and other older persons. They place great emphasis on respect for elders, who are seen as having hindsight and wisdom. Most families expect young children to treat others well, to obey family rules, and to work hard in school.

❑ African American families tend to use an approach to child-rearing that is more authoritative than in some other groups (Tannen, 1994). Many families believe strongly in discipline to teach children appropriate behavior.

❑ Many African Americans believe that children must be loved, guided, protected, and disciplined; all responsible adults in many communities partake in the discipline and training of children.

❑ In many African American families, infants are nurtured warmly and affectionately; young children are given the opportunity to "be children" and to enjoy play (Willis, 1998). In contrast, Anglo Americans tend to push children towards early independence and self-reliance.

❑ African American families tend to be flexible about family roles. Fathers and mothers share child care responsibilities, and older siblings carry out household chores and help care for younger siblings.

❑ "African Americans are not as concerned about sex role identities as European Americans...they are more concerned with overcoming obstacles based on racial membership than with gender affiliation" (van Keulen et al., 1998, p. 218).

EDUCATION AND LITERACY

❑ Education is viewed as an important and desirable achievement by many African Americans. Children in African American families are often taught that an education is something that no one can take away.

❑ Unfortunately, educational barriers are often experienced by African Americans. Conflicts may occur because of differences between school values and peer group values (Ogbu, 1992). In addition, there may be mismatches between home and school that contribute to lack of success for African American children.

❏ Some African American students have difficulty in school because the language used in instruction and in books differs from the spoken language as it is used in their community. These children may use African American English in their community and home, although school teachers conduct classes in Mainstream American English and often expect students to use "standard English" at school.

❏ This can put African American students at a disadvantage in school, and may be a factor contributing to the overrepresentation of African American students in special education.

❏ The overrepresentation of African American students in special education has occurred most often in school districts with a high percentage of Anglo students (van Keulen et al., 1998).

❏ Van Keulen et al. (1998) likened African American English-speaking students to second language learners in that these students have conversational language proficiency, but struggle with academic English used in textbooks.

❏ Gifted and talented African American students may be under-identified in schools because of assessment procedures that do not adequately reflect the strengths of individuals from African American backgrounds. Traditional intelligence tests are notoriously biased against African Americans.

HEALTH CARE AND DISABLING CONDITIONS

❏ Many African Americans lack access to adequate health care and do not have medical insurance (Terrell & Jackson, 2002).

❏ The African American population tends to have a higher mortality rate than other groups in some communities. Infant mortality is 20 per 1,000 African American live births as opposed to 10.5 per 1,000 White live births (Willis, 1998). Lower income, less frequent prenatal care, poorer maternal nutrition, and other factors make it more difficult for many African Americans to raise healthy children.

❏ Jaundice may not be noticed in African American infants because the typical symptom is yellow skin; some infants go untreated and experience varying degrees of brain damage.

❏ Death from nutritional deficiency in infancy is 10 times more likely among African American children than among White children (Willis, 1998).

❏ Approaches to health vary depending on income and the educational level of individual families. Some African Americans, especially in the rural south, rely on home remedies or holistic health approaches in which herbs, roots, teas, and natural foods are used (Willis, 1998).

❏ Some low-income families may not understand and/or have access to the traditional health care system. Thus, they may only receive care when they are seriously ill. Preventative health care may not be available or utilized.

❏ Health care may differ in quantity and quality for African Americans than for other groups. For example, some African Americans have been forced to experience longer waiting periods in doctors' offices than Whites and delays in transfer times from emergency rooms to critical care units in hospitals (Ghali, Cooper, Kowatly, & Liao, 1993).

❏ Sickle cell disease, a hereditary disease of the red blood cells affecting Blacks worldwide, has been associated with sensorineural hearing loss (Scott, 1998).

❏ Major inner city areas of the United States are comprised primarily of African Americans. These areas have limited services, poor housing, unemployment, crime, poverty, overcrowding, and illegal drug activities (Willis, 1998). All of these phenomena have negative implications for health.

❏ Many African American children under 6 years of age have an elevated level of lead in the blood. This is due in part to lead levels in low-income housing. High lead levels are linked to many learning problems and health risks.

❏ Elderly African Americans are at greatest risk for heart disease and hypertension, and they are also at risk for strokes.

❏ Some African Americans believe that disabling conditions are due to evil spirits, the work of the devil, punishment for disobeying God, and/or bad luck (Willis, 1998).

❏ African American families are often able to accept children who have disabilities. This acceptance may result, in part, from support within the extended family and strong ties with the church.

AFRICAN AMERICAN COMMUNICATION STYLES

❏ Approval and agreement between participants in a conversation may be expressed through touching or physical contact. African Americans, during interactions, touch each other more than they touch Anglo Americans. This is especially true of African Americans from lower socioeconomic backgrounds (van Keulen et al., 1998).

❏ Eye contact is used as a form of nonverbal communication. However, rolling of the eyes during conversation may be viewed as offensive (Willis, 1998).

❏ Some African American students make little eye contact with adults, who may view such behavior as disrespectful.

❏ Public behavior can be intense and demonstrative; it may appear to be unrestrained by other groups (Willis, 1998).

❏ African American students often speak in a manner that is animated, interpersonal, and confrontational. This manner of speaking contrasts with that of Anglo students who often speak in a manner that is dispassionate, non-challenging, and impersonal (van Keulen et al., 1998).

❏ Traditional turn-taking may not be observed in conversations between participants. If a participant feels a need to add valuable information, an interruption and/or change of topic may occur.

❏ Individuals are expected to participate verbally in conversations and not to remain silent. Conversations may be quite competitive, with the most assertive participants doing most of the talking. Mainstream professionals must be careful not to label this behavior as "rude" or as "lacking in pragmatic skills."

❑ Among many African Americans, charismatic speech with distinctive intonational patterns and rhythm is rewarded and valued. African Americans frequently speak with emotional vitality.

❑ Because of the relatively continuous presence of music or words among African Americans, some people would characterize them as loud or shallow. These pejorative terms indicate a lack of understanding of African American values. Both systems of values are legitimate (Willis, 1998).

❑ African American culture contains many communication rituals and distinctive styles that affirm cultural identity and allegiance to the group.

❑ One example is "call and response," where the listeners echo part of the speaker's previous utterance. For example, in a church setting, the preacher might say "And the Lord told Noah to build an ark." The congregation might respond "Build an ark." (see van Keulen et al., 1998, for more details regarding communication rituals).

❑ African American students' narrative styles often differ from those of mainstream Anglo students who speak Standard American English (SAE). These differences can lead to incorrect judgments about behavior (Gutierrez-Clellen & Quinn, 1993; Terrell & Jackson, 2002; van Keulen et al., 1998).

1. African American students often rely on gestures to accompany verbalizations or narratives.
2. When African American students tell stories, they may include personal judgments and evaluations about the characters.
3. In mainstream school programs, students are expected to tell stories in a topic-centered style, characterized by topic elaboration, structured discourse on a single topic, and lack of presupposed shared knowledge. African American students often use a topic-associating style, characterized by lack of consideration for detail, presupposition of shared knowledge between the speaker and listener(s), and structured discourse on several linked topics. Unfortunately, use of the topic-associating style can cause examiners to view African American children as disorganized and as language-disordered.

AFRICAN AMERICAN ENGLISH CONSIDERATIONS

African American English (AAE), the language spoken by some residents of the United States, has undergone many changes in nomenclature (LeMoine, 1993). AAE has been referred to using terms such as Black Dialect, Black English, Black English Vernacular, African American Vernacular, African American Language, and Ebonics (Craig, Washington, & Thompson-Porter, 1998; van Keulen et al., 1998). The changes in nomenclature have been due, in part, to an increasingly sophisticated understanding of AAE, and to changes in sociolinguistic theory. Because it contains much similarity to SAE, AAE is considered by most experts today to be a dialect of SAE, not a separate language (Terrell et al., 1998).

The extent to which African American English is used is influenced by a number of factors:

❑ Use of AAE is influenced by geographic region, socioeconomic status, education, gender, age, and other factors.

❑ Middle-class African Americans generally use AAE less than working class African Americans, especially in formal settings.

❑ African American children from low-income homes use more "dialectal forms" than their peers from middle class homes. The discourse of boys shows more evidence of use of these forms than that of girls (Craig et al., 1998).

❑ Syntax is the area in which differences between AAE and SAE are most apparent (Willis, 1998).

❑ There are a number of West African languages that have impacted modern-day African American English: Bambara, Ewe, Fanta, Fon, Fula, Ga, Ibo, Ibibio, Kimbundu, Longo, Mandinka, Mende, Twi, Imbundu, Wolof, and Yoruba.

❑ Prior to 3 years of age, it is difficult to detect differences in the language development of children who speak SAE and children who speak AAE. During this period, the morphosyntactic development of children who speak AAE differs very little from that of children who speak SAE. However, between 3 and 5 years of age, children who are acquiring AAE begin to use a greater number of "nonstandard" grammatical forms (Wyatt, 1998b).

❑ As many as 39% of the utterances of African American preschoolers from low-income, urban homes include morphosyntactic forms that are characteristic of African American English (Washington & Craig, 1994).

❑ Isaacs (1996) found that a dialect shift/decline occurred between grades 3 and 5 in White and African American children who spoke non-standard dialect. The transition tended not to occur in children who failed to make the shift in the elementary school grades. Thus, one may extrapolate from the research that children who speak AAE use it most heavily between ages 3 and 8; after age 8, use of AAE may decline as the children are exposed increasingly to SAE within the school setting.

MISCONCEPTIONS ABOUT AFRICAN AMERICAN ENGLISH

There are numerous misconceptions about AAE that professionals must be aware of if they are to interact effectively with AAE speakers:

Misconception #1. All African Americans speak AAE.

Some African Americans speak AAE and some do not. Some codeswitch back and forth between SAE and AAE depending on context (van Keulen et al., 1998).

Profile

Dr. Ndidi Johnson is Chair of the Nursing Department in a university setting. She shared with this author that she codeswitches between SAE and AAE depending upon the situation. In Dr. Johnson's words, "When I'm at work, I speak White English because that's what I need to do. When I get home, I switch to Black English. [Linguistically], it's like wearing high heels all day—when I get home, I kick them off and put on a pair of comfortable tennis shoes."

Misconception #2. AAE is only spoken by African Americans.

AAE can be spoken by people of any ethnic and linguistic background. Non-African Americans may speak AAE if their primary peer group is composed of African Americans. For example, some Puerto Rican students in New York City speak AAE as do some Anglo students in Oakland, California. African Americans who are socialized primarily with Anglos will generally speak Mainstream American English.

Misconception #3. AAE is a substandard form of Mainstream American English.

Historically, the language patterns of African Americans were viewed as "deficient." A major premise of this view was that African Americans were cognitively unable to learn SAE. Currently, AAE is viewed as a fully developed language with a system of rules governing its structure and use.

Misconception #4. AAE needs to be eradicated so that children can learn the language as it is used in school.

It is possible to learn Standard American English without eradicating African American English. Some experts believe that speakers of AAE should become "bilingual" or "bidialectal" so that they can speak both AAE and SAE fluently (LeMoine, 1993; van Keulen et al., 1998). In this optimal situation, students can preserve their culture, heritage, and community dialect as they learn the style of speaking required in school and in various types of social interactions.

Misconception #5. Speakers of AAE can be adequately assessed with standardized tests of intelligence, language, etc. if a representative sample is included in the norming population.

Many published assessment instruments used in schools were developed and standardized on student populations consisting primarily of Anglo, middle class, monolingual English speakers. These tests, especially those designed to assess aspects of grammar and sentence production, have been criticized by numerous experts as being inappropriate for use with African American children and other cultural groups. Including a small sample of AAE speakers in the norming population does little to make the test appropriate for these students (Craig & Washington, 2000; Smith, Lee, & McDade, 2001; Wyatt, 1997).

BIAS IN ASSESSMENT MEASURES

When AAE speakers are tested, it is critical to know which aspects of their speech and language are reflective of AAE rules and which aspects are indicative of a disorder. It is illegal for speech-language pathologists in the public schools to enroll AAE speakers for "remediation" of speech-language "disorders" if the goal of intervention is to teach standard English grammar. An understanding of AAE and how it differs from SAE is critical if speech-language pathologists are to distinguish between a language difference and a language disorder. Important morphosyntactic and articulatory-phonological characteristics of AAE are presented in Tables 4.1 and 4.2 respectively. Additional examples of bias are presented below:

❏ Bias in articulation and phonological tasks

Most tests of articulation and phonology are normed on Anglo children. The unique characteristics of AAL must be considered when assessing articulation and phonology.

Table 4.1

CHARACTERISTICS OF AFRICAN AMERICAN ENGLISH MORPHOLOGY AND SYNTAX

AAL Feature/Characteristic	Mainstream American English	Sample AAE Utterance
Omission of noun possessive	That's the woman's car. It's John's pencil.	That *the woman* car. It *John* pencil.
Omission of noun plural	He has 2 boxes of apples. She gives me 5 cents.	He got 2 *box* of *apple*. She give me 5 *cent*.
Omission of third person singular present tense marker	She walks to school. The man works in his yard.	She *walk* to school. The man *work* in his yard.
Omission of "to be" forms such as "is, are"	She is a nice lady. They are going to a movie.	*She a* nice lady. *They going* to a movie
Present tense "is" may be used regardless of person/number.	They are having fun. You are a smart man.	*They is* having fun. *You is* a smart man.
Utterances with "to be" may not show person number agreement with past and present forms.	You are playing ball. They are having a picnic.	You *is* playing ball. They *is* having a picnic.
Present tense forms of auxiliary "have" are omitted.	I have been here for 2 hours. He has done it again.	I been here for 2 hours. He done it again.
Past tense endings may be omitted.	He lived in California. She cracked the nut.	He *live* in California. She *crack* the nut.
Past "was" may be used regardless of number and person.	They were shopping. You were helping me.	They *was* shopping. You *was* helping me.

AAE Feature/Characteristic	Mainstream American English	Sample AAE Utterance
Multiple negatives (each additional negative form adds emphasis to the negative meaning.)	We don't have any more. I don't want any cake. I don't like broccoli.	We **don't** have **no** more. I **don't never** want **no** cake. I **don't never** like broccoli.
"None" may be substituted for "any."	She doesn't want any.	She don't want **none.**
Perfective construction; "been" may be used to indicate that an action took place in the distant past.	I had the mumps last year I have known her for years.	I **been had** the mumps last year. I **been known** her.
"Done" may be combined with a past tense form to indicate that an action was started and completed.	He fixed the stove. She tried to paint it.	He **done fixed** the stove. She **done tried** to paint it.
The form "be" may be used as the main verb.	Today she is working. We are singing.	Today **she be** working. **We be** singing.
Distributive "be" may be used to indicate actions and events over time.	He is often cheerful. She's kind sometimes.	**He be** cheerful. **She be** kind.
A pronoun may be used to restate the subject.	My brother surprised me. My dog has fleas.	My brother, **he** surprise me. My dog, **he** got fleas.
"Them" may be substituted for "those."	Those cars are antiques. Where'd you get those books?	Them cars, they be antique. Where you get **them books**?
Future tense "is, are" may be replaced by "gonna."	She is going to help us. They are going to be there.	She **gonna** help us. They **gonna** be there.
"At" is used at the end of "where" questions.	Where is the house? Where is the store?	Where is the house **at**? Where is the store **at**?
Additional auxiliaries are often used.	I might have done it.	I **might could have** done it.
"Does" is replaced by "do."	She does funny things. It does make sense.	**She do** funny things. **It do** make sense.

Table 4.2

CHARACTERISTICS OF AFRICAN AMERICAN ENGLISH ARTICULATION AND PHONOLOGY

AAE Feature/Characteristic	Mainstream American English	African American English
/l/ phoneme lessened or omitted	tool always	too' a'ways
/r/ phoneme lessened or omitted	door mother protect	doah mudah p'otek
f/voiceless "th" substitution at end or middle of word	teeth both nothing	teef bof nufin'
t/voiceless "th" substitution in beginning of a word	think thin	tink tin
d/voiced "th" substitution at the beginning, middle of words	this brother	dis broder
v/voiced "th" substitution at the end of words	breathe smooth	breave smoov
consonant cluster reduction	desk rest left wasp	des' res' lef' was'
Differing syllable stress patterns	guitar police July	**gui** tar **po** lice **Ju** ly

AAE Feature/Characteristic	Mainstream American English	African American English
Verbs ending in /k/ are changed	liked walked	li-tid wah-tid
Metathesis occurs	ask	aks ("axe")
Devoicing of final voiced consonants	bed rug cab	bet ruk cap
Final consonants may be deleted	bad good	ba' goo'
I/E substitution	pen ten	pin tin
b/v substitution	valentine vest	balentine bes'
diphthong reduction	find oil pound	fahnd ol pond
n/ng substitution	walking thing	walkin' thin'

Note: Characteristics may vary depending on variables such as geographic region.

Articulation differences such as the substitution of /f/ for the initial sound in *thumb*, for example, may result in an "error" being scored.

❏ Bias in sentence repetition tasks

Examiner: "Repeat these sentences after me. Remember to say them EXACTLY like I say them!"

1. Neither child is using the swings.
2. They had been hungry.
3. She looks at the big, brown dog.

❏ Bias in grammatic closure tasks

Examiner: "I am going to say some sentences. I want you to fill in the word that is missing. For example, "A rose is a flower and a daisy is a flower. Daisies and roses are both _____." Now you do some:

1. Today I play the marimba; yesterday I _____the marimba.
2. I have a cat, and you have a cat; we have two _____.
3. Today Sue is going to the store; yesterday she _____ going to the store.

❏ Bias in receptive grammatical tasks

Examiner: "We are going to look at some pictures. Each page has three pictures. When I say a sentence, you point to the picture that goes with the sentence I say. Here's the first picture."

1. Show me, "The cats are playing in the garden."
2. Show me, "He played baseball."
3. Point to, "They have been painting the fence."

✐ *REFLECTION* ✐

Ms. Smith had a number of African American students in her class. One day she was overheard talking with an African American child who was leaving her room to go back to the school library.

"Bye, Ms. Smith," he said cheerfully. "We be goin' back to the library now."

"DeJon!" she exclaimed. "That's the bad grammar! We are learning to use the good grammar. Say 'We ARE going back to class now.' "

Why was the comment made by Ms. Smith inappropriate? What might she have said instead?

_____

_____
_____
_____
_____

❏ **Bias in grammatical judgment tasks**

Examiner: "Tell me whether the following sentences are correct or incorrect."

1. Them girls is having a good time.
2. The boys is going to the party.
3. We don't have no time to talk to you.

Although the sentence examples above are "incorrect" in standard English, they are not abnormal among speakers of African American English. Additional examples of language differences affecting sentence production are presented in Table 4.3.

FACTORS TO CONSIDER IN ASSESSMENT

❏ There are many considerations to keep in mind when assessing the speech and language of African American students. Professionals must be nonjudgmental, open, and knowledgeable about linguistic and cultural issues that can impact the evaluation of African American students.

❏ It is sometimes necessary to avoid asking personal and direct questions during the first meeting with African American students. Questions of this type may be viewed as offensive and intrusive. The question "Can you tell me about your family" may be insulting to an African American student who does not know the interviewer.

❏ If an African American student feels intimidated when asked questions by a school professional, responses to these questions may provide limited information. The professional may conclude, inappropriately, that the student has poor expressive language skills.

❏ Researchers have recommended alternative forms of assessment (nonstandardized measures) that can be used to assess the presence of communication disorders in African American students. These include contrastive analysis (McGregor, Williams, Hearst, & Johnson, 1997), a description of children's functional communication skills (Campbell, 1996), and language sample analysis (Bliss, 2002; Seymour, Bland-Stewart, & Green, 1998; Stockman, 1996).

❏ Culturally fair, dialectically nonbiased methods for analyzing information obtained from language samples have been described (Craig & Washington, 2000; Smith, Lee, & McDade, 2001). The measurement of C-unit length has been found to be more useful than traditional measures such as mean length of utterance. C-units consist of independent clauses plus their modifiers (see Craig et al., 1998 for information about measuring C-unit length).

❏ Washington, Craig, and Kushmaul (1998) compared two language sampling situations for young African American children entering school. They found that African American English language production was more diverse and frequent during a picture description activity than it was in a free play situation. Picture description was also found to be more efficient than free play for language sampling. Washington et al. thus recommended that for young African American children entering school, picture description is an excellent way to obtain a "more ecologically valid picture of the African American child as a classroom dialect user. Picture description more closely resembles the kinds of tasks that might be encountered in an SAE classroom environment than free play." (p. 112)

❏ The development of social interaction skills may be viewed as having greater importance than the development of a large vocabulary in many African American families. Students who have

Table 4.3

EXAMPLES OF ACCEPTABLE UTTERANCES
BY SPEAKERS OF AFRICAN AMERICAN LANGUAGE

Mainstream American English	African American Language
That boy looks like me.	That boy, he look like me.
If he kicks it, he'll be in trouble.	If he kick it, he be in trouble.
When the lights are off, it's dark.	When the lights be off, it dark.
It could be somebody's pet.	It could be somebody pet.
Her feet are too big.	Her feet is too big.
I'll get something to eat.	I will get me something to eat.
She is dancing and the music's on.	She be dancin' an' the music on.
What kind of cheese do you want?	What kind of cheese you want?
My brother's name is Joe.	My brother name is Joe.
I raked the leaves outside.	I rakted the leaves outside.
After the recital, they shook my hand.	After the recital, they shaketed my hand.
They are standing around.	They is just standing around.
He is a basketball star.	He a basketball star.
They are in cages.	They be in cages.
It's not like a tree or anything.	It not like a tree or nothin'.
He does like to fish.	He do like to fish.
They are going to swim.	They gonna swim.
Mom already repaired the car.	Mom done repair the car.

had limited experience with activities in which they are asked to "name" objects may do poorly on vocabulary assessment measures, giving the false impression that they have a disorder that affects language learning ability.

❑ Washington and Craig (1999) found that the Peabody Picture Vocabulary Test, third edition (PPVT-III) was more culturally fair than the earlier edition (PPVT-R) and that the changes in the PPVT-III made it possible to obtain unbiased outcomes for at-risk African American subjects as a group. They did caution, however, that the overall high group scores masked lower scores that were common among subjects from homes in which the mother had limited educational experiences.

❑ Despite the fact that the PPVT-III appears to be one of the better tests available for nonbiased assessment of the receptive vocabulary skills of African American students, Stockman (2000) cautioned that more research is needed and that the PPVT-III should be used in conjunction with other measures of vocabulary knowledge and use.

❑ When assessing speech sound production, it must be remembered that misdiagnosis is likely to occur if the presence of an articulation disorder is based entirely on the results of formal articulation tests. It is important to examine the child's speech in everyday situations and to consider how others in the local community react to the child's speech.

IMPLICATIONS FOR PROFESSIONALS

❑ Professionals should always address family members formally, using titles and surnames, unless specifically invited to do otherwise (Terrell & Jackson, 2002).

❑ Professionals should address students' needs with a family-focused approach to intervention. Families may be experiencing stress because of health and safety hazards, poverty, lack of access to medical care, etc. It is best to utilize the strong family support systems that exist within many African American families when helping them to achieve specific goals.

❑ Local religious organizations, supported by the family, can often be used as allies in intervention. Their assistance may be of greater value than that provided by agencies that the family has never used.

❑ In order to help families to follow intervention suggestions appropriately, Willis (1998) maintained that professionals may need to do the following:

1. Make sure that at least two family members understand recommendations.

2. Design take-home materials and treatment plans so that they can be used without complications.

3. Follow up on the family's progress and make appropriate adjustments.

4. Be sure that the family can obtain necessary materials and equipment to carry out instructions.

❑ When working with families, remember that poverty is not necessarily an indicator of dysfunction; many low-income families provide stable, loving environments for their children.

❑ However, because disproportionate numbers of African American families in the U.S. experience poverty, the need for educational services and rehabilitation often are viewed as less important than the need for food, clothing, shelter, and medical care (Terrell et al., 1998). Professionals should not judge these families as being uncaring or indifferent.

❑ When working with families of African American children, it is important to consider the family's socioeconomic status (SES) as an important variable impacting communication patterns in the home. For example, Wallace, Roberts, and Lodder (1998) showed that mothers from low-income families scored lower on measures related to care-giving than did mothers who were not experiencing financial hardship.

❑ Hammer and Weiss (1999), in their study of low- and mid-SES African American mother-child dyads, showed that mid-SES mothers tended to include significantly more language goals (e.g., labeling objects) in their interactions than did low-SES mothers.

❑ Hammer and Weiss speculated that as the children in the low-SES group grew older, they might be at risk for lower language gains as measured by standardized tests. When home interaction styles differ from what is expected in school, children may not develop the skills needed to perform well on the tests administered in the school setting.

❑ Additionally, it was seen that low-SES African American mothers initiated play interactions to teach their children less frequently than did mid-SES African American mothers; instead, low-SES children often initiated play interactions with their mothers (Hammer & Weiss, 2000).

❑ Hammer and Weiss recommended that these parents be provided with strategies to help them facilitate play within child-initiated interactions.

❑ African American parents often interact with their children through story-telling. They should be encouraged to stimulate their children's interaction with print by reading to them frequently (van Keulen et al., 1998).

❑ Parents can also be encouraged to provide responsive and stimulating home environments. Jackson & Roberts (2001) found that the responsiveness of the home environment predicted the amount of complex syntax children from AAE homes used at 4 years of age. Complex syntax use was not affected by use of AAE.

❑ Some researchers have found that African American infants are more advanced in their motor development than infants from other ethnic groups; this is an important consideration when looking at case history information relating to motor development (Erickson, 1992).

❑ When using published assessment instruments with African American students, an effort should be made to select measures that have been found to be linguistically and culturally appropriate for this population. The Communication and Symbolic Behavior Scales (Wetherby & Prizant, 1993), for example, has been shown (in one study) not to be culturally biased (Roberts, Medley, Swartzfager, & Neebe, 1997).

❑ Educators in regular and special education programs should be flexible in identifying the special talents of their African American students. Identification of students' strengths and limitations should be based, to a greater degree, on observations made by teachers and parents than on scores obtained from standardized tests.

❏ Among African Americans, the cultural emphasis on verbal expectations can lead some parents to perceive a language or articulation problem as a fluency problem. They hear a disruption in their child's speech and attribute it to abnormalities in the speech flow. Thus, it is important in these cases to carefully elicit parents' or clients' perception of the presenting communication problem in order to ascertain the precise nature of that problem (Robinson & Crowe, 1998).

❏ Because of the strong emphasis African Americans place on oral communication, they may feel the need to speak fluently, rapidly, and without struggle. This can cause some African Americans, especially males, to do everything possible to conceal their stuttering (van Keulen et al., 1998).

❏ If African American students qualify for intervention, professionals should work to ensure that service delivery is culturally sensitive to and appropriate for these students.

❏ Professionals should remember that some young African American children learn best when the teaching strategies emphasize interpersonal interaction rather than independence. Child-rearing practices in African American culture have been described as "people oriented" and highly affective (Terrell & Hale, 1992). Teaching styles that emphasize open affection, encouragement, and praise are highly effective with many African American children.

❏ African American students often show a relational cognitive style in which gestalt learning, opportunities for muscular movement, and variation in learning activities positively affect performance (Robinson & Crowe, 1998; Terrell & Hale, 1992; van Keulen et al., 1998).

❏ Because African American culture emphasizes cooperation and sharing rather than competition, cooperative learning activities benefit many African American students.

❏ African American students tend to be more responsive in educational situations in which the professional (e.g., teacher, speech-language pathologist) is charismatic and encourages sharing, team work, and open discussions. These students tend to be least responsive in situations in which they are expected to sit still, be passive, and refrain from interaction (van Keulen et al., 1998).

❏ Because African American students often prefer a field-dependent learning style, peer interaction and aspects in the surrounding environment facilitate learning. Feelings of low self-esteem and mistrust might be experienced if the student is isolated from opportunities to interact with others during instruction (Terrell et al., 1998).

❏ When teaching African American students, professionals should remember that learning may be enhanced through the use of auditory and kinesthetic techniques in a high-energy, fast-paced atmosphere with a varied format (Terrell et al., 1998).

❏ Professionals should incorporate African American music, literature, art, and history into learning activities. Experiences of this type have been shown to enhance pride and to enhance learning. King (1993) recommended the use of rap music and African American proverbs to cultivate students' sense of history and culture.

❏ African American students who are accustomed to "call and response" may respond verbally in class to the teacher's question without first raising their hands. These students may be viewed as disrespectful, rude, and aggressive (van Keulen et al., 1998). Although "school rules" may need to be explained to these students, school professionals should be understanding when such behaviors do occur.

❏ Phrases as "raise your hand," "take a seat," or "line up" are not necessarily familiar to African American students when they enter school. Professionals can help these children adjust to the school setting by teaching the language of the classroom.

❏ Within the African American culture, the name given to a child is considered extremely important (Terrell & Jackson, 2002). Professionals should always ask students the name that they prefer to be called. If the pronunciation of the name appears unique to mainstream professionals, these professionals should make every attempt to memorize this unique pronunciation and use it appropriately.

❏ Most experts agree that it is not the province of school-based speech-language pathologists or special education teachers to provide services for "remediation" of AAE. It is important to remember that use of AAE is not a "disorder" and that students may not be enrolled in any type of special education program without evidence of a disorder or disability. It is recommended that classroom teachers help these students learn SAE.

❏ Teachers and other professionals should not overtly correct or criticize the oral language of students who speak AAE. However, professionals can model SAE. For instance, if a student says "Hey, he cool" the professional might reply, "Yes, he is cool. I think he is cool, too." Professionals can also teach the differences between "home talk" and "school talk" in a nonperjorative manner that helps students become bidialectal in both oral and written language (Campbell, 1993). Specific, instructional strategies have been described by van Keulen et al. (1998). Although it is important for students to learn SAE, teachers should respect the use of AAE within the African American culture.

❏ Speech-language pathologists can provide inservice programs to enhance teachers' knowledge of specific ways to differentiate between language difference and disorder in speakers of AAE. In this inservice, strategies for teaching SAE in the classroom can also be shared. Such inservice programs are likely to result in fewer inappropriate referrals as illustrated in the school situation below:

> The student population at Apple Elementary School in California consisted primarily of Anglo speakers of SAE. Recently, there had been a large influx of African American students. Several dozen speakers of African American English were referred inappropriately to the speech-language pathologist for testing. One teacher told the speech-language pathologist that "someone has to teach these kids how to talk right!"
>
> In an effort to reduce the number of inappropriate referrals, the speech-language pathologist held an hour-long inservice for the teachers. She explained that it is legal to enroll students for speech and language services only if a disorder has been identified. She provided the teachers with a detailed handout to help them distinguish communication differences from disorders in speakers of AAE. The next year, inappropriate referrals of AAE-speaking students decreased substantially, and teachers became more accepting of individual differences within their classrooms.

STUDY QUESTIONS

1. Briefly describe factors in the history of African Americans in the United States that have led to feelings of anger and mistrust toward Anglo Americans.

2. List characteristics that are common to many African American families. What values do many of them hold regarding child-rearing?

3. Describe educational barriers that African American students may experience when they attend traditional U.S. schools. In what ways has African American English been described as a barrier to achievement? Do you agree or disagree that AAE is a barrier?

TRUE-FALSE

Circle the number beside each statement that is true.

4. African American English (AAE) is a substandard form of the English language characterized primarily by limited use of grammatical rules.
5. African American students who interrupt others during conversations typically have significant pragmatic language difficulties or internalized feelings of anger.
6. African American mothers from low socioeconomic backgrounds tend to interact with their infants and small children differently than African American mothers from middle income backgrounds.
7. When collecting case history information, one must remember that African American infants are often slower to develop gross motor skills than infants from other ethnic groups.
8. A speaker of AAE who said "He do like to play with the other kid" is showing signs of a difference, not a disorder.
9. Sickle cell disease in African Americans has been associated with sensorineural hearing loss.
10. When speakers of AAE tell stories, they tend to use a topic-associating style characterized by structured discourse on a single topic.

MULTIPLE CHOICE

Circle the letter beside each of the choices that is correct.

11. Many African American students respond best to intervention methods that:
    A. Require that they sit still and demonstrate "good" behavior.
    B. Incorporate many kinesthetic and auditory cues.
    C. Include African American music, history, and cultural materials.
    D. Allow students to receive individual therapy so they get one-to-one attention from an adult.
    E. Are fast-paced and varied.

12. Which of the following are recommended as nonbiased, valid assessments of the communication skills of speakers of AAE?
    A. Language samples
    B. Analysis of C-units
    C. Mean length of utterance
    D. Norm-referenced tests standardized on a national sample
    E. Sentence repetition tasks

13. Ganesha T., a 6-year-old first grade speaker of AAE, is referred by her classroom teacher for testing. The referral form says that "Ganesha is disruptive in class. I'm wondering if she needs therapy for her social communication skills." Which of the following indicate that Ganesha is manifesting a communication difference (not disorder) based on her cultural background?
    A. When the teacher asks a question in class, Ganesha answers without raising her hand first.
    B. When Ganesha tells a story, she assumes that the listener has enough background information to understand what she is talking about.
    C. Ganesha looks down when she is talking with teachers and administrators (e.g., the principal).
    D. Ganesha has difficulty sitting still and listening to the teacher lecture to a group of students.
    E. Ganesha tends to talk loudly with her peers and (to the Anglo teacher) appears to be "in your face."

14. On this same form, the teacher states that "Ganesha also has poor grammar. I'm concerned that this will interfere with her reading and writing." He gives several examples. Which one of the following utterances would NOT be typical for a speaker of AAE?
    A. My daddy done buy the groceries.
    B. They ain't no be gonna havin' a good time.
    C. That might be my friend pencil.
    D. We be readin' our book in class.
    E. Those mice is gettin' chased by the cat.

15. Which of the following would be considered inappropriate in service delivery to African American students and their families?
    A. Giving students nicknames to help them feel special (e.g., calling Ganesha "Nesha")
    B. Calling family members by their first names to establish a cordial, comfortable relationship
    C. Helping families develop strategies for reading and telling stories to their children
    D. Asking for the parent's consent to conduct an assessment
    E. Expecting the student to answer questions that can be answered by the parent

ANSWERS TO STUDY QUESTIONS
    4. False
    5. False
    6. True
    7. False
    8. True
    9. True
    10. False
    11. B, C, and E
    12. A and B
    13. A, B, C, D, and E
    14. B
    15. A and B

Chapter 5

FAMILIES FROM HISPANIC BACKGROUNDS

Outline

General Background Information
Hispanic Family Life
Hispanic Education and Literacy
Cultural Customs, Courtesies, and Beliefs
Health Care and Disabling Conditions
Hispanic Communication Styles
Spanish Language Characteristics and Considerations
Implications for Professionals

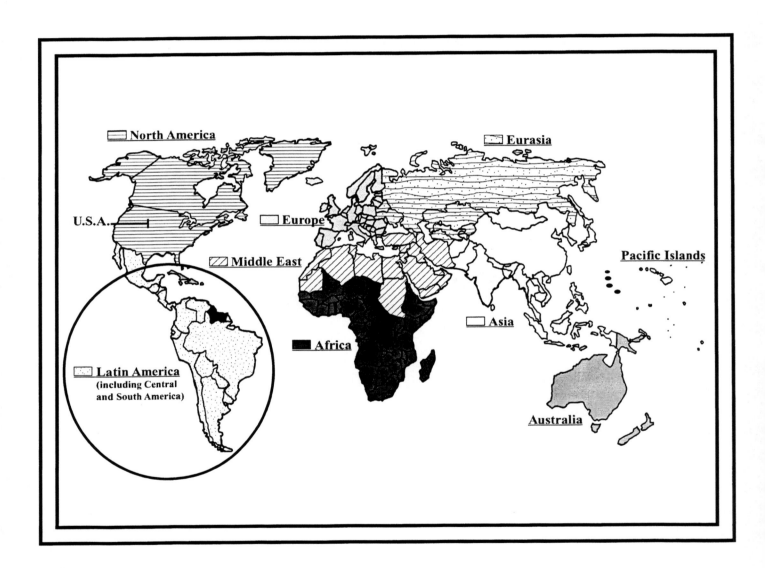

The Hispanic population in the United States is growing rapidly. Many Hispanic students come to school speaking only Spanish. Although bilingual education programs are available in many school districts, few programs are available to meet the needs of the growing population of Spanish speakers with special learning needs.

The term "Hispanic" is used to refer to individuals who were born in or trace the background of their families to one of the Spanish-speaking Latin American nations or to Spain. Hispanics may also come from Caribbean countries such as Puerto Rico and Cuba. The largest portion of the Hispanic population in the United States is Mexican.

Spanish is the language most often spoken in Mexico and throughout most countries in Central and South America (see Figure 5.1).

Figure 5.1

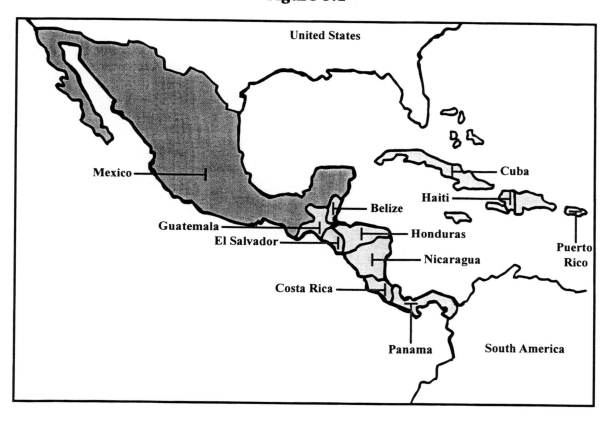

GENERAL BACKGROUND INFORMATION

❑ The term "Hispanic" is used as an ethnic label by the U.S. Bureau of the Census; it does not denote a race, because most Hispanics are racially mixed. The majority are Mestizo, having both European and Indian heritage.

❑ Some individuals from Spanish language backgrounds do not like the term "Hispanic." Many prefer to be called "Latino." (Iglesias, 2002). Others prefer a reference to their family's country of origin. For example, some Hispanics like to be called Cuban Americans, Mexican Americans, etc.

❑ Many Hispanics are born in the United States; others immigrate for reasons such as family reunification and economic opportunity. Many individuals from Central and South America have come to the United States to escape from politically unstable situations in their native countries.

❑ Immigrants tend to settle in parts of the United States where others from their country have established residence. Most Mexican Hispanics live in the Southwestern states. The majority of Puerto Rican Hispanics live in New York and New Jersey. Many Cubans live in Florida. Although most Hispanics in California are of Mexican descent, other groups are also represented in large numbers. Many Central Americans, for example, reside in San Francisco.

❑ Hispanics comprise one of the fastest-growing segments of the population. The U.S. Hispanic population has grown 58% in 10 years to 35 million people. Today, the Hispanic population constitutes the largest minority in the United States (U.S. Bureau of the Census, 2000).

❑ Hispanics comprise 12.1% of the U.S. population. Thirty-five percent of them are under 18 years of age (U.S. Bureau of the Census, 2000).

❑ The importance of Hispanics in the United States work force is increasing because of their youth and numbers relative to the aging Anglo European American population. For example, in the future, Hispanics will comprise 40% of California's work force (U.S. Bureau of the Census, 2000).

❑ Many Hispanics live in poverty. In California, 67% of children from Hispanic households were found to be living below poverty level as compared to 15.4% of White children (U.S. Bureau of the Census, 1999).

❑ Consequences of poverty include poor housing conditions, educational and employment barriers, and health problems (Brice, 2002).

❑ Despite numerous social and economic disadvantages, many Hispanics have benefited from improved educational opportunities, a strong work ethic, strong families, high labor force participation, and low reliance on welfare (Hayes-Bautista, Hurtado, Valdez, & Hernandez, 1992, Iglesias, 2002).

❑ Many Hispanics are Catholic. The church often plays an important role in their lives.

HISPANIC FAMILY LIFE

❑ Family life is a high priority among most Hispanics. Familialism is a cultural value in which individuals have a strong identification with and attachment to their nuclear and extended families, and values of solidarity, loyalty, and reciprocity among family members.

❑ Most Hispanic homes (70%) are maintained by married couples (Kayser, 1998b).

❑ In some families, bearing children is viewed as the purpose of marriage. Children may be expected shortly after marriage (Zuniga, 1998).

❑ Large and extended families are common. Divorce is relatively uncommon due, in part, to the influence of Catholicism.

❑ The father is generally the authority figure. The welfare of the family is the responsibility of the father (Zuniga, 1998). The husband may make decisions without consulting his wife.

❑ In some families, the man is the breadwinner and the woman cares for the family. This is changing because many Hispanic women now need to obtain jobs outside the home.

❑ Many Hispanic children are taught to listen, obey, and not to challenge authority. In many families, girls have restricted freedom and are taught that they need to be protected (Langdon, 1992; Zuniga, 1998).

❑ Families may travel frequently from the United States to the home country to be with family members.

❑ Experiences associated with age are held in high regard and children are expected to show respect for their elders, regardless of status or formal education (Zuniga, 1998). The advice of elderly grandparents, for example, is often solicited and followed because grandparents are integral and important family members.

❑ Parents may be indulgent and permissive with young children, especially infants, and often do not push them towards achievement to the extent that Anglo families do (Brice, 1993). For example, preschool-age children may drink from baby bottles and pre-teens may sit on their mothers' laps. Direct physical closeness is the norm for many families (Zuniga, 1998).

Profile

Carlos G. was born to parents who came to Texas as refugees from El Salvador. When Carlos was born, the umbilical cord was wrapped around his neck and he suffered from severe fetal anoxia. He experienced hydrocephalus and was eventually diagnosed with severe mental retardation. Doctors told his parents that Carlos would never walk or talk, much less learn to read or write. His mother sought as many early intervention services for Carlos as possible, and Carlos did learn to walk and talk, albeit very slowly. However, his father did not participate in meetings or in carrying out the recommendations made by professionals. The mother felt that she carried the entire burden of Carlos' rehabilitation. Eventually, the parents divorced.

As Carlos grew older, he received special education services in elementary and junior high schools and eventually learned to read and write at a basic level. However, his mother would not allow him to participate in events such as field trips or to socialize with other students. She felt that social interactions caused too much stress for the child. No effort was made in the home to help Carlos develop independent living skills. The child was not taught how to catch a bus, order food in a restaurant, etc. In fact, his mother did everything for him.

When Carlos was in 10th grade, he began manifesting symptoms of serious depression and mentioned suicide several times. He told the psychologist, "It would be better for me to die than for all these people to be working so hard for me." At his IEP meeting, 15 people were in attendance, including his mother. The meeting lasted for several hours. The team managed to persuade his mother to allow Carlos more social freedom and to allow school district personnel to teach the "basic life skills" he would need to support himself in a sheltered vocational setting.

❏ Communication styles in many Spanish-speaking families differ somewhat from styles in mainstream Anglo families. For example, when Anglo mothers go shopping, they often talk constantly with their children about what they are doing. Hispanic parents often do not comment or verbalize about ongoing events (Langdon, 1992).

❏ Many parents do not participate in their children's play activities and may view play as a distraction from household chores, etc. (Langdon, 1992). Children are often expected to work toward goals that are viewed as critical for the family's survival (Zuniga, 1998).

❏ Many children are raised to value cooperation within the family unit more than individual achievement (Brice, 2002).

HISPANIC EDUCATION AND LITERACY

❏ Many families hold teachers in high regard.

❏ Education is very important to families and is often viewed as the route to upward mobility (Brice, 1993).

❏ If the family moves frequently, educational opportunities for the children may be sporadic and limited.

❏ A "field-sensitive" cognitive style is common among Hispanic children (Nellum-Davis et al., 1998). These children are sensitive to nonverbal indicators of feelings.

❏ Many Hispanic children learn best when interacting in situations where they experience warmth, responsiveness, and frequent attention (Zuniga, 1998). They often respond well to physical touch and affection.

❏ Parents often encourage children to be responsible for their own learning and only offer help with homework when provided with specific instructions (Langdon, 1992).

❏ Some girls are not encouraged to complete school or to train for a career. They are expected to marry and to bear children.

❏ In most Hispanic countries, education is compulsory for children from about 6 years of age to at least 12 years of age. Some classes have up to 58 students (Langdon, 1992).

❏ Students who immigrate to the United States may vary considerably in their school experiences and literacy skills.

❏ Many Hispanics in the United States have not had educational opportunities commensurate with those of Anglo European Americans. Thus, their educational attainment has been limited by these constraints (Padilla, 1992).

❏ Dropping out of school is common among Hispanic adolescents. In the 25-34 year age group, 58% of Hispanics have attained a high school education, compared to 89% of non-Hispanics (Riquelme, 1994).

❏ Possible reasons for the less-than-optimal educational attainment of Hispanics include: 1) culture shock and difference in home and school expectations, 2) sporadic school attendance due to high family mobility, and 3) fluctuating funding for programs designed to assist students learning English as a second language. Moreover, over 55% of Spanish-speaking children in the U.S. come from families with annual incomes of $20,000 or lower (Hammer & Miccio, 2001).

❑ Hispanic students may be under-represented in gifted programs in schools because of cultural and/or linguistic bias in the assessment procedures used.

❑ Hispanic students have traditionally been over-represented in special education, especially in classes for the mentally handicapped and learning disabled (Argulewicz & Sanchez, 1983).

✐ REFLECTION ✐

Describe two characteristics relating to family life and two characteristics relating to the educational experiences of many Hispanic students in the U.S.

_____

_____

_____

_____

_____

CULTURAL CUSTOMS, COURTESIES, AND BELIEFS

❑ Allocentrism (collectivism) is a fundamental Hispanic value that emphasizes the objectives and needs of an in-group rather than emphasizing competition and individualism.

❑ Families strive to be friendly, to welcome guests to their homes, and to offer refreshments.

❑ Many Hispanics have a flexible attitude about time and the importance of maintaining schedules. Thus, appointments are often not kept with the precision expected by school professionals. Hispanics tend to place greater value on interpersonal relations than on factors related to time.

❑ Girls are often encouraged to be modest and feminine (Buell, 1984c).

HEALTH CARE AND DISABLING CONDITIONS

❑ Many Hispanic families have limited access to health care. For example, Roseberry-McKibbin, Peña, Hall, and Smith-Stubblefield (1996) found that of 254 migrant Hispanic families surveyed, 90% had no health insurance. These families were the "working poor" who had no work-related health benefits and who could not afford private health insurance.

❑ Hispanics are less likely to have adequate insurance coverage than any ethnic group in the United States (Riquelme, 1994).

❑ Various types of acute, chronic, communicable, and traumatic diseases are more common in the Hispanic population than in most other groups (Latino Legislative Caucus Hearings, 1991).

❏ Poverty and poor prenatal care lead to disproportionate numbers of Hispanic children who are sick or undernourished from birth. Mexican American mothers experience maternal risk factors and inadequate prenatal care more frequently than non-Hispanic white mothers (Balcazar, Hartner, & Cole, 1993).

❏ An estimated 2.3 million Hispanics in the United States need speech, language, and/or hearing services (Langdon, 1992).

❏ Families may believe in "curanderismo," a healing process that occurs when folk medicine practices are used (Langdon 1992). Often these beliefs are more prevalent in groups with less access to modern health care (e.g., individuals who live in rural areas).

❏ Among some Hispanics, there may be resistance to institutionalization (Meyerson, 1983). Due to the extended family situation in many homes, individuals with illnesses or disabilities may be cared for within the family (Madding, 2002).

❏ Families differ in their reactions to disabilities. In some families, a visible disability (e.g., cleft palate, cerebral palsy) is often attributed to an external, non-medical cause such as witchcraft. Some parents may believe that they are being punished for their own wrong-doing (Zuniga, 1998). Many Catholic parents accept disabilities stoically, as part of a larger divine plan that is not comprehensible to humans (Maestas & Erickson, 1992).

❏ Families may have more difficulty accepting invisible disabling conditions such as learning disabilities or reading disorders than disabling conditions that are visible.

❏ If families greatly prize vitality and health, they may hide a disabled child and, therefore, deprive that child of treatment.

❏ Family and friends may indulge children with disabilities. These children are often not expected to participate actively in their own treatment and care.

❏ The roles of health agencies may cause confusion for family members. Families may prefer small clinics to large medical centers.

❏ Some families turn to spiritualists to seek healing and dispel evil spirits (Zuniga, 1998).

Profile

Juan Jaramillo, a handsome, courteous 10-year-old Hispanic fourth grader, was referred for assessment by his classroom teacher because he was struggling academically. Psychoeducational testing in both Spanish and English revealed that Juan had a learning disability. His mother came to the IEP meeting and was informed in Spanish that special education services appeared to be necessary. During the meeting she said, "Juan is just lazy—I know he can do the work. Look at him—he's a normal boy." The IEP team explained that although Juan was normal in appearance, he had a clinically significant learning disability that was hampering his academic progress. Mrs. Jaramillo was visibly dubious about this conclusion, but signed the IEP and agreed to special education services for her son.

HISPANIC COMMUNICATION STYLES

❏ Many Hispanics utilize the social script of "simpatica," which emphasizes positive personal interactions that convey empathy for others, harmony in interpersonal relations, and de-emphasize negative behaviors in circumstances of conflict. People often initiate conversations on a personal note before proceeding with business.

❏ Embraces are common between friends. Members of the same sex may have physical contact in public.

❏ Standing close and touching during conversations is acceptable. Hispanics tend to stand closer during conversation than Anglos and other groups. Many Hispanics feel insulted when someone steps away from them during conversation.

❏ Due to differences in cultural norms for physical distance or space (proxemics), some Hispanics view Anglos as being uninterested, aloof, or cold. Anglos may view Hispanics as being too pushy or close (Irujo, 1988).

❏ One may beckon another person by producing a "psssst" sound; this is not considered rude.

❏ As a sign of respect, children may look away or lower their heads when talking to adults. Avoidance of eye contact may be a sign of respect and deference; sustained eye contact may be seen as a challenge to authority.

❏ Children often learn through observation and hands-on participation rather than through verbal interactions with adults .

❏ When adults are talking, children are not to interrupt. They are not expected to participate in adult conversations, and they show respect for adults by considering themselves as "non-equals" during interactions.

❏ Children interact verbally more often with siblings or peers than with adults. Peers are considered equal partners in conversation (Kayser, 1998a).

❏ Hispanic children tend to use gestures much more often than non-Hispanic children (Kayser, 1990).

❏ In many Hispanic homes, parents do not verbalize about ongoing events; they don't relate actions to words (Mann & Hodson, 1994).

❏ Usually, adults do not ask children to voice their preferences or to give their personal evaluations of situations (Langdon, 1992).

❏ Adults usually do not ask children to foretell what they will do or to repeat facts (Heath, 1986).

❏ Some Hispanic parents do not consider the learning of colors, shapes, or letters to be a high priority for their children. Instead, respect and politeness are emphasized. Many Mexican mothers regard themselves as "mothers" rather than "teachers" (Madding, 1999).

❏ Some Spanish-speaking children, especially those from the Caribbean or Central America, come from homes where narratives are frequently characterized by a de-emphasis on actions and event sequencing (Bliss, McCabe, & Mahecha, 2001).

SPANISH LANGUAGE CHARACTERISTICS AND CONSIDERATIONS

Numerous dialects/varieties of Spanish are spoken in the United States. The two major Spanish dialects in the U.S. are the Caribbean (e.g., Cuban and Puerto Rican) and southwestern (Mexican/Mexican American) dialects (Goldstein & Iglesias, 1996). However, many other dialects exist, and it is imperative to remember that the diversity among Spanish speakers is great (Mahecha, 1991). Although Spanish is spoken in Spain and most of Central and South America, there are variations from country to country that are reflected in pragmatics, syntax, morphology, and phonology (Goldstein, 2000). The word *gordo* (fat), for example, is pronounced "goldo" by many Spanish speakers in Puerto Rico. In Argentina, the word *pollo* may be pronounced "po-sho."

Thus, professionals must consider the individual student's background when evaluating language performance. Some norms are available for Spanish articulation and phonological development (Acevedo, 1991; Goldstein & Iglesias, 1996; Jimenez, 1987; Merino, 1992). An accent is to be expected and should not be viewed as a disorder. It is important for professionals who work with Spanish-speaking students to understand the language differences commonly observed when these students learn English. Information about articulation and language differences commonly observed when Spanish speakers speak English is presented in Table 5.1 and Table 5.2.

Table 5.1

LANGUAGE DIFFERENCES COMMONLY OBSERVED AMONG SPANISH SPEAKERS

Language Characteristics	Sample English Utterances
1. Adjective comes after noun.	The house green.
2. 's is often omitted in plurals and possessives.	The girl book is... Juan hat is red.
3. Past tense -ed is often omitted.	We walk yesterday.
4. Double negatives are required.	I don't have no more.
5. Superiority is demonstrated by using *mas*.	This cake is more big.
6. The adverb often follows the verb.	He drives very fast his motorcycle.

Table 5.2

ARTICULATION DIFFERENCES COMMONLY OBSERVED AMONG SPANISH SPEAKERS

Articulation Characteristics	Sample English Patterns
1. /t, d, n/ may be dentalized (tip of tongue is placed against the back of the upper central incisors).	
2. Final consonants are often devoiced.	dose/doze
3. b/v substitution	berry/very
4. Deaspirated stops (sounds like speaker is omitting the sound because it is said with little air release).	
5. ch/sh substitution	chew/shoe
6. d/voiced th, or z/voiced th (voiced "th" does not exist in Spanish).	dis/this, zat/that
7. t/voiceless th (voiceless "th" does not exist in Spanish).	tink/think
8. Schwa sound is inserted before word initial consonant clusters.	eskate/skate espend/spend
9. Words can end in 10 different sounds: a, e, i, o, u, l, r, n, s, d	may omit sounds at the ends of words
10. When words start with /h/, the /h/ is silent.	'old/hold, 'it/hit
11. /r/ is tapped or trilled (tap /r/ might sound like the tap in the English word "butter").	
12. There is no /j/ (e.g., judge) sound in Spanish; speakers may substitute "y."	Yulie/Julie yoke/joke
13. Spanish /s/ is produced more frontally than English /s/.	Some speakers may sound like they have frontal lisps.
14. The ñ is pronounced like a "y" (e.g. "baño is pronounced "bahnyo").	

Spanish has 5 vowels: a, e, i, o, u (ah, E, ee, o, u) and few diphthongs. Thus, Spanish speakers may produce the following vowel substitutions:

15. ee/I substitution	peeg/pig, leetle/little
16. E/ae, ah/ae substitutions	pet/pat, Stahn/Stan

> ## Profile
>
> Rosa S., an 8-year-old girl from a migrant Hispanic family, was being tested by the school psychologist. He noticed that she seemed to be unusually quiet and he tried unsuccessfully for 15 minutes to encourage her to speak to him. Finally he asked her if anything was wrong. She responded by telling the psychologist that a snake had been found in her house and that snakes in the home are viewed in Mexico as a sign of bad luck. The psychologist sympathized with Rosa, and said that luckily, in California, finding a snake was considered to be good luck. After several minutes of conversation about California's "good luck snakes," Rosa brightened considerably and was much more verbal in the testing situation.

IMPLICATIONS FOR PROFESSIONALS

❑ Professionals need to include the entire family in any procedures involving an individual student and should encourage active family participation (Brice & Roseberry-McKibbin, 1999a).

❑ Professionals should use formal titles with Hispanic adults to show respect. Adults should be addressed with the formal *you* (*Usted*) rather than the less formal *you* (*tu*). It is acceptable to use *tu* with children.

❑ Professionals should attempt to communicate with both parents in meetings. It is important to understand that, in many families, the father is the spokesperson and the primary decision maker (Zuniga, 1998).

❑ Professionals will more readily gain the trust of family members if they have a humanistic orientation rather than a task orientation. Informal, friendly chatting can set the stage for work to be done. Discussing business immediately or appearing hurried may be considered rude. Professionals may need to allow extra time for the meeting to accommodate Hispanic families (Brice, 2002).

❑ Relationships are very important to Hispanic families; they may care more about the professional's personal qualities (e.g., approachability, interest in and respect for the family) than about the professional's technical qualifications (Kayser, 1998a).

❑ Some Hispanic families may be uncomfortable collaborating with professionals because they do not see parent participation as necessary (Goldstein, 2000). They may prefer to leave decisions to school personnel. Thus, professionals should ascertain that families truly understand their role in assessment and treatment plans.

❑ Because of their respect for professionals, parents may not openly disagree with them or question them. Parents may not follow suggestions that they have agreed to follow. Professionals should always follow up when suggestions are given.

❑ Professionals should define terms such as language disorder and learning disability to ensure that parents understand their meanings. Terms that are undefined may lead parents to believe that professionals are talking about mental retardation or mental illness (Harry, 1992).

❏ Families may appear to be passive about accepting treatment for conditions they believe are the result of external forces. Professionals must work within the framework of the family's culture to foster confidence and trust.

❏ Professionals should state their expectations and should explain the importance of maintaining schedules. Families may be late for or miss appointments due to different perspectives about time and/or lack of understanding about the importance of schedules.

❏ Professionals need to remember that there may be child-rearing norms among some Hispanic families that do not fit the Anglo mainstream timeline for developmental milestones. For example, some Puerto Rican children may be weaned off the bottle at 3 years; some Mexican American preschool-age children may still use pacifiers or bottles.

❏ Because of the relaxed attitude toward child rearing, some parents may be resistant to the concept of early intervention, believing that children will eventually "catch up" to their peers.

❏ If families are grieving about a child's disability, they may find comfort at a local church. Professionals can consider presenting this option when appropriate.

❏ Professionals may need to assist families so that they can be assertive in obtaining needed services (e.g., educational, medical).

❏ It is important to choose interpreters with care, as the use of friends and family members may violate the family's privacy.

❏ Professionals should accept gifts, food, or drink within ethical boundaries. Families may be insulted if professionals refuse these gifts.

❏ Clients may sit or stand close to the professionals with whom they are interacting. It is important not to move away.

❏ Parents may believe that an all-English program is superior to bilingual programs that enhance Spanish skills (Langdon, 1992). It is important to emphasize to parents that initial literacy instruction in Spanish often enhances future academic success.

❏ Professionals should do what they can to promote bilingual education opportunities for Hispanic students. Ideally, Hispanic students, especially those with language learning disabilities, should receive bilingual instruction that maintains and promotes their Spanish skills while helping them learn English (Gutierrez-Clellen, 1998; Restrepo & Kruth, 2000).

❏ Unfortunately, many Hispanic students are placed into all-English classrooms with no support in Spanish; this is very detrimental to their learning and progress. Language loss in Spanish is a major issue for these students, especially as they get older (Kohnert, Bates, & Hernandez, 1999). Students who have limited opportunities for continued use of Spanish are likely to become less proficient in the language over time.

❏ When interacting with students at home, parents who don't speak English well should continue to use Spanish. Parents should be encouraged to speak the language in which they feel most comfortable (Gutierrez-Clellen, 1999a; Patterson, 1999). It is better for children to hear fluent Spanish than "broken" English. Interacting in Spanish in the home will help Hispanic students to prevent language loss and consequent negative cognitive and linguistic effects (Madding, 2002).

❏ Patterson (1999) and Brice (2000a) stated that parents should also be reassured that modeling the behavior of codeswitching (alternating languages over phrases or sentences) is not detrimental to their children's language development in English or Spanish.

❏ Professionals can also help parents carry out home activities that will promote their children's cognitive and linguistic development.

❏ A study by Gonzales, Ezell, & Randolph (1999) found that migrant Mexican-American families provided literacy experiences for their children in the home. However, these families generally engaged in story-telling or book-reading no more than a few times each week. It was recommended that parents be encouraged to provide literacy experiences daily and to make efforts to enhance their children's awareness of print.

❏ Madding (1999) found that Mexican Hispanic mothers in her study were not highly verbal or directive in interactions with their children. When asked whose job it was to teach their children concepts such as colors or shapes, the mothers indicated that instruction of this type was the responsibility of teachers. In addition, the mothers believed that it was not appropriate to begin reading to their children prior to kindergarten. Thus, professionals may need to encourage mothers to read to their children prior to kindergarten and to stimulate the development of basic language concepts.

❏ Bliss et al. (2001) recommended that professionals help parents understand that talking with children about past experiences is an important foundational skill for literacy achievement. Parents should be taught to elicit narratives from their children.

❏ Professionals should try to avoid making recommendations that conflict with the family's cultural values and practices. However, as Zuniga (1998) emphasized, many Hispanic parents come to the U.S. specifically to obtain better educational opportunities for their children and, therefore, it is a disservice to withhold information that can facilitate language development and learning. Professionals need to be sensitive to the values and beliefs of parents when making recommendations that will affect their interactions with the child at home.

❏ Professionals must consider a variety of options other than standardized tests when attempting to identify gifted and talented Hispanic students.

❏ Many standardized tests require children to name pictures; however, many Spanish-speaking children will provide functions for objects rather than names (Mann & Hodson, 1994). Clinicians may need to rephrase questions or present prompts to elicit appropriate responses.

✐*REFLECTION*✐

Describe two language interaction patterns commonly observed between parents and children in Spanish-speaking homes that differ from those observed in mainstream English-speaking families. How might these differences impact the performance of Spanish-speaking children in our schools?

_____

_____

_____

_____

_____

❑ Professionals need to be extremely careful when using standardized tests with Hispanic children because of the bias inherent in these measures.

❑ Pena and Quinn (1997) assessed the language skills of preschool Spanish-speaking children. They found that a task requiring descriptive responses (e.g., "What are stoves used for?") was more sensitive than a labeling task (e.g., "Tell me what's in this picture") in differentiating preschoolers who were developing typically from those who had low language skills.

❑ Professionals must also remember that many Hispanic students have stronger vocabulary skills in English in some areas and stronger vocabulary skills in Spanish in others. For example, these students often know school vocabulary in English and home vocabulary in Spanish (Gutierrez-Clellen, Restrepo, Bedore, Peña, & Anderson, 2000). Professionals can dual-score vocabulary tests, using both Spanish and English responses to achieve a total score for the test.

❑ Some Hispanic children may not perform well on tasks that require repeating facts or foretelling what they will do. They may have little experience with these activities in the home (Langdon, 1992).

❑ In addition, Hispanic children may remain silent when interacting with unfamiliar adult professionals who are attempting to assess and/or treat them. It is important not to misinterpret the children's silence as indicative of a language disorder.

❑ Experts recommend the use of information from parent interviews and language samples when assessing Spanish-speaking children with possible communication disorders (Gutierrez-Clellen et al., 2000; Patterson, 2000; Restrepo, 1998). (see Gutierrez-Clellen et al., 2000 for specific details regarding language sampling techniques)

❑ When conducting parent interviews to ascertain the language skills of young children, professionals may consider utilizing the Fundación MacArthur Inventario del Desarrollo de Habilidades Comunicativas: Palabras Enunciadoes (IDHC: PE; Jackson-Maldonado, Bates, & Thal, 1992). However, research has only shown this instrument to be valid with monolingual, Spanish-speaking children living in Mexico in educated, middle- and upper-class families (Thal, Jackson-Maldonado, & Acosta, 2000). Professionals should use caution when using this instrument with children from families that do not fit that profile.

❑ When Hispanic students are served in educational settings, professionals should remember to be sensitive to cultural and linguistic phenomena that impact service delivery to these students.

❑ In educational settings, children may be more comfortable with cooperative, group learning than with individualistic, competitive learning situations. Many Hispanic children perform best in cooperative learning situations where they experience warmth and enthusiasm.

❑ There is little research available relating to the nonverbal skills of Hispanic students (Roseberry-McKibbin & Brice, 1999).

❑ Brice & Montgomery (1996) found that older Hispanic students with and without language-learning disabilities needed assistance in learning how to perform according to U.S. school expectations during classroom instruction, These students needed to learn how to ask questions, interact with teachers, and participate actively in classroom settings.

❑ Westby, Dezale, Fradd, & Lee (1999) studied several classrooms taught by Hispanic teachers. It was observed that the students were encouraged to engage in overlapping discourse to co-construct their understanding of tasks. The teachers used social communication to relate personal experiences to academic context. Humor was used to create a positive atmosphere that encouraged students to participate. Thus, teachers of classrooms with Hispanic students should be encouraged to use successful strategies such as these in their teaching.

❑ Restrepo (1998) found that Spanish-speaking children with language impairments used fewer complex sentences than Spanish-speaking children who were developing according to expectations. Thus, it was recommended that Spanish-speaking students with language impairments be encouraged to use complex sentences more frequently.

❑ Hispanic students with language-learning disabilities may also need direct assistance in learning to figure out word definitions during literacy activities in the classroom. Professionals can utilize dictionaries for this purpose (Gutierrez-Clellen & DeCurtis, 1999).

❑ Several researchers have studied the narrative skills of Spanish-speaking children with language impairments. Brito, Perez, Bliss, and McCabe (1999) found that these children produced narratives characterized by a reduced number of evaluation statements. They suggested that professionals elicit evaluative statements more frequently so that communication becomes more personal and emotionally expressive.

❑ Gutierrez-Clellen (1998) studied Mexican Spanish-speaking children with language impairments and found that the task of re-telling a story based on a short, silent movie elicited more complex language than story-retelling based on a wordless book. She suggested that professionals use movies to promote development of narrative skills in language-impaired Spanish-speaking children.

❑ Bedore and Leonard (2000) suggested that professionals overlay new information onto what is already known when teaching Hispanic students. For example, if a professional is teaching a new inflectional form to a Spanish-speaking child, this form should be introduced in a context in which familiar vocabulary is used. In this way, the professional maximizes the resources available and makes learning relevant to the student's previous learning experiences.

❑ When working with Hispanic students, it is critical that professionals learn to interact with family members in a culturally appropriate manner. Brice (2002) put forth excellent suggestions for working effectively with Hispanic families.

Profile

Jorge, a 17-year-old high school sophomore, had a documented bilateral 50 dB sensorineural hearing loss. His family moved to California from rural Mexico when Jorge was 16 years old. In Mexico, Jorge had not learned sign language or lipreading, and he had never had hearing aids. The school district tested Jorge's hearing and attempted to make the parents aware that he would need hearing aids to function effectively in school and in a vocation.

Jorge and his family were angry because of the school district's "interference," and denied that the hearing loss existed. Thus, Jorge received no additional assistance and was floundering in high school. The speech-language pathologist contacted Jose R., a Mexican professional from the State Department of Vocational Rehabilitation, who himself had come from a migrant Mexican family. Mr. R. met with Jorge and his parents, and found that they actually knew about Jorge's hearing loss but denied it, believing that the hearing loss meant that they (the parents) had sinned against God. The parents believed that Jorge's "defect" was punishment for their sins. They had accepted their fate and believed that no intervention was appropriate.

Mr. R. arranged a meeting with Jorge's family and the local priest to discuss the situation. After this meeting, the priest assured the parents that Jorge's hearing loss was not an indication of sin on their part. The parents then informed the school district that they would agree to the use of hearing aids. Jorge was subsequently fitted with aids and his academic performance improved markedly.

STUDY QUESTIONS

1. Describe three ways in which cultural expectations within the Hispanic culture differ from cultural expectations within the mainstream Anglo culture in the United States (e.g., degree to which punctuality is important). How might these differences impact service delivery to Hispanic students and their families?

2. Traditional language assessment measures are often biased in favor of mainstream Anglo students. Describe two strategies, recommended by researchers, that can be used to conduct assessments with Hispanic students in a nondiscriminatory manner.

3. Describe health considerations that are relevant to many Hispanic families in the U.S.

TRUE-FALSE

Circle the number beside each true statement below.

4. Puerto Ricans are the largest Hispanic group in the U.S.

5. When assessing vocabulary proficiency levels in Spanish-speaking students, tasks that require the description of objects are more helpful than tasks that require the naming of objects.

6. At the beginning of a meeting, most Hispanic families prefer that professionals "cut to the chase" and not waste time on social preliminaries or chit-chat.

7. Researchers have found that Mexican mothers have their children practice using basic concepts such as colors, shapes, and numbers in the home so that they will be prepared for kindergarten.

8. The utterance, "This cake chocolate is more big than that cake" would suggest a language difference rather than a disorder, in a Spanish-speaking child.

9. Young Hispanic children often respond better in educational situations that promote feelings of warmth, physical closeness, and cooperative learning than in situations that encourage competitive, individualistic learning.

10. Hispanic families are often quite "relaxed" in promoting the development of skills prior to school entry and may oppose recommendations for early intervention.

MULTIPLE CHOICE

11. Unfortunately, Hispanic students often experience academic difficulties and fail to complete high school. Possible reasons for this failure are:
    A. Fluctuating funding for programs designed to assist students in learning English as a second language
    B. Sporadic school attendance due to high family mobility
    C. Culture shock and other differences in home and school expectations
    D. Bilingualism is a detriment to learning.

12. Which of the following recommendations reflect "best practice" for professionals who work with Hispanic children and their families?
    A. Tell parents to speak only English in the home so that children can learn faster and experience greater academic success.
    B. Encourage parents to teach their young children basic concepts and to read to them in the early years (e.g., before kindergarten).
    C. Rely on nationally normed language tests to ensure that language skills are measured precisely when differentiating language differences from disorders in Spanish-speaking children.
    D. Encourage Hispanic students to be assertive in the classroom (e.g., raise their hands, interact with teachers).
    E. State expectations and let families know about the importance of keeping to a schedule (e.g., for meetings).

13. A teacher has referred a Spanish-speaking child to you for assessment. In the teacher's words, "This child has trouble pronouncing his sounds in English. I think he may need speech therapy." Which of the following English productions are indicative of an articulation difference rather than an articulation disorder?
   A. My tum (thumb) got cut when I was eskating wit (with) my friends in de (the) park.
   B. The pawk (park) had a bun (bunch) of dwied (dried) gwass.
   C. Dere (there) was a leetle peeg (little pig) in de (the) park and I wanted to as' (ask) if I could pet it.
   D. Lat (that) TV tow (show) is not bunny (funny).

14. Which one of the following general statements is NOT true about Hispanics in the U.S.?
   A. Most Hispanics have strong family values.
   B. Most Hispanics receive welfare services because poverty impacts so many of them.
   C. Most Hispanics are Catholic.
   D. Young Hispanic children tend to interact more often with other children at home than with adults.
   E. Hispanics may experience inadequate medical care because they frequently do not have health insurance.

15. Many Hispanic families do not:
   A. Emphasize education for girls
   B. Respect and listen to older family members
   C. Emphasize cooperation and the welfare of the whole family
   D. Question professionals out of respect
   E. Eat food that is not kosher

ANSWERS TO STUDY QUESTIONS

   4. False
   5. True
   6. False
   7. False
   8. True
   9. True
   10. True
   11. A, B, and C
   12. B, D, and E
   13. A and C
   14. B
   15. A and D

Chapter 6

FAMILIES FROM ASIAN BACKGROUNDS

Outline

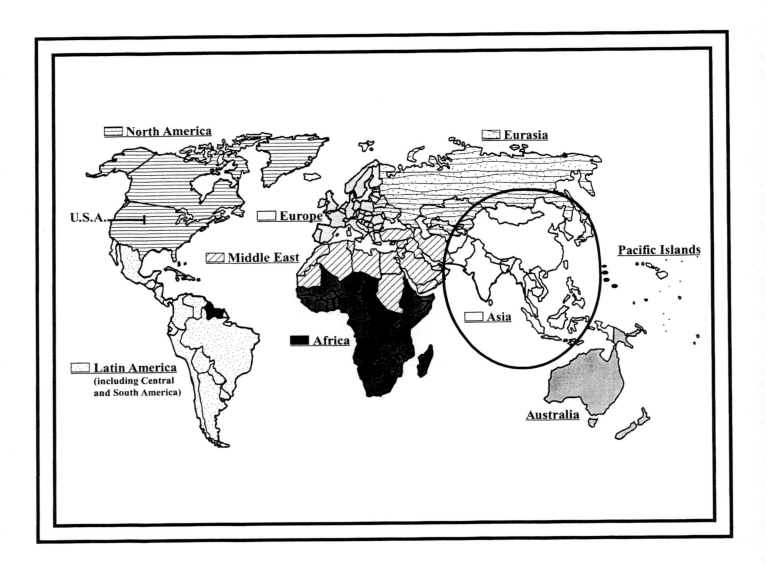

M any families from Asian countries have come to live in the United States in recent years. Students who are classified as "Asian" come from three primary geographic regions:

East Asia:	Japan, Korea, China
Southeast Asia:	Philippines, Laos, Cambodia, Thailand, Indonesia, Singapore, Myanmar (Burma), Vietnam, Malaysia
South Asia:	Sri Lanka, Pakistan, India

A large number of Asians originate from countries in the Pacific Rim. The Pacific Rim includes all nations and regions touching the Pacific Ocean. As shown in Figure 6.1, China is the largest country in Asia. Although most countries in Asia are fairly small in physical size, some (e.g., Japan) have large populations.

Figure 6.1

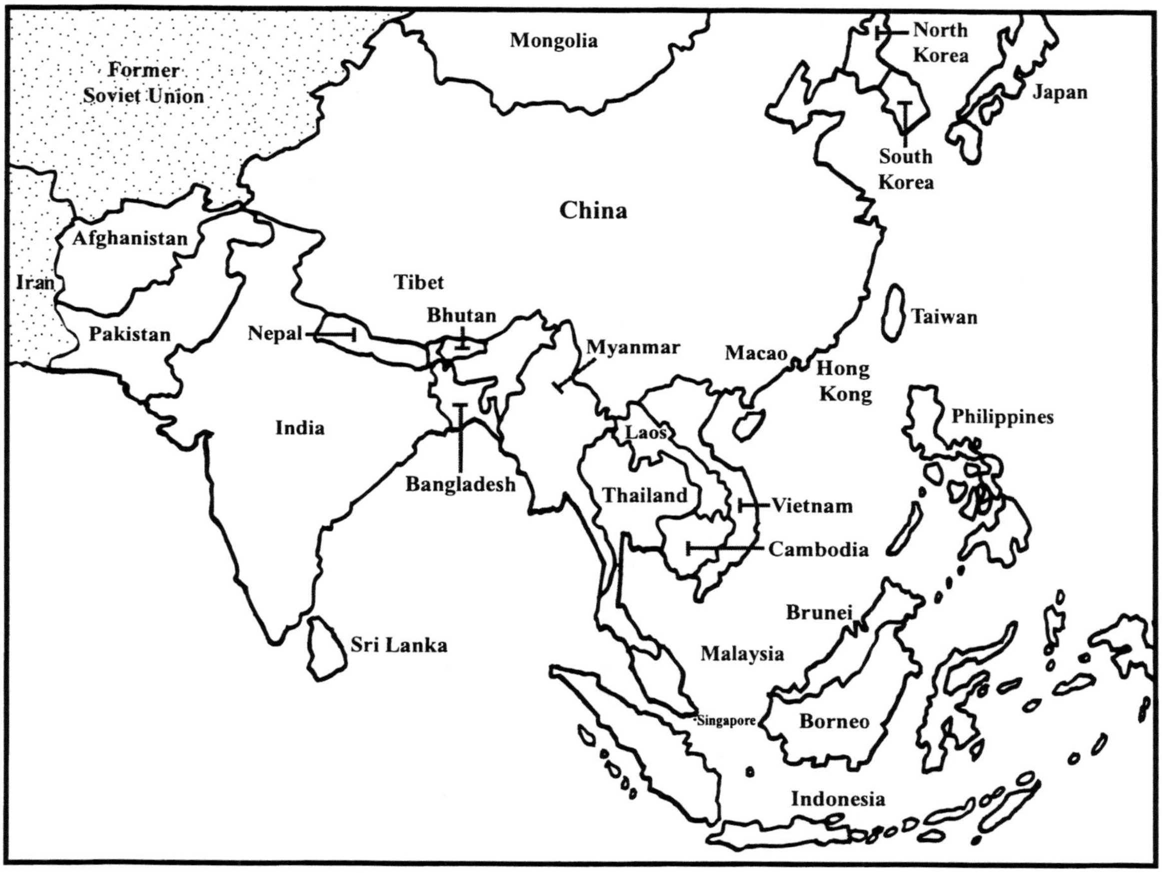

GENERAL BACKGROUND INFORMATION

❑ Some Asian cultures (Korean, Chinese, Vietnamese) are rooted in civilizations that are over 4,000 years old (Chan, 1998a).

❑ Common religions in Asia are Buddhism, Taoism, and Confucianism; other religions include animism (all forms of spirit worship, including the spirits of nature), Hinduism, Islam, and Shintoism.

❑ Residents of the Philippines are primarily Roman Catholic. Many Southeast Asians are Buddhist, and some groups believe in fortune-telling, astrology, shamanism, and ancestor worship.

❑ The majority of Indians are Hindus. The caste system is a unique feature of Hindu life. There are four castes, with Brahmins being the highest caste and Sudras being the lowest caste or "menials." The traditional caste system is not promoted today, but individuals from different castes commonly do not maintain contact (Cheng, 2002).

❑ Indian Hindus regard the cow as sacred and pure because it gives milk, one of the purest substances. Most Hindus do not eat beef.

❑ There are now more than 10 million Asian American residents.

❑ Between 1990 and 2000, using the category of "race alone," the number of Asians in the U.S. increased by 48.3%. If one uses the figures from the category of "race alone or in combination," the number of Asians in the United States grew by 72.2% between 1990 and 2000, reaching a total of 11,898,828 persons in the U.S. in 2000 (U.S. Bureau of the Census, 2000).

❑ There are approximately 722,000 Indians in the U.S. Only 6% of Indian immigrants live below the poverty line. Fewer than 1% use public assistance (Center for Immigration Studies, 2001).

❑ Filipino Americans are the fastest-growing ethnic group in the U.S., and among Asian Americans, have the highest percentage of their population in the labor force (Chan, 1998b).

❑ Asians in the United States are often referred to as the "model minority." For example, Steinberg (1996; cited in Johnston, 2001) stated that "It is more advantageous to be Asian than to be wealthy, to have nondivorced parents, or to have a mother who is able to stay home full time." The "model minority" belief can cause many problems such as the following:

1. Asians may be targets of resentment because they are put into an uncomfortable comparative position with other ethnic groups.
2. Social problems such as gang membership among Asian youth, poverty, substance abuse, domestic violence, and mental illness may be ignored, making it difficult for Asians to receive help in dealing with these problems.
3. Needs of Asian students often go unrecognized by the educational system, and their needs in schools may consequently be unmet. This can contribute to a higher dropout rate (Chan, 1998a). Asian students may be under-represented in special education programs. Johnston (2001) pointed out that not all Asian students perform equally well in the educational system. In 1998-1999, Asian Americans accounted for 8% of California's K-12 enrollment, but represented 40% of the student body at University of California at Berkeley. However, groups such as Cambodians and Laotians tend to have less money and perform more poorly in school than Japanese and Korean students. Thus, when all Asian students are viewed as a group, the needs of the lower-achieving students often are not met.

ASIAN FAMILY LIFE

❑ The family is the basic societal unit and the central focus of an individual's life.

❑ Most, but not all, Asian cultures are patriarchal; the family structure in the Philippines, for example, is matriarchal (Roseberry-McKibbin, 1997b).

❑ Extended families, with several generations living under the same roof, are quite common.

❑ Role relationships within hierarchies are often considered important. Individuals within the family are expected to fill their roles according to gender, age, and position. For example, wives may submit to husbands, younger male children may submit to older male children, and female children may submit to everyone.

❑ Fathers may hold the highest authority in the family. Eldest sons also frequently have high positions of respect.

❑ Children are encouraged to defer to adults and other authority figures. Respect for elders is expected.

❑ If a child behaves badly, the entire family may lose face.

❑ Children may be strictly controlled and punished physically (Fung & Roseberry-McKibbin, 1999).

❑ Children may stay in the home as long as they are unmarried, even if they have reached adulthood. These individuals may help care for nieces and nephews.

❑ Older siblings commonly care for younger siblings.

❑ Among some groups, it is common for girls to marry between 13 and 16 years of age.

❑ Marriage may be a concern of the entire family rather than a private matter between the two people involved.

❑ In some groups, the whole family's reputation may be in danger if a young woman has a boyfriend before she is married.

❑ Women in some groups bring honor to themselves and their families by bearing sons. Some families value sons more than daughters.

❑ Divorce is often viewed as being unacceptable.

❑ Many Asian students come from two-parent homes. In the U.S., single-parent families are rarest among Asian Americans (Shekar & Hegde, 1995).

❑ The viewpoint that children "should be seen and not heard" is common. Talking at the family dinner table is generally viewed as impolite. Many Asians believe that "a quiet child is a good child" (Van Kleeck, 1994, p. 70).

❑ Parents often control the direction of the conversation, length of time children can talk, and the topics discussed.

❑ Parents tend to initiate conversation with children, verbally explain tasks, verbally monitor children's activities, and ask children factual questions.

REFLECTION

Pa, a Hmong 12-year-old child, was referred for a special education assessment because of academic problems. Her family had come to the U.S. as refugees when Pa was 7 years old, and she had no schooling in the Southeast Asian refugee camps where her family lived. She told the speech-language pathologist that she shared a house with 12 other people (none of whom spoke English). She said, "My mommy pick strawberry for money and my daddy don't work." The speech-language pathologist needed to determine whether or not Pa's academic difficulties were due to limited exposure to English or to a genuine language-learning disability. Finding a program that would help Pa to acquire basic skills quickly was also a concern. Girls from Hmong families tend to marry when they are fairly young, and Pa talked about getting married in three or four years. How might the school help Pa's family to support her academically?

EDUCATION AND LITERACY

As a student who attended Asian schools, the author of this book learned much about the educational system. Additional information for this section was obtained from interviews with individuals from Asian cultures, and an extensive review of the literature (Chan, 1998a; Cheng, 2002).

❏ Many Asians have great respect for learning. Education is viewed as a means of advancement for the individual and represents honor for the family.

❏ Asians have high expectations for their children's educational attainment. Okagaki and Frensch (1998) studied educational expectations of parents from Asian, Hispanic, and European American groups and found that the Asian parents set higher expectations for their children as well as higher standards for achievement. Asian parents also expected their children to complete more years of schooling than they themselves did.

❏ Thirty-three percent of Asians in the United States have completed four or more years of college (Wallace, 1994).

❏ Educational levels vary widely among Asian immigrants. For example, only 3% of persons arriving from India lack a high school education, and 75% of working Indians are college graduates (CIS, 2001).

❏ Asian Indians and Filipinos in the U.S. have the highest educational attainment of all ethnic groups (Chan, 1998b; Shekar & Hegde, 1995). Conversely, many refugees from other countries may be preliterate (Cheng, 1999).

❑ In some groups, the greatest honor children can bestow on their parents is academic achievement.

❑ Many Asian parents see themselves as active agents in their children's learning and work diligently at home with their children.

❑ In some countries, boys are separated from girls for instruction.

❑ Some Asian schools do not require students to move from classroom to classroom—only the teachers move.

❑ Students and their families accord teachers great respect. In some countries, teachers are revered as much as doctors.

❑ In some schools students are expected to stand up and bow when the teacher enters the room. Students sit down only when given permission to do so.

❑ Some Asian schools rely heavily on rote learning and memorization.

❑ Conformity may be viewed as more important than creativity.

❑ In some Asian schools, corporal punishment is acceptable.

❑ Many Asian students are accustomed to authoritarian teachers. Asian students are expected to maintain a proper social distance from their teachers (Cheng, 1998).

❑ Teachers often lecture to students without offering opportunities for discussion of the information presented.

❑ Many Asians consider it rude for students to volunteer or to ask questions in class.

❑ Asian students are unlikely to correct a teacher or to hear a teacher admit that an error was made.

❑ Students tend to avoid eye contact with teachers because direct eye contact is considered rude.

❑ Some schools do not provide textbooks to individual students. Students are expected to copy information from the blackboard or to take oral dictation.

❑ In some schools, teachers have complete responsibility for the care of students. They may even take students to the doctor if medical care is needed.

❑ Some Asian schools require students to wear uniforms. Schools are generally not considered places to display the latest fashions.

❑ In many countries, students go home for lunch because food is not served at school.

❑ Southeast Asian immigrants/refugees have high rates of middle ear problems. These problems can contribute to problems learning in the school environment.

CULTURAL CUSTOMS AND COURTESIES

❏ Hospitality is highly valued.

❏ Many Asians bow slightly when greeting others.

❏ In some homes, guests are expected to remove their shoes.

❏ Public hand holding or touching between same-sex members may be acceptable.

❏ Public displays of affection between members of the opposite sex may be frowned upon and seen as distasteful. Holding hands in public may be considered daring. In contrast, in one study, Americans reported nearly twice as much physical contact as did Japanese, most of it being with friends of the opposite sex (Irujo, 1988).

❏ Among some groups, dating is not permitted and premarital sex is frowned upon.

❏ Modesty in dress and appearance are highly valued; American clothing may be seen as immodest and revealing.

❏ Modesty and humility are highly valued; "blowing your own horn" may be seen as arrogant and unseemly.

❏ Other important personal qualities for many Asians include self-restraint, self-sacrifice, inner strength, perseverance, and patience.

❏ Authority figures of any kind generally should not be questioned.

❏ Hierarchical relationships tend to be viewed as important. Conventions can be based on age, gender, social status, etc.

❏ Many Asian groups show reverence for the elderly. Advancement in age is approached with respect, dignity, and pride. The number of grandchildren one has may be viewed as a measure of one's success in life.

❏ Some students (e.g., Vietnamese) may wear a Buddhist symbol that is shaped like a swastika. They may be aware only of the Buddhist meaning of this symbol.

HEALTH CARE AND DISABLING CONDITIONS

❏ In the U.S., lack of health insurance is a significant problem for many Asian immigrants and refugees. This is particularly true for those from China and Korea (Center for Immigration Studies, 2001).

❏ Many Asian parents believe that children who are "disabled" show physical evidence of the disability. Conditions that are not visible (e.g., stuttering, learning disability) are believed to result from "not trying hard enough." Parents may not see any need for therapy or rehabilitation (Bebout & Arthur, 1992).

❏ Many Asians only consider physical disabilities to be worthy of treatment (Matsuda, 1989).

❑ Among many Asians, there is a tendency to define the causes of health-related problems and disabilities in spiritual terms. For example, problems may be attributed to spoiled foods, demons or spirits, or a bad wind (Cheng, 1999).

❑ Fadiman (1997) told the story of a Hmong girl with epilepsy who lived in central California. Doctors wanted to treat the epilepsy with traditional Western medical methods. But her family believed the condition was caused by spiritual forces, and described the girl's condition as "the spirit catches you and you fall down."

❑ Some Asians feel that disabling conditions occur because of one's "fate" and that nothing can or should be done to interfere.

❑ Some families believe that birth defects and disabilities result from sins committed by parents and even remote ancestors.

❑ If a child's defects represent a punishment for sins, the child may be looked upon as an object of shame for the entire family and consequently isolated from society.

❑ To "save face" some families are hesitant to seek medical care for children with disabilities.

❑ Many groups believe that caring for the disabled is the responsibility of the family rather than the school.

❑ Health practices may involve acupuncture, herbs, massage, and baths in hot springs.

❑ Some Western practices such as collecting blood, surgery, performing biopsies, etc. may be alien to the family.

❑ Some groups may visit religious shrines or temples to seek healing.

❑ Attitudes toward rehabilitation are often influenced by acculturation; first generation immigrants may feel more "hopeless" than Asians born and raised in the United States (Huer, Saenz, & Doan, 2001).

Profile

Melanie, an 8-year-old Filipino girl, was born with a cleft palate. She had undergone several surgeries for repairs, but her speech continued to be affected by hypernasality and poor articulation. The surgeon had recommended pharyngeal flap surgery for Melanie to resolve the velopharyngeal incompetence that was causing Melanie's hypernasality, but the family refused the surgery. At the triennial IEP meeting, the speech-language pathologist informed Melanie's parents that the student's speech had become more intelligible as a result of treatment, although she still exhibited hypernasality.

The speech-language pathologist expressed the concern that further therapy to modify Melanie's resonance would not be effective unless she had pharyngeal flap surgery. The father was very angry, and refused to allow Melanie to come back for more speech therapy. He smiled as he left, however, and thanked the speech-language pathologist for the work she had done with Melanie over the last 3 years.

ASIAN COMMUNICATION STYLES

❏ Many Asian languages have formal rules of communication propriety based on the relative status of the participants in the interaction.

❏ Much information is conveyed nonverbally through subtle gestures, postures, positioning, facial expressions, eye contact, and silence (Fung & Roseberry-McKibbin, 1999).

❏ "Saving face" or avoiding public embarrassment is very important.

❏ Smooth and harmonious interpersonal relationships are a high priority.

❏ Asians may avoid public confrontations and open competition.

❏ Many Asians are indirect in their communication, giving the impression that they are evasive and noncommittal (Chan, 1998b).

❏ Interrupting a conversation may be considered impolite.

❏ Many Asians believe that it is inappropriate and offensive to display anger publicly or to contradict others (Roseberry-McKibbin, 1997b).

❏ Among some groups (e.g., the Japanese), a hiss may be considered a sign of approval rather than contempt or rejection (Irujo, 1988).

❏ A slap on the back may be considered insulting.

❏ Individuals may say "yes," to show that they are listening and paying attention even when they are in disagreement.

❏ Direct eye contact may be considered an open show of rudeness or challenge between individuals who are conversing.

❏ When asked to do something, Asians often give a positive response in an effort to be polite. They, however, may not follow through (Chan, 1998b).

❏ It is considered proper to keep one's outward composure, no matter how one may feel inside.

❏ Many groups (e.g., the Japanese and Indians) value silence and think that Westerners are verbose. Silence may be used to avoid expressing disagreement (Irujo, 1988).

❏ Some Asians smile or laugh in situations in which embarrassment is experienced.

❏ Smiling does not necessarily imply happiness or pleasure; it can connote many positive or even negative emotions.

❏ Personal questions may be considered appropriate (e.g., it is acceptable to ask one's age, marital status) to ascertain relative status between speakers.

❏ Among some groups, it is considered unacceptable to touch others on the head.

❑ Some groups, such as the Japanese, may be accustomed to more personal space than that commonly experienced during interactions with Anglo Americans. It is important not to violate space boundaries.

❑ There may be very little touching during conversations. The Japanese, for example, generally exhibit limited physical contact during social interactions in public places (Irujo, 1988).

❑ Among many traditional Japanese, honorifics and formalities are the norm. Such formalities might seem excessive to Americans.

ASIAN LANGUAGE CONSIDERATIONS

❑ Some of the most widely spoken Asian languages in the United States are Chinese, Filipino, Vietnamese, Japanese, Khmer, and Korean (Cheng, 1998).

❑ Many Asian languages have numerous dialects that may or may not be mutually intelligible; for example, there are over 87 dialects in China and the Philippines (Cheng, 1991). Most Philippine dialects spoken in the Philippines are mutually unintelligible (Roseberry-McKibbin, 1997b).

❑ The Indian constitution recognizes 15 major languages, but India has over 700 dialects. Hindi is recognized as the national language, although many Indians do not speak it.

❑ Kannada is another major language of India. English is the official language of education and the government (see Shekar & Hegde, 1995, for a complete description of the phonetics, phonology, and grammar of Hindi and Kannada).

❑ Students from some countries, such as Vietnam and Cambodia, may speak French in addition to their primary language.

❑ Some groups have politeness conventions that dictate the use of certain word forms depending upon the relative status of the participants in the interaction. For example, Japanese has more than 100 words for "I" and "me" that are selected based on one's social status (Cheng, 1991).

❑ Vietnamese, Chinese, and Laotian are tonal languages. Each tone change is phonemic in nature and represents a meaning change. For example, in Mandarin, the word "ma" can mean *mother, horse, scold, flax,* or *curse* depending on the tone used.

❑ Mandarin has four types of tones that affect meaning. These are referred to as tonemes. Cantonese has seven tonemes; Northern Vietnamese has six tonemes; Central and Southern Vietnamese each have five tonemes.

❑ Japanese, Khmer, and Korean are not tonal languages.

❑ Written Asian language systems vary widely. The Vietnamese, for example, use a modified Roman alphabet whereas the Chinese use symbols to represent concepts.

❑ When stating their names in writing, the last name precedes the first name in most Asian cultures (see Table 6.1).

❑ Chinese, Vietnamese, and Laotian are basically monosyllabic.

Table 6.1
Information About Asian Family Names

Characteristics of names most often given to members of various Asian populations are summarized below.

Cambodian: Names consist of two parts. Family name precedes personal name. Middle names are rare.

Chinese: Names consist of two parts. Family name precedes personal name. Most Chinese names consist of only one syllable. Common Chinese names: Chan, Chang, Chiang, Chin, Chow, Chung, Lee, Louie, Lum, Wong, Woo.

Hmong: Most names consist of two parts. Family name precedes personal name. Common Hmong family names: Chang, Chue, Fang, Her, Khang, Kue, Lor, Lee, Moua, Thao, Vang, Vue, Xiong, Yang.

Indonesians: Names consist of two parts. Many are polysyllabic and thus quite lengthy by American standards (e.g., "Pranawahadi"). Many Indonesians have Muslim names.

Japanese: Most names consist of two parts. Family name precedes personal name. To be polite when interacting with an authority figure, "san" is added to the end of the individual's last name. Japanese names often consist of more than one syllable. Common Japanese surnames: Kawaguchi, Nakamura, Tanaka, Watanabe, Yamamoto.

Koreans: Most names consist of a family name that precedes a two-part personal name. Common Korean surnames are: Kim, Park, Lee.

Laotians: Family name precedes personal name. Names may consist of more than one syllable, and some are quite lengthy by American standards (e.g., Souphanouvong).

Thais: Personal name precedes the surname. Some names are quite long (e.g., Suvarnarami).

Vietnamese: Names consist of three components: family, middle, and given names. The family name is followed by the middle name and personal name respectively. The name, Nguyen Van Thieu, for example, begins with the family name "Nguyen" and ends with "Thieu," the name that the individual is called by family members and friends. Approximately 52% of Vietnamese individuals have the family name "Nguyen"; 31% have the family name "Tran." Other common family names are Pham, Le, Ngo, Do, Dao, Vu, Hoang, Dang, Dinh, and Duong.

Source: Information included in this table was obtained from the *Asian American Handbook* (1991).

❑ Chinese and Vietnamese have no consonant blends.

❑ Many Asian languages do not have inflectional markers.

❑ Some languages (e.g., Indonesian, Japanese, Tagalog) do not have specific gender pronouns such as "he" or "she."

❑ Prosody or intonation in English may sound very "choppy" and monotonous.

❑ Some speakers may sound nasal when speaking English.

It is very difficult to provide generalities about Asian speakers' English language patterns because of the variety of languages and dialects spoken by this population. Some of the commonly observed characteristics of the English of Asian speakers are listed in Table 6.2 and Table 6.3 based on information reported in the literature (Chan, 1998b; Cheng, 1987, 1991, 1994, 2002; Fang & Ping-An, 1992; Goldstein, 2000; Li, 1992; Yoshinaga-Itano, 1990).

✐ REFLECTION ✐

A classroom teacher has referred a Chinese 5-year-old kindergarten student to you. She stated that the child "sounds nasal and choppy." He also leaves the ending sounds off of his words and can't pronounce long words very well. Pronouncing the /r/ and /l/ sounds is very difficult for him. What will you share with this teacher? Does this student have a communication difference, or a communication disorder?

_____

_____

_____

_____

IMPLICATIONS FOR PROFESSIONALS

Much diversity exists among Asian populations. Among the cultural variables that may be important to consider are the following:

❑ Asians generally prefer to be referred to as "Asians" rather than "Orientals."

❑ Shaking hands with someone of the opposite sex may be considered unacceptable.

❑ Use of one's left hand to touch someone or to hand something to someone may be frowned upon. Some Asians consider the left hand to be unclean.

❑ The older members of the family should be addressed first, as a sign of respect.

❑ Because of the great value Asians place on education, they respect educated professionals. This respect may lead them to revere the professional as an "expert," and they may not volunteer opinions or responses. Asian individuals may agree to carry out recommendations although they have no intention of actually doing so (Liam & Abdullah, 2001).

Table 6.2

Language Differences Commonly Observed Among Asian Speakers

Language Characteristics	*Sample English Utterances*
Omission of plurals	Here are 2 piece of toast. I got 5 finger on each hand.
Omission of copula	He going home now. They eating.
Omission of possessive	I have Phuong pencil. Mom food is cold.
Omission of past tense morpheme	We cook dinner yesterday. Last night she walk home.
Past tense double marking	He didn't went by himself.
Double negative	They don't have no books.
Subject-verb-object relationship differences/omissions	I messed up it. He like.
Misordering of interrogatives	You are going now?
Misuse or omission of prepositions	She is in home. He goes to school 8:00.
Misuse of pronouns	She husband is coming. She said her wife is here.
Omission and/or overgeneralization of articles	Boy is sick. He went the home.
Incorrect use of comparatives	This book is gooder than that book.
Omission of conjunctions	You _____ I going to the beach.
Omission, lack of inflection on auxiliary "do"	She _____ not take it. He do not have enough.
Omission, lack of inflection on forms of "have"	She have no money. We_____been the store.

Table 6.3

Articulation Differences Observed Commonly Among Asian Speakers

Articulation Characteristics	*Sample English Utterances*	
In many Asian languages, words end in vowels only or in just a few consonants; speakers may delete many final consonants in English.	ste/step ro/robe	li/lid do/dog
Some languages are monosyllabic; speakers may truncate polysyllabic words or emphasize the wrong syllable.	efunt/elephant **di**versity/diversity (emphasis on first syllable)	
Possible devoicing of voiced cognates	beece/bees luff/love	pick/pig crip/crib
r/l confusion	lize/rise	clown/crown
/r/ may be omitted entirely.	gull/girl	tone/torn
Reduction of vowel length in words	Words sound choppy to Americans.	
No voiced or voiceless "th"	dose/those zose/those	tin/thin sin/thin
Epenthesis (addition of "uh" sound in blends, ends of words).	bulack/black	wooduh/wood
Confusion of "ch" and "sh"	sheep/cheap	beesh/beach
/ae/ does not exist in many Asian languages	block/black	shock/shack
b/v substitutions	base/vase	Beberly/Beverly
v/w substitutions	vork/work	vall/wall

❏ When family members say "yes," they may mean "I hear you" rather than "I agree." Professionals need to encourage open communication as much as possible (Roseberry-McKibbin, 1999).

❏ It is best if professionals establish rapport before venturing into frank discussions of specific problem areas.

❏ It may be considered disloyal or disgraceful to the family for parents to openly discuss a child or family-related problem such as a disability. Professionals need to be sensitive when asking personal questions and may need to be indirect when discussing areas of concern.

❏ In some Asian countries (e.g., Malaysia), it is considered rude to say "yes" when first offered an item or service; to be polite, one should say "no." The person who makes the offer then tries to persuade the other person to accept it. Thus, professionals may need to offer services many times before these services are accepted (Liam & Abdullah, 2001).

❏ Families may offer gifts in exchange for professional services, and may feel offended if professionals do not accept these gifts.

❏ Professionals should dress formally, even when making home visits, because informal dress may be seen as a sign of disrespect.

❏ Some parents may believe that ESL or bilingual classes are inferior to classes without these special programs (Yiquang & Wink, 1992). Professionals should provide parents with information about bilingual programs of instruction.

❏ Parents may feel uncomfortable about sex education programs offered in schools. Many families do not openly discuss sex at home (Chan, 1998a).

❏ Professionals should understand that some immigrant Asian students may be unaccustomed to participating in groups of mixed gender.

❏ Professionals can help immigrant students (especially in junior high and high school) to become accustomed to moving from classroom to classroom for different subjects.

❏ Professionals should gently ease students into tasks requiring them to express opinions, form judgments, and solve problems. Such activities may be a new experience for students who had been taught to sit quietly in class (Cheng, 1994).

❏ Some immigrant Asian students may not be accustomed to being called upon in class and may feel uncomfortable speaking up or even reading in front of the group.

❏ The informal atmosphere in American schools may be disconcerting to Asian students and parents. Professionals can offer guidance to help students feel more comfortable in the classroom.

❏ Parents often expect students to bring home large amounts of homework. Professionals may be asked to account for "too little" homework.

❏ Students may need help in learning how to use libraries.

❏ Students may not "take initiative" in the classroom. Many Asian students have grown accustomed to being told what to do by authoritarian teachers and may seem "passive" in the classroom.

❏ Students may be unaccustomed to physical contact in the classroom.

❏ Students may appear to have "expressive language problems" because they have been taught to be quiet and respectful.

❏ The concept of winning a game may be unfamiliar to some students (Cheng, 2002). Professionals can help students for whom this is the case.

❏ When working with Hindu Indian students, professionals must be sensitive about pictures depicting beef or about offering beef as part of a snack or general eating activity.

Profile

A teacher in Stockton, California was teaching in a classroom that had many Vietnamese students. The teacher spelled the name of one of the boys incorrectly numerous times in the first half of the school year. The boy saw his name spelled incorrectly on his name card, and proceeded to misspell his name on all his papers from then on. Some months later, the teacher became aware of her error and asked the boy why he didn't tell her she had spelled his name incorrectly. He said, "I thought that was the way you wanted me to spell it." The boy did not dare challenge his teacher!

STUDY QUESTIONS

1. Why are Asians often called the "model minority?" Describe problems that this label creates for them.

2. Compare and contrast mainstream U.S. beliefs about causation of disabilities and the need for intervention with the beliefs commonly held within Asian countries.

3. You will be meeting with the family of a 9-year-old Asian boy who needs special education services. Describe four things that need to be considered to ensure that you interact with family members in a culturally appropriate manner.

TRUE-FALSE

Unless indicated otherwise, circle the number beside each statement that is true.

4. Among Asians, laughter and smiling generally indicate happiness and pleasure.

5. Among Asian Americans, Filipinos have the highest percentage of their population in the labor force.

6. Many Asians attribute the causes of disabilities to spiritual etiologies (e.g., a bad wind).

7. When working with Asian students, professionals must remember that modesty and humility are not highly valued by them, so it is important to help Asian students realize the importance of these qualities.

8. Some of the most widely spoken Asian languages in the United States are Chinese, Filipino, Vietnamese, Japanese, Khmer, and Korean.

9. The family structure in Asian countries is always patriarchal.

10. Asian parents often feel relieved by the informal structure of American schools because it allows opportunities for a high level of participation and interaction with the teacher.

11. Which one of the following is FALSE?
    A. Japan, Korea, and China are in East Asia.
    B. Sri Lanka, Pakistan, India, and Saudi Arabia are in South Asia.
    C. The Philippines, Laos, Cambodia, Thailand, Indonesia, Singapore, Burma, Vietnam, and Malaysia are in Southeast Asia.
    D. Most Indians are Hindus.
    E. The Asian American population in the U.S. is now over 10 million.

12. The following statements describe communication styles observed frequently among Asian cultures:
    A. Personal questions (e.g., asking one's age) are considered highly inappropriate.
    B. Direct eye contact may be considered an open display of rudeness or challenge between individuals who are conversing.
    C. Periods of silence during a conversation are considered awkward and should be avoided if at all possible.
    D. Many Asians avoid open competition and public confrontation.
    E. To maintain harmony when they disagree with others, many Asians will not outwardly express their feelings of disagreement.

13. A teacher refers a child to you for assessment. This student recently moved to this country from China. Which of the following would indicate a communication difference, not a disorder?
    A. Omission of articles (e.g., "Little dog is playing in water.")
    B. Difficulty with consonant clusters
    C. An a/ae substitution (e.g., substituting "block" for "black" by saying, "The sky gets <u>block</u> at night.")
    D. Substitution of /r/ for /n/

14. Which statements about Asian education are true?
  A. In Asia, teachers are often formal and tend to maintain a distance from students.
  B. Teachers are not highly respected.
  C. Many Asian parents see themselves as active agents in their children's learning and work diligently at home with their children.
  D. Teachers in Asian schools tend to discourage rote learning and memorization so that divergent thinking and creativity can be promoted.
  E. Many Asians believe that the greatest honor children can bestow on their parents is academic achievement.

15. Which of the following beliefs or actions would suggest lack of "cultural awareness" during interactions with the parents of an Asian child?
  A. The professional is aware that Asians often agree to recommendations out of respect, although they have no intention of following through on these recommendations.
  B. The professional assures parents that little homework will be given to prevent stress in the home environment.
  C. The professional is direct and forthright when informing the family that the student has a communication disorder.
  D. The professional speaks in a stern voice when making recommendations to earn the respect of the parents.

ANSWERS TO STUDY QUESTIONS

  4. False
  5. True
  6. True
  7. False
  8. True
  9. False
  10. False
  11. B
  12. B, D, and E
  13. A, B, and C
  14. A, C, and E
  15. B, C, and D

Chapter 7

FAMILIES FROM NATIVE AMERICAN BACKGROUNDS

Outline

There are approximately 650-700 separate and distinct Native American tribal entities with distinct languages and cultures (Westby & Vining, 2002). Thus, there is considerable heterogeneity within and across tribes; they may differ in terms of cultural, sociological, linguistic, and demographic variables. When reading this chapter, it is important for readers to remember that not all Native American groups have the same customs, beliefs, and values.

GENERAL BACKGROUND INFORMATION

❑ In 1990, approximately 1.9 million people identified themselves as Aleuts, American Indians, or Eskimos (U.S. Bureau of the Census, 1992).

❑ Between 1990 and 2000, the population of Native American and Alaska Natives in the U.S. grew 26% based on the 2,474,956 identified during the census as Native American by "race alone." Those who identified themselves as Native American by "race alone or in combination" totaled 4,119,301. If one uses the latter figure, there was a 110.3% rate of growth among Native Americans between 1990 amd 2000 (U.S. Bureau of the Census, 2000).

❑ There are approximately 500 separate and distinct tribal entities with distinct languages and cultures (Harris, 1998). Thus, there is considerable heterogeneity within and across tribes; they may differ in terms of cultural, sociological, linguistic, and demographic variables.

❑ There are various names for Native Americans (e.g., First People). Some prefer to be called American Indians, feeling that "Native American" is a generic term for anyone born on American soil (Murphy, 2001).

❑ Historically, most Native Americans lived in nations that were made up of tribes and clans.

❑ When Europeans came to North America, millions of Native Americans were slaughtered or died of disease and starvation.

❑ Many Native American children were, in the past, removed from their families and forced to attend government-run boarding schools, where a major goal was to eliminate the children's language and culture (Leibowitz, 1971). This practice, viewed by many Native Americans as cultural genocide, has led to renewed efforts to preserve Native American family unity (Mannes, 1993).

❑ The Indian Relocation Act resulted in efforts to assimilate Indians into white society by moving them into cities for jobs or job training. The years of relocation substantially increased the probability that many Indian families would spend part or all of their lives in "ghettoized" urban poverty (Fixico, 1986).

❑ The Indian Education Act (IEA) of 1972 led to improved educational opportunities for Native Americans (Tonemah & Roanhorse-Benally, 1984).

❑ The Native American population is young; a greater number are under 20 years of age than in most other ethnic groups.

❑ Poverty is endemic among Native Americans. "American Indian groups are ranked at the bottom of virtually every social status indicator with regard to health, income, and education. Twice as many Indian families live in poverty and are headed by women than in the general U.S. population" (Harris, 1998, p. 138).

❏ Native American reservations have a 31% poverty rate, the highest in the U.S. Currently, the unemployment rate for Native Americans is 46% (Murphy, 2001).

❏ Most Native American religious traditions emphasize a universal spirituality that is integral to all of life. Native Americans believe that all things, supernatural and natural, are interconnected.

❏ Members of many tribes believe in one Creator or Great Spirit. They have great respect for Mother Earth.

❏ Anglo European Americans have been most concerned with harnessing and controlling nature; Native Americans have attempted to live in harmony with nature (Gilliland, 1988).

❏ Historically, Native Americans did not believe in private or individual ownership of land, but rather viewed (and continue to view) themselves as caretakers of it.

❏ Today, most tribes teach respect for the land and forbid destruction of their ancestral lands.

❏ In some tribes, medicine people serve a dual role as religious leaders and doctors for physical illnesses. Many medicine people believe in treating the whole person, not just the affected part of the body.

❏ Long hair has spiritual significance for some Native American males.

NATIVE AMERICAN FAMILY LIFE

❏ Seventy-eight percent of Native Americans live in urban areas. Oklahoma and California have the greatest number of Native American residents in the United States. (Robinson-Zañartu, 1996).

❏ Close-knit, extended families are common.

❏ To many Native Americans, family ties are more important than anything, including money, school, and prestige.

❏ Members of the extended family often care for children and provide long-term nursing care for elderly family members.

❏ Each family member is expected to support others in the family. Working members of the family may be expected to care for needy brothers and sisters, elderly parents, and even more distant kin.

❏ Often, the grandparents and other elders are in positions of authority and assume more responsibility for the training of children than either the mother or father (Tafoya, 1989).

❏ Because the family is so close-knit, many Native Americans do not leave their children in the care of people outside the family or tribe. Baby-sitters and day-care workers are never used by some families (Harris, 1985).

❏ Native Americans tend to be affectionate with their children. Touching and closeness are integral in parent-child relationships.

❏ Children are often accorded great respect and given individual responsibility. They may even be allowed to make decisions for themselves about matters that other cultural groups might consider too important to be left to a child or young adult. There is tolerance for mistakes, and little censure or punishment (Anderson & Fenichel, 1989).

❏ Native American children are encouraged to become independent and master self-care skills at an early age; children who help around the house are praised.

❏ Many Native Americans do not shower babies with compliments because such behavior draws attention that is believed to be harmful (Joe & Malach, 1998).

❏ Many Native American children live in out-of-home placements; 85% of those placements are with non-Native American families (Robinson-Zañartu, 1996).

✐ REFLECTION ✐

Describe three characteristics of Native American family life that are important for professionals to remember as they work with these families.

_____

_____

_____

_____

_____

NATIVE AMERICAN EDUCATION AND LITERACY

❏ Information is often passed down from one generation to the next by story-telling. Some Native American groups had no system for writing down information until recently. Reading is not always culturally reinforced (Kay-Raining Bird & Vetter, 1994).

❏ Many Native American children begin school at an academic disadvantage when compared to other children. They may have difficulties in school resulting from cultural and linguistic differences between the home and school.

❏ Use of a language other than English in the home by one or more family members is common; many Native Americans enter school with limited knowledge of English.

❏ Students may miss school because of traditional family obligations. Poor attendance can cause them to fall behind academically and can create a conflict between family loyalties and school expectations.

❏ Only 8% of Native Americans have finished four or more years of college as compared to 16% of the general U.S. population (Harris, 1998).

❏ The Native American drop-out rate (50%) is the highest of any ethnic group. In some areas, the drop-out rate is 96% (Robinson-Zanartu, 1996).

❏ Many Native Americans value patience and the ability to wait quietly. Thus, in school, the continuous flurry of activities according to a rigid schedule can cause confusion for a child.

❏ Native American students are often thought to have a reflective rather than impulsive learning style (Phillips, 1983).

❏ In many Native American tribes, such as the Chippewa tribe, it is stressed that children should learn through observation and that they should display knowledge later (Kay-Raining Bird & Vetter, 1994).

❏ Native American students have been disproportionately represented in special education (Harris, 1998).

CULTURAL CUSTOMS, COURTESIES, AND BELIEFS

❏ It is considered culturally unacceptable in some tribes to seek outside assistance when a family is in need; the extended family is supposed to provide everything that is needed.

❏ Many Native Americans are taught not to interfere in the affairs of others (Joe & Malach, 1998). Thus, they may give advice or information only if it is specifically asked of them.

❏ Most groups teach their younger members to show respect for authority and for the elderly, who are regarded as valuable sources of knowledge and experience (Westby & Vining, 2002).

❏ Anglo American society emphasizes competition and winning. Native Americans believe in doing their best, but they do not want to stand out as being "superior" to others. Native Americans strive to avoid competing with peers (Swisher & Deyhle, 1989).

❏ Native Americans are often reluctant to exalt themselves above others in their community; high achievers may downplay or even mask their talents in order to be accepted. Bragging about oneself and one's abilities is considered rude (Tafoya, 1989).

❏ Happiness and harmony between individuals, society, and nature is emphasized.

❏ Many tribes emphasize generosity in the sharing of resources, possessions, and self. Honor and respect are obtained through sharing and giving rather than accumulating material goods (Bridges & Midgette, 2000).

❏ Many young Native Americans experience conflict between the old and new ways of doing things. They may feel that they are on a "bridge between two worlds." Parents and grandparents often hold certain beliefs that are rejected by the "younger generation" because of a desire to assimilate into white culture. This can lead to pain, frustration, and conflict within families (McWhirter & Ryan, 1991).

❑ Ceremonies and traditional activities have an important place in the lives of many Native Americans. Some activities are highly religious while others are social and recreational. The latter might include Pow Wows, giveaways, rodeos, and competitive dance contests.

❑ The establishment of human relationships is considered to be far more important than adherence to schedules. Punctuality and planning may be de-emphasized and even viewed negatively (Bridges & Midgette, 2000).

HEALTH CARE AND DISABLING CONDITIONS

❑ There is a lack of effective, comprehensive health and prevention programs for Native Americans (Stewart, 1992).

❑ Many Native Americans live on reservations that are geographically remote from available health, education, and vocational services.

❑ Native Americans, as a group, have the highest infant mortality rate in the United States.

❑ The average Native American life span is 54 years (Whitney & Friedlander, 1994).

❑ A high incidence of alcoholism among Native Americans is a well-documented phenomenon (Carney & Chermak, 1991; Friedlander, 1993; Harris, 1998). Almost half of Native American deaths are due to cirrhosis of the liver.

❑ Most Native American drinkers range in age from 25 to 44, and are women in their child-bearing years (Clark & Kelley, 1992).

❑ The number of alcohol-related deaths among Native Americans is five times greater than among Americans as a whole (Whitney & Friedlander, 1994).

❑ The incidence of Native American babies born with Fetal Alcohol Syndrome (FAS) is six times higher than the incidence within the general population; approximately 20% of American Indian babies are born with FAS.

❑ Other diseases common among Native Americans include diabetes, gastrointestinal disease, malignant neoplasms, and tuberculosis.

❑ Higher than average prevalences of certain health conditions associated with communication disorders are reported for the Native American population. Otitis media, bacterial meningitis, fetal alcohol syndrome, and cleft lip and palate, for example, are all more prevalent among Native Americans than among other groups.

❑ Many Native American children have otitis media and related hearing problems. Studies indicate that the prevalence rate of otitis media among Native American children ranges from 17% to 76% (Pang-Ching, Robb, Heath, & Takumi, 1995). The high incidence of otitis media is due, in part, to the limited availability of appropriate health care services.

❑ Native Americans who qualify for health care may only receive services while residing on the reservation; if they live in urban areas, they do not qualify for "reservation health care" and sometimes their health needs go unattended.

❑ Healing and purification ceremonies are quite common among many tribes (Joe & Malach, 1998).

❑ Some Native Americans accept a disabled child as the Great Spirit's gift; others may believe that the handicapping condition resulted from witchcraft or moral transgressions (Harris, 1986).

❑ Some Native American groups are able to accept disabled individuals because of a strong belief that these individuals still have a viable role to play in the community.

❑ Some Native Americans believe that a child is born with a disability because that child has made a choice prenatally to be disabled. Other beliefs about causality cited by Vining (1999) include:

1. Events and experiences encountered by the Holy People

2. Not honoring traditional teachings

3. Curses placed on the child

4. Taboos violated by parents (e.g., mother viewed a solar or lunar eclipse during pregnancy)

❑ Many Native Americans are unaware of services provided by speech-language pathologists. Some, such as the Navajo, believe that certain types of communication disorders can be treated by performing such rituals as breaking a pot over a child's head, having a child eat roasted corn with straight kernels, holding a purification ceremony, and others (Vining, 1999).

Profile

An early intervention team was made aware of a Cherokee girl who had been born with cerebral palsy and had been recently enrolled in the local preschool. The team head arranged to visit the family at home to talk about services for the child (speech, occupational, and physical therapy). Upon visiting the home, the team leader found that the family expressed gratitude for the child's cerebral palsy. The mother shared that this condition was a gift from the Great Spirit to help her become a more patient person. She added that she had also been given the opportunity to appreciate every minor development her child made. The family stated that they would like to postpone rehabilitative efforts until their daughter was in school.

NATIVE AMERICAN COMMUNICATION STYLES

❑ Respect is highly valued; one way of signifying respect for another person is to avoid eye contact by looking down.

❑ Children's communication with adults is respectful and discrete. To show respect, there is little eye contact. Making eye contact is viewed as a way of showing defiance or rudeness.

❑ Native American mothers, especially those in the Navajo population, may be silent during interactions with their infants (van Kleeck, 1994).

❑ Most children are taught that one learns more by listening and observing than by speaking.

❑ Parents often feel that their children's auditory comprehension skills are more advanced than their expressive language skills (Wilson, 1994).

❑ Speech, language, and hearing difficulties occur five times more frequently among Native Americans than in the general population (Friedlander, 1993).

❑ Children are generally discouraged from speaking the tribal language before they are capable of correct articulation. Opportunities for oral practice in the language may be limited (Harris, 1985).

❑ In some families, children communicate primarily through pointing and "gesturing for a long period of time before they begin using words" (Wilson, 1994, p. 5).

❑ Among some Western Apache Indians, children may be rebuked for "talking like a white man" if they speak English or talk too much in the village (Harris, 1985).

❑ In many families, adults do not carry out verbal exchanges with infants or they respond to infants' vocalizations as if these vocalizations carry no meaning.

❑ Native American etiquette requires a lapse of time between the asking and answering of a question. Some Native Americans believe that an immediate answer to a question implies that the question was not worth thinking about (Gilliland, 1988).

❑ Children often do not answer a question unless they are confident that their answer is correct.

❑ Children do not express opinions on certain subjects because they first need to earn the right to express such opinions.

❑ In many groups, it is considered inappropriate for a person to express strong feelings publicly. Adults usually express grief around outsiders only during official mourning ceremonies (Gilliland, 1988).

NATIVE AMERICAN LANGUAGE CONSIDERATIONS

❑ Among the Navajo, a child's "first laugh" is very significant. Parents may be more concerned about physical development than about communication milestones (Wilson, 1994).

❑ Many Native American children speak a language other than English.

❑ There are over 200 American Indian languages spoken in the United States, and dialectal variations exist within each of these languages.

❑ Leap (1993) estimated that there are more than 760,000 speakers of Native American languages in the United States.

❑ Six general "families" of Native American languages are Eskimo-Aleut, Algonquin, Penutian, Na-Dane', Macro-Siouan, and Aztec-Tanoan (Goldstein, 2000). Some of the most commonly spoken American Indian languages are Teton Sioux, Cherokee, and Dinneh.

❑ Many Indian languages have no word for time, contain no future tense verbs, and are based almost entirely on the present tense (Gilliland, 1988).

❑ Many American Indian languages contain fewer vowel sounds than English. The English sound system is often difficult for students to master.

❑ Native American languages contain some sounds that do not occur in English. For example, there may be voiceless stops in combination with velar fricatives, ejectives (sounds made with a glottalic egressive airstream), and implosives (sounds made with an ingressive glottalic airstream). In addition, many vowels are nasalized (Goldstein, 2000).

❑ There are other differences between Native American languages and Standard American English (SAE) that make SAE difficult to master. For example, word order may change, even in the same language, depending on the speaker's intended meaning. Pronoun deletion is also common (Robinson-Zanartu, 1996).

❑ Harris (1998), in her extensive description of the Navajo language, details other differences, such as Navajo's lack of distinction of grammatical gender as its intricate verb system. Professionals should be aware that students may struggle in school because Native American languages are so different from English.

❑ It is beyond the scope of this book to describe characteristics of the more than 200 Native American languages spoken in the United States. Consultation with native speakers is important in situations where a problem is suspected. For more specific information about Native American languages, see Westby & Vining (2002).

✐REFLECTION✐

Communication styles differ between many Native Americans and Anglo Americans. Describe two common characteristics of Native American communication styles that professionals might interpret inaccurately as signs of a communication disorder.

_____

_____

_____

_____

_____

IMPLICATIONS FOR PROFESSIONALS

❑ Many Native Americans believe in taking life as it comes and accepting all circumstances; professionals should not interpret this as passivity and as resistance to change.

❑ If a member of an urban-dwelling family needs health care that can only be obtained on a reservation, the entire family must relocate, sometimes resulting in a situation in which children miss school for a period of time.

❑ Parents may remove their children from school to take them to Pow-Wows, ceremonies, and events considered important within the culture.

❑ Some tribal groups are forced to constantly choose between White people's modern medicine and traditional Native American approaches. This can cause uncertainty and guilt for some tribal members.

❑ It is often appropriate to consult with an Indian medicine person before recommending a therapeutic intervention or medical procedure.

❑ Professionals should not be surprised if grandparents show up for conferences instead of parents.

❑ Some families may be reluctant to take advantage of aid and services that are available, such as health care, welfare, legal aid, and counseling (Clark & Kelley, 1992). Pride is often a factor contributing to their reluctance to accept help from outside agencies.

❑ Some Native Americans may be unwilling to discuss family affairs freely. They may believe that words have power to hurt as well as heal, so they feel that if they even discuss a disabling condition, the discussion itself can bring greater problems to the person or the family as a whole.

❑ Thus, it may be difficult or impossible to gather important case history information. Personal questions may be viewed as prying into one's personal affairs. It is important to explain the reasons for asking specific questions.

❑ It is critical to reach out to the families, both immediate and extended (especially the grandparents), of Native American students. One should not attempt to treat the student in isolation. Many Native American families view rehabilitation as a family-centered rather than client-centered affair (Westby & Vining, 2002).

❑ Professionals should be flexible when scheduling meetings. It is also important for Native Americans to understand that schools within the United States are "time-oriented" institutions with schedules that professionals need to maintain. Developing an understanding of our time-dominated mainstream social system is critical (Gilliland, 1988).

❑ Professionals should address all family members during meetings, rather than addressing only the parents.

❑ At the beginning of meetings and visits with families, it is important for professionals to engage in small talk to establish rapport with family members.

❏ When families do seek health care or services such as speech-language remediation, they may be slow to open up to professionals. It is important to take time to build trust.

❏ U.S. schools have historically viewed the language and culture of the Native American as detrimental to the child's future. Thus, parent involvement has been viewed as negative.

❏ Because of the consequent adversarial relationship between parents and schools, parent involvement has often been limited and parents viewed as "apathetic" (Robinson-Zanartu, 1996). Thus, professionals should be careful to avoid this judgment and encourage parental/family involvement.

❏ If families feel that personnel are hurried, they may not discuss their true concerns. Allow plenty of time for meetings so that families will not feel rushed.

❏ Malach, Segal, & Thomas (1989) found that the families of the Pueblo Indian children in their study valued the professional's emotional support and respect for them much more than they valued the professional's title or the agency's status. Thus, professionals must be especially careful to take time to build rapport.

❏ Family members may feel that it is a sign of respect to avoid eye contact with school professionals and to refrain from asking them direct questions (Joe & Malach, 1998).

❏ Professionals should always ask families to share concerns that they have regarding the use of interpreters; families may be uncomfortable with interpreters selected by school professionals.

❏ Professionals should help families to coordinate services through various agencies; this process may seem overwhelming to families.

❏ Support groups should be provided when possible. The traditional group approach to problem-solving in some tribes fits ideally with the support group concept, and professionals can take advantage of this.

❏ Some families (e.g., Navajo) do not attach great importance to developmental milestones. They feel that children will develop individually at their own pace (Wilson, 1994). Thus, during the gathering of the case history, parents/caretakers may not be able to provide details about children's acquisition of specific skills.

❏ Research has found that Native American infants may achieve gross motor developmental milestones (e.g., walking) later than infants from other ethnic groups (Harris, 1998). Professionals must keep this in mind and avoid labeling these children inappropriately as "delayed."

❏ The concept of special education may be unfamiliar to Native Americans, who often have little knowledge about specific available services. The little that is known about special education tends to be negative, and some parents have removed their children from school rather than allowing them to be placed into special education (Robinson-Zañartu, 1996).

❏ Because of this, professionals should ensure that families truly understand the nature of services that are being offered. Working with a member of the particular tribe, who can serve as a cultural mediator, is recommended.

❑ Efforts should be made to preserve students' traditions as much as possible. For example, native styles of dress should be accepted as much as possible within the school setting.

❑ Students may experience religious conflict in educational situations in which they are asked to complete culturally inappropriate activities (e.g., dissecting animals in traditional biology classes). Professionals should give Native American students alternate assignments in these situations.

❑ School professionals need to be aware that certain markings or objects (e.g., amulets) may be placed on Native American students during sacred ceremonies. It is important to learn about these customs so that students are not criticized or punished for culturally appropriate behavior.

❑ Professionals should visit the students' homes if possible. Much can be learned by observing the child's interactions with others in the home environment.

❑ When professionals arrive at the home for a previously scheduled meeting, they should make sure that the family is ready for their visit. If family members are involved in a religious ceremony or some other activity, they may not wish to be interrupted (Joe & Malach, 1998).

❑ During home visits, professionals should not assume that they can sit anywhere. They should ask the family if there is a place to sit.

❑ In the home, it is customary to address all who are present.

❑ Professionals may be offered food or coffee in the home. If offerings of food or drink are refused, professionals should provide an explanation (e.g., "I have just finished eating.").

❑ Children with special needs may not be disciplined because the family feels that they have suffered a great deal already. Professionals need to clearly delineate their own role and the roles of family members in providing discipline (Joe & Malach, 1998).

❑ Some studies have shown that Native American students tend to do better on tests of spatial ability and visual skills than on tests of verbal and/or auditory skills (Brescia & Fortune, 1988; Harris, 1985; McAvoy & Sidles, 1991). Professionals should be aware of this in assessment situations.

❑ Certain pictures, toys, dolls, and animals may be viewed as causes of evil or bad luck within certain tribes. The family should be consulted to make certain that the materials used in assessment and intervention are appropriate.

❑ It is culturally appropriate within many Native American groups for children to avoid eye contact with adults. Professionals may misinterpret this as evidence of shyness or as a deficit in interpersonal language skills.

❑ Some Navajo children may not respond when asked for their name.

❑ Native American students may be incorrectly diagnosed as having language disorders if they do not interact with adult examiners or if they give limited responses. These behaviors, however, are often culturally appropriate for situations in which children are asked to respond to questions from an adult authority figure (Harris, 1985).

❏ During assessment and intervention, silence is often a culturally appropriate response. Remember, students are taught to reflect before answering a question. Students should not be penalized when they fail to respond immediately to questions that are asked (Phillips, 1982).

❏ In many tribes, children observe while elders tell stories. Thus, when asked to perform narrative tasks in an assessment, young Native American students may not respond in the desired manner. Kay-Raining Bird and Vetter (1994) emphasized that traditional Chippewa-Cree children—those who have had limited interaction with mainstream culture—produced longer, more complex stories with increasing age.

❏ Scores on formal tests may fall "below the norm" because of a variety of factors. Low parental education, poverty, nonstandard English usage, lack of facility with English, poor health and nutrition, limited experience in taking formal tests, and other factors are likely to influence the test performance of Native American students (Palcich, 1992; Tomchak & Bain, 1994). This is especially true of tests that emphasize auditory and verbal skills (Robinson-Zañartu, 1996).

❏ Because there is such wide variation in the extent of native language use among populations in specific villages and reservations, language status needs to be ascertained for each individual community (Inglebret, 1994).

❏ Many Native American children will not respond to a question if the answer is something that the person asking the question already knows. The child, for example, might not respond to the test question, "What color is a banana?" Thus, in testing situations, they may be nonresponsive (Harris, 1998).

❏ Native American students tend to have strengths in the visual modality and often learn quickly by observing the behavior of others. Professionals can make use of these strengths to enhance learning.

❏ Many Native American students perform more readily when learning activities are presented in a group situation (Swisher & Deyhle, 1989). Individual instruction may, therefore, be less effective than group instruction.

❏ Many Native American students feel uncomfortable in competitive situations—they believe they should not stand out from the group (Robinson-Zañartu, 1996). Thus, they should be provided with cooperative rather than competitive learning experiences. The cooperative learning model is ideal for many Native American students.

❏ Native American students often do not wish to be singled out from the group and, therefore, should be praised for special accomplishments in situations where others are not present.

❏ Some children may give less feedback than Anglo children during interactions (e.g., nodding, smiling, looking at the speaker). It is important not to judge these children as having clinically significant pragmatic language problems.

❏ Professionals should use materials in assessment and intervention that are culturally relevant. Native American children and children from other cultural backgrounds may enjoy learning about local Indian history and traditions.

❏ Celebrations of holidays such as Thanksgiving and Columbus Day may be perceived as "prejudiced" by Native Americans.

❏ Professionals should avoid materials and terms that portray Native Americans in ways that promote negative stereotypes (e.g., "squaw, savage, papoose, brave;" singing of songs such as "Ten Little Indians;" collecting scalps, making a whooping war cry).

❏ To reduce prejudice, professionals can discuss the stereotypes of Native Americans and other minorities as portrayed through the popular media.

❏ Many Native American students are "whole concept" rather than linear learners. They may understand explanations more easily when they progress from the whole to the parts, rather than from the parts to the whole. Multi-sensory, whole language activities are likely to be successful with Native American students.

❏ Many Native American students will observe an activity repeatedly before attempting to do it themselves (Harris, 1998). In the European-American culture, children are encouraged to use the trial-and-error method of learning; for some Native American children, however, the cultural norm is that competence should truly precede performance. Thus, professionals should allow Native American students to watch activities several times before asking them to do the activities.

❏ In addition, Native American students may respond more often if they are allowed longer "wait times" (Harris, 1998). Because of the cultural emphasis on silence, these students often do not answer a question immediately—but they will respond eventually if professionals are willing to wait.

❏ Culturally, because of the emphasis on cooperation rather than competition, Native American students may feel uncomfortable defending themselves verbally or openly disagreeing with others. Thus, Native American students may need extra support when situations are encountered that require one to show disagreement or to defend a position.

❏ Because of cultural differences in the importance of time and punctuality, some Native American students may not understand the importance of turning in assignments by a specific date. This should not be interpreted as laziness or irresponsible behavior (Robinson-Zanartu, 1996).

❏ Story-telling is important within Native American families and can be used as a tool for teaching vocabulary. Stories should be accompanied by clear, non-biased, realistic illustrations. Some students may prefer to hear a story in its entirety before discussing it or answering questions about it.

Profile

Luis, a five-year-old Native American child from the Shoshone tribe, was referred to the special education team by his kindergarten teacher for assessment. She stated that Luis was "non-participatory, extremely shy, and lacked social skills." In addition, he seemed to "catch on very slowly to new information" and was "slow to process directions."

The special education team contacted a member of the Shoshone tribe for a consultation. Joy Buffalo Earthwoman, the tribal member, observed Luis in class on several different occasions. When she reported back to the team, she indicated that Luis was behaving in a manner that was consistent with what he had learned growing up on the reservation. She cautioned that his parents had told him that he shouldn't talk too much or he will "sound like a White person." Thus, the team was unable to carry out an evaluation of Luis' cognitive and linguistic skills.

A Shoshone tutor was hired to work with Luis for 30 minutes each day in the classroom. At the end of the year, Luis was performing at grade level and had learned to be "bicultural" by speaking more in the classroom, although he still remained quiet, as was culturally appropriate, when in the presence of adults on the reservation. Luis said, "At school, I talk like White people. At home, I'm an Indian."

STUDY QUESTIONS

1. Describe health issues that tend to impact members of the Native American community. What impact might these issues have on communication skills?

2. Briefly outline the history of Native Americans in the U.S. Why might some of them experience feelings of fear and mistrust toward Anglo professionals and Anglos in general?

3. You are giving an inservice to some student interns who are going to begin working in a Head Start program attended by many Native American children. List and describe five recommendations to help them provide services in a culturally sensitive and appropriate manner.

TRUE-FALSE

Circle the number beside each statement that is true.

4. Native American infants tend to be somewhat slower in their gross motor development than infants from other ethnic groups.

5. Native Americans emphasize spirituality and the interconnectedness of all living things.

6. Native American mothers encourage their children to speak as much as possible from early on because this will help the children perform better in school.

7. In many Native American languages, vowels are nasalized.

8. Fetal Alcohol Syndrome is a common problem within the Native American population.

9. Historically, the mainstream American establishment (e.g., government, schools) has strongly encouraged Native American families to retain their linguistic and cultural roots.

10. When working with Native American children, professionals should encourage competitive games to help them feel more comfortable.

MULTIPLE CHOICE

Unless indicated otherwise, circle the number beside each choice that is correct.

11. Which one of the following is NOT considered characteristic of Native American communication styles?
    A. There is a great deal of nodding, smiling, and interjecting during conversations.
    B. Children look down or away to show respect for elders.
    C. In many families, adults do not carry out verbal exchanges with infants or respond to their vocalizations, acting as if these vocalizations carried no meaning.
    D. It is polite to hesitate for a period of time before answering a question.
    E. Children may be rebuked for talking too much.

12. With regard to health care and longevity, the following statements are true:
    A. Native Americans have a high incidence of otitis media.
    B. Diseases common among Native Americans include diabetes, gastrointestinal disease, malignant neoplasms, and tuberculosis.
    C. The average life span within the Native American population is 82 years.
    D. Alcohol consumption is viewed as sinful and occurs rarely in Native American populations.

13. Native American students often experience challenges with the education system for the following reasons:
    A. There are many differences between Native American languages and mainstream English.
    B. Impulsivity is a common characteristic of their behavior.
    C. Confusion may result from a rigid classroom schedule packed with activities.
    D. Their competitive nature often results in disruptions within the classroom.
    E. They may not respond to a question if they are confident that the adult already knows the answer.

14. Culturally sensitive service delivery to Native American students and their families would include the following:
    A. One must realize that families tend to be passive and rarely participate in planning for intervention.
    B. It is important to engage students in non-competitive, cooperative learning activities.
    C. Teachers should single out children so that they can be praised in front of their peers.
    D. The professional should ask a wide range of questions to demonstrate a sincere interest in what family members know.

15. Which one of the following is NOT commonly observed among Native Americans?
    A. They may be very reluctant to discuss personal affairs.
    B. They try not to interfere in the affairs of others.
    C. They believe that a child's disability is a gift.
    D. Happiness and harmony are valued highly.
    E. They greatly value the accumulation of material possessions.

ANSWERS TO STUDY QUESTIONS

    4. True
    5. True
    6. False
    7. True
    8. True
    9. False
    10. False
    11. A
    12. A and B
    13. A, C, and E
    14. B
    15. E

Chapter 8

FAMILIES FROM PACIFIC ISLAND BACKGROUNDS

Outline

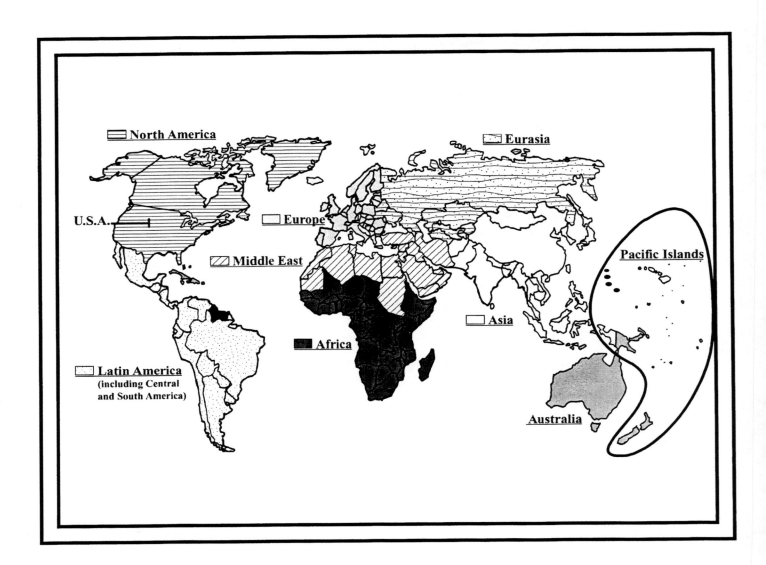

The Pacific Islands include three major geographic areas: Melanesia, Micronesia, and Polynesia (See Figure 8.1). Within each area are several island groups. Each island nation has a unique history that has influenced the customs and way of life of its inhabitants.

Figure 8.1

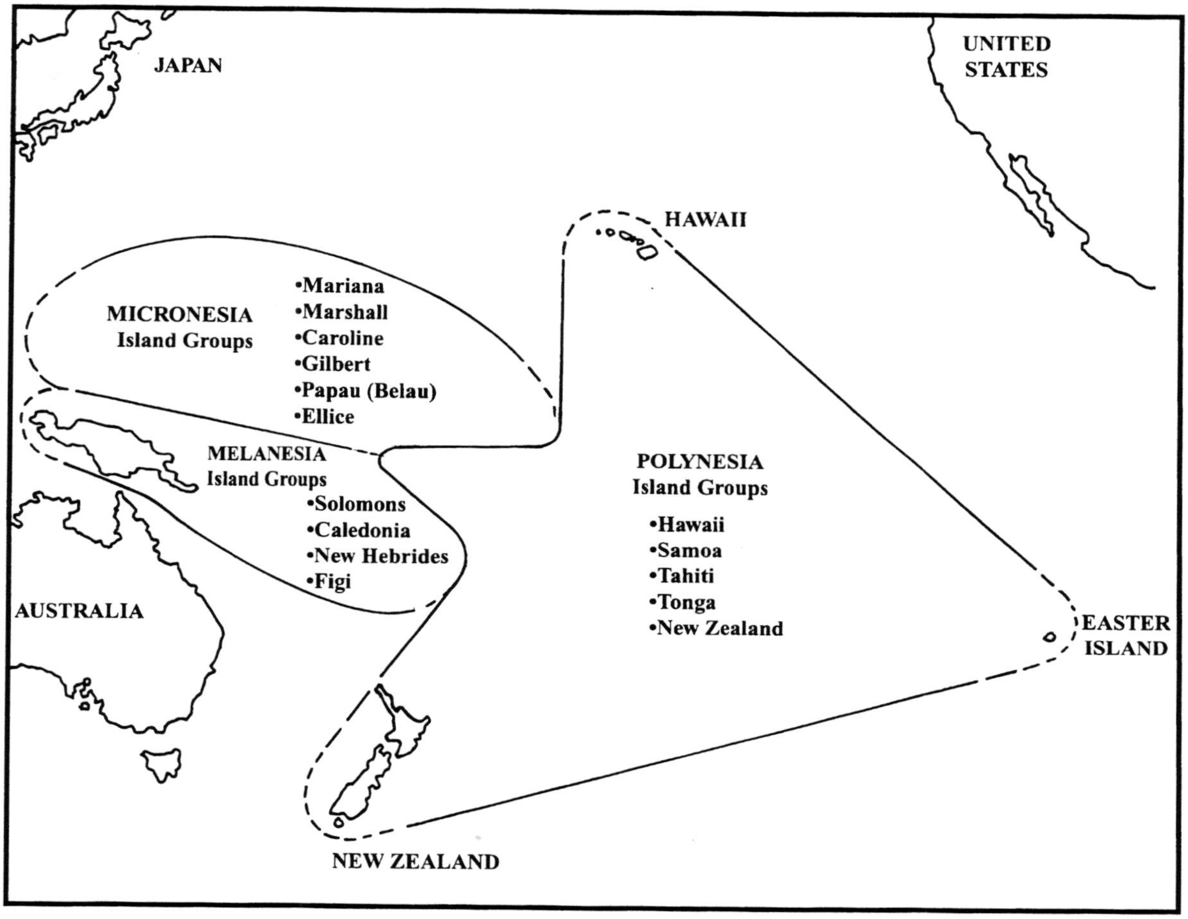

Melanesia

1. includes the following island groups: Solomons, New Caledonia, New Hebrides, and Fiji.

2. has natives who tend to be heterogeneous in culture and language (Dodge, 1976).

Micronesia

1. includes the following island groups: Mariana, Marshall, Caroline Gilbert, Palau (Belau) and Ellice.

2. includes Guam of the Marianas; Guam is the most populous island in all of Micronesia, with over 90,000 inhabitants.

3. has populations that are culturally more uniform than in Melanesia (Campbell, 1989).

Polynesia

1. includes the following island groups: Hawaii, Samoa, Tahiti, Tonga, New Zealand.

2. has greater linguistic and cultural homogeneity than either Micronesia or Melanesia (Dodge, 1976).

3. encompasses the Hawaiian Islands, all areas that have been heavily influenced by Filipino, Chinese, Korean, and Japanese cultures.

GENERAL BACKGROUND INFORMATION

☐ The combined population of all of the Pacific Islands is seven million people. Four million of these people live in Papua, New Guinea.

☐ The Pacific Islands have been influenced by cultural groups from many countries, including France, the United States, Spain, Portugal, Germany, and Japan. Many areas in the Pacific Islands have a history of colonialism.

☐ Many religions are practiced in the Pacific Islands. Christianity is widespread, and many Pacific Islanders consider the Bible a major source of inspiration (Cheng, 2002).

☐ Forms of Christianity (e.g., Catholicism, Protestantism) may be combined with folk medicine which may include faith healing, herbs, etc. Magic and sorcery also are practiced in some places, particularly in Melanesia.

☐ Most Samoans have strong religious beliefs; Samoa's motto is "Samoa is founded upon God" (Wallace, 1994).

☐ The largest populations in the Pacific Islands are the Hawaiians, Samoans, and Chamorros (Cheng, 2002).

☐ In the U.S., the Native Hawaiian and Other Pacific Islander group increased considerably between 1990 and 2000. If one counts "race alone" as indicated by the census, this population has grown 9.3% over this 10-year period. If one counts "race alone or in combination," this population has grown 139.5% between 1990 and 2000 (U.S. Bureau of the Census, 2000).

☐ The census data indicate that Asian Americans in combination with Pacific Islanders in the U.S. (AAPI) comprise 4% of the total U.S. population.

☐ AAPIs are the fastest-growing racial/ethnic group in the United States and are expected to represent 10% of the U.S. population by the year 2050 (U.S. Bureau of the Census, 2000).

PACIFIC ISLAND FAMILY LIFE

☐ Children are often viewed as gifts of God (Mokuau & Tauili'ili, 1998).

☐ Extended families of several generations are quite common.

❑ Childcare is frequently provided by multiple caretakers.

❑ Among Western Samoans, siblings may become primary caregivers.

❑ The Chamorro and Carolinian societies are matriarchal with clearly defined roles for members of the nuclear family. "Fathers are responsible for making financial decisions, and mothers hold the responsibility for raising the children and housekeeping" (Hammer, 1994, p. 6).

❑ In some Chamorro families, daughters live at home until they are married. Living alone can have negative sexual connotations for a single woman.

❑ When a couple is married in the Northern Marianas, they will usually live with the groom's parents and conceive their first child within the first few years of the marriage (Hammer, 1994).

❑ Villagers often have close ties and help one another in many situations.

❑ Reciprocity, interdependence, and cooperation are inherent values of many groups.

❑ Islanders place a strong emphasis on authority and respect. Children and subordinates must comply with the wishes of elders.

❑ Islanders are more concerned about the well-being of the family than about the rights of individuals. In Samoa, for example, a person is expected to help other members of the family, regardless of the cost (Cheng & Ima, 1989).

❑ Although Samoans may appear to be poor in the eyes of outsiders, there is no "homelessness" in Samoa. Extended families and family networks freely share food, material goods, and shelter. The Samoan language has no word for "person" because individual people are considered to be part of the whole group (Cheng, Nakasato, & Wallace, 1995).

❑ The welfare of the family is considered a much higher priority than the welfare of individual children; children are often preoccupied with pleasing their parents.

❑ Many Hawaiian families are quite physically affectionate with their children.

❑ Mothers may not leave the home for at least one week after a child is born; in some groups, babies do not leave the house for the first month of life (Mokuau & Tauili'ili, 1998).

❑ Physical punishment is very common among Samoans and some other groups in the Pacific Islands; rulers, belts, and other implements may be used regularly to discipline children.

❑ In many of these families, physical discipline begins at about 3 years of age and continues through mid-adolescence (Markoff & Bond, 1980). Many Samoans use corporal punishment to ingrain respect into their children so that, as adults, the children will fit into society's hierarchical structure.

✐REFLECTION✐

Describe four patterns of behavior commonly observed within Pacific Islander families that are observed much less frequently within mainstream U.S. families.

_____

_____

_____

_____

_____

PACIFIC ISLAND EDUCATION

❑ The educational style in the Islands is generally relaxed; absenteeism among both teachers and students is common (Cheng & Ima, 1989).

❑ Classes may be quite unstructured and so informal that teachers do not necessarily arrive at school with lesson plans for the day, and there may be a minimal amount of work that occurs in the classroom.

❑ There are six universities in the Islands.

❑ Books and other educational resources are often in short supply because many areas are remote.

❑ The educational tradition emphasizes oral learning.

❑ Some schools provide bilingual education in the native language and English.

❑ For many students, it is a major adjustment to go from Island schools to mainland schools in the United States (Cheng & Ima, 1989); Island students often experience "...persistent disproportionate school failure" (Ogbu & Matute-Bianchi, 1990, p. 73).

❑ It is quite difficult for Pacific Islander students to go from relaxed schools in which orally-based learning and rote memorization are stressed to U.S. schools in which individual excellence and creativity are emphasized (Cheng, 2002).

❑ Educators in the United States have been concerned about the high percentage of Islander students who fail in school and/or drop out. In 1988, Islanders had the highest school dropout rate of any ethnic group in California (Cheng & Ima, 1989).

❑ Some Islander families want their children to go to work as soon as possible, feeling that children who continue in school selfishly drain the family's resources instead of contributing to the family's well-being. Many families encourage their children to enter the job market before completing high school (Cheng & Ima, 1989).

❑ Samoans in the United States want very much for their children to be educated; however, values emphasized in school often conflict with those of the home (Wallace, 1994).

CULTURAL CUSTOMS AND COURTESIES

❑ Many Islanders have a "collective rights" attitude in which generosity and sharing are valued. Collectivism and cooperation are important, and individualism and privacy are usually not priorities.

❑ In Samoa, many homes are comprised of one large, communal room. Adjusting to American homes with many rooms can be difficult and very divisive to Samoan families (Wallace, 1994).

❑ Hospitality is important among many groups.

❑ Festive occasions and celebrations in which food is served are very common.

❑ It is considered inappropriate, by some Samoans, to drink or eat while walking or standing (Mokuau & Tauili'ili, 1998).

❑ "Compared to U.S. standards, the pace in the Northern Marianas is slow. There is a tacit belief that if something is not done today, it will be done tomorrow, and if it is not done tomorrow, it is very possible that it does not have to be done at all. This notion is observed in all aspects of life, including work settings, the government, and access to speech and language services" (Hammer, 1994, p. 7).

HEALTH CARE AND DISABLING CONDITIONS

❑ When people are sick, families may call upon faith healers or practitioners of folk medicine.

❑ Among some groups, massage and the use of fruits, roots, and leaves in treatment are common.

❑ Some Islanders have poor access to health care.

❑ Infant mortality rates in the U.S.-associated Pacific Island jurisdictions exceed the U.S. rate, and may be twice as high (Singh, 2001).

❑ Diabetes, lung cancer, and heart disease are prevalent (Cheng at al., 1995).

❑ Hearing problems due to factors such as impacted wax and otitis media are common among some groups. High rates of otitis media are common among Samoan and Hawaiian children (Pang-Ching, Robb, Heath, & Takumi, 1995).

❑ Some families protect disabled children and do not expect them to be independent.

❑ Some Hawaiian families attribute physical disabilities to spiritual causes; the disabilities may be viewed as beyond the control of human beings.

❑ Some members of the Carolinian and Chamarro cultures believe that spirits can cause disabilities in children (Hammer, 1994).

❏ "Some cultures (e.g., the Chamorro culture) view a disability as a gift from God, and hence the individual is to be protected and sheltered" (Cheng & Hammer, 1992, p. 8).

❏ Parents may acquiesce to their children's desires, particularly if the children have experienced a number of medical difficulties.

❏ Among the Samoans and some other groups, there is a tendency toward intolerance for disabilities. Families may try to conceal the disability (Stewart, 1986).

❏ Some Samoans believe that the birth of a handicapped child is a sign of God's displeasure with the family (Mokuau & Tauili'ili, 1998).

Profile

Lee T., a 16-year-old Chamorro, was diving off a cliff into the ocean with his friends. He struck his head on the rocks below and experienced a profound head injury. He was flown by helicopter to Hawaii, where doctors were able to save his life. However, after awakening from a coma two months later, Lee was experiencing major cognitive and linguistic deficits as well as difficulty walking and dressing himself. The hospital staff offered the family both in- and out-patient rehabilitative services that included occupational, physical, and speech therapy. The family thanked the staff and declined to accept any services, saying that they would take care of Lee from that point on. The family did not feel that it was appropriate to try to "force" Lee to become independent again. They felt that he had suffered enough already, and they believed it was their job to protect him from now on.

PACIFIC ISLAND COMMUNICATION STYLES

❏ To avoid offending others, some Islanders may say what they think the listener wants to hear.

❏ Some groups (e.g., Hawaiians) tend to favor interpersonal communication styles that emphasize cooperation rather than competition.

❏ Children may be unaccustomed to interacting with adults on a one-to-one basis because their primary communication experiences are with other children, not adults (Cheng & Ima, 1989).

❏ It may be considered inappropriate to touch a child on the top of the head because this area is considered sacred.

❏ Oral language proficiency and story-telling are often highly prized.

❏ Nonverbal cues in interactions are important to most Islanders.

❏ Some Islanders may view prolonged eye contact as a sign of disrespect (Cheng & Hammer, 1992).

❑ Persons from the Carolinian and Chamorro cultures use their eyebrows extensively to communicate meaning (Hammer, 1994).

❑ Among many Samoans, it is inappropriate to walk past a person of status or authority without a display of deference such as downcast eyes.

❑ In some Samoan families, children, as a sign of respect, are to sit down when addressing an older person.

❑ In the Samoan culture, movement of the shoulders often indicates ambivalence or confusion (Mokuau & Tauili'ili, 1998).

❑ In the Samoan household, the mother has power and authority as chief caregiver. Since Samoan children are expected to accommodate to adults, most Samoan mothers don't simplify their vocabulary by using "baby talk" when interacting with their children. If a child says something unintelligible, the Samoan mother may call attention to the problem and might even ignore the utterance (Tannen, 1994).

❑ Samoan mothers play with their infants and cuddle them, but do not respond to their vocalizations as intentional or social. Thus, there is little emphasis on early language development (Cheng et al., 1995).

PACIFIC ISLAND LANGUAGE CONSIDERATIONS

❑ The Pacific Island languages fall within the Austronesian language family.

❑ Over 1,200 indigenous languages are spoken in the Pacific Islands (Campbell, 1989). Major languages include Fijian, Hawaiian, Samoan, Tahitian, Chamorro, Carolinian, Korean, Palauan, Marshallese, Papua New Guinean, Yapese, Trukese, and Pompean. Most languages are mutually unintelligible.

❑ The linguistic variety is great in some areas. For example, more than 800 languages are spoken on Papua, New Guinea.

❑ The languages of Polynesia have more homogeneity than the languages of Melanesia (Campbell, 1989).

❑ Languages spoken in Hawaii include Mandarin, Tagalog, Samoan, Ilocano, Korean, Cantonese, Japanese, and Hawaiian. English is spoken by almost all Hawaiians.

❑ Some Hawaiians speak a fluent dominant language (e.g., English, Japanese) as well as pidgin. Pidgin is a restricted form of language used only in certain settings for simple transactions (Komenaka, 1994).

❑ The three major languages spoken in many areas of Micronesia are English, Chamorro, and Carolinian.

❑ Language use is influenced by culture. In the Carolinian language, for example, there are more than 10 words that depict the various stages of a coconut's growth.

❑ Samoa's schools are bilingual (Samoan and English).

❏ Some cultures (e.g., Samoan and Hawaiian) place a strong emphasis on oral traditions.

❏ Many Pacific Islanders understand English but speak a pidgin form of the language. Many need assistance in acquiring formal written and oral English skills (Cheng & Ima, 1989).

❏ In the writing systems of languages spoken in the Pacific Islands, letters for vowels represent one sound only (Campbell, 1989).

❏ In general, consonants are identical or close approximations to their English equivalents. The g is always hard; in Samoan, g is always pronounced as "ng" (e.g., Pago Pago becomes Pango Pango) (Erickson, 1979).

❏ The apostrophe within a word (e.g., ali'i) is pronounced as a glottal stop (momentary stopping of the breath in the throat) (Campbell, 1989).

❏ Characteristics of several languages spoken in the Pacific Islands are described below:

Hawaiian language (see Cheng, 1991; Cheng & Ima, 1989; Campbell, 1989):

1. The language is alphabetical and polysyllabic, with stress being placed on the next to last syllable.
2. Five vowels are used: a, e, i, o, u.
3. Eight consonants are used: w, p, n, m, h, l, k and the glottal stop.
4. The language has no consonant clusters.
5. The language is characterized by words that always end in vowels.
6. w is pronounced as v when it follows an e or i.

Tahitian language (see Erickson, 1979, p. 19):

1. The alphabet has only 13 letters.
2. Five vowels are used:
   a (as in father)
   e (as in May; may also be pronounced as in egg)
   i (pronounced "ee" as in tree)
   o (pronounced "o" as in goat)
   u (pronounced "u" as in flute)
3. Eight consonants are used: f, h, m, n, p, r, t, v; these are pronounced like their English equivalents, but they are never used at the end of syllables.
4. Syllables end in vowels.
5. Vowels are often grouped together; each should be pronounced separately (e.g., Faaa is pronounced "Fa-ah-ah").
6. Most words are accented on the next to last syllable, except when an apostrophe separates the final vowel from the vowel preceding it; in this case, both vowels are given equal emphasis (e.g., mataura'a [custom] is pronounced "mah-tah-oo-ra-ah").

Fijiian language (see Erickson, 1979, p. 63; Campbell, 1989):

1. b is pronounced as if it is preceded by m (e.g., "ba" is pronounced as "mba").
2. c is pronounced as "th" (e.g., "Yanuca" becomes "Yanu tha").
3. d is pronounced as "nd" (e.g., "Nadee" becomes "Nan dee").
4. g is pronounced as "ng" (e.g., "Sigatoka" becomes "Singatokaî").
5. q is pronounced as "ngg" (e.g., "Beqa" becomes "Mbeng-ga").

Chamorro language (spoken on Guam) (see Cheng, 1991, pp. 79-80; Cheng & Ima, 1989, p. 7):

1. The language has six vowels and 11 allophonic variations of these vowels. Vowel sounds in Chamorro include: *i, e, ae, a, o, u.*
2. The language has 18 consonants and the glide *w.*
3. Most consonants are pronounced as they are in English with some exceptions.
4. *ch* is pronounced "ts" as in "tsar."
5. *y* is pronounced "ds" as in "goods."
6. *ñ* is pronounced "ny" as in "Bunyan."
7. *w* is pronounced "gw" as in "Gwendolyn."

✐ REFLECTION ✐

List two verbal and two nonverbal characteristics commonly observed in the communication of Pacific Islanders. Why is it important to be aware of these characteristics?

_____

_____

_____

_____

_____

IMPLICATIONS FOR PROFESSIONALS

❑ Professionals should remember that families may be late for meetings or may not come at all if a family matter arises; family needs are generally a higher priority than meetings.

❑ Professionals should not automatically assume that the biological parents are in charge of a student because care-taking may rotate between relatives (e.g., aunts, uncles, grandparents, older siblings). Thus, when contacting the home, professionals may need to find out who is currently in charge of the student.

❑ It is imperative to involve the entire family in any processes and decisions, not just the student. Some parents may even want elders to be present during decision-making.

❑ Professionals should be formal when addressing authority figures within the family.

❑ In the matriarchal Carolinian and Chamorro societies, an elder female such as the paternal grandmother may have the final say in some family matters. Professionals should relate positively with this person because the opinions expressed may determine whether or not a child receives services (Hammer, 1994).

❑ Professionals may observe bruises on students or hear reports of physical punishment. It is critical for parents to be informed about American laws regarding child abuse. In addition, professionals should be aware that physical punishment may occur at home when the parents learn that discipline has been provided at school (Cheng & Ima, 1989). In cases such as these, parents will want to work with the local community and local churches in order to intervene in culturally appropriate ways in matters relating to discipline.

❑ The importance of keeping students in school until graduation may need to be emphasized during interactions with parents. By remaining in school, students will be better equipped to find jobs in the work force.

❑ Some students (e.g., Carolinian) may come from an environment in which several languages are spoken. Thus, the identification of a "primary" language may prove to be a challenge. When assessing these students, professionals must rely heavily on parent and information from teachers and on natural, informal, environmental assessment methods.

❑ It is considered culturally appropriate for professionals to show their concern and interest in the welfare of the entire family.

❑ Professionals should not venture immediately into frank discussions about personal problems or difficulties.

❑ Among some groups, it is considered rude for people to converse when they are standing.

❑ Professionals must remember that families may say "yes" to indicate that they acknowledge receiving information. A "yes" response does not necessarily indicate agreement with what has been said. Thus, it is better to ask open-ended questions than *yes-no* questions (Cheng & Hammer, 1992).

❑ Professionals should respect the family's spiritual values and beliefs about healing. Western professionals can work in collaboration with traditional folk healers.

❑ Professionals must fully explain forms that require signatures. Many parents are accustomed only to signing documents relating to major life events such as births and deaths. They may not understand why signatures are needed on school forms (Cheng & Hammer, 1992).

❑ When parents are asked to come to school for a meeting, they may feel that their child is being criticized. The purpose of the meeting should be explained clearly.

Considerations that are important for professionals to consider when working with Asian students (see Cheng & Ima, 1989; Cheng et al., 1995) include the following:

1. Remember that students who are proficient in basic conversation do not necessarily have the language skills necessary to perform effectively in classroom reading and writing activities.

2. Remember that students may come from low socioeconomic backgrounds in which there have been few opportunities for language stimulation.

3. Encourage a "buddy system" in which students are paired with peers from the same background.

4. Increase knowledge of the home language (e.g., learning basic vocabulary).

5. Become familiar with the sociolinguistic/pragmatic rules of discourse within the child's language (e.g., leave-taking, greeting, complimenting, etc).

6. Remember that at home, students are often taught to be quiet, observant, and not to challenge authority. The classroom learning environment, however, may require the child to criticize, evaluate, speculate, and render judgments. Such behaviors conflict with behavioral expectations in the home environment.

7. Teach students how to interact with adults if they are not accustomed to such interactions at home.

8. Use a collective rather than individual story-telling method. A number of students should be included.

9. Teach students story-telling skills.

10. Teach students problem-solving skills.

11. Providing opportunities for contextualized learning.

Profile

Alisi, a Samoan 7-year-old, recently moved to the U.S. with her family. She was quiet in class, and struggled academically, so the speech-language pathologist collaborated with the teacher to help Alisi increase linguistic and cognitive skills in English. Alisi was learning to raise her hand, give opinions, ask questions of the teacher, and engage in verbal problem-solving.

One day Alisi came to school with bruises on her face, arms, and back. The teacher noticed the bruises immediately, and the case was referred to Child Protective Services (CPS). When the CPS worker came to the school and spoke with Alisi, she told him that her parents had beaten her for asking too many questions and challenging their authority at home.

Alisi's parents were called to court for breaking U.S. child abuse laws. They defended their actions, saying that Alisi needed to keep respecting her elders. They stated that she was becoming too "mouthy" and Americanized.

After this incident, the teacher and speech-language pathologist arranged a meeting with the pastor of the local Samoan church that Alisi's family attended. The pastor explained U.S. child abuse laws in further detail to Alisi's parents. The need for the child to be verbally assertive in the classroom was also stressed. The parents did not agree with this recommendation, but indicated that they would find other ways to discipline the child. They also indicated that they would make an effort to be more understanding of differences in how the school expected children to interact with others.

STUDY QUESTIONS

1. List the three major geographic areas of the Pacific Islands. Which area is the most homogeneous?

2. Discuss health concerns that are typical for many Pacific Islanders. How might these concerns impact communication skills, if at all?

3. Describe educational practices of schools in the Pacific Islands. How do these practices impact the adjustment of students who move to the U.S. and enroll in school?

TRUE-FALSE

Circle the number beside all statements that are true.

4. Persons from the Samoan culture use their eyebrows extensively to communicate meaning.

5. When professionals discuss personal problems or difficult areas with families, it is best to address these issues immediately or the families will think professionals are "beating around the bush."

6. The apostrophe within a word (e.g., ali'i) is pronounced as a glottal stop (momentary stopping of the breath in the throat).

7. Samoans tend to be very lenient with their children, using verbal reprimands as a last resort to punish undesirable behaviors.

8. Middle ear infections are more common among Samoan and Hawaiian children than among children from most other cultures.

9. Professionals can help students in school by encouraging a "buddy system" in which these students work with peers who come from a similar cultural background.

10. Most families are very comfortable signing forms because, in the Pacific Islands, placing a signature on a document is a way of showing one's status.

MULTIPLE CHOICE

Circle the letter beside each of the choices that is correct.

11. The following may be observed in the Pacific Islands:
    A. Some Hawaiian families attribute physical disabilities to spiritual causes; the disabilities may be viewed as beyond the control of human beings.
    B. Some Samoans feel that the birth of a disabled child is a sign of God's displeasure with the family.
    C. Some cultures (e.g., the Chamorro culture) view a disability as a gift from God, and hence the individual is to be protected and sheltered.
    D. Most Pacific Islanders believe that a disabled individual should be given as many rehabilitative services as possible.
    E. Healers or folk medicine practitioners may be called upon by some groups.

12. When professionals work with Pacific Islander students, they can be most helpful by thinking about and doing the following:
    A. They should remember that students who are proficient in basic conversation do not necessarily have the language skills necessary to perform effectively in classroom reading and writing activities.
    B. They should understand that many of these students come from middle class socioeconomic backgrounds that have supported learning experiences in schools.
    C. They should focus on critical thinking and evaluation tasks because students are encouraged to give opinions and render judgments at home.
    D. They should use collective story-telling methods.
    E. They should teach problem-solving skills.

13. Which of the following are TRUE?
    A. The Pacific Island languages fall within the Austronesian language family.
    B. Hawaiian is alphabetical and polysyllabic, with stress being placed on the next to last syllable.
    C. Vowels are often grouped together in the Tahitian language, but each should be pronounced separately.
    D. Samoan is the most widely used language in the Philippines.

14. Aspects of communication that are important to remember when working with families from the Pacific Islands include the following:
    A. Oral language proficiency and story-telling are often highly prized.
    B. Nonverbal cues are relatively unimportant; verbal cues carry most of the meaning.
    C. Samoan mothers often cuddle and physically care for their babies, but do not respond to the infants' vocalizations as meaningful attempts to communicate.
    D. The frequent asking of questions is encouraged in the classroom in all cultural groups within the Pacific Islands.

15. A Chamorro child has been found to have a communication disorder, and you need to discuss the assessment with his family. What should you be aware of in planning your meeting?
    A. The family will arrive promptly to avoid experiencing feelings of shame that are often associated with tardiness.
    B. The grandmother may be the primary decision maker.
    C. The biological parents are in charge of the child, so questions should be directed to them first.
    D. It is best to ask *yes-no* questions (rather than open-ended questions) to reduce feelings of anxiety that family members might experience.
    E. If family members agree to have the child placed in a special education program, it is highly likely that they will make sure that all homework assignments are completed.

ANSWERS TO STUDY QUESTIONS

 4. False
 5. False
 6. True
 7. False
 8. True
 9. True
10. False
11. A, B, C, E
12. A, D, E
13. A, B, C
14. A, C
15. B

Chapter 9

FAMILIES FROM MIDDLE EASTERN BACKGROUNDS

Outline

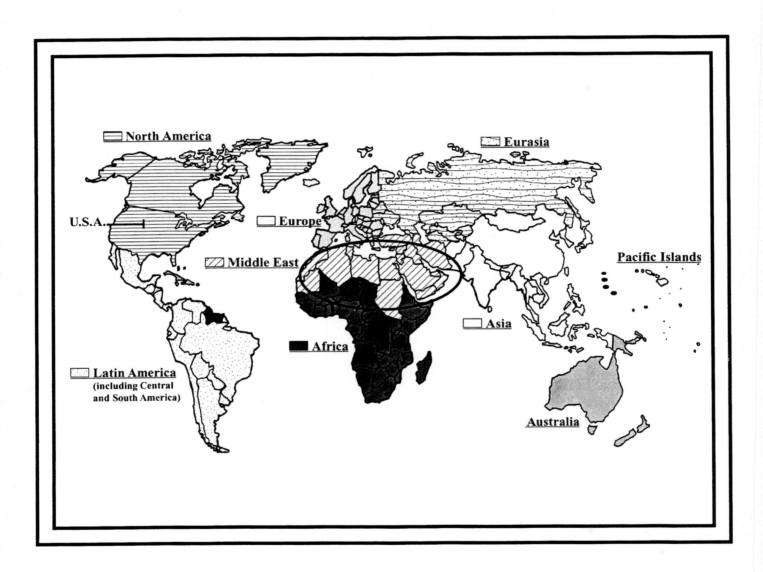

The Middle East is often called the cradle of civilization. Countries included in this area are Israel, Syria, Lebanon, the Occupied Territories, Iraq, Iran, Jordan, Saudi Arabia, Bahrain, Kuwait, Qatar, Oman, Yemen, the United Arab Emirates, Egypt, Turkey, and Sudan.

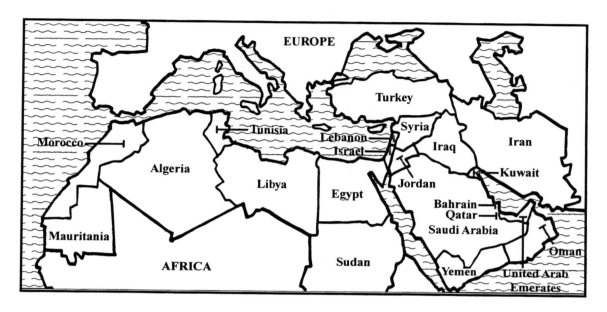

GENERAL BACKGROUND INFORMATION

❏ A large number of Middle Eastern immigrants have come to the United States since the 1980s.

❏ The Middle East stretches over a large area, approximately the size of the United States, where the continents of Africa, Asia, and Europe come together.

❏ Most of the Middle East is comprised of deserts.

❏ The largest city in the Middle East is Cairo, Egypt.

❏ The largest country in the Middle East is Saudi Arabia. It is one million square miles in size, roughly one-third the size of the United States. Saudi Arabia is often considered a bridge between Asia and the Western world.

❏ The Muslim holy cities of Mecca and Medina are located in Saudi Arabia. Thousands of Muslims journey to these cities annually (especially Mecca) to pray and worship.

❏ The Arab population in the Middle East is larger than that of any other group. Thus, the majority (but not all) of Middle Easterners are Arabs.

❏ The Arab countries include: Morroco, Mauritania, Algeria, Tunisia, Libya, Chad, Sudan, Egypt, Syria, Iraq, Jordan, Lebanon, Kuwait, Saudi Arabia, Bahrain, Qatar, United Arab Emirates, Yemen, and Oman.

❑ The Arabic language provides a linguistic bond to the Arab countries. Anyone who speaks Arabic as a native is considered to be an Arab, no matter what country he or she is from.

❑ Wilson (1998, pp. 197-198) states that "...the term *Arab* itself is not strictly definable. In a purely semantic sense, no people can be classified as *Arab* because the word connotes a mixed population with widely varying ethnologic and racial origins...Hence, *Arab* is best used within a cultural context. Arab countries are those countries in which the primary language is Arabic and the primary religion is Islam." (*Note: In this chapter, the terms "Arab" and "Middle Easterner" are used interchangeably although readers need to be aware of the distinctions between the two groups.)

❑ More than 95% of Arabic speakers in the Middle East are Muslim (Wilson, 1998). In Lebanon, however, approximately half of the population is Christian. Most residents of Israel are Jewish.

❑ Most Middle Eastern Jews live in Israel.

❑ Other religious groups include the Bahais and Zoroastrians.

❑ The Bahai faith is derived from Islam, but Bahais take Bahaullah as their prophet and they emphasize modernization and equality. Bahais in Iran are persecuted by Shi'ite Muslims, and many Iranian Bahais have fled to other countries (Mohtasham-Nouri, 1994).

❑ It is not possible to report the numbers of Arabs living in the U.S. at the present time because Arabs were not counted in the U.S. Census 2000.

❑ Key values for many Middle Easterners include family and religion. Religion is an integral part of everyday life and activity.

❑ For Arabs, religious affiliation is essential; it is not acceptable to be an agnostic or atheist. Arabs respect religious people, and lose respect for people who have no religious affiliation or who do not believe in God (Omar Nydell, 1996).

❑ Many Middle Easterners live in small villages; over 30% live in cities or large towns. There are small numbers of semi-nomadic or nomadic people who live in sparsely populated areas.

❑ Some nomads in Saudi Arabia are called "Bedouins" (Arabic for "people who live in the open country"); many of them are shepherds who live in clans and tribes. There are fewer than 500,000 Bedouins (Grossier, 1982).

❑ A difficulty for many Middle Easterners in the U.S. is the negative stereotypes placed upon them by many Americans. These stereotypes are caused by several phenomena, which include actions in Middle Eastern countries by extremist Muslim groups (Bozorgmehr, 2001).

❑ In a survey of Americans by Kamalipour (2001), it was found that the terms associated most with Middle Easterners were "oil, mean people, dark skin, terrorism."

❑ The negative stereotypes that many Americans have about Iranians have caused many to identify themselves according to their "specific ethno-religiosity" (e.g., Armenian, Bahai, Jewish) rather than by their Iranian ethnicity (Bozorgmehr, 2001).

✐REFLECTION✐

Describe four general characteristics that are commonly observed among individuals from the Middle East.

_____

_____

_____

_____

_____

_____

MIDDLE EASTERN FAMILY LIFE

❑ The family is the primary focus of loyalty for many Middle Easterners; families are usually considered the pillars of society.

❑ Extended, multigenerational families are quite common.

❑ In many marriages, procreation is a higher priority than marital love and intimacy. Children are greatly valued and not having children may be a cause for unhappiness (Sharifzadeh, 1998).

❑ Younger members of the family respect and care for the elderly. Many children support their parents in old age.

❑ The achievements of any individual in the family affect how the family is perceived by others in the community.

❑ Parents may continue to provide for children even after the children have married.

❑ In Saudi Arabia and some other areas, marriages are often arranged by the parents of the bride and groom. Sometimes the bride and groom meet one another before the wedding, but this is not always the case.

❑ Among Muslim Arabs, especially in nomadic and rural communities, people prefer to marry first or second cousins. In 1996, 58% of Iraqis married their cousins, followed by 55% of Saudi Arabians, 54% of Kuwaitis, and 50% of Jordanians. Intermarriage ensures that the spouse is a "known quantity" and that money and possessions stay within the family (Omar Nydell, 1996).

❑ Polygamy is practiced in some areas. In Iran, for example, men are often allowed to have up to four wives if they can provide for them. Each wife is supposed to be treated equally in all respects.

❑ Generally, the father is the head of the household; most Middle Eastern societies are patriarchal.

❏ In many families, the primary roles and responsibilities of women are to care for their husbands and to raise their children.

❏ Husbands often take little responsibility for the care of very young children and infants; however, when boys reach the age of 4 or 5, fathers often assume a more active role (Sharifzadeh, 1998).

❏ Arab boys are expected to be decisive and aggressive, and girls are expected to play a passive role.

❏ Arab adults generally do not reason with young children. They tell them to do things because "that is how it is done" or teach their children to avoid certain actions because of the fear of what others might think or say. Children are taught that it is important to conform to an expected social image (Omar Nydell, 1996).

❏ Children are not to interrupt when adults are talking and may not question rules relating to obedience and authority.

❏ Among Arabs, the most important aspect of acceptable conduct among children is respectful behavior in front of adults.

❏ Divorce is rare and, in some groups, brings shame upon the woman and her family. A divorced woman may not be permitted to marry again.

❏ Traditionally, girls stay at home until they are married. In some groups, women may not be allowed to speak to strangers until after marriage.

❏ In some countries (e.g., Iran and Saudi Arabia), dating and premarital sex are not tolerated for women but are allowed and even encouraged for men (Mohtasham-Nouri, 1994; Sasson, 1992).

❏ There is a direct relationship between the number of children in a family (especially boys) and the amount of prestige experienced by the father and his family. A large family is a sign of prestige.

❏ Male children are often preferred over female children, in part, because boys carry on the family tradition and name. In agricultural societies, the male's potential for economic contribution is greater than that of the female (Sasson, 1992).

❏ Many mothers in the Middle East emphasize attachment and parent-child bonding rather than individualism and independence (Sharifzadeh, 1998).

❏ Children are encouraged at early ages to take on family and household responsibilities. Girls are expected to take on household chores at about 5 years of age, but boys are generally exempt from these chores (Sharifzadeh, 1998).

❏ Many young Arabs admire and prefer Western entertainment, dress, and liberal thought. This is distressing to older, more traditional Arabs, and has created an increasing generation gap in the Arab world (Omar Nydell, 1996).

> ### *Profile*
>
> Omar Y., a 4-year-old Middle Eastern boy, was brought to the local preschool by his mother. She wanted him to learn English (his primary language was Yemeni) and socialize with other children. Her husband traveled much of the time on business, and she was concerned that Omar was exposed primarily to her at home and was not receiving enough outside stimulation. The American preschool teachers noticed that Omar expected them to help him complete tasks such as putting on his sweater and throwing out leftovers from his snacks. They also noticed that Omar was extremely respectful to the point where he never asked questions or interacted with the teachers at all, even when he started learning some English.
>
> One of the teachers, who had lived in the Middle East for several years as a Peace Corps volunteer, asked Omar's mother to meet with her after preschool for tea and snacks while Omar played nearby. The teacher shared her challenging experience of raising American children in the Middle East, with its different cultural mores, and discussed the changes that had to be made in her parenting while the family lived in Saudi Arabia. The teacher also discussed U.S. expectations for children's independence as well as the American school system's expectation that children initiate interactions with teachers.
>
> Omar's mother was open and receptive to the teacher's suggestions, so the teacher invited her to observe classroom instruction. Mrs. Y. observed for 20 minutes each day, and the teachers began to see an increase in Omar's social interaction skills and independent activity in the classroom.

EDUCATION AND LITERACY

❑ Educational opportunities and teaching styles vary greatly from country to country as does literacy.

❑ The literacy rate in Kuwait is 79%; in Israel it is 92%; in Yemen it is 39% (Johnstone, 1993).

❑ Classes are often quite large and may have as many as 60 students (elementary level).

❑ Formal Arabic is taught in many schools.

❑ The education of children is a high priority in many families. Parents see education as a means of professional and financial advancement.

❑ Some girls do not continue their education beyond elementary school because of the fear that they will be exposed and unguarded in social situations within the school environment (Sharifzadeh, 1998).

❑ Traditionally, females were not encouraged to attend college. Higher education for women, however, is viewed more positively than in previous years and is becoming more common (Sharifzadeh, 1998).

❑ Schools are often not co-educational.

❏ Compulsory education usually begins at around 6 or 7 years of age.

❏ Story-telling is very common in schools in the Middle East.

❏ Children from middle class, educated families often learn poems and share storybook reading activities with their parents.

CULTURAL CUSTOMS, COURTESIES, AND BELIEFS

❏ Some of the most important character traits, to Middle Easterners, include generosity, bravery, friendship, and hospitality.

❏ Guests generally are treated with kindness; food is available in abundance.

❏ Some groups (e.g., Saudi Arabians) generally do not talk much during meals; these groups prefer to talk after meals.

❏ Women in some cultures may be expected to eat in separate rooms from men.

❏ Some groups (e.g., Saudi Arabians) consider the left hand to be unclean. It is to be used for lavatory purposes only. Some people may be offended if the left hand is used when greeting others.

❏ Among Arabs, there is no concept of privacy. When translated, the Arabic word that most closely resembles the concept of privacy is "loneliness" (Omar Nydell, 1996).

❏ Arabs tend to have a relaxed attitude about time and are not expected to apologize when they arrive late for meetings or events.

❏ In some countries (e.g., Kuwait), birthdays have traditionally not been celebrated (Micek, 1992). Birthdays, however, are now celebrated in some families.

❏ Arab society is conservative and demands conformity from its members. Arabs have a high regard for tradition, and they are not as mobile as Westerners (Omar Nyell, 1996).

❏ It is acceptable in most places for friends of the same sex to show public affection (e.g., holding hands). Members of the opposite sex, however, generally do not show affection in public.

❏ In some areas, women are not to talk to strangers and may not leave the home without permission from the husband. Males are not supposed to approach women in some parts of the Middle East.

❏ There is a great emphasis on premarital chastity, especially for girls. Some immigrant Middle Eastern families may leave the United States because of a fear that their daughters will engage in premarital sexual activity (Sharifzadeh, 1998).

❏ Engaging in extramarital sex is often considered a crime. Women have, in some cases, been put to death for this activity (Sasson, 1992).

❏ In some areas, women cover themselves in clothing from head to toe before going out in public. Many women wear modest clothes and do not show the face. Dress, however, varies from country to country. Women in Iran, for example, are being allowed greater freedom in exposing their faces. In Afghanistan, members of the Taliban religious group have been known to beat a woman to death if she accidentally exposed a body part such as the arm in public.

❑ Traditional Arabs view clothing restrictions for women as a means of providing protection from the competition, stress, temptations, and indignities found in outside society. Many Arab women feel that the present social system gives them protection, security, and respect (Omar Nydell, 1996).

❑ Many Middle Easterners do not wear bright colors.

❑ In the Arabian Gulf states, Yemen, and Saudi Arabia, few women work outside the home. The few with employment outside the home work in all-female environments or in the medical professions.

❑ Some Middle Eastern women in the United States have found paying work outside the home. This has led to a reversal of roles for many women who did not work outside the home in their countries of origin. Some Middle Eastern men have difficulty accepting the greater freedom that women are allowed in the U.S. (Mohtasham-Nouri, 1994).

HEALTH CARE AND DISABLING CONDITIONS

Sharifzadeh (1998) described issues relating to health care in the Middle East:

❑ Health conditions and the availability of health care vary from country to country.

❑ In some war-torn countries (e.g., Iraq), thousands of children have died because of lack of adequate health care, embargoes on food, and other war-related problems.

❑ In many traditional Muslim families, it is considered unacceptable for women to be examined by male doctors. Often, experienced older women provide health care to female patients.

❑ Minor health problems experienced by children may be treated using nutritional remedies. For example, pediatricians in Iran may put children with chicken pox or small pox on a strict watermelon diet.

❑ Many Middle Eastern parents, especially those from cold climates, have their children cover themselves in warm attire to ward off illnesses.

❑ If a child is born with a disability, it is common for the mother to feel shame and guilt; the father may view the child's disability as a personal defeat and a blemish on the family's pride.

❑ Reactions to a child with disabilities may include denial, isolation, overprotection, or in some cases, total abandonment.

❑ Many Middle Eastern families have strong beliefs about the causes of serious mental disabilities. Families with children who have these disabilities may become isolated from everyone except other family members.

MIDDLE EASTERN COMMUNICATION STYLES

Middle Eastern communication styles have been described by a number of authors (see Abdrabbah, 1984; Battle, 2002; Irujo, 1988, Omar Nydell, 1996; Samovar & Porter, 1991, 1994; Sasson, 1992; Sharifzadeh, 1998; Wilson, 1998).

❏ It is generally acceptable to speak loudly in conversation. Loudness in the Arab culture connotes sincerity and strength; speaking softly implies that one is frail (Samovar & Porter, 1991). Observers may think that conversational partners are angry because of the loudness level of the communication.

❏ Arabs tend to speak rapidly. Americans may view their speaking rate as "too fast."

❏ Gestures, intonation, and facial expressions are important factors in communication.

❏ In the Arab world, a good personal relationship is the most important factor in successfully conducting business. A few minutes at the beginning of a meeting may be devoted to developing such a relationship by discussing recent activities and matters relating to the well-being of others (Omar Nydell, 1996).

❏ Arabs look directly into the eyes of the people they are communicating with, "and do so for long periods of time. They believe that such contact shows interest in the other person and also helps assess the truthfulness of the words the other is speaking" (Samovar & Porter, 1991, p. 199). However, in many Arab cultures it is taboo for a woman to look a man in the eye.

❏ Among Arabs, verbal eloquence is highly prized. Common rhetorical patterns include repetition, overassertion, and exaggeration. Emphatic assertions are common.

❏ In communication, Arabs highly value displays of emotion that Westerners may regard as immature. Westerners may label Arabs as too emotional, while many Arabs find Westerners inscrutable and cold (Omar Nydell, 1996).

❏ Poets are held in very high esteem in Arabic societies; many educated Arabs, at some point in their careers, will attempt to write poetry.

❏ Arab writers look to the Koran as the ultimate book of grammar and style, in much the same way that U.S. writers rely on the King James version of the Bible (Samovar & Porter, 1994).

❏ It is often difficult to obtain a direct answer from an Arab; a common answer is *inshalla* (God willing).

❏ Usually it is considered discourteous to say "no." Words such as "perhaps" or "maybe" are often used in place of the word "no."

❏ An alveolar click (*"tsk, tsk"*) can mean "no" to an Arab.

❏ Communication is often indirect and, therefore, listeners must be sensitive to the underlying meaning of the speaker's message.

❏ It may be unacceptable, in some groups, to cross one's legs or stretch one's legs in a group setting.

❑ Among some groups, it is acceptable during conversations to retreat into silence and internal reflection. "Tuning out" is accepted and valued.

❑ During conversations, many Middle Easterners stand or sit close to other persons. Americans tend to maintain a distance of approximately five feet between themselves and their conversational partners, but for Middle Easterners, a distance of two feet is typical. Touching during conversations is common.

❑ It is generally expected that people will show proper respect to others. Titles and last names are used in greetings.

❑ Lack of eye contact between men and women during conversation is common to maintain respect and proper distance between genders.

✐REFLECTION✐

Compare and contrast two communication style differences between Americans and Middle Easterners. Why is it important to be aware of these differences?

_____

_____

_____

_____

_____

MIDDLE EASTERN LANGUAGE CONSIDERATIONS

❑ Middle Eastern languages are divided into three different language families: the Altic, the Hamito-Semitic, and the Indo-European.

❑ Arabic, the language spoken most widely in the Middle East, is the world's sixth most common language, and is spoken by over 160 million people worldwide.

❑ Arabic falls under the Semitic subdivision of the Hamito Semitic language family.

❑ Other common Middle Eastern languages are Kurdish, Farsi (Persian), and Turkish. Hebrew is the official language of Israel.

❑ Farsi is the official language of Iran. Farsi shares 28 of its 32 letters with Arabic and is written from right to left.

❑ Arabic, as it is used during conversation, differs in important ways from the written form of the language. Written, formal Arabic is unchangeable and is used everywhere. Written Arabic is more grammatically complex and includes a richer vocabulary than spoken Arabic. There are many spoken dialects, some of which are mutually unintelligible.

❏ Most educated Arabs are bilingual, and speak Modern Standard Arabic as well as their local Arabic dialect.

❏ There are 29 letters in the Arabic alphabet. All but one of the letters is a consonant. The Arabic language is written from right to left.

❏ The most common word order in Arabic is *verb + subject + object.*

❏ Some consonants in the Arabic language are not used in English. Among these consonants are glottal stops, voiceless and voiced uvular fricatives, and voiced and voiceless pharyngeal fricatives (Goldstein, 2000).

Characteristics of the Arabic speaker's articulation and language are presented in Table 9.1.

IMPLICATIONS FOR PROFESSIONALS

The information reported by Battle (2002), Omar Nydell (1996), Sharifzadeh (1998), and Wilson (1998) has important implications for professionals:

❏ Professionals should begin meetings with inquiries about the family and an informal, light conversation. Most Arabs regard people who discuss business immediately as being brusque. Arabs mistrust people who do not appear to take an interest in them personally. If Arabs do not like or trust someone, they will often not listen to that person.

❏ Professionals may be more successful in communicating with families if they are informal and perceived as "family friends" rather than authority figures. It may be difficult for some families to trust those outside the extended family circle.

❏ Some families may be offended if professionals offer their left hand in greeting, as the left hand is often considered unclean.

❏ It may not be considered appropriate for female professionals to shake hands with male family members.

❏ Most Arabs accept Western female professionals and especially admire those that are well-educated. Thus, female professionals may want to find a comfortable, non-threatening way to share their professional education and credentials with families.

❏ Professionals should sit with good posture and dress formally to indicate respect for the family. It is considered disrespectful to talk when slouching, leaning against a wall, or holding one's hands in one's pockets.

❏ Families may be late for appointments or may not keep appointments at all. Professionals should emphasize the need for promptness so that families can receive the time and support that they need within the professional's schedule.

❏ Many professionals speak to the student's mother first. In some Middle Eastern families, the father is the official liaison between the family and any "strangers." Thus, professionals may need to consult with the father first.

Table 9.1
ARTICULATION AND LANGUAGE DIFFERENCES COMMONLY OBSERVED AMONG ARABIC SPEAKERS
(see Battle, 2002; Omar Nydell, 1996).

Articulation Characteristics	*Possible English Errors*
n/ng substitution	son/song, nothin'/nothing
sh/ch substitution	mush/much, shoe/chew
w/v substitution or f/v substitution	west/vest, Walerie/Valerie fife/five, abofe/above
t/voiceless "th" substitution or s/voiceless "th" substitution	bat/bath, noting/nothing sing/thing, somesing/something
z/voiced "th" substitution	brozer/brother, zese/these zhoke/joke, fuzh/fudge
retroflex /r/ doesn't exist;	speakers of Arabic will use a tap or trilled /r/
There are no triple consonant clusters in Arabic, so epenthesis may occur	kinduhly/kindly, harduhly/hardly
o/a substitutions	hole/hall, bowl/ball
o/oi substitutions	bowl/boil, foble/foible
uh/a substitutions	snuck/snack, ruck/rack
ee/i substitutions	cheep/chip, sheep/ship

Language Characteristics	*Possible English Errors*
Omission of possessives 's and "of"	That Kathy book. The title the story is...
Omission of plurals	She has 5 horse in her stable. He has 3 pen in his pocket.
Omission of prepositions	Put your shoes.
Omission of form "to be"	She ___ my friend.
Inversion of noun constructs	Let's go to the station gas.

❑ Case history information may be somewhat challenging for a female interviewer to gather. The father, the family spokesperson, might not want to be questioned by a female interviewer. Male interviewers are likely to experience greater success.

❑ It is important to find out family members' titles and use them—omission of a title is an insult.

❑ Professionals should not be surprised if Arab families communicate emotionally, because this is an accepted and common pattern among Arabs.

❑ Arabs are quite aware of social class, and upper-class Arabs may not socialize with those from lower socio-economic backgrounds. If an interpreter is from a social class different from that of the family, feelings of alienation may affect their interactions.

❑ Arabs are uncomfortable during discussions that focus directly on death, illness, or disasters; they use euphemisms or avoid these topics altogether. Thus, professionals will want to approach discussions of disabilities with tact and diplomacy.

❑ Disabilities are often associated with feelings of denial, shame, and guilt that impede communication in a formal interview situation.

❑ Arabs may deny the existence of conditions that threaten their personal dignity (e.g., a child's disability) because honor is more important than facts.

❑ It is often helpful for professionals to supplement arguments with personal comments when trying to persuade parents to accept the school's recommendations. Most Arabs respond far more readily to personalized arguments than to "logical" conclusions.

❑ Professionals should not be shocked if personal questions are asked such as, "What is your salary?" or "Why do you have no children?"

❑ Professionals who are used to keeping physical distance when interacting with others may feel uncomfortable when Arabs stand close to them or touch them during conversations. It is important not to move away or to appear disturbed by these communication patterns.

❑ The limited knowledge that many Arabs have about speech, language, and hearing services can affect their willingness to accept and participate in service delivery. They may feel uncomfortable utilizing services provided by a non-Arab.

❑ Many American professionals emphasize that both parents need to work together to help their children. Some Middle Eastern men may resist child-rearing activities because they do not see child-rearing as their responsibility. Child care is generally the province of women.

❑ The mastery of self-help skills at an early age is often not considered critical in Middle Eastern families. Professionals should not label children as "delayed" based on developmental expectations for American born, Anglo children.

❑ The emphasis on interdependence within the family may conflict with the professional's goal of independence for a student with a disability.

❑ Some families indicate agreement with the recommendations of professionals because the expression of disagreement is considered rude. A "yes" response may be an expression of good will rather than an indication that recommendations will be followed.

❑ Rather than saying "no" directly, most Arabs will give a noncommittal answer.

❑ Professionals need to have frequent contacts with families to make sure that appropriate action is being taken to meet the needs of children.

❑ Because families are expected to take care of the needs of its members, problems may be encountered when outside agencies intervene to provide assistance. Professionals need to help families understand how these agencies can help them.

❑ Because of the frequent use of exaggeration, assertion, and repetition among Arabs, professionals should use repetition and emphasis to convey to families that what is said is truly meant to be taken seriously. "If you speak softly and make your statements only once, Arabs may wonder if you really mean what you are saying" (Omar Nydell, 1996, p. 118).

❑ Some Middle Easterners may view the term "Middle East" as ethnocentric. Thus, professionals may wish to avoid this term when communicating with families.

❑ Arabs who are Muslim often rely on religiously-based rather than medically-based explanations about the cause of a disability (Langdon & Cheng, 2002).

Profile

Mahbohbah K., a 9-year-old girl, came to the U.S. from Kuwait with her parents. Mahbohbah had been diagnosed with cerebral palsy in Kuwait, and had been kept at home and cared for by her mother. Mahbohbah had never attended school, and her family ensured that her needs were met.

In the Colorado city where the family settled, school personnel became aware of Mahbohbah and told her parents that school attendance was required in the U.S. The parents objected strongly. The school met with the parents, discussed all the special education options that were available to Mahbohbah, and recommended placement in a special education program. The family refused to sign the program enrollment forms.

Finally the speech-language pathologist was able to obtain assistance from Abdullah S., a respected member of the local Muslim mosque. After much discussion in Arabic between the family and Abdullah, the family agreed to allow Mahbohbah to attend school and to receive special education services. Abdullah later told the speech-language pathologist privately that Mahbohbah's father felt that it was the duty of the family to care for this child's needs. The father didn't view education as being important for girls. Abdullah had worked hard to convince the family of the importance of educating both boys and girls. The family was informed that Mahbohbah would be at a severe disadvantage without the services offered by the school district.

STUDY QUESTIONS

1. Describe the traditional roles of men and women in the Middle East. How might these roles impact the relationship and communication between a female professional and a Middle Eastern man?

2. Discuss views of disabilities that are common in the Middle East.

3. List three practical suggestions that will help professionals communicate more effectively with Middle Eastern families.

TRUE-FALSE

Circle the number beside all statements that are true.

4. There are few differences between spoken Arabic and written Arabic.

5. Most Middle Eastern women work in jobs outside the home.

6. Muslim Arabs, especially in the big cities, prefer to marry first and second cousins.

7. Many Arabs communicate in an emotional manner, and professionals should be prepared for this.

8. Families may experience feelings of guilt, shame, and denial if a family member has a disability.

9. In the Middle Eastern countries, Yemen has one of the highest literacy rates.

10. Arab society tends to be conservative and emphasizes conformity among its members.

MULTIPLE CHOICE

Circle the letter beside all choices that are correct.

11. Which countries are referred to as either Middle Eastern or Arab countries?
    A. Kuwait
    B. Iran
    C. Yemen
    D. Israel
    E. Argentina

12. A Middle Eastern child has been referred to you. Farrah is 5 years old and her teacher suspects a developmental delay. You need to meet with the special education team and the child's family to discuss the need for a full psychoeducational assessment. What are some important things you will keep in mind before and during this meeting?
    A. Most Middle Eastern parents strongly encourage early independence in their children.
    B. It will be best to direct the questions to Farrah's father during the meeting.
    C. To help family members relax so that they will not feel intimidated, you should dress informally and slouch slightly during the meeting.
    D. The family may deny the existence of any disability because it is a discredit to their honor.
    E. You need to repeat yourself and emphasize important points several times.

13. Which one of the following is/are true about Farsi?
    A. Farsi is the official language of Iraq.
    B. Farsi shares 28 of its 32 letters with Arabic.
    C. Farsi is written from right to left.
    D. Farsi is the smallest country in the Middle East.
    E. Farsi is a city that separates two very different cultures.

14. Consonants that occur in Arabic but not in English include:
    A. Voiceless and voiced uvular fricatives
    B. Glottal stops
    C. Alveolar laterals
    D. Voiced and voiceless pharyngeal fricatives
    E. Voiced bilabial fricatives

15. Which of the following are TRUE statements about education in the Middle East?
    A. Schools are often co-educational.
    B. Formal Arabic is taught in many schools.
    C. Traditionally, most females were not encouraged to attend college.
    D. The education of children is a high priority in many families.
    E. Compulsory education usually begins at around 5 years of age.

ANSWERS TO STUDY QUESTIONS

4. False
5. False
6. False
7. True
8. True
9. False
10. True
11. A and C
12. B, D, and E
13. B and C
14. A, B, and D
15. B, C, and D

Chapter 10

FAMILIES FROM RUSSIAN BACKGROUNDS

by Celeste Roseberry-McKibbin, Ph.D. and Lisa Domyancic, M.S.

Outline

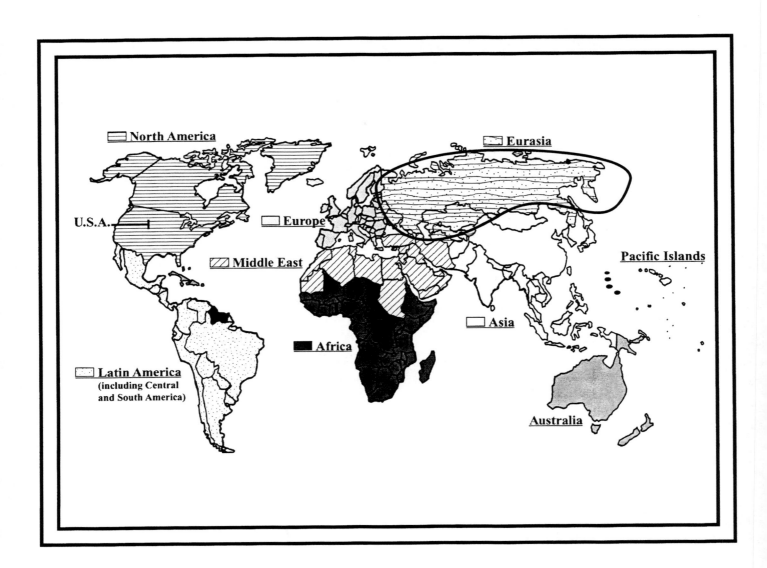

The increasing numbers of immigrants from the former United Soviet Socialist Republics (USSR) has resulted in a need for many professionals in special education to learn about the language and cultural background of this population. In 1989, the U.S. Lautenberg amendment broadened the definition of refugees to include "a presumption of persecution." Thus, Soviet citizens could gain refugee status by stating that they feared religious persecution in the Soviet Union. Since that time, 350,000 religious refugees from the former USSR (80% Jews, 20% Christians) have resettled in the United States.

In this chapter, immigrants from the former USSR are referred to as "Russians." It is important, however, to remember that much diversity exists within the individual republics that were once part of the Soviet Union (see Figure 10.1) and that changes affecting the map below may occur in the future.

Figure 10.1

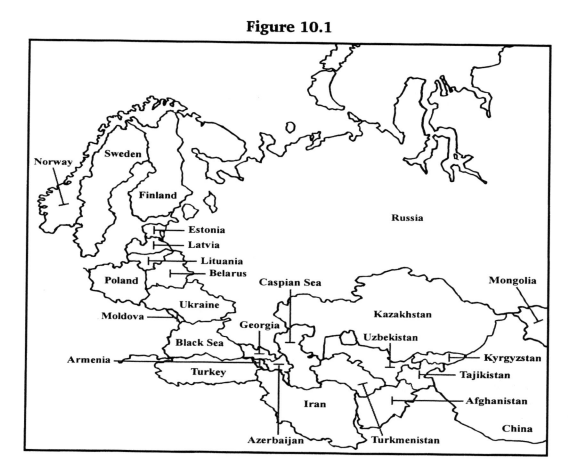

GENERAL BACKGROUND INFORMATION

❑ According to the U.S. Immigration and Naturalization Service, approximately 62,800 immigrants from the former USSR entered the U.S. in 1996. Of these immigrants, 4,300 were from Belarus; 1,800 were from Moldava; 19,700 were from Russia; and 21,100 were from Ukraine (U.S. Bureau of the Census, 1999).

❑ There are great numbers of Russians in certain areas of the U.S. An informal study estimated that in New York City there are over 200,000 Russian immigrants (Helfman, 1999).

❑ In Sacramento, California and nearby areas, it is estimated that there are 100,000 Russian residents. Approximately 14,538 students of Russian background were enrolled in the public schools in California in the 1998-1999 school year (California Department of Education, 1999).

❑ Most Russians have come to the U.S. because of religious persecution, economic hardship, and limited educational and vocational opportunities for themselves and their children (Katz-Stone, 2000; Minochin, 1999).

❑ Young Russians have value systems that are quite different from those of older Russians whose formative and early adult years occurred during Communist rule.

❑ The general area of the Russian Federation is 17,075,000 square kilometers, extending across 11 time zones between the Pacific and the Baltic. The capital of the Russian Federation is Moscow.

❑ Russia, the largest of the former Soviet republics, is nearly twice the size of the U.S. and is the largest country in the world.

❑ The Russian Federation has 89 administrative units, and 31 are autonomous entities where most of the non-Russians live (Richmond, 1996). In 1990, the former USSR had a population of 290 million people. Population shifts, however, have occurred in recent years.

❑ During World War I, Czar Nicholas II abdicated due to popular unrest among the people. The 1917 revolt was led by Vladimir Lenin, head of the Bolshevik party, and the Communists came to power in 1922. At this time, they formed the USSR and forcibly incorporated Belarus, Azerbaijan, Georgia, Ukraine, and Armenia. Many Russians died when Lenin reorganized Russian geographical and political boundaries.

❑ Trotsky became the ruler after Lenin's death in 1924. However, in 1925, Joseph Stalin assumed power as a dictator and forced the people into a lifestyle of industrialization and collective agriculture.

❑ In the mid-1930's, Stalin initiated the Great Purge, a program of terror designed to crush opposition by Soviet citizens who disagreed with his policies. It is estimated that 20 million Russians died as a result of the Great Purge.

❑ Russians lived in great fear of the KGB (secret police) under Stalin and his successors, especially Kruschev and Brezhnev.

❑ Mikhail Gorbachev became head of the USSR in 1985 and was generally viewed as the first of a new generation of leaders. He instituted the policy of *perestroika* (restructuring) to improve economic conditions and performance. Unfortunately, this policy failed; inflation grew worse and shortages increased.

❑ *Glasnost,* a policy of openness that resulted in increased, widespread freedom to express opinions and critically discuss issues of concern (even if these issues differed from those of the Communist leaders) was introduced by Gorbachev.

❏ The USSR was formally dissolved on December 25, 1991 when Gorbachev resigned as Soviet president. In September, 1991, the three Baltic republics were recognized as independent by Moscow (Richmond, 1996).

❏ Powerful leaders announced the formation of a new, loose confederation, headed by Boris Yeltsin, that was called the Commonwealth of Independent States (CIS).

❏ The CIS consisted of independent republics: Armenia, Azerbaijan, Belarus, Kazakhstan, Kyrgyzstan, Moldova, Russia, Tajikistan, Turkmenistan, Ukraine, and Uzbekistan. President Vladimir Putin was elected on March 27, 2000. (Note: for purposes of efficiency, all geographic areas are referred to as "Russia" in this chapter although there are many other republics and protectorates.)

❏ Approximately 70% of Russians belong to Slavic ethnic groups. The largest Slavic group is the Russians, who comprise approximately half of the Russian Federation's population. The second and third largest Slavic ethnic groups are the Ukrainians and the Belarusians respectively.

❏ Turkic peoples comprise the second largest ethnic group in the Russian Federation. The largest Turkic groups include the Uzbeks, the Kazakhs, the Kyrgyz, and the Turkmens. In Russia today, people are very proud of their distinct ethnic heritage.

❏ Russians have a history of invasion, persecution, and suffering. During the past thousand years, Russia has been repeatedly invaded and occupied by different ethnic groups such as the Mongols, Germans, Turks, and others. Entire Russian villages have been slaughtered or, at least, brutally occupied and ruled (Samovar & Porter, 1991).

❏ From 1917-1991, under Soviet Communism, as many as 61 million people were purged as "enemies of the state." This included Christians, Jews, Muslims, and followers of other faiths.

❏ Communist control resulted in restrictions in every aspect of life until 1991. Before 1991, it was considered a great honor to be accepted into the Communist party.

❏ Career advancement was most likely to occur among individuals who were members of the Communist party; in fact, people in high positions were expected to be members of this party (Dabars, 1995). Conversely, people who refused to belong to the Communist party often remained at a low point on the career ladder, with little or no opportunity for advancement.

❏ To survive within a country that had a long history of totalitarianism, many Russians developed a fatalistic attitude toward life. Prior to 1991, Russians were under such oppressive rule that they had few opportunities to make their own decisions.

❏ For Russians raised in previous eras, the state suppressed personal initiative, personal responsibility, and the desire to work independently. Citizens had to conform to the government's opinions and dictates.

❏ Although Russia has great potential wealth, the long-term impacts of a Marxist centralized command economy have been devastating. Collectivization and industrialization of farms was achieved with great cruelty and oppression.

❏ In the last two decades, the Russian government's efforts to reduce state ownership and liberalize the economy have had variable success because of the resistance of the vast bureaucracy and entrenched leadership structures that are threatened by change. Decline and hyper-inflation have resulted (Johnstone, 1993).

❏ Some perceive their current government as not being strong enough to run the country because laws and decrees are regularly disobeyed (Sperling, 1999). Millions of Russian citizens are dissatisfied with the current economic and political situation.

❏ Older people especially miss the times when Russia was under Communist rule and things were stable, understandable, and predictable. Under the Soviet regime, there was little unemployment. Although the Soviet regime was oppressive in many ways, most Russians viewed life during that time as being more economically stable than it is today.

❏ Russian Orthodoxy has been the state religion in Russia for almost 1,000 years. However, the Communists greatly restricted religious practices in the former USSR prior to 1990.

❏ Officially, the Communists were atheists and viewed religion as an anti-Communist force and as a form of mental enslavement from which people must be liberated. For over 75 years, Russians were told that religion was the "opium of the people" by Marxist-Leninist leaders.

❏ After the revolution in 1917, the Communists instituted separation of church and state; many churches were forced to close during the Lenin and Stalin eras. Gorbachev was the first Soviet leader to change official policy and tolerate religion.

❏ In the 1990s, the Russian Orthodox Church began to attain increased visibility and freedom. Today, the Russian Orthodox church is viewed by most Russians as the state religion (Kornblatt, 1999).

❏ Many Russians are Orthodox. Other religions in Russia include Islam, Buddhism, Judaism, and various sects/cults.

❏ With the demise of the Soviet Union in 1991 and the discrediting of the Communist philosophy, there emerged a moral and spiritual vacuum in the former USSR. Many religions attempted to fill this vacuum and began proselytizing in Russia (Kornblatt, 1999).

❏ As stated, a number of Russians have come to the U.S. because of religious persecution in their country. Jews experienced persecution in Russia before 1991 due to the Soviet Union's policy of state-sponsored anti-Semitism (Minochin, 1999).

❏ Evangelical Christians in the former USSR have historically been killed, put into prison, tortured, harassed, exiled, and denied an education for themselves and their children because of their faith in God (Johnstone, 1993; Soldatenkov, personal communication, May, 2000). Pentecostal Christians have especially been persecuted and many have attempted to emigrate to the U.S. This situation has improved since the USSR formally dissolved.

✐REFLECTION✐

What impact does the history of the former USSR have on the life of people living there today?

_____

_____

_____

_____

_____

RUSSIAN FAMILY LIFE

❑ Historically, Russians have married at an early age. This was especially prevalent among peasants in earlier centuries, where extended families were common and much intergenerational help and assistance occurred (Worobee, 1991).

❑ Early marriage is still prevalent today. For young Russian women, marriage at 17 or 18 years of age is common. If a Russian woman is not married by age 22 or so, she may be considered an "old maid."

❑ Marriage is a primary concern for young women. Society dictates that they marry and raise children to help increase the population. Thus, Russian women tend to start families at younger ages than American women. Most urban couples have only one or two children, whereas rural families are larger.

❑ Extended families are quite common in Russia even today, with several generations living under one roof. Most families are strongly united and mutually interdependent; they tend to rely on each other a great deal.

❑ Historically in Russia, the people could not trust anyone outside their families (especially during the Stalin years), and to this day, many people feel safe with and close to their families and do not trust outsiders.

❑ Russians value their families greatly. Unfortunately, however, the divorce rate in Russia is high (over 30 percent) and is rising. Reasons associated with the high divorce rate include alcoholism, adultery, personality and cultural differences, and lack of privacy due to the housing shortage (Dabars, 1995).

❑ Because it is hard to obtain housing, young couples often live with their parents for some time, even up to several years. Urban apartments are small by American standards, and a family of three people or more may live in one room.

❑ In many Russian families, both parents work outside the home. Nearly 40% of parents work nine or more hours a day and face lengthy commutes on crowded public transportation. Few families can afford to own cars.

❑ After a full work day and long commute, mothers may spend several hours in line trying to buy food for their families. Because household appliances (e.g., microwaves and automatic washing machines) are not common, housekeeping duties can take up quite a bit of time. Thus, many families have few free hours.

❑ Grandparents or other relatives often care for children when the parents are working. If their assistance is not available, children go to child care centers or nurseries while their parents work.

❑ Day care has become increasingly hard to find. In 1988, 70% of children attended child care centers. In 1994, only 56% of children attended these centers and 370,000 children were on waiting lists (Sperling, 1999). Hundreds of mothers have been forced to abandon their jobs because of this situation.

❑ Many Russian men hold very traditional views of women. For decades there has been economic discrimination against Russian women. Women tend to work in branches of industry with low prestige and low pay.

❑ Although the overall level of education of women is generally higher than that of men, women work mainly in the low-skill areas and rarely attain an executive or managerial level (Sperling, 1999). Although three-fourths of doctors are women, women seldom are seen in supervisory or management positions (Richmond, 1996).

❑ The roles of men and women in Russia tend to be more separate and specifically defined than the roles of men and women in the U.S. For example, Sperling (1999) cited the Russian Orthodox Church as stating that "A man is more aggressive, more active, more curious, more risk-taking...Women create continuity, peace, reliability. Man creates, woman reproduces" (p. 77).

❑ However, attitudes toward women vary from region to region. For example, in Ukraine (in contrast to Russia), authority in the home is shared by husband and wife (Richmond, 1995).

❑ During the Soviet period most women worked outside the home, and many women continue to work outside the home today. As in the past, many women in Russia take on the "double burden" of working full time outside the home for a salary and also taking the primary responsibility for maintaining the household and raising the children (Dabars, 1995; Richmond, 1996; Sperling, 1999).

❑ Fathers may spend much less time with children than mothers, and many Russian men are minimally involved in household maintenance activities (Dunn & Dunn, 1977; Sperling, 1999). Changes in the roles of men within the family unit, however, are beginning to occur.

❑ Many Russian men prefer that their wives work inside the home managing the household and caring for children (Panansenko, personal communication, April, 2001). Generally, women in Russia hold much responsibility and little authority.

❑ At 18 years of age, Russians obtain full citizenship rights including the right to vote, marry, and obtain a driver's license. Although Russians must be 18 to marry, girls may marry younger if special permission is granted (Dabars, 1995).

❑ An issue affecting many Russians is birth control. Abortion is free in Russia, while birth control is expensive and often not effective. It is estimated that the average Russian woman has between three and eight abortions due to these circumstances. Abortions among girls during the teen-age years are increasing in Russia, a country in which permission from parents is not required.

❑ Two-thirds of Russian pregnancies end in abortion (Richmond, 1996). Individuals who do not believe in abortion often have large families. Sometimes children are placed in orphanages by families that do not have the financial resources to support them.

❑ In many Russian families, parents attempt to "let children be children" for as long as possible. Zelensky (1999) quoted many Russian parents who stressed that "I want to create a fairy tale environment for my child" (p. 140).

❑ Many Russian parents have suffered so many hardships that they long for their children to live better lives. Therefore, the upbringing of many Russian children is characterized by a prolonged childhood in which they are allowed to remain emotionally and physically dependent and in which they are separated from "objective reality" by parents who withhold information (Zelensky, 1999).

❑ The emphasis on becoming independent at an early age is not as strong in Russia as it is in the United States. Discipline may be quite lax by American standards (Barker, 1999). Boys are permitted a considerable amount of behavioral freedom, although the level of permissiveness varies from republic to republic (Borodovsky, personal communication, May, 2001).

❑ Today, unemployment is rampant and is especially so for women (Sperling, 1999). Under the Soviet rule, women had a 90% employment rate. In 1995, 55% of Russian single mothers were living below the poverty line. Today, women comprise 90% of the ranks of the unemployed.

❑ The high unemployment rate in Russia has been related to the sharp rise in crime that occurred after the 1991 dissolution of the former USSR. It is estimated that in Russia, at least one-third of the population lives in poverty (Richmond, 1996).

❑ For those who are employed, particularly by the government, salaries are often paid weeks or months after they are due even though late payment is illegal (Sperling, 1999).

❑ Many Russian families suffer economic hardship, and the infamous "bread lines" still exist in some places today. Russians may stand in line for hours to purchase common items such as tea or a loaf of bread.

❑ Prices for food are about the same as prices in the U.S., but many Russians receive what is equivalent to $100.00 a month in salary (Soldatenkov, personal communication, May, 2000). Disposable diapers, considered affordable by most Americans, are a luxury item in Russia (Barker, 1999).

❑ Most Russians in cities and towns live in tall apartment buildings. Some families live in their own apartments. Others live in communal housing, and as many as 18 families may share a building. In communal housing, everyone shares one or two bathrooms, and food is prepared in one big kitchen (Dabars, 1995).

> ## Profile
>
> Alexi D., an Uzbeki 6-year-old male, was being evaluated by both a speech-language pathologist and a psychologist. The teacher had referred Alexi for attention and behavior problems, saying that "he is immature and he can't sit still." Attention Deficit Disorder with Hyperactivity (ADHD) was suspected. The speech-language pathologist was supervising a student intern from Uzbekistan, who observed Alexi during the evaluation. She also spoke with Alexi in Uzbeki, taking and later analyzing a language sample. The speech-language pathologist and psychologist felt that Alexi had symptoms of ADHD, although no language problems in Uzbeki were noted.
>
> The team discussed referring Alexi to a physician for a medical evaluation. The intern shared with the team that in Uzbekistan, Alexi's behavior would be viewed as quite normal and that for his cultural background, she did not think he had a clinically significant attention problem. It was recommended that the classroom teacher pair Alexi with a peer tutor and increase the level of structure in his program. Under the supervision of the speech-language pathologist, the intern made suggestions to the parents designed to help Alexi improve his attention skills.

EDUCATION AND LITERACY

❑ The literacy rate in Russia is greater than 98% (Johnstone, 1993). Russians read a lot, and books are inexpensive. Many people can afford to buy between five and 10 books a month, even on limited budgets.

❑ During the Stalin era, the importance of education was stressed and even today, many Russian men and women hold college degrees.

❑ School generally starts on September 1. Children begin first grade at 6 years of age and most attend school until they have completed 11th grade. Only nine grades are compulsory. Elementary, junior high, and senior high students usually study together in one building with multiple stories.

❑ From the beginning of first grade, students are assigned to a home room where they will stay until 11th grade. If a school is a newer, populated area, it may have six or seven home rooms per grade level (Dabars, 1995).

❑ Educational reform in Russia is progressing slowly. However, there still are many obstacles to this reform such as low salaries for teachers and lack of basic necessities (in some schools) such as heat, indoor plumbing, sewer systems, and textbooks (Richmond, 1996). Despite this, many students continue on to universities.

❑ When students are admitted to universities, they have already chosen their specialties. Most of the courses taken are required; few elective courses are available. Students study between four and six years, and must write and defend a thesis in the final year.

❑ The final degree earned is somewhat higher than a Bachelor's degree in the U.S. After students graduate, they are expected to work in a government-assigned position for two or three years. Tuition in universities is free, and most students receive stipends (Dabars, 1995).

❏ Russian schools have traditionally been responsible for moral education or *vospitaniye* (upbringing) (Richmond, 1996). Values that are considered important in the school setting include discipline, needs of the collective (as opposed to the individual), and the need to show great respect for teachers and elders in general.

❏ Critical thinking skills are often not emphasized in the curriculum. Students are told what the answers are, and there is no other "right" answer. Information is often not evaluated, and "why" questions are rare in classrooms.

❏ Discipline is strict, and there is little to no discussion (Richmond, 1996). Even in universities, students are often taught to accept only one answer as correct and do not express their individual viewpoints (Richmond, 1995). Instruction in universities is theoretical, and students rarely challenge their professors (Richmond, 1996).

❏ However, statistics indicate that Russian children are often between two and three years ahead of American children in math and science; they are also more advanced than American children in literature and history (Richmond, 1996).

CULTURAL CUSTOMS, COURTESIES, AND BELIEFS

❏ Russians try to avoid *nyekulturno* (bad manners).

❏ When people enter Russian homes, they immediately remove their shoes and put on special slippers to wear in the home. It is important not to show the soles of one's shoes by crossing legs with an ankle on a knee or putting one's feet on furniture.

❏ It is considered bad luck to shake hands across the threshold of a door step. People always take off their gloves when shaking hands.

❏ If a guest makes a complimentary statement about an item in the home of a Russian, that item may be given to the guest.

❏ If a guest eats dinner in a Russian home, it is customary to bring a gift such as alcohol, candy, or flowers. There should never be an even number of flowers in a bouquet; even numbers are reserved for funeral arrangements.

❏ Russians eat breakfast in the morning and a "dinner" around one o'clock that is the main meal of the day. This main meal includes appetizers, a main course, potatoes/noodles/rice, vegetables, and dessert.

❏ A popular feature of many Russian meals is the many appetizers (*zakuski*) that are served. Many Russians eat an afternoon snack at around four o'clock. A light meal is consumed in the evening. Most Russians do not use the word "lunch," and have difficulty understanding this American concept (Dabars, 1995).

❏ Russians will often leave some food on the table and on their plates at the end of a meal to indicate abundance.

❏ Russians are famous for their "*gostepriimstvo*" (hospitality). They often expect that guests will eat several helpings of everything put in front of them, and may be offended if guests turn down food. Guests should leave some food on their plates to indicate that they have had a hearty meal.

☐ Russian cuisine is internationally considered to be varied and of high quality. Regular mainstays in the Russian diet include bread, meat, potatoes, soups, and pickled fish. Due to food shortages, it is almost impossible to obtain vegetables and fruits in winter. Russians on limited incomes (such as the elderly) eat mainly bread.

☐ Scientists consider approximately one-fourth of Russia's water to be unsafe, and ice is not served in cold drinks. Tea is the most popular nonalcoholic drink in Russia, and is consumed after meals and during mid-afternoon breaks. In some families, it is considered inappropriate to drink tea with a meal.

☐ Punctuality in Russia is viewed as less important than punctuality in the U.S. In Russia, time is not money and many Russians have a very relaxed attitude toward timelines and deadlines (Richmond, 1995). Patience is far more valued than punctuality. "Americans are oriented toward doing; Russians, toward contemplating" (Richmond, 1996, p. 130).

☐ When Russians arrive for a meeting or appointment, they may engage in a number of rituals before getting down to business. Discussions relating to family and personal issues, small talk, and refreshments (e.g., something to drink) may precede a business meeting.

☐ For many Russians, when dealing with professionals, the person comes first; his ideas are secondary.

☐ Relationships are all-important to Russians, and good personal relationships take priority over business (Richmond, 1996). Also, many Russians welcome inquiries about their families and are genuinely interested in knowing about the families of others.

☐ Russian women tend to dress conservatively, and they are not supposed to be assertive in public. Older Russians generally dress conservatively.

☐ Many Russians do not believe that one must shower or bathe daily. Taking a bath no more than once a week is common in some areas. Most Russians find it difficult to understand the American habit of daily hair washing (Dabars, 1995).

☐ In Russia, important holidays include:

January 7 - Russian Orthodox Christmas

February 23 - Soviet Army Day. All young men are still required to give some military service; on the 23rd of February, it is customary for women to give men small gifts.

March 8 - International Women's Day. Men phone female friends to wish them well, and give flowers to those whom they are close to.

April/May - Russian Orthodox Easter. Orthodox Russians are not supposed to do any menial labor on Easter Sunday and the two days that follow.

May 1 - International Workers' Solidarity Day

May 9 - Victory Day

May 27 - St. Petersburg's Birthday

June 12 - Independence Day

September 1 - Day of Knowledge. This is the first day of school and children bring gifts to teachers.

December 12 - Russian Federation Constitution Day

December 31 - January 1- New Year

Note: If a person is having a birthday, she will stay at home in the evening while friends and relatives come by with congratulations. The person having the birthday provides the food for the guests.

✐*REFLECTION*✐

Describe three communication practices commonly observed among Russians that are important for professionals in the U.S. to understand. Why should professionals be especially aware of these practices?

_____

_____

_____

_____

HEALTH CARE AND DISABLING CONDITIONS

❑ Although free medical care is available in the former USSR, the quality of service is often poor. Doctors are well trained but do not have modern supplies or equipment.

❑ At the present time, the Russian health care system is in a fluctuating and uncertain state. The state medical system predominated until 1987, and all medical care (except for prescription drugs purchased at pharmacies) was free.

❑ Unfortunately, the scarcity of prescription drugs and the lack of adequate medical equipment have made medical care difficult.

❑ There continues to be a shortage of necessary medicine and equipment. Also, unfortunately, maternal mortality rates are rising in Russia and increasing numbers of children are born with medical problems (Sperling, 1999).

❑ The 1986 explosion in Ukraine's Chernobyl nuclear power plant caused three immediate fatalities. However, in 2000, there were three million children who continued to require medical treatment for radiation exposure as a result of the Chernobyl explosion.

❑ Smoking in Russia is extremely common. It is estimated that 70% of Russian adults smoke (Richmond, 1996). One Russian cartoon portrays a restaurant with two sections: Smoking and Chain Smoking.

❏ Alcoholism is rampant in Russia and is often associated with social and health problems. From 1992 to 1993, deaths related to alcoholism rose by 100% (Richmond, 1996). Many Russians, especially males, start drinking as early as 12 years of age.

❏ Vodka is the most common alcoholic beverage consumed in Russia. Vodka is distilled by using water and is, typically, 40% grain alcohol with 80 proof strength. The average life expectancy of Russian men is 58 years, and this short life span may result, in large part, from copious vodka consumption.

❏ Due to economic circumstances and other variables, poor health among Russian citizens has increased. The most common illnesses among Russians are the flu and the common cold.

❏ Though Russians believe that colds are spread by viruses, both patients and doctors think that cold drinks, drafts, or sitting on cold surfaces are also significant causes of colds (Dabars, 1995). Thus, if a Russian with a cold is offered a cold drink, he or she will probably decline it.

❏ In 1995, there were 36,000 cases of diphtheria. Other prevalent diseases in Russia include cholera, typhoid fever, tuberculosis, bubonic plague, measles, and whooping cough (Richmond, 1996).

❏ The incidence of venereal disease has increased since the end of the Soviet era. Incidences of HIV and AIDS are also on the rise.

❏ Russia has no nationwide sex education program; the Russian Orthodox Church has vocally opposed such programs. The Orthodox Church encourages abstinence, but young people are often sexually active.

ADOPTED RUSSIAN CHILDREN

Because increasing numbers of people in the U.S. are adopting children from Russian institutions (e.g., orphanages), it is important to understand the following facts about these children:

❏ Parents of these children may be deceased or may not have the financial resources necessary to care for children. Children are often sent to orphanages by parents who are unable to provide for them.

❏ There are approximately 200,000 children in Russia who live in institutions (Burnett, 2000). Many of these children have little variety in their diets; in some orphanages in Ukraine, for example, the diet consists primarily of macaroni, although an occasional piece of candy is provided as a treat (Soldatenkov, personal communication, May 2000).

❏ Children who have craniofacial anomalies such as cleft palates may be severely neglected. They may be "routinely confined to 'lying down' rooms where they receive no medical care and limited staff attention...if they are not adopted, they may remain institutionalized for life" (Burnett, 2000, p. 26).

❏ Many institutionalized Russian children without overt physical disabilities are adopted by American parents. For children who have come from these institutions, the professionals may expect an average of one month of growth for every three to four months of orphanage care (Glennen & Masters, 1999).

❏ In many orphanages, infants and toddlers are put into cribs twice a day for three-hour naps. Thus, much time is spent in an isolated, physically restricted space (Glenne, personal communication, November 2001).

❏ For children cared for in orphanages, language is the primary area of noted delay. Children adopted from Russian institutions generally lose their Russian language skills within a few months of arriving in the U.S. These children frequently have challenges in learning English because they do not have a solid foundation in their native languages. For example, it was found that institutionalized older children adopted from Russia and other Eastern European countries had never attended school prior to adoption, and a number of these children had moderate to severe delays in their native languages (Glennen & Masters, 1999).

COMMUNICATION STYLES

❏ People in Russia usually shake hands when being introduced. However, if a new person joins a group, introductions are not considered necessary. The person who just joined the group usually takes the initiative and introduces himself (Dabars, 1995).

❏ Many Russians consider it rude to cross one's arms behind one's head or drape an arm over the back of a chair.

❏ It is rude to say that one is going to the rest room; the norm is to just excuse oneself.

❏ It is considered discourteous to talk with one's arms folded across one's chest or with one's hands in one's pocket, especially during interactions with an older person.

❏ In addition, age is respected in Russia and some older Russians might not want to take advice or directions from younger people (Richmond, 1995).

❏ Russians, when speaking to others, are likely to stand closer than Americans (Richmond, 1995, 1996). A distance of 12 inches from the other person is common.

❏ Russians have more physical contact with one another in their daily lives than do Americans. Females may walk arm-in-arm on the street and may stand physically close during conversations.

❏ Some Russian men will embrace and kiss (on the cheek) an acquaintance they have not seen for a while. Many Russians touch the person they are talking with; some Americans would consider this invasive (Dabars, 1995).

❏ The Russian language does not have a word for "privacy." In contrast to individualistic Americans, Russians live by the philosophy of "sobornost" (togetherness, communal spirit) and believe that the needs of the group or collective are paramount (Richmond, 1996).

❏ Touching others and sharing space are considered positive values.

❏ In prior times, those who lived an isolated life often were visited by authorities. The belief was that one does not need privacy if one has nothing to hide (Dabars, 1995).

❑ Russians often enjoy group activities. The individual's business is everyone's business, and some Russians are blunt in giving their personal opinions about other lifestyles and activities. Richmond (1996) wrote:

> Russians seem compelled to intrude into the private affairs of others. Older Russians admonish young men and women—complete strangers—for perceived wrongdoings...On the streets, older women volunteer advice to young mothers on the care of their children...In a collective society, everybody's business is also everyone else's. (pp. 19-20)

❑ Russians are often straightforward and usually don't mince words when speaking their minds. Also, some Russians may inform others of wrongdoing in an emotional manner; maintaining a calm atmosphere is not as high a priority in Russia as it is in the United States.

❑ Russians value face-to-face communication; placing a phone call in Russia is much more logistically difficult than it is in the United States. One must often shout to be heard even when local calls are made.

❑ In Russia, it can be difficult to communicate with someone who is far away. Many Russians relate well to people, but not nearly as well to phone calls, letters, faxes, or e-mails (Richmond, 1996).

❑ As has been mentioned, Russians have a long history of suffering and hardship. Thus, to Americans, some Russians may appear cautious, conservative, skeptical, and negative, appearing as "defenders of the status quo" (Richmond, 1996, p. 38).

❑ Americans may become impatient with the desire of many Russians to cautiously maintain the status quo rather than venture into the unknown. However, Russians have learned to live with misfortune and are known for their resiliency, strength, and endurance.

LANGUAGE CONSIDERATIONS

❑ The official language in Russia is Russian, which was also the official language of the former USSR. Russian, Ukrainian, and Belarusian are Slavic languages. Russian uses the Cyrillic alphabet, which consists of 33 letters. Many of these letters are unlike any in the Roman (Latin) alphabet.

❑ There are also many languages indigenous to specific geographic locations. For example, the residents of Ukraine speak Ukrainian, Tartars speak Tartar, and Chuvashes speak Chuvash.

❑ Speakers of these languages are bilingual, speaking Russian as well as their native language. Individual languages such as Ukrainian are taught at schools in each individual republic in which the majority of people use the language.

❑ It takes about 10% longer to say something in Russian than in English. Experienced interpreters often say they need two or three Russian words to interpret a single English word.

❑ Words are inflected for number, gender, case, tense, mood, and person. Many negatives are used; for example, a small object will be described as "not big;" something that is good will be described as "not bad."

❑ A double negative does not create a positive, as in English, but rather increases the overall negativity of the utterance (Richmond, 1996).

IMPLICATIONS FOR PROFESSIONALS

❏ Never automatically refer to a family as "Russian" in their presence. It is very important for professionals to ask the families for information about where they came from. Families that are Ukrainians, for example, may be offended if referred to as "Russians." As one Ukrainian said, "We have fought wars and died in order to be called according to our individual nationalities" (Dubya, personal communication, March 2001).

❏ It is also important to remember that the term "Soviet" is only used today in a derogatory sense—professionals should not use the term.

❏ Because Russians have been accustomed to obeying the government without question or argument, it is a great change for them to learn to discuss issues, compromise, be creative, and take risks. Thus, if professionals are working with middle-aged and older Russian parents, they might appear to have a "fatalistic" attitude and to not question the professional's decisions.

❏ The parents might accept everything the professional says without question, and rely almost completely on the professional for their child's special needs. It is important that these parents be encouraged to be contributing partners in the clinical relationship.

❏ Many Russians, even today, have a great distrust of the police, government, and military. Professionals should remember that some Russians may not feel comfortable responding to personal questions; under Communist rule, providing answers to these questions could lead to prison or even death. It is ideal to work with a Russian interpreter or cultural mediator in these situations. Family members can also be very helpful.

❏ Female professionals who work with traditional Russian fathers may need to expend extra effort to be taken seriously. Helpful strategies include informing the father and family that the professional possesses an advanced degree; an expensive-looking business card is also helpful (Richmond, 1996).

❏ Professionals must be careful not to mislabel Russian boys as having conduct/behavioral disorders or ADHD because the boys may be acting in a way that is considered normal and acceptable in their culture.

❏ Professionals must be careful not to label Russian children as "overprotected" or "sheltered" by parents who are working hard to give their children a better life than they themselves had.

❏ Because the Russian educational system emphasizes conformity and lack of questioning, immigrant children may need help in using "higher level" thinking skills.

❏ Although many Russian immigrants are very grateful to be in the U.S., they encounter challenges that may leave them discouraged. Professionals need to be sensitive to these challenges.

❏ Limited proficiency in English is an obvious barrier for many Russian immigrants (Domyancic, 2000). A related problem for many Russian immigrants is that their skills and educational background are not acknowledged in the U.S. For example, Russian doctors and architects may work as custodians in the U.S. because of differing laws for licensing and professional practice. It is critical for professionals to be sensitive to this; the mother who is washing dishes at a restaurant in the U.S. might have been a heart surgeon in Russia.

❏ Many Russians have not had the same access to technology as Americans. Few homes have computers; computers are available in university libraries. Some families may own typewriters. Thus, professionals may see Russian immigrant students who are unfamiliar with even the basic technological information that most Americans take for granted.

❏ Domyancic (2000) found that approximately half of families that she studied from the former USSR did not have health insurance. Thus, some Russian students may not be receiving adequate health care. Professionals can help Russian families by having a list of affordable or free local resources.

❏ A major challenge for some families is accepting the egalitarian views of the roles of men and women that exist in the U.S. The balance of power in the marriage is shifting as women become more actively involved in the work force.

❏ Professionals may need to work with Russian families and clients who are having difficulty adjusting to the American emphasis on punctuality and time schedules (Dabars, 1995).

❏ Because Russians care so much about personal relationships, professionals should spend the first few minutes of any meeting in "small talk" so as not to appear rude or uncaring.

❏ By sharing information about his or her family, professionals can create an environment in which families feel comfortable talking about their child.

❏ Gift-giving is important to Russians, and they may bring a small gift to break the ice with the professional at the beginning of a relationship. It is important to be culturally sensitive when gifts are offered.

❏ Professionals who work with older Russian parents and grandparents may be expected to dress conservatively.

❏ Professionals who work with Russian children and adolescents may need to inform them about the school's expectations regarding personal hygiene. Issues relating to bathing need to be discussed in a culturally sensitive manner.

❏ Some evangelical Christian Russian immigrants and their children may have been denied a formal education in Russia because of their faith. Thus, the language skills and conceptual knowledge of these students may be below that of peers.

❏ Russian Christians who refused to join the Communist party because of religious beliefs generally were denied opportunities for career advancement and remained at a low socio-economic level. Professionals need to be sensitive to situations in which immigrants have experienced job discrimination and financial hardship because of their refusal to give up religion.

❏ Professionals need to be aware that adopted children with craniofacial anomalies who have been institutionalized may have severe cognitive-linguistic delays as well as unresolved medical problems resulting from neglect in the institution.

❏ Professionals should also be aware that adopted Russian children with histories of institutionalization may exhibit language delays that impact the acquisition of oral and written English.

❑ Individuals from Russian backgrounds often stand in close proximity and touch one another during interactions. Professionals should be careful not to move away or judge Russians as being rude or intrusive when such behaviors are observed.

❑ If a Russian family member becomes openly emotional during an encounter, the best solution for the professional is to take an immediate break. After the break, the professional should resume the relationship by using "small talk" to create a comfortable atmosphere for the meeting.

❑ Russian families may have limited experience with modes of communication commonly used in the U.S. (e.g., fax machines, e-mail). It is often best to meet directly with family members when information needs to be shared.

❑ Russians may promise more than they can deliver because they want to please the professional. "Da" or "yes" might mean "maybe" or even "no." It is critical for professionals to follow through with families and clients to be sure that they are doing as they said they would.

❑ When working with interpreters, it is important for professionals to realize that more words are generally required to communicate an idea in Russian than in English.

❑ Russian mothers read to their children more often than do fathers. Professionals should encourage both parents to read to their children (Domyancic, 2000).

Profile

Janey and Mike T., an American couple, adopted Viktor from a Ukrainian orphanage when he was 8 years old. Viktor spoke little English and was extremely shy with his adoptive parents. He was put into a third grade classroom in the U.S. but showed little progress during the course of the year. Viktor also had frequent nightmares and showed signs of angry, aggressive behavior. Mike and Janey were quite concerned, and sought an evaluation of Viktor's emotional as well as cognitive and linguistic skills.

The speech-language pathologist found an Ukrainian interpreter, who spoke extensively with Viktor about his past life in Ukraine. Viktor shared that he spent a great deal of time alone in the orphanage, and that if he committed even a slight infraction, he was hit quite hard in the face by the orphanage caretakers. He told the interpreter that once he was hit so hard on the side of the head that he could not hear anything for a while (subsequent audiological testing revealed a 30 db sensorineural hearing loss in the left ear). There was little to eat at the orphanage, and Viktor was afraid to ask for more food. There were no toys or books, and the children spent much of the day watching television. Viktor indicated that he was happy in the U.S., although he did not understand much of what went on in the classroom. He also talked about nightmares involving his experience in the orphanage.

The interpreter shared this conversation with the school team, and counseling services were set up for Viktor with the help of the Ukrainian interpreter. In addition, Viktor was enrolled in the after-school Homework Club and was placed in the school's daily Reading Clinic to help him develop English literacy skills. A family from the local Russian church agreed to spend time with Viktor each week, taking him on outings and talking with him about his previous experiences in the homeland.

STUDY QUESTIONS

1. Discuss ways in which the former Soviet Union's history of Communist rule continues to influence the lives of Russians today.

2. Summarize health matters that are of concern to Russians today. What is one health problem that might especially impact the communication skills of children?

3. Although many Russians are highly educated, several educational practices can make it difficult for Russian immigrant students to adjust to American educational expectations. What are these practices?

TRUE-FALSE

Circle the number beside each statement that is true.

4. The vast majority of Russians are opposed to Communism because of the instability that resulted from Communist rule.

5. Alcohol consumption, a problem that begins at around age 12 for many males, is a major health concern in Russia.

6. The literacy rate in Russia is above 98%. Russians read quite a bit, and books are inexpensive.

7. Many students do not go on to attend universities because of the deplorable condition of the schools.

8. When interacting with family members, professionals may refer to the household as a Russian family, but should not refer to it as a Soviet family.

9. The concept of "school lunches" is difficult for Russian families to comprehend.

10. Most Russians strongly encourage early independence so that children will be able to cope with the problems of daily life at an early age.

MULTIPLE CHOICE

Unless specified otherwise, circle the number beside each choice that is correct.

11. Features of the Russian language include the following:
    A. A double negative is used to produce an affirmative statement.
    B. Russian is a tonal language.
    C. Russian uses the Cyrillic alphabet, a symbol system that includes 33 letters.
    D. Words in the Russian language usually end in the consonant /n/ or /v/.
    E. Only one verb tense is used.

12. Which of the following are TRUE statements about Russian children who live in institutions?
    A. Children who have craniofacial anomalies receive multidisciplinary team intervention designed to help them achieve their full potential.
    B. For children who have come from institutions, professionals may expect an average of 1 month of growth for every 9 months of orphanage care.
    C. Most children in institutions receive schooling and become fluent in their native languages even if they do not know English.
    D. Children adopted from Russian institutions generally lose their Russian language skills within a few months following their arrival in the U.S.
    E. For children cared for in orphanages, language is the primary area of delay.

13. Which one of the following is NOT a true statement about Russian communication styles?
    A. Many Russians stand quite close and often make physical contact when conversing.
    B. Privacy is critical, and people like to do things individually rather than in groups.
    C. Russians tend to be blunt in giving their personal opinions about other people's lifestyles and activities.
    D. Russians often become quite emotional when informing others that they are "wrong" about something.
    E. During conversation it is considered discourteous for one to fold arms across the chest or to keep hands in pockets, especially when speaking to an older person.

14. Health issues for many Russians include the following:
    A. Cholera, typhoid fever, tuberculosis, bubonic plague, measles, and whooping cough are prevalent among Russians.
    B. Maternal mortality rates are rising and increasing numbers of children are being born with medical problems.
    C. The most common illnesses among Russians are the flu and the common cold.
    D. Walking pneumonia is the leading cause of death among adolescents and has become a major epidemic in recent years.
    E. There are no female physicians and medical treatment for women is inadequate, especially in heavily populated regions.

15. Professionals who work with Russian students and their families should remember the following:
    A. Evangelical Christian families have had especially good opportunities to receive an education, and their children's linguistic and cognitive skills tend to be highly developed.
    B. Parents, especially older ones, will often question the professional's decisions.
    C. Many Russians will promise more than they intend to deliver because of the desire to please the professional.
    D. Most Russians prefer face-to-face conversations rather than communication through the use of the telephone or e-mail.
    E. An effort should be made to encourage fathers to spend time reading with their children.

ANSWERS TO STUDY QUESTIONS

    4. False
    5. True
    6. True
    7. False
    8. False
    9. True
    10. False
    11. D
    12. D and E
    13. B
    14. A, B, and C
    15. C, D, and E

PART 2

ASSESSMENT OF LINGUISTICALLY AND CULTURALLY DIVERSE STUDENTS

Chapter 11

BILINGUALISM AND SECOND LANGUAGE LEARNING

Outline

Normal Processes of Second Language Acquisition
Affective Variables in Second Language Acquisition
Second Language Learning Styles and Strategies
Types of Language Proficiency
Additive and Subtractive Bilingualism
Developing Bilingual Language Proficiency
The Importance of Comprehensible Input
Simultaneous vs. Sequential Bilingualism
Conclusion

Whenassessing a child because of a possible language-learning disability, it is necessary to know what "normal behavior" is (Roseberry-McKibbin, 1994). A major challenge confronting professionals is that normal behavior varies widely even among monolingual children. When working with culturally diverse student populations, the picture becomes far more complex.

In spite of the enormous complexity of the situation confronting professionals who work with linguistically and culturally diverse students, there are certain general facts about second language acquisition and bilingualism that can be outlined and then used to tailor assessment and treatment to individual students. In this chapter, these facts will be discussed.

NORMAL PROCESSES OF SECOND LANGUAGE ACQUISITION

The processes of second language acquisition must be understood if one is to differentiate between a language difference and a language-learning disability (Goldstein, 2000; Saenz, 1996). Normal second language acquisition processes often result in differences that can impede communication. These differences need to be recognized as normal behaviors for students who are not yet proficient in English. Some of the most commonly observed processes are described in this section.

1. Interference (Transfer)

Interference (referred to by some authors as *transfer*) refers to a process in which a communicative behavior from the first language is carried over into the second language. Interference can occur in all areas: syntax, morphology, phonology, pragmatics, and semantics. Dulay and Burt (1974) analyzed the responses of 179 Spanish-speaking children between 5 and 8 years of age on the Bilingual Syntax Measure and found that less than 5 percent of the children's errors in English resulted from Spanish language interference. Other researchers (e.g., Politzer & Ramirez, 1974), however, believe that many English errors made by students acquiring English as a second language can be traced directly to the influences of the first language. Although there is disagreement among researchers about the extent to which interference occurs in second language acquisition, educators need to be aware that some speech and language characteristics from the first language may be carried over into the second language (Brice, 2002).

Language patterns from the first language may influence how one phrases a particular message in the second language. In German, for example, "Ich habe Hunger" means "I'm hungry." A literal translation of the German, however, would be "I have hunger." Thus, a German-speaking student who says "I have hunger" would be manifesting interference from German. In Visayan (a dialect spoken in the Philippines), "Ambot sa iya" translates to "I don't know to you." But a Filipino would use this expression to mean "I don't know—it's completely up to you." A Filipino student who says, "I don't know to you" could easily be diagnosed as abnormal if assessment personnel do not consider the influences of the first language on the learning of a new language.

Ervin-Tripp (1974) stated that interference occurs more often when children are attempting to use complex rather than simple structures in the second language. Thus, a student is more likely to demonstrate interference when using English in a formal setting, such as a testing situation, than on the playground. McLaughlin (1984) stated that when the second language is not the language of the student's social milieu, interference is greater. Thus, when second language learners produce errors in English, it is important to consider the possibility that these errors result from language interference or from the student's limited experience in using English.

Information about the student's first language can sometimes be obtained from a local library or possibly from a local university with a foreign language program. Bilingual paraprofessionals can be of great assistance in helping the professional determine the presence of first language interference. One must be careful, however, that the paraprofessional is familiar with the dialect spoken by the student.

2. Fossilization

Fossilization occurs when specific second language "errors" remain firmly entrenched despite good proficiency in the second language (Pica, 1994). For example, an individual from Cuba was observed to say "the news are that..." This same individual, however, had flawless grammar most of the time. Fossilized items can be idiosyncratic to a child, or can be common within a linguistic community. It is important to conduct a comprehensive evaluation of the student's communicative capabilities rather than focusing on isolated aspects of language that have little effect on communication.

3. Interlanguage

Interlanguage is defined as a separate linguistic system resulting from the learner's attempts to produce the target language (Selinker, 1972). Interlanguage is constantly changing and is developmentally idiosyncratic (Gorbet, 1979). When learning a second language, the learner tests hypotheses about how language works and forms a personal set of rules for using language. The individual's production changes over time as language is experienced in different contexts. Inconsistent errors reflect the progress that the student is making in learning a new language and should not be viewed as evidence of an abnormality.

4. Silent Period

Some students, when learning a second language, go through a *silent period* in which there is much listening/comprehension and little output (Krashen, 1992; Brice, 2002). It is believed that students are learning the rules of the language during this silent period; the silent period can last anywhere from three to six months, although estimates vary. Practitioners might be led to believe that a student has an expressive language delay, when in reality the student's attention is focused on learning the language. Tabors (1997) stated that generally, the younger the child is when exposure to the second language occurs, the longer the silent period lasts. Tabors gave the example of a child who came to the U.S. from Greece when he was 2 years old. His silent period lasted almost 1.6 years. The silent period for elementary school children who began learning a second language at 5 or 6 years old, however, lasted between six and eight weeks.

Profile

Arisbel R., a 3-year-old Spanish-speaking girl, was brought to a local preschool where only English was spoken. According to Arisbel's mother, Arisbel had no problems acquiring Spanish and her Spanish acquisition skills were commensurate with those of her siblings. However, the preschool teachers contacted the local speech-language pathologist after two months because Arisbel "isn't talking and we think she might have a language delay."

After assessing Arisbel in Spanish in both the home and preschool settings, and gathering an extensive case history from Arisbel's parents, the speech-language pathologist concluded that Arisbel was a normal language learner who needed more exposure to English before she began speaking it. The speech-language pathologist explained to the preschool teachers that because Arisbel was so young when she was exposed to a second language, an extended silent period was normal and could be expected. Six months later Arisbel was making functional use of the second language and interacting effectively with the other children in the preschool setting.

5. Code-switching

Alternating between two languages in discourse is commonly observed among bilingual speakers and is not necessarily an indicator of a problem. *Code-switching* is the alternation between two languages within a single constituent, sentence, or discourse. Language alternation within a sentence is also called *code-mixing*. Code-switching/mixing behavior is used by typical, proficient bilingual speakers throughout the world (Langdon & Cheng, 2002). During the early stages of second language learning, the learner may substitute structures, forms, or lexical items from the first language for forms in the second language that have not yet been learned. Bilingual children commonly use code-switching as a strategy, and the use of code-mixing seems to help bridge the two languages that a child is learning (Brice & Anderson, 1999). Although code-switching is a normal communicative behavior, it may occur excessively in situations where an individual lacks competence in one language (Langdon, 1992).

6. Language Loss

If use of the first language decreases, it is common for the learner to lose skills in that language as proficiency is acquired in the second language (Anderson, 1999; Brice, 2002; Schiff-Myers, 1992). Berko-Gleason (1982, p. 13) stated that "language...is a social and interactive skill, and in the absence of a supportive social environment it becomes surprisingly vulnerable." Many LCD children hear and speak only English in the school environment; bilingual education is often nonexistent, especially for students who speak languages that are not spoken by any of the teachers. Since English is the dominant language of society in the United States, children often experience language loss in the first language and a gradual replacement of that language by English (Langdon & Cheng, 2002). This is particularly true for children whose languages have minority status (e.g., those of working class immigrants) or those spoken by people who have limited access to the political and economic institutions of the dominant group (Anderson, 1999).

If a student has experienced language loss and is still acquiring English, the student may appear to be low-functioning in both languages (see Figure 11.1). Based on language test scores, one might be led to conclude that the student has a language learning disability. Differentiating

Figure 11.1
English-Language Learners at Risk

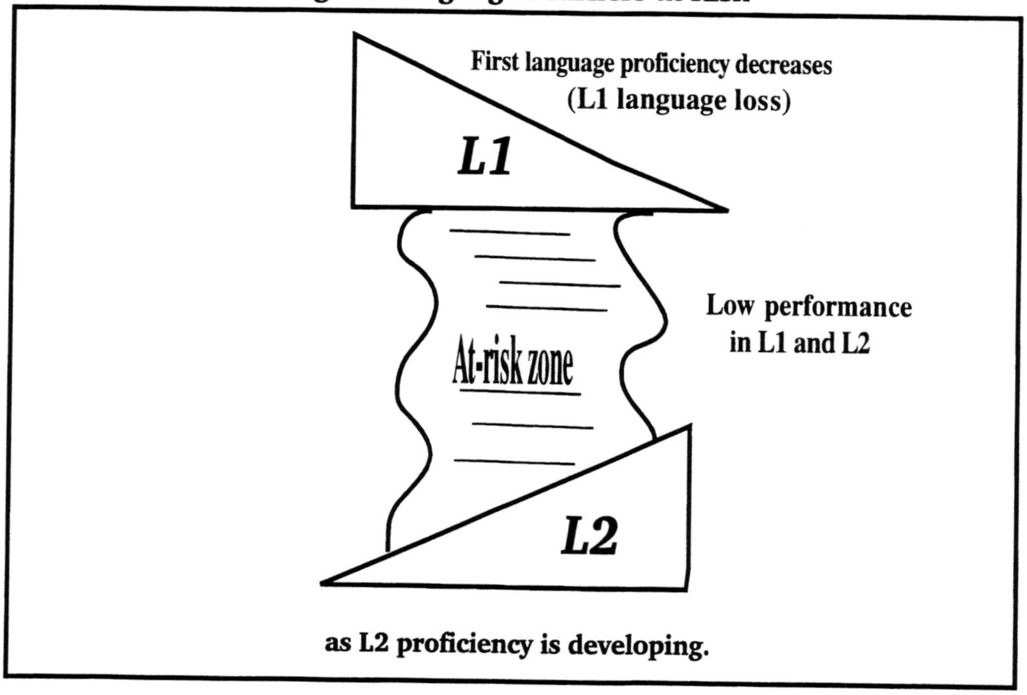

First language proficiency decreases
(L1 language loss)

L1

At-risk zone

Low performance
in L1 and L2

L2

as L2 proficiency is developing.

between language differences and language learning disabilities in a situation where language loss has occurred is challenging.

AFFECTIVE VARIABLES IN SECOND LANGUAGE ACQUISITION

The influence of affective variables in second language acquisition has been documented by many researchers (Cummins, 1988; Hearne, 2000; Langdon, 2000; Schumann, 1986). In this section, these variables are described in terms of their effect on the academic and linguistic performance of culturally diverse students.

1. Motivation

When attempting to determine a student's level of motivation, the following questions can be asked:

A. ***Is the student becoming acculturated into the English language environment?*** *Acculturation* refers to psychological integration with speakers of the second language (Schumann, 1986). Schumann proposes that second language learners acquire the second language to the degree that they acculturate. Thus, if a student is not integrated into situations with English-speaking peers, he or she may not be very motivated to learn English. Some parents of LCD students discourage them from playing and interacting with American English-speaking students. In these cases, motivation to learn English may be quite low. In other situations, peers may discourage a student from learning English.

B. ***How much enclosure exists between the student's culture and the American culture?*** *Enclosure* refers to the degree to which ethnic groups share the same things in life: schools, churches, recreational facilities, professions, leisure activities, etc. If a student comes from an ethnic-linguistic community that has little enclosure or little in common with the dominant English-speaking community, the acquisition of English will usually not take place as rapidly (Schumann, 1986).

C. ***Is there congruence between the student's cultural group and the dominant group?*** The more similar two cultures are, the greater the likelihood that one will experience the social contact necessary for success in learning the second language.

D. ***What are the attitudes of the LCD student group and the dominant group toward one another?*** If the feelings toward one another are positive, second language learning is usually facilitated.

E. ***How long does the LCD student's family intend to stay in the United States? Will the family be going back to the home country?*** In families that plan to remain in the United States, motivation to learn English is often higher than in families that plan to return to their homeland.

F. ***Does the student feel that learning a second language will threaten his or her identity?*** If a student is rejected by family and/or peers for speaking English, motivation will be affected.

2. Personality

Brown (1980) outlined several personality factors and how they relate to second language acquisition.

    A. ***Self-esteem***. The student's feelings and judgments relating to his/her own abilities and worthiness have an effect on second language acquisition. To maximize learning, students need to have a positive self-concept and a positive attitude. The more positive that students feel about themselves, the more rapidly and completely second language acquisition is likely to take place. Students whose first language and culture are rejected may have low self-esteem and consequently learn English more slowly than children whose backgrounds are accepted (Cummins, 1994).

    B. ***Extroversion***. There is some evidence that extroverted students learn English conversational skills faster than introverted students (Wong Fillmore, 1976; Ventriglia, 1982). Shy students may take longer to develop conversational competence than outgoing students.

    C. ***Assertiveness***. Being assertive can be very helpful in facilitating second language learning, as assertive learners avail themselves of increased opportunities for second language practice. If a student is non-assertive, there may be fewer opportunities to practice English skills with native speakers.

3. Anxiety Level

Motivated individuals with a low anxiety level are more readily able to benefit from language input in the second language. Krashen (1992) described such students as having a low affective filter. These students learn better because they are in an environment that is relatively stress-free and accepting.

4. Socioeconomic Status

LCD students who come from a socioeconomic background different from that of most other students in their school may experience difficulty developing friendships with native English speakers and may not interact with them frequently enough to learn a second language.

SECOND LANGUAGE LEARNING STYLES AND STRATEGIES

Students bring a variety of language learning styles and strategies to the second language learning situation. This section delineates learning styles and strategies that might influence students' oral communication.

1. Avoidance

A student may avoid communicating in the second language to avoid ridicule from others. This strategy could result in the student's language *performance* appearing to be inadequate when language *competence* might be adequate. Students don't want to be laughed at when they speak. This may be particularly true of older students who speak English with a pronounced accent.

2. Use of Routines

Routines are phrases such as "Have a good day" that are learned as a whole. Second language learners may use these phrases appropriately, although they may not know the meaning or grammatical function of individual words within the phrases (Ventriglia, 1982). Students who use these memorized phrases are often able to initiate and sustain simple conversation and, therefore, give the false impression that they are fluent speakers of the language.

3. Practice Opportunities

Much of a student's progress in second language acquisition depends on the availability of functional opportunities for second language practice. Some students speak English in the classroom but not in any other contexts. The learning of a second language is likely to be slow if the student makes little use of that language with family and friends outside of the classroom.

Profile

P. B. is a Laotian kindergarten student who came to school speaking only Laotian. The Home Language Survey in her school file indicated that only Laotian was spoken in the home. P. B.'s refugee family came to the United States when P. B. was one year old. When P. B. came to school, she was evaluated with an oral language proficiency test and classified as "non-English speaking." A language dominance test, administered one month later, showed the student to be a "Limited Bilingual," with limited skills in English and Laotian. Laotian was found to be the dominant language.

P. B. was retained in kindergarten. At the end of her second year in kindergarten, she showed little progress in acquiring English skills although she apparently got along quite well in class. Her teachers were not concerned at this point because P. B. was a cooperative child who followed the daily curriculum and was good at art. The teachers did not feel that P. B. was a child with special education needs. Nevertheless, the speech-language pathologist was concerned because P. B.'s basic English conversational skills continued to be quite limited. Pre- and post-testing during the second year of kindergarten revealed little progress in learning English.

P. B. interacted almost exclusively with Laotian-speaking students at school and in her neighborhood. She received no instruction in English. Her parents, monolingual speakers of Laotian, were illiterate and gave her no help with homework.

Is P. B. a potential special education child? Should she undergo special education testing because of her limited progress in acquiring English? This would be an easy conclusion to reach; however, P. B.'s limited opportunities for practice in English must be considered. Since she rarely spoke English inside or outside of the classroom, her opportunities for acquiring English were limited indeed. Should special education testing occur anyway?

The speech-language pathologist felt that P. B.'s limited progress in acquiring English may have resulted from limited experiences in using the English language. The clinician recommended tutoring to develop Laotian language skills and skills in using English. It was also recommended that her oral language proficiency be tested again, following a period of instruction, to assess progress in learning English. Finally, the speech-language pathologist spoke with the site ESL specialist and asked him to monitor P. B. for problems that might be indicative of a disability. Although the possibility of a language learning disability was not ruled out, it was felt that classroom language instruction should be attempted before implementing any type of special education assessment.

4. High vs. Low Input Generators

Students who are *high input generators* avail themselves of many opportunities for language practice. These students are often extroverted and initiate conversations with speakers of the second language. This initiation, in turn, generates an interchange that gives the students increased opportunities to practice communication. *Low input generators*, on the other hand, are usually not assertive, generate few opportunities for language practice, and acquire language skills more slowly than high input generators.

5. Modeling

When conducting assessments, it is important for professionals to familiarize themselves with the student's daily speech and language models. Many professionals have had the experience of assessing a student and subsequently talking with a parent about the child's performance. It is often discovered that the parents' speech and language patterns sound very similar to those of the child! In addition to considering the impact of parents as language models, it is important to consider the influence of siblings, peers, grandparents, baby-sitters, and others in the student's environment. Some students come from extended families in which they spend much time with grandparents or baby-sitters who are not native speakers of English.

Profile

L. M., a first grade boy, was referred for speech-language screening by his first grade teacher. The speech-language pathologist assessed L. M. informally in the classroom setting. The student conversed readily and confided that he wanted to be a pediatrician in the future. Language comprehension appeared to be good. Some morphosyntactic errors were noted during conversation. In addition, L. M. was slightly difficult to understand due to misarticulated speech sounds. The speech-language pathologist reviewed the Home Language Survey in the student's school file. The survey, filled out by his mother, indicated that English was the language used most often by the student and other family members. Because this was the case, the speech-language pathologist felt that L. M. should be formally tested to determine if he was eligible for speech and language intervention.

After receiving information about the proposed assessment, the student's father came to the school and informed the speech-language pathologist that the child's mother spoke several Filipino dialects in the home, although use of these languages was not indicated on the Home Language Survey. The mother was not a proficient English speaker, but she tutored her child in English on a daily basis. The father was from Cuba, spoke rapidly, was difficult to understand, and made frequent grammatical errors in English.

It appeared that L. M.'s speech and language patterns were influenced by the language models available to him in the home. L. M.'s parents did not feel that the child was having difficulty learning language. The student did not appear to be self-conscious about his speech, and his classmates did not make fun of him. Although the student made some expressive errors in English, it was felt that his needs could be met within the classroom language curriculum. The problems did not appear to stem from a disorder and, therefore, placement in special education would not be appropriate.

TYPES OF LANGUAGE PROFICIENCY

Language proficiency is a complex phenomenon that has been defined in a variety of ways. In this section, several models of language proficiency are described. When differentiating between a language difference and a language learning disability, knowledge of what constitutes language proficiency in the two languages is critical.

Separate Underlying Proficiency versus Common Underlying Proficiency

Cummins (1992c) described the Separate Underlying Proficiency (SUP) and the Common Underlying Proficiency (CUP) models. In the SUP model, language proficiency in the first language is entirely separate from proficiency in the second language and, therefore, skills learned in the first language will not transfer to the second language. One implication of this model is that language development activities in the first language will not enhance learning of a second language. Supporters of this viewpoint have often tried to eradicate languages other than English by encouraging students and their families to speak English only. Children who learn English from models who lack proficiency in the language will speak the language as they hear it used in their environment. Supporters of the SUP model believe that exposure to poor language models in English will be more beneficial to the child in developing English language skills than a language environment in which only the first language is used.

There, however, is no evidence to support the SUP model (Cummins, 1988, 1992b). As children learn their first language, they acquire concepts and strategies that will facilitate the learning of a second language. Concepts are acquired through interaction with the environment and the nature of this interaction may vary from culture to culture. High quality exposure enhances the learning of concepts that are important for cognitive and linguistic development (Cummins, 1988; 1989). As children hear and use their native language in a variety of contexts, they develop the conceptual knowledge and cognitive strategies necessary for success in acquiring new information and linguistic skills.

Cummins (1992c) described the CUP model as an alternative to the SUP model (see Figure 11.2). In describing the CUP model, Cummins stated that "...the literacy-related aspects of a bilingual's proficiency in L1 and L2 are seen as common or interdependent across languages...experience with either language can promote development of the proficiency underlying both languages, given adequate motivation and exposure to both either in school or in the wider environment" (Cummins, 1992c, pp. 23-25). This underlying proficiency is that which is involved in cognitively demanding communicative tasks, and it is interdependent across languages (Cummins, 1991b).

The CUP model has major implications for professionals working with LCD children. If a student has had limited exposure and experience in the first language, the conceptual foundation necessary for success in the classroom will be underdeveloped. Cummins (1991a, 1992b) recommended strengthening the foundation in the first language before instruction is attempted in the second language. Negative cognitive consequences may result if efforts are made to switch the child to English before the first language is fully developed (Wong Fillmore, 1993).

Using the second language for instruction when the first language has not yet been fully developed is like building a house on an unstable foundation (see Figure 11.3). By building a solid foundation in the first language, the child acquires concepts and strategies that will facilitate learning another language. By suddenly switching the child to a new language, school professionals deprive students of opportunities to make use of their previously acquired knowledge when confronted with learning situations in the classroom. When children have difficulty relating new experiences to what they already know, learning is a slow process.

Rather than eradicating the first language, efforts should be made to help students become fluent bilingual speakers. By helping students to develop high levels of proficiency in the first and second languages, students may experience growth in various cognitive skills that have been

Figure 11.2

TWO MODELS OF LANGUAGE PROFICIENCY

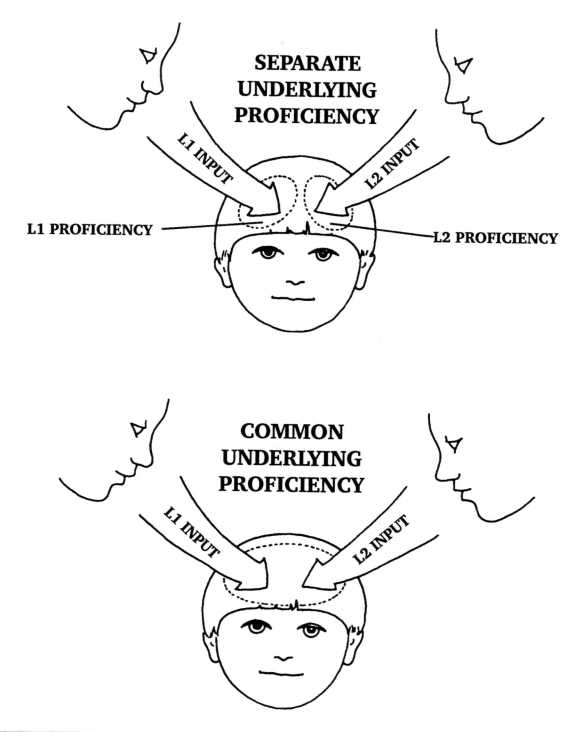

Source: Adapted from Cummins, J. (1992). The role of primary language development in promoting educational success of language minority students. In California State Department of Education, *Schooling and language minority students: A theoretical framework.*

Figure 11.3

Thresholds of Bilingual Development

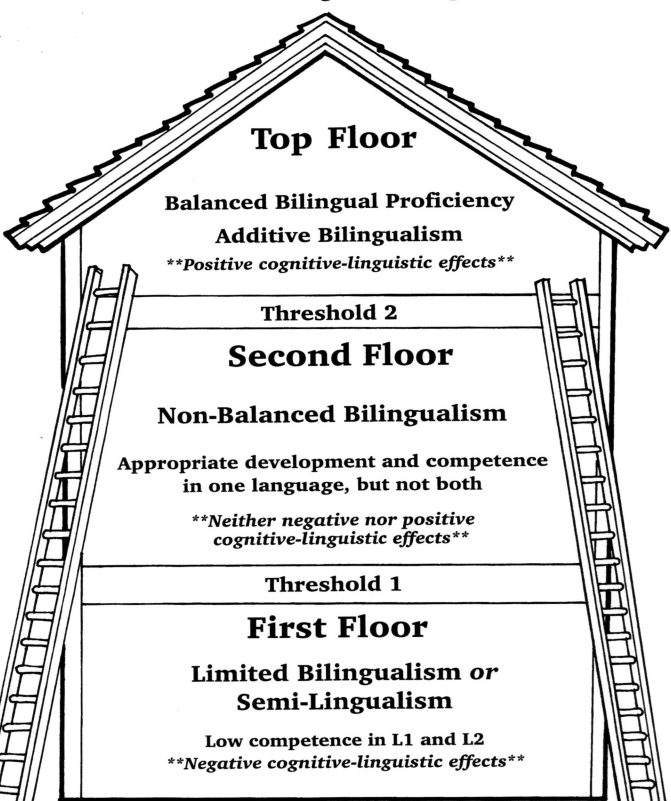

Top Floor

Balanced Bilingual Proficiency

Additive Bilingualism

Positive cognitive-linguistic effects

Threshold 2

Second Floor

Non-Balanced Bilingualism

Appropriate development and competence in one language, but not both

Neither negative nor positive cognitive-linguistic effects

Threshold 1

First Floor

Limited Bilingualism *or* Semi-Lingualism

Low competence in L1 and L2
Negative cognitive-linguistic effects

First Language   *Second Language*

associated with success in school. Children who speak two or more languages fluently have been found to outperform monolingual children in various cognitive and linguistic tasks (Thomas & Collier, 1998). Individuals who are bilingual can also make greater contributions to society. Being a fluent bilingual individual has many advantages (Brice, 2000).

The ramifications for LCD students are clear. If a student is struggling academically or not learning English as rapidly as would be expected, one is likely to suspect that the student needs special education services. However, it can be seen from the above discussion that limited progress in school is often due, at least in part, to weak skills in the first language and lack of opportunities for continued development of skills in that language. Thomas and Collier stated that the average English speaker generally gains 10 months of academic growth in a 10-month school year. Second language learners must show more growth than native speakers by making one and one-half years' progress on academic tests in English for six successive school years. Thus, in order to perform at a level commensurate with that of native speakers, ESL learners must make nine years progress in six years. It is no wonder that schools create deficits in students that are not related to language-learning disabilities, but rather to an educational system that does not even begin to adequately meet the needs of students who are learning English as a second language.

Cummins (1988, 1992a) reported that there is a strong correlation between reading skills in the first and second language; the better the reading skills in the first language, the better will be the reading skills in the second language. Also, the student who does not read in the first language at all is likely to have a more difficult time reading in English than the student who reads fluently in the first language (Ramirez, Yuen, & Ramey, 1991).

Additive and Subtractive Bilingualism

Additive bilingualism occurs when both languages spoken by the student are reinforced, resulting in high levels of proficiency in the two languages. The student's first language continues to be nurtured and encouraged as the child learns the second language. The goal is to help the student become a fluent and balanced bilingual speaker. By becoming fully bilingual, individuals develop high level metalinguistic skills, enhance their employability, and increase their potential for making valuable contributions to society. In today's global economy, bilingualism is a great asset. In many parts of the world, multilingual individuals are considered educated and cosmopolitan.

What occurs much more frequently is *subtractive bilingualism*, a phenomenon in which the student's first language is replaced by the second language (Lambert & Tucker, 1972). In this situation, language loss in the first language occurs, and the student gradually becomes a monolingual speaker of English or the majority language. However, if English skills continue to be considerably below those of their monolingual peers, the student's cognitive and linguistic growth is likely to be negatively affected (Brice, 2002).

LCD students who struggle academically and linguistically from year to year are often those who have experienced subtractive bilingualism, consequent negative cognitive effects, and are left with a reduced conceptual foundation on which to build academic and linguistic skills. These students do not have "disabilities" and, therefore, are not appropriate candidates for special education. Instructional activities that build conceptual knowledge in the first language can help students with limited proficiency in English acquire cognitive strategies that will facilitate learning English and functioning effectively in the classroom learning environment. These students also need comprehensible second language input and interactive experiences that promote functional use of English (Roseberry-McKibbin, 2002).

REFLECTION

Compare and contrast the SUP and CUP theories. What effects might widespread implementation of programs based on the SUP theory have within school districts? How can professionals help school districts subscribe to and implement the CUP theory instead?

_____

_____

_____

_____

DEVELOPING BILINGUAL LANGUAGE PROFICIENCY

Ideally, students with limited proficiency in the language of the school should participate in bilingual education throughout the elementary years and beyond if possible (Cummins, 1992b; Ramirez, Yuen, & Ramey, 1991). Such instruction provides students with culturally appropriate learning experiences, opportunities for continued use of the first language, and experiences designed to promote the learning and effective use of a second language. Programs of bilingual education appear to promote the greatest linguistic, cultural, and cognitive benefits when there is active parent and community involvement. Some European countries are even promoting a policy of trilingualism in their schools (Beardsmore, 1993).

Most professionals are aware that the optimal situation of "maintenance bilingual education" rarely exists in school in the United States. Some U.S. citizens have a negative attitude toward bilingualism and believe that being bilingual has negative cognitive and social effects on children. Malakoff & Hakuta (1991, p. 141) described the monolingual-norm assumption—the belief that monolingualism is the cognitive-linguistic norm and that the child's cognitive system is fragile and only designed to cope with one language. The monolingual-norm assumption gave rise to the negative myths surrounding bilingualism—bilingualism has been blamed for cognitive, social, and emotional damage to children.

Bilingual programs in the schools are often transitional programs wherein the first language is used to teach academic subjects, but an emphasis is placed on transitioning the student into English as quickly as possible. Some schools have Sheltered English classrooms, where an effort is made to teach subject matter using English that is comprehensible to the students. Some school programs do not have ESL (English as a second language) services at all. Thus, the problem becomes one of determining how to best educate linguistically and culturally diverse students when the staff and resources needed for instruction in the first language are limited or perhaps even nonexistent.

BICS AND CALP

A second model of language proficiency that is useful in working with linguistically and culturally diverse children distinguishes *Basic Interpersonal Communication Skills* (BICS) from *Cognitive Academic Language Proficiency* (CALP) (see Figure 11.4). According to Cummins (1992c), BICS take approximately two years (in an ideal situation) to develop to a level commensurate with that of native speakers of the language; CALP takes between five and seven years to develop to a native-like level). This 5-7 year time frame is common for students from enriched backgrounds. Some researchers are even maintaining that it can take between seven and ten years for CALP to develop to a native-like level under less than optimal conditions (Peregoy & Boyle, 1997).

Figure 11.4

LENGTH OF TIME REQUIRED TO ACHIEVE AGE-APPROPRIATE LEVELS OF CONTEXT-EMBEDDED AND CONTEXT-REDUCED COMMUNICATIVE PROFICIENCY

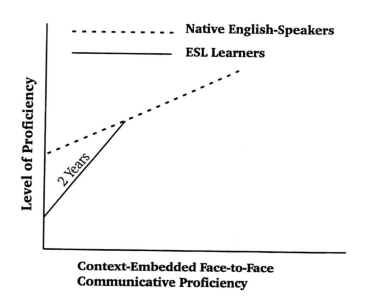

Context-Embedded Face-to-Face Communicative Proficiency

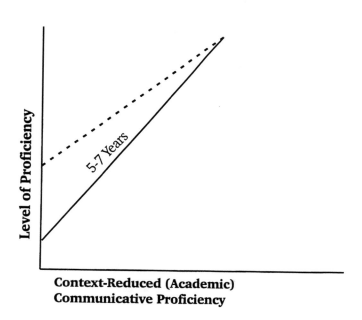

Context-Reduced (Academic) Communicative Proficiency

Source: Cummins, J. (1992). The role of primary language development in promoting educational success of language minority students. In California State Department of Education, *Schooling and language minority students: A theoretical framework.* Reprinted with permission.

In cross-sectional studies conducted in the United States, it was found that students took between three and six years to perform at the 50th percentile in English in academic areas. The students, in all cases, received instruction in both languages in equal proportion (see Langdon, 1992). One can conclude from these results that if the students in these studies took between three and six years to achieve at the 50th percentile after being in bilingual programs, how much longer might it take for children who are placed in monolingual English-speaking programs?

The Basic Interpersonal Communication Skills involve cognitively undemanding, context-embedded forms of communication. Cognitive Academic Language Proficiency refers to cognitively demanding, context-reduced forms of communication (see Figure 11.5). In context-embedded communication, participants have a shared reality and can actively negotiate meaning. Context-embedded communication is typical of that found in the everyday world outside the classroom, where language is supported by a wide range of meaningful situational cues and paralinguistic gestures. For example, in a discussion about a field trip, there is a shared reality and participants can negotiate meaning with one another. Gestures and facial expressions facilitate the communication of meaning in this context-embedded situation. Context-reduced communication, on the other hand, does not assume a shared reality. It may rely exclusively on linguistic cues for meaning (Cummins, 1992c; Hatch, 1992).

Cognitive involvement refers to the amount of information that needs to be processed simultaneously or in close succession by a student in order to do an activity (Cummins, 1992c). Cognitively undemanding tasks are those that are generally automatized and require little active cognitive involvement for adequate performance. For instance, a cognitively undemanding task for most people is to state their name, address, and phone number when asked for this information. Cognitively demanding tasks, however, involve situations in which knowledge is not automatized and the person must make use of various cognitive strategies to perform the task. For example, writing an essay in a foreign language is cognitively demanding for a student who has not yet mastered that language.

Thus, when professionals are assessing a student because of a suspected language learning disability, it is important to examine the school environment. Is the student in a classroom situation where cognitively demanding tasks are presented regularly? How much contextual information is available to facilitate comprehension? If the student has not yet had opportunities to develop the cognitive strategies necessary to perform context-reduced classroom activities, educational professionals need to be aware of this fact. Students will struggle if they have not yet acquired the cognitive academic skills necessary to complete classroom assignments.

Professionals in the United States who work with culturally and linguistically diverse students in public schools know that these students are often placed into submersion or sink-or-swim classrooms where only English is spoken and no special provisions are made to help students learn the English they need for school. Students who speak no English are often expected to learn English in the classroom setting where the linguistic input is often context-reduced and cognitively demanding. Because a student's initial exposure to English is often of this nature, many students fail to acquire a solid conceptual foundation and end up struggling academically. The acquisition of CALP is difficult if the student's primary exposure to the language occurs within situations in which contextual cues are limited. Helping students to develop a basic conceptual foundation is critical if students are to acquire the strategies necessary for academic success.

Many English proficiency tests administered in school evaluate only BICS. The student may be asked to respond to simple questions such as, "What do you like to watch on TV?" A problem occurs when professionals use the results to determine whether or not the student has the language skills necessary to function appropriately in an English-only program of academic instruction. Another related problem is that many professionals administer English tests to "English Proficient" students, believing that a label of "English Proficient" based on English proficiency tests means that the students have the language skills necessary to perform adequately on tests standardized

Figure 11.5
ILLUSTRATION OF CUMMINS' GRID OF COGNITIVE DEMANDS

Cognitively Undemanding

A

Asking permission to go to the rest room

Following directions to line up for recess

Participating in various art, physical education, and music activities

Discussing a class field trip

BICS

B

Talking on the phone

Following written instructions without an illustration

Listing categorical items (e.g., "Tell me all of the fruits you can think of.")

CALP

C
Context-Embedded

Projects and hands-on activities

Basic math computations

Lab experiments and demonstrations

Lessons using visuals (e.g., charts, overheads)

BICS

D
Context Reduced

Algebra

Teacher lectures

Most textbooks

Standardized tests (Special education)

Statewide achievement tests

CALP

Cognitively Demanding

on monolingual, English-speaking children. A student who is identified as English Language Proficient based on BICS-type language proficiency measures can easily be misdiagnosed as having a language learning disability if CALP has not been fully developed. When assessing language proficiency, it is important to assess performance on the types of language tasks that are used in the classroom setting.

When professionals make judgments about overall proficiency in English based on a student's performance in face-to-face communication situations, they risk the possibility of creating academic deficits in these students (Cummins, 1992c) (see Figure 11.6). It is important to keep in mind that skill in BICS is acquired in about two years, but CALP takes much longer.

Profile

P. S., a male student from India, was referred to the Student Study Team by his teacher because of problems in reading and math. The teacher reported that the child had good receptive and expressive language skills. P. S. was described as cooperative, courteous, and helpful, and he frequently asked questions when he did not understand classroom assignments. Areas of concern included sight word vocabulary, knowledge of phonics, basic word attack skills, sentence structure, written expression, spelling, and math concepts. P. S. was able to do well in math when manipulatives were used, and was ahead of some of his classmates in math manipulative skills. When the speech-language pathologist asked about the student's language background, no one on the team was able to provide this information. The speech-language pathologist left the meeting briefly to check the student's school records. A review of the Home Language Survey revealed that Hindu was the primary language of the home and the language used most often by P. S. The student had been exposed to English for 2.5 years, but spoke only his native language when he entered kindergarten. The speech-language pathologist brought this information back to the Student Study Team.

Team members told the teacher about the CALP versus BICS distinction. Rather than testing the student for special education, it was concluded that he should receive increased tutoring in the first language and increased ESL support.

In looking at the student's profile, it was clear that he had mastered the basic interpersonal communication skills. He, however, was having difficulty with the context-reduced, cognitively demanding aspects of English academics. This is very typical of children who enter kindergarten speaking only their first language. Thus, this case illustrates the need for utilizing language proficiency models when attempting to determine the cause of a child's difficulties in the classroom. The case of P. S. also underscores the great importance of taking the time to gather information about children's language backgrounds. The speech-language pathologist was able to obtain this information in five minutes. If that five minutes had not been spent, the student might have been inappropriately placed into special education.

THE IMPORTANCE OF COMPREHENSIBLE INPUT

The extent to which children experience success in learning is influenced by their past experiences. The more experiences that students have had, the more they will learn (see Figure 11.7). It is important to provide second language learners with comprehensible input in the second language (Krashen, 1992). Krashen (1993) proposed that people acquire language structure by understanding messages and that the learner's focus is the function of the utterance rather than

Figure 11.6

LANGUAGE PROFICIENCY MISDIAGNOSIS MODEL

ADEQUATE BICS

BICS takes approximately 2 years to develop to native-like level under optimal conditions.

The child can:

* Use English phrases, chunks
* Carry on intelligible conversations about context-embedded, cognitively undemanding topics (e.g., TV, classroom activities, friends, family)
* Interact with English-speaking peers
* Pass simple, "BICS-oriented" language proficiency tests

Appropriate diagnosis → BILINGUAL EDUCATION, SHELTERED ENGLISH, ESL

Inappropriate diagnosis ← - BICS/CALP GAP

INADEQUATE CALP

CALP takes between 5 and 7 years to develop to native-like level under optimal conditions.

The child with developing CALP may have difficulty:

* performing well on standardized tests of academic skills (state school tests)
* performing well on standardized IQ, academic, and language tests that would be administered by psychologists, speech pathologists, resource specialists
* performing adequately in context-reduced, cognitively demanding classroom activities such as writing, reading, spelling, test-taking

SPECIAL EDUCATION REFERRAL

SPECIAL EDUCATION PLACEMENT:

* resource room
* speech/language program
* special day class

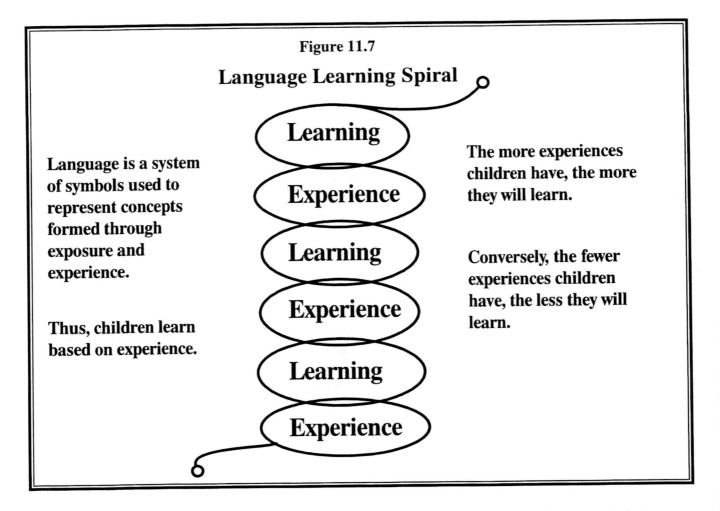

Figure 11.7

Language Learning Spiral

Language is a system of symbols used to represent concepts formed through exposure and experience.

Thus, children learn based on experience.

The more experiences children have, the more they will learn.

Conversely, the fewer experiences children have, the less they will learn.

the form. According to Krashen, optimal comprehensible input in the second language includes the following:

1. It includes "*i + 1 input*" that is slightly above the learner's current level, but comprehensible enough to be mostly understood.

2. Concrete referents are available (e.g., extra-linguistic aids such as visuals, hands-on materials, etc.)

3. It is interesting, meaningful, and relevant to the learner.

4. It occurs naturally and the learner has practice opportunities in natural, conversational, everyday situations that are communicatively meaningful.

5. It is not grammatically sequenced, but rather occurs naturally.

6. There are sufficient quantities of this input to ensure optimal learning.

The comprehensible input hypothesis runs counter to the traditional language teaching approach in which language structures are taught first. Krashen (1992) stated that language is acquired best by aiming first for meaning. Language structures develop as the student gains proficiency in using language for specific purposes to communicate meaning. Success in acquiring a second language requires that comprehensible input be provided frequently in situations where language is used for a purpose.

While Krashen's idea regarding comprehensible input makes sense, several researchers have criticized his claim that comprehensible input alone is sufficient for optimal second language acquisition. Selinker (1986, personal communication) argued that there is no evidence that understanding input will effect positive changes in a language learner's second language output. Larsen-Freeman (1985) stated that, at least in terms of expressive grammatical competence, no quantity of comprehensible input may be enough. Swain (1985) stated that while comprehensible input may be essential to second language acquisition, it is not enough to ensure that the outcome will be native-like performance. According to Swain, comprehensible output is a necessary mechanism of successful second language acquisition; she argued that second language learners must engage in interactions in which meaning is negotiated. This interaction gives the learners necessary practice in production of the second language, not just in passive reception of comprehensible input. Second language learners must be active agents in their environment in terms of language output.

The necessity of comprehensible output can further be explained using the ZPD theory of development proposed by Vygotsky (1962). Vygotsky defined the ZPD as the distance between a child's actual level of development as determined by independent problem solving and the individual's potential level of development through problem solving, either in collaboration with more capable peers or with guidance from an adult. Proponents of this theory maintain that children will show growth when they interact with others and when information is provided for them. This interaction and provision of information helps children learn more and helps them advance to a higher level of learning.

Thus, when linguistically and culturally diverse students appear to be having academic and/or linguistic difficulty, professionals can ask if the classroom language input is comprehensible to the students. If not, the student's difficulties may stem directly from a lack of comprehension. Professionals can also ask if there are adequate comprehensible output situations available to the student.

✐ *REFLECTION* ✐

Define "comprehensible input." Why is comprehensible input so important for LCD students? What happens when they do not receive comprehensible input in the classroom?

_____

_____

_____

_____

_____

_____

SIMULTANEOUS VERSUS SEQUENTIAL BILINGUALISM

Researchers have broadly delineated two types of bilingualism: *simultaneous* and *sequential*. *Simultaneous acquisition* occurs when two languages are acquired simultaneously from infancy.

When two languages are spoken to children beginning in early infancy, the phenomenon of *infant bilinguality* occurs (Schiff-Myers, 1992). The bilingual development observed in these children closely parallels monolingual development (Dulay et al., 1982; Gorbet, 1979; McLaughlin, 1984). Simultaneous acquisition has also been defined as the acquisition of two languages before age 3. McLaughlin stated that children initially appear to work from a single set of rules and go through a stage of language mixing, but eventually the two sets of rules become differentiated. Children who acquire two languages simultaneously in naturalistic situations seem to do so with minimal interference (Genesee, 1988; Kessler, 1984). If the situation is one of additive bilingualism, children experience cognitive-linguistic and social benefits. Simultaneous acquisition results in equivalent levels of language proficiency in both languages more often than does sequential acquisition (Bliss, 2001).

Students who experience *sequential acquisition* of the second language show greater diversity in rates and stages of acquisition (Kayser, 2002; Langdon, 1992). Researchers generally believe that similar developmental sequences occur in both first- and second-language learners of a target language (Felix, 1978; Mace-Matluck, 1971; Prakash, 1984). Although some students may acquire the second language with minimal interference, others may experience difficulties. If a student is introduced to a second language before the first language threshold has been reached, the development of the first language may be arrested or may regress while the child is focused on the learning of a second language (Schiff-Myers, 1992). Since, as Cummins (1988, 1992b) has stated, proficiency in the second language is partially a function of competence in the first language, a condition of semilingualism may occur in which the student does not fully develop either language. Schiff-Myers pointed out that for a period of time, these students may obtain low test scores in both languages and consequently appear language-learning disabled. Furthermore, students from low socioeconomic backgrounds who have had little experience with decontextualized language may have difficulty learning a new language readily.

Thus, when professionals are working with linguistically and culturally diverse students in the schools, it is necessary when a student appears "low functioning" to find out if language development occurred simultaneously or sequentially. If languages were acquired sequentially, what was the effect of second language acquisition on the development of proficiency in the first language? Did the children develop a high enough level of language proficiency in the primary language to respond to the cognitive demands of the classroom? If the student was "switched" to English before acquiring these cognitive abilities, it is likely that many classroom tasks will be difficult. Moreover, students who have had limited exposure to decontextualized language in the home are often at risk for academic difficulties (Weiner, 2001).

CONCLUSION

When professionals evaluate linguistic, intellectual, and academic performance, they must take into account factors relating to second language acquisition and bilingual development. In many cases, errors in judgment and the consequent inappropriate placement of students in special education programs can be avoided. The greater the understanding that professionals have of normal second language learning and bilingualism, the more unbiased and appropriate will be the services provided to culturally and linguistically diverse students in the schools.

STUDY QUESTIONS

1. Describe three affective variables that are critical in second language acquisition.

2. Define the terms *simultaneous acquisition* and *sequential acquisition*. Will the child who is a simultaneous language learner or the child who is a sequential language learner be more likely to experience difficulty in the classroom? Why?

3. Discuss the negative myths about bilingualism in the U.S. How have these negative myths impacted actual practice in U.S. school systems?

TRUE-FALSE

Circle the number beside each statement that is true.

4. Code-switching is generally a sign of linguistic confusion and is thus frequently indicative of a language-learning disability.
5. The younger the child is when first exposed to the second language, the longer the silent period typically lasts.
6. Enclosure refers to the degree to which ethnic groups share the same things in life.
7. Most Europeans believe that it is better to be monolingual rather than bilingual.
8. Proficient bilinguals frequently outperform monolinguals on tests of metalinguistic skill.
9. Students with a high affective filter can be described as motivated individuals with a low anxiety level who are readily able to benefit from language input in the second language.
10. The term "interlanguage" refers to a phenomenon in which specific second language "errors" remain firmly entrenched despite good proficiency in the second language.

MULTIPLE CHOICE

Circle the letter beside each choice that is correct.

11. Which term refers to a process in which a communicative behavior or structure from the first language is carried over inappropriately into the second language?
    A. fossilization
    B. interference/transfer
    C. interlanguage
    D. silent period
    E. enclosure

12. Which of the following statements are TRUE?
    A. Under optimal conditions, the development of BICS to a native-like proficiency level takes

approximately two years for second language learners.
B. Under optimal conditions, the development of CALP to a native-like proficiency level takes approximately three to four years.
C. BICS involves cognitively undemanding, context-embedded forms of communication.
D. CALP refers to the cognitively demanding, context-reduced forms of communication.
E. Most English language proficiency tests assess CALP.

13. Which one of the following is NOT a feature of comprehensible input according to Krashen?
A. The input is slightly below the learner's current level, making it comprehensible enough to be mostly understood.
B. Concrete referents are available (e.g., visuals).
C. It is not grammatically sequenced, but rather occurs naturally.
D. It is interesting, meaningful, and relevant to the learner.
E. There are sufficient quantities of this input to ensure optimal learning.

14. For children who are learning two languages, which of the following are true?
A. It is ideal to learn both languages from infancy.
B. A strong first language base contributes positively to learning the second language adequately.
C. Students who do not learn either L1 or L2 adequately often face a state of semilingualism which leads to negative cognitive effects.
D. Bilingualism almost always has detrimental effects whenever two languages are learned simultaneously.

15. Francisco L., a 5-year-old Spanish-speaking boy, has just entered an all-English kindergarten classroom. He has lived his whole life in a trailer with his parents, grandparents, and six siblings. Francisco has never been to preschool, and his parents are migrant workers who are non-literate in both Spanish and English. Following three months of kindergarten, the teacher refers Francisco for a special education evaluation because she thinks he may have a language-learning disability. The student speaks occasionally in class and has friends, but he is having difficulty with writing, spelling, and math. What would be the best course of action for the special education team to take?
A. Use English special education tests because Francisco is in an all-English-speaking school and he will eventually need to perform at the same level as his English-speaking peers.
B. Test Francisco in both Spanish and English using BICS- and CALP-oriented special education tests.
C. Assess Francisco's level of proficiency in both English and Spanish, provide him with ESL services in Spanish, assign a Spanish-speaking aide to the classroom to assist him, and re-evaluate him in a year to assess progress.
D. Do not assess Francisco in any way at this time because his limited language exposure will invalidate any tests that are given.
E. Place Francisco in special education so that he can receive an individualized program of English language instruction that targets the conceptual skills necessary for success in the general education curriculum.

ANSWERS TO STUDY QUESTIONS

4. False	11. B
5. True	12. A, C, D
6. True	13. A
7. False	14. A, B, C
8. True	15. C
9. False	
10. True	

Chapter 12

INTRODUCTION TO ASSESSMENT: FOUNDATIONAL PRINCIPLES

Outline

THE DIAGNOSTIC CHALLENGE

When assessment personnel are confronted with linguistically and culturally diverse students who appear to be struggling in school, the first question that they usually ask is: "Does this student have a language difference or a language disorder?" Language differences are behaviors commonly observed among second language learners. Differences in sentence structure, speech sound production, vocabulary, and the pragmatic uses of language are to be expected when a child learns a new language. Unfortunately, children with language differences that result from limited experience in using a language are often misidentified as "language disordered" (Roseberry-McKibbin, 1995). The "language disorder" diagnosis is appropriate only for students with disabilities affecting their underlying ability to learn any language.

Distinguishing a language difference from a language disorder is often a challenge. In this chapter and the one that follows, strategies are presented for identifying language disorders in multicultural populations.

Bloom and Lahey (1978) defined language as a system of symbols that is used to represent concepts formed through exposure and experience. Exposure and experience are critical for success in acquiring a language. Children must hear the language and must be provided with experience in using it. Language can be experienced through oral communication or through literacy experiences. Teachers typically assume that students entering school have had opportunities to listen to stories, to explore books, to cut with scissors, to color pictures with crayons, and to use language for a variety of purposes. It is assumed that children have been taken to stores, parks, zoos, libraries, and other places in the community.

Some students come from backgrounds where they have had all of these experiences. Children who immigrate to the United States may have traveled to a variety of countries and may speak and write in several languages. These students have much to share about their cultural backgrounds and their experiences when they interact with mainstream American students in the school setting.

Other students, however, have had limited experiences with books and limited opportunities for language enrichment. These students and their families may be non-literate for one or more reasons. Perhaps family members have not had the opportunity to attend school or their experience in school is limited. There are some students who come from backgrounds in which there is no written form of the language. In the Netherlands, for example, some students from isolated areas speak Berber languages that do not have a tradition of literacy. These students struggle in school. Some Native American groups and speakers of Haitian Creole have predominantly oral traditions with no formal written language.

When "problems" observed in school result from differences in the student's experiences and the school's expectations, educational professionals may assume that there is something inherently wrong with the student. In assessment, an emphasis is often placed on searching for a disability to "explain" the problem. Disabilities are often "created" for students who, in reality, need greater exposure and experience to meet the demands of the classroom curriculum.

If a student's background experiences are different from those of most other children in the school system, he or she may exhibit language behaviors that stand out as being "different." The student may not be learning because of lack of exposure to new experiences or to experiences that are not commensurate with what the school expects. If the expectations of school professionals do not consider what the student has experienced in the past, misdiagnosis may occur and this misdiagnosis may result in an inappropriate special education placement.

The "diagnostic pie" in Figure 12.1 is a simple conceptual framework that assessment personnel can use to distinguish language differences from language disorders in bilingual students who are learning English as a second language. The importance of considering the child's language experiences is critical in evaluating language proficiency.

Figure 12.1

DIAGNOSTIC "PIE"

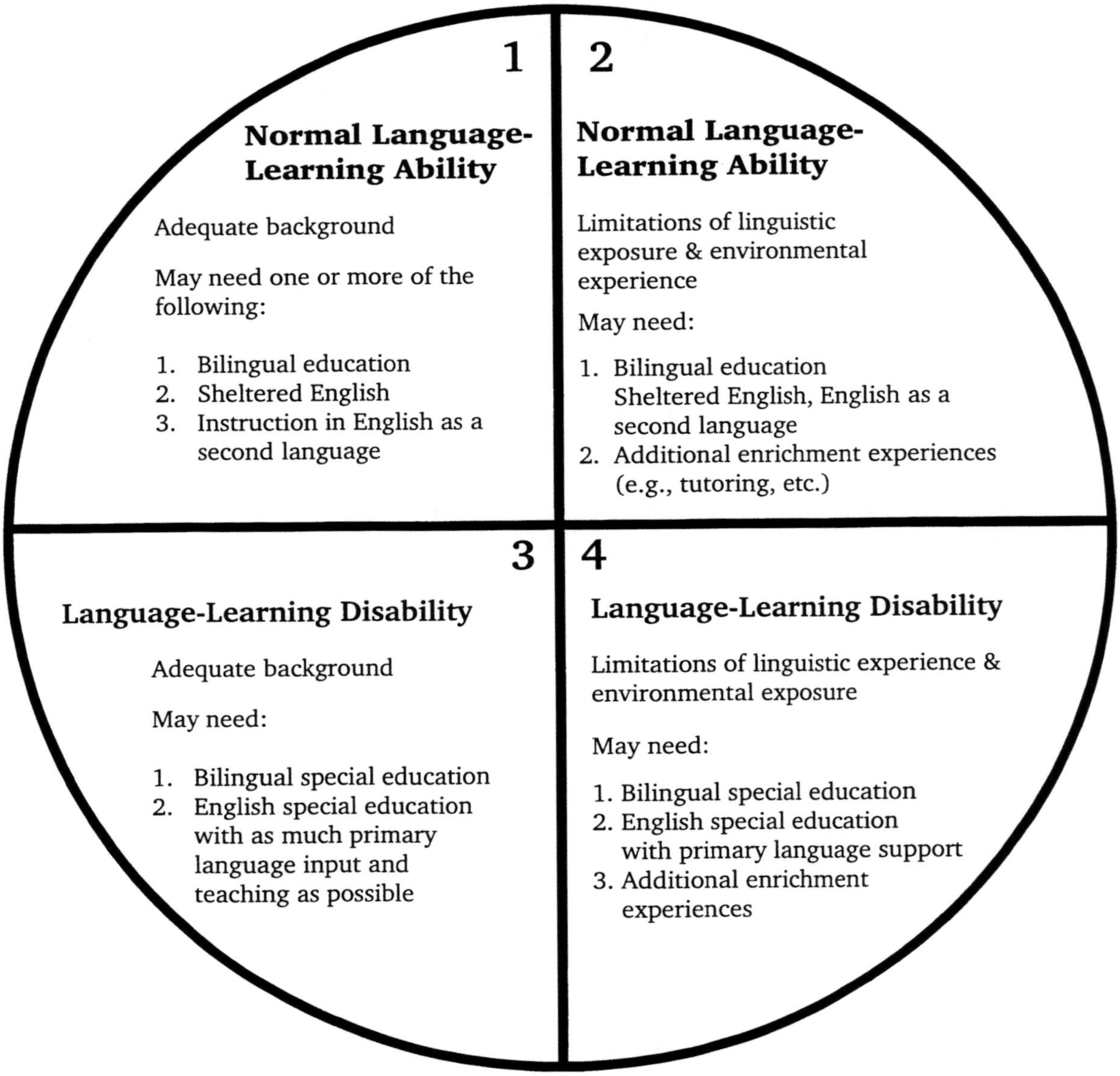

1 — Normal Language-Learning Ability

Adequate background

May need one or more of the following:

1. Bilingual education
2. Sheltered English
3. Instruction in English as a second language

2 — Normal Language-Learning Ability

Limitations of linguistic exposure & environmental experience

May need:

1. Bilingual education
   Sheltered English, English as a second language
2. Additional enrichment experiences (e.g., tutoring, etc.)

3 — Language-Learning Disability

Adequate background

May need:

1. Bilingual special education
2. English special education with as much primary language input and teaching as possible

4 — Language-Learning Disability

Limitations of linguistic experience & environmental exposure

May need:

1. Bilingual special education
2. English special education with primary language support
3. Additional enrichment experiences

QUADRANT 1

Students who fall into this quadrant of the pie have no abnormalities in their ability to learn language. They come from backgrounds that may be rich in stimulation and general experiences, but their experiences have not been consistent with expectations in mainstream U.S. schools. These students generally have the conceptual foundation necessary for academic success. The needs of these students can usually be served best in bilingual classrooms that provide opportunities for language development both in English and in the primary language.

If bilingual education is not available, these students can benefit from Sheltered English (academic content taught in English that is comprehensible) or, barring this, a program that teaches English as a second language (ESL). Again, if these students are given time, attention, and support, they will generally succeed in school.

QUADRANT 2

These students have normal language learning abilities. However, they come from backgrounds where they may have experienced some limitations in environmental stimulation and linguistic exposure. Society may have placed them and their families in an economically disadvantageous situation. This author has worked with many children from this type of background. The students have the ability to learn, but life circumstances have curtailed their opportunities to learn and their experiences prior to entering school.

These students often do poorly on standardized tests that are based on mainstream, middle-class expectations. If these students have not had the experiences necessary to perform well on tests, they may appear to be "language disordered."

Students in Quadrant 2 are likely to make adequate progress in school if they receive enough input, exposure, and stimulation. Bilingual education, ESL, and/or Sheltered English programs may be effective because they enhance skills in both the primary language and English. Unfortunately, these students are sometimes placed into special education programs. Special education programs for language intervention are inappropriate for students whose underlying language-learning ability is intact (Roseberry-McKibbin, 1995).

QUADRANT 3

Students in Quadrant 3 come from backgrounds in which they have had adequate exposure and language stimulation. The life experiences of some of these students are consistent with those expected in mainstream schools. Often, parents have given these students as much help as possible in the home, and the students still do not succeed in school. Other students may not have had life experiences and opportunities that are commensurate with school expectations. However, the school has provided much additional help and support over time to assist these students in developing academic skills (e.g., tutoring, ESL programs). Despite the fact that school personnel have provided supplemental activities within the regular education curriculum in an effort to stimulate academic growth, the students continue to acquire new information more slowly than peers from similar cultural and linguistic backgrounds, and continue to manifest learning difficulties. Students with these characteristics have underlying language-learning disabilities that prevent them from learning and using any language adequately, despite backgrounds that have provided opportunities for appropriate environmental and linguistic stimulation. These students need to receive special education services so that their unique disabilities can be appropriately addressed by personnel with specialized training. Opportunities for instruction in the primary language should be provided, if possible, so that the child can make use of his or her previously acquired knowledge to learn new information.

> ## Profile
>
> Tanveer D., a sixth-grade speaker of Urdu from a Pakistani family, was referred for special education assessment. His teacher was especially concerned about his written language skills. His parents, who did not speak English, were unable to assist Tanveer with his homework. Thus, the school had provided Tanveer with an Urdu tutor who had worked with him weekly on an individual basis for two years. Tanveer had participated in the school's Homework Club, an after-school program for students who needed extra academic support. In addition, Tanveer had attended Reading Clinic (a non-special education program to provide reading support for struggling students) for the last year. Despite this extra support, Tanveer was unable to recite the alphabet and could not identify simple printed words such as "cat" and "the." The other Urdu-speaking students in the school had surpassed Tanveer academically, and the Urdu interpreter confided that Tanveer was "much lower than other Urdu students I have worked with in this district."
>
> Extensive testing revealed evidence of a language-learning disability affecting both Urdu and English, as well as a clinically significant reading disability. Tanveer was placed in special education so that he could receive the necessary services to address the disability that was negatively affecting learning in both languages.

QUADRANT 4

Students in Quadrant 4 come from backgrounds in which there are known limitations in experiences that may be contributing to problems identified in the school setting. These children, however, also have problems learning new language skills. When assessing these students, it is difficult to determine whether the students' low test scores are due to background/environment, an underlying disability, or both. Most professionals wrestle with the issue of whether to place these students into Quadrant 2 or Quadrant 4. Determining why a child is not performing well in the classroom is difficult. Children, however, should not be considered to have a "disability" if their needs can be met by providing a culturally and linguistically appropriate program of instruction in the regular classroom.

Students in Quadrant 4 ideally need bilingual special education with additional enrichment activities to compensate for limited learning opportunities in their environments. Students in Quadrant 4 should be provided with opportunities for support in the primary language to the maximum extent possible. They can also benefit from participating in whatever additional enrichment experiences are available.

How do assessment personnel know which section of the "diagnostic pie" the student falls into? Examining the child's background is critical. Professionals must also look at the effects of second language acquisition and bilingualism on the student's performance. Understanding the processes of second language acquisition and the nature of bilingualism will help educational professionals assess students in a nonbiased manner. Then, professionals must understand what constitutes a language-learning disability in a linguistically and culturally diverse (LCD) student, and must be familiar with laws governing the assessment of these students. If professionals use standardized tests to assess LCD students, they must be familiar with the biases and limitations inherent in these measures. Professionals must also understand the importance of going through a pre-evaluation process that includes the classroom teacher's evaluation, the gathering of a case history, and the determination of the student's primary language, dominant language, and level of proficiency in each language (Brice & Roseberry-McKibbin, 1999).

DEFINITION OF LANGUAGE-LEARNING DISABILITY

Students should not be considered to have language learning disabilities if "problems" are observed only in the English language. If the student is truly language-disordered, problems in communication should be evident in BOTH ENGLISH AND THE PRIMARY LANGUAGE. A language disorder is a disability that affects the child's ability to learn any language. Exposure to two languages is not the cause of the disability. Bilingual children with language disorders will have difficulty learning English, Spanish, or any other language.

Students who speak a language other than English should never be diagnosed as language-learning disabled based solely on results obtained from tests administered in English. Information about language functioning in both the primary language and English should be obtained before educational decisions are made.

POSSIBLE INDICATORS OF A LANGUAGE-LEARNING DISABILITY

Culturally and linguistically diverse students with language-learning disabilities demonstrate problems in both the primary language and English. These problems may be observed in the following areas:

1. Difficulty in learning language at a normal rate, even with special assistance in both languages
2. Deficits in vocabulary
3. Short mean length of utterance
4. Communication difficulties at home
5. Communication difficulties when interacting with peers from a similar background
6. Auditory processing problems (e.g., poor memory, poor comprehension)
7. Lack of organization, structure, and sequence in spoken and written language; difficulty conveying thoughts
8. Slow academic achievement despite adequate academic English proficiency
9. Family history of special education/learning difficulties
10. Slower development than siblings (as per parent report)
11. Reliance on gestures rather than speech to communicate
12. Inordinate slowness in responding to questions
13. General disorganization and confusion
14. Difficulty paying attention
15. Need for frequent repetition and prompts during instruction
16. Need for a program of instruction that is more structured than that used with most other students
17. Difficulties affecting grammar and sentence structure

18. Difficulties in the use of precise vocabulary and overuse of words such as *stuff, things, you know*, etc.

19. Inappropriate social use of language (e.g., interrupts frequently, digresses from topic, is insensitive to the needs or communication goals of conversational partners, cannot stay on the topic of discussion, cannot take turns in conversation)

20. Poor sequencing skills. Communication is disorganized, incoherent, and leaves listener confused

21. Overall communication skills that are substantially poorer than those of peers

If a LCD student manifests many of these characteristics, professionals may choose to carry out a comprehensive assessment. When doing so, there are legal considerations that must be kept in mind.

LEGAL CONSIDERATIONS

Recent federal legislation (IDEA, 1997) has emphasized the prevention of inappropriate identification and mislabeling of ethnically and linguistically diverse students. Professionals responsible for conducting special education evaluations need to be aware of legal mandates governing the assessment of LCD children. The key mandates are summarized below (for more detailed information, see Moore-Brown & Montgomery, 2001; Silliman & Diehl, 2002; van Keulen, Weddington, & DeBose, 1998):

❑ *1973 Diana vs. State Board of Education.* Testing must be carried out in the student's primary language. Assessment teams must document the appropriateness of special education placement by collecting extensive supportive data.

❑ *1974 Lau vs. Nichols.* Schools need to provide primary language programs to ensure equal education opportunities for LCD students.

❑ *1974 PL 93-380. Educational Amendments of 1974.* Testing must be conducted in a nondiscriminatory manner.

❑ *1975 PL 94-142. The Education of All Handicapped Children Act* (updated in 1990 to the Individuals with Disabilities Education Act, re-updated in 1997). This law contains provisions designed to ensure that nondiscriminatory evaluations are conducted:

1. Personnel must make reasonable accommodations for students with disabilities and may not exclude any school-aged children solely because of the disability.

2. All children, regardless of handicap, are entitled to an appropriate and free education.

3. Informed consent must be obtained in the primary language.

4. Testing and evaluation materials and procedures must be selected and administered in a nondiscriminatory manner.

5. Testing and evaluation materials must be provided and administered in the language or other mode of communication in which the child is most proficient.

6. Accommodations may include alternative forms of assessment and evaluation.

7. Tests must be administered to a child with a motor, speech, hearing, visual or other com-

munication disability, or to a bilingual child, so as to reflect accurately the child's ability in the area tested, rather than the child's impaired communication skill or limited English language skill.

8. Personnel must prepare an appropriate individualized education plan that meets the needs of the individual child.

9. Schools must educate children with disabilities in the least restrictive environment (LRE).

10. According to procedural due process, parents must be provided with the opportunity to object or consent to their child's identification, classification, placement, or individualized education plan.

❑ *1986 PL 99-457 - Education of All Handicapped Children's Act Amendment of 1986*

1. Programming for handicapped children down to age 3 is mandatory.
2. Incentives should be provided for programming beginning at birth.
3. An IFSP (individualized family service plan) is required that describes the services to be provided for children and their families.
4. All services must be provided by qualified personnel.

ASSESSMENT DOCUMENTATION

When conducting assessments, it is important to document the procedures used to ensure that legal mandates are being followed. Each state has specific regulations governing the assessment of LCD students. Examples from the California Education Code (CA EC) are presented below with their implications for report writing:

1. *Legislative Requirements*: Identification procedures must be coordinated with school site procedures for referral of pupils with needs that cannot be met with modification of the regular instructional program. (CA EC 56302).

A pupil shall be referred for special educational instruction and services ONLY AFTER the resources of the regular education program have been considered and where appropriate, utilized. (CA EC 5630).

Implications for Assessment: Document what regular education support services, programs, and strategies have already been utilized to help this student. Were they successful or not?

2. *Legislative Requirements*: Testing and assessment materials and procedures used for the purposes of assessment and placement of individuals with exceptional needs are selected and administered so as not to be racially, culturally, or sexually discriminatory. (CA EC 56320.a)

Implications for Assessment: Document validity and adequacy of the tests and procedures used in assessment.

3. *Legislative Requirements*: Tests and other assessment materials are provided and administered in the pupil's primary language or other mode of communication, unless the assessment plan indicates reasons why such provision and administration are not clearly feasible. (CA EC 56320.b.1)

Implications for Assessment: Indicate which language was used in assessment. If the student's primary language was not used, explain the reasons why it was not used.

4. *Legislative Requirements*: No single procedure is used as the sole criterion for determining an appropriate education program for an individual with exceptional needs. (CA EC 56320.e)

Implications for Assessment: Do not report the results of just one test or procedure. Use a number of procedures to justify findings.

5. *Legislative Requirements*: The assessment report shall include but not be limited to the following:

...a determination concerning the effects of environmental, cultural, or economic disadvantage, where appropriate. (CA EC 56327.g)

Implications for Assessment: Address any possible effects of the student's socioeconomic status, cultural differences, or lack of environmental opportunities that may be affecting performance.

6. *Legislative Requirements:* A pupil shall be assessed as having a specific learning disability which makes him or her eligible for special education and related services when.... a severe discrepancy exists between intellectual ability and achievements....and the discrepancy is due to a disorder in one or more of the basic psychological processes and is not the result of environmental, cultural, or economic disadvantages. (CA EC 56337.a.c)

Implications for Assessment: If the professional concludes that a LCD student has a learning disability, he or she must document the fact that the learning disability is not caused by any of the above disadvantages.

If school programs are to follow legal mandates, it is important to include a variety of approaches to assessment. Standardized tests are not appropriate measures of performance for many students who come from multicultural backgrounds. However, if professionals do use standardized tests, it is important to be aware of the many biases and limitations of these measures.

✐ *REFLECTION* ✐

Summarize two legal requirements relating to the assessment of LCD students. What are the implications of these requirements for writing reports?

_____

_____

_____

_____

_____

NONBIASED ASSESSMENT AND STANDARDIZED TESTS

Many professionals rely almost entirely on the use of standardized tests to evaluate the language abilities of LCD students and plan intervention/service delivery. When speech and language evaluations are conducted, standardized tests are often the primary measure used in determining whether or not students qualify for special education intervention. The procedures commonly used in determining students' eligibility for special education programs are shown in Figure 12.2. Many school districts require the use of standardized measures in determining students' eligibility for special education programs. Reasons for reliance on standardized testing include *legal considerations* (e.g., percentile ranks and standard deviations used as cut-offs to determine special education eligibility), *time constraints* (standardized tests are perceived as faster to score and administer than informal measures), *caseload constraints* (many schools have large numbers of students who are referred for testing due to academic difficulties), and *convenience* (standardized tests are often easier and more automatic to administer than less structured, informal measures). Many public school professionals believe incorrectly that federal law requires the use of standardized tests to determine eligibility for special education services. Kratcoski (1998) emphasized that the IDEA (1997) states that assessment tools display equity, validity, and nondiscrimination. The law allows for subjective and qualitative measures; norm-referenced tests are not required. However, because many professionals continue to rely heavily on use of standardized tests to assess LCD students, this section addresses considerations in the use of these tests. If professionals continue to use these tests with LCD students, they need to at least be aware of the tests' potential legal, psychometric, cultural, and linguistic limitations in terms of validity and reliability.

As mentioned previously, LCD students who have been classified "English proficient" based on conversational English language proficiency measures are often not appropriate candidates for the standardized tests used in special education evaluations. These instruments are often biased in favor of native English-speaking children from middle class backgrounds and, therefore, should never be used as the sole basis for identifying students' language-learning abilities and needs.

FORMAL TEST ASSUMPTIONS

The development of standardized, formal tests has grown out of a framework that is Western, literate, and "middle class." Kayser (1989, p. 232) stated that "the standardized approach to testing limits the minority student to a stimulus-response set that is considered to be a western European social communication event." For these and many other reasons, formal tests are often highly biased against LCD students.

It is important for professionals to be aware of the underlying assumptions upon which many formal tests are based. These inherent assumptions are extremely important to consider when working with LCD students (Heath, 1984; Lund & Duchan, 1993, p. 332). These assumptions hold that test-takers:

❑ follow the cooperative principle: perform to the best of their ability and try to provide relevant answers;

❑ attempt to respond even when test tasks don't make sense;

❑ understand test tasks (e.g. fill in the blank, point to the picture);

❑ have been exposed to the information and experiences inherent in the test;

❑ feel comfortable enough with the examiner in the testing setting to perform optimally.

These assumptions do not hold true for many LCD students. In some cultures, individuals are expected to greet unfamiliar events with silence or to be silent in the presence of an adult (Matsuda, 1989). Many Native American children are expected to learn by listening and watching, not by verbalizing; they are not encouraged to guess when they are unsure of an answer.

Many students have had no previous experience in a testing situation. Many have had experiences that are not consistent with the experiences assumed within the test design. In addition, some

Figure 12.2

TYPICAL REFERRAL AND ASSESSMENT PROCEDURES

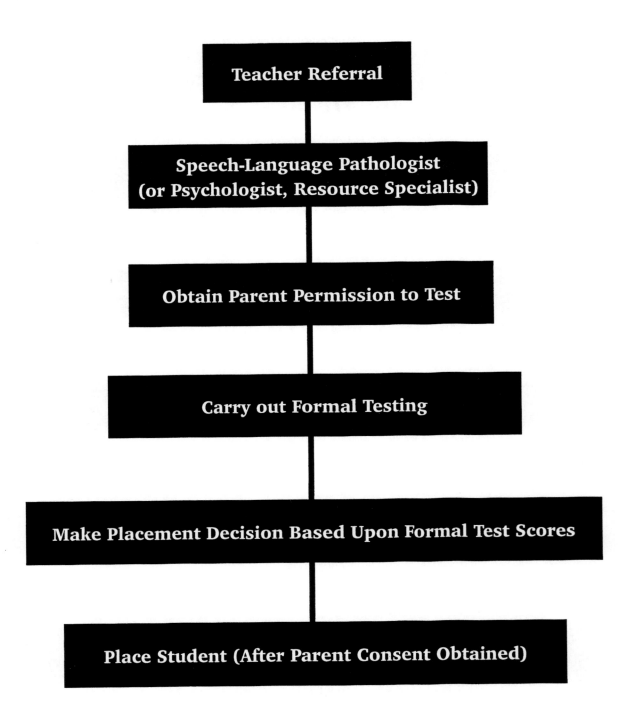

LCD students do not perform optimally when the testing setting and/or examiners are unfamiliar to them and/or from a different ethnic background.

SOURCES OF BIAS IN STANDARDIZED TESTING

The bias in standardized tests can take many forms when these tests are being used with LCD students. Some of these forms of bias are described below.

Potentially Unfamiliar Items (Cultural Bias)

Cultural bias occurs when the examiner uses items and activities that do not correspond with the child's experiential base (Anderson, 2002). Cheng (1991) listed test items that might be unfamiliar to LCD students, especially those who have immigrated to the United States:

1. Various household objects (e.g. blenders, microwaves)
2. Vehicles (e.g., dune buggies, subway trains)
3. Sports, especially those involving snow and cold weather. Sports such as football are not played in every country.
4. Musical instruments
5. Types of clothing (e.g. suspenders, galoshes, mittens)
6. Professions/occupations
7. Historically related events & people (e.g. Thanksgiving, Christmas, Abraham Lincoln)
8. Foods: apple pie, yogurt, American fruits, and vegetables
9. American nursery rhymes, fairy tales
10. Geography (e.g. New York, Midwest)
11. Games (tag, hopscotch, Monopoly)

Items Translated from English

Translated versions of English tests are often used with LCD students. There are many problems inherent in the use of translated English tests.

1. Differences in structure and content between English and the primary language raise questions about the comparability of scores. Many words cannot be directly translated from one language into another. For example, some Asian languages do not have pronouns; translating "she" or "he" or "it" into these languages is impossible. Also, the difficulty level of a specific word may differ in the two languages. For example, German has three different words for "the" depending on the noun (e.g. *das Buch* =the book; *der Mann* = the man; *die Frau* = the woman). English test translations cannot test a German student's knowledge of these important distinctions. (see Langdon & Cheng, 2002).

2. Information relating to test validity, reliability, and normative data cannot be used if a test is translated.

3. Differences in background and life experiences are not considered when direct translations of tests are used.

Bias in Tests Developed in the Primary Language

Many professionals feel that they can obtain valid assessments of LCD students' language skills if they use tests specifically developed in the primary language. For example, Spanish-speaking students can be given Spanish tests, etc. One major problem with this assumption is that much heterogeneity exists among populations that speak a particular language. For example, many dialects of Spanish exist, and Spanish-speaking children may come from such different countries as Cuba, Mexico, Puerto Rico, the Dominican Republic, and Spain (Brice, 2002; Goldstein, 2000; Goldstein & Iglesias, 2001). Spanish-speaking students raised in different parts of the United States have different vocabulary words for some items (Mattes & Omark, 1991). The Philippines has over 100 different mutually unintelligible languages and dialects. Therefore a Filipino student who speaks Odionganon (the local dialect spoken in the town of Odiongan) can be expected to perform poorly on a test written in Tagalog, the national language.

A second difficulty is that developmental data on languages other than English is limited. Some Spanish norms for articulation and language have been developed (e.g., Goldstein & Iglesias, 1996; Jimenez, 1987; Merino, 1992) but few easily-accessible established language development norms exist for languages other than English.

There are also differences in the vocabularies and linguistic knowledge bases of students who are born in the United States and those who immigrate here at a later age. Thus, test norms obtained on students born and raised in Mexico are not valid for Spanish-speaking students born and raised in the United States.

Examiner Bias

Examiners may show bias in how they administer or interpret assessment instruments. There are several potential forms of examiner bias:

❑ *Overinterpretation bias.* This type of bias occurs when examiners reach conclusions about a student's abilities based on a small sample of a student's behavior.

❑ *Examiner sensitivity bias.* Examiners may be unfamiliar with cultural and linguistic issues affecting the student's test performance.

❑ *Examiner expectations bias.* Examiners may have low expectations for LCD students and thus not provide them with adequate opportunities to respond.

Leung (1993) stated that the evaluator is the most important instrument in the assessment of LCD students. Thus, it behooves professionals to try to ensure that they are as free from bias as possible when testing LCD students.

CONSIDERATIONS IN TEST SELECTION

Variables described as important to consider in selecting assessment instruments (see Mattes & Omark, 1991; Respeto & Silverman, 2001; Roseberry-McKibbin & Hegde, 2000) are the following:

❑ *Purpose of the test.* Is the instrument used for screening or in-depth evaluation?

❑ *Construct validity.* What theory was used in the test's creation? Is one mentioned? Is it appropriate for the student being tested?

❑ *Appropriateness of test content.* Professionals should have native speakers of the student's language review the test whenever possible. Field-testing can be helpful in evaluating the appropriateness of test items.

❑ *Adequacy of norms.* How was the standardization sample selected? Are the students being tested represented in the norming and standardization?

CONSIDERATIONS IN TEST ADMINISTRATION

Professionals must consider formal test assumptions and how these assumptions might negatively impact individual test-takers. There are ways in which professionals can alter the administration of standardized tests so that LCD students will perform optimally in ways that reflect their true abilities (Erickson & Iglesias, 1986; Kayser, 1989; Van Keulen et al., 1998; Wilson, Wilson, & Coleman, 2000). Suggestions of altering test administration procedures include the following:

❑ Provide instructions in both English and L1.

❑ Explain the reason for testing.

❑ Change pronunciation of test items to reflect the language or dialect of the child.

❑ Rephrase confusing instructions.

❑ Give extra examples, demonstrations, and practice items.

❑ Give the student extra time to respond.

❑ Repeat items when necessary.

❑ If students give "wrong" answers, ask them to explain and write down their explanations. Score items as correct if they are culturally appropriate. RECORD ALL RESPONSES.

❑ Omit biased items that are likely to be difficult for students.

❑ Continue testing even after the ceiling has been reached.

❑ Devote more than one session to the testing.

❑ Have a parent or another trusted adult administer test items under the professional's supervision.

❑ Use a "dual scoring" system designed to provide two scores: the score the child would have obtained using the exact scoring format of the test (as per the examiner's manual) and the child's actual responses that would be considered correct in his culture (or, if the child answers some items in L1 and some items in English, use a combined score that reflects answers in both languages).

Gutierrez-Clellen, Restrepo, Bedore, Peña, and Anderson (2000) emphasized that students often demonstrate language proficiency in L1 for certain situations and proficiency in L2 for other situations. For example, young children often know "school" vocabulary (e.g., shapes, colors) in English and "home" vocabulary (e.g., body parts, certain foods) in L1. Thus, a dual-scoring system that uses answers in both languages to compute a total score is more reflective of a child's actual language knowledge than a system that only accounts for answers in one language or the other.

CONSIDERATIONS IN TEST INTERPRETATION

When professionals administer standardized tests, there are ways to interpret these tests that can effectively reduce bias:

❑ Do not identify a student as needing special education solely on the basis of test scores. Use informal measures to supplement standardized test scores!

❑ Ascertain if students' errors are typical of those observed among other students from similar backgrounds.

❑ Review test results with family members and/or other persons from the student's background to gain additional insights that may be helpful in educational decision-making.

❑ Interpret overall test results in a team setting. If professionals review and interpret results alone, errors are more likely.

❑ When writing assessment reports, be sure to include cautions and disclaimers about any departures from standard testing procedures. In addition, discuss how the student's background may have influenced testing results.

Profile

Soua L., a shy kindergartner from a Hmong family, was referred for a special education assessment. At the end of his kindergarten year, Soua was still designated as "Limited English Proficient." However, the special education team used standardized English tests to assess Soua's speech-language, cognitive, and academic skills. Each professional commented on how Soua was unwilling to speak or make eye contact during testing. Soua's scores on each test were significantly below the norm for the sample tested, and Soua was labeled "disordered in oral and written language." He then was placed into both speech-language and resource services for remediation.

The next year, a new speech-language pathologist came to the school and reviewed Soua's reports and IEP from the previous year. When it was time for Soua's annual review, the speech-language pathologist carried out a comprehensive pre-evaluation process that included gathering an extensive case history from the student's parents and re-evaluating his language proficiency in English and Hmong.

A home visit was conducted with a Hmong interpreter whom the family knew and trusted. Soua's parents shared that they had been in the U.S. for only two years and that they did not know English. They confided to the interpreter that they did not understand why Soua was receiving "extra help" but that they were grateful that he was "learning more English." Soua's parents said that he learned Hmong rapidly and easily in comparison with his five siblings, and that they had no concerns about his ability to learn or remember in the Hmong language. Soua's first grade teacher stated that he was progressing well in class, and the interpreter shared that in his five years of experience working with Hmong students in the school district, Soua "looks normal to me when he speaks in Hmong—and he remembers everything I tell him."

Soua was dismissed from special education services, but continued to receive support in Hmong from a interpreter who came into his classroom twice a week. Soua was also signed up for the after-school literacy program that allowed him to work in a small group with a tutor who helped LCD students become grade-level proficient in reading. Soua's teacher was given suggestions for use in the classroom.

There are many hazards to using standardized, formal tests with LCD students. However, if professionals use these tests, they should be aware of potential forms of bias and try to control for them as much as possible. If professionals are extremely cautious in the way they use standardized tests, and if they administer and interpret them in sensitive and nonbiased ways, the results may help to provide part of the answer to questions regarding the presence or absence of a "disorder."

Rather than relying solely on standardized tests to differentiate between a language difference and a language-learning disability, a thorough pre-evaluation process is recommended to determine whether or not a comprehensive assessment is even necessary.

THE PRE-EVALUATION PROCESS

As stated, relying solely on the typical assessment process depicted in Figure 12.2 is inappropriate when LCD student populations are referred for testing. When assessing these students, a team approach should be implemented and a variety of strategies should be used to collect the assessment data. When a team approach to assessment is used, the possibilities of a misdiagnosis are greatly diminished.

There are several steps that should be completed before a student undergoes a formal evaluation. The pre-evaluation process consists of the following components:

1. comprehensive teacher evaluation of the student's classroom performance

2. ethnographic interviewing and the collection of a case history

3. language proficiency testing

Again, these steps should be carried out BEFORE conducting a formal evaluation. When the pre-evaluation process is carried out by a team of professionals, the information gathered will facilitate decision making regarding the student's need for special education intervention. The prereferral model shown in Figure 12.3 can be used as a guide when collecting information about a student's performance.

Teacher Evaluation of Classroom Performance

It is crucial for teachers to give detailed descriptions of the student's performance in various aspects of classroom life. The Bilingual Classroom Communication Profile (BCCP) (Roseberry-McKibbin, 1993), published by Academic Communication Associates, is an informal tool for collecting information about the student's history, background, and use of language in the classroom environment. The BCCP includes guidelines for administering the instrument and a package of record forms for use in recording responses. The record form includes specific questions that should be explored prior to conducting formal testing. The information reported on the BCCP record form can be helpful in determining whether or not the student is an appropriate candidate for diagnostic testing.

The components and questions contained within the BCCP are described in Table 12.1. The record form includes space for recording responses and comments related to the questions asked. The Bilingual Classroom Communication Profile can be used in conjunction with other informal measures to provide a comprehensive picture of the student's use of language. An informal assessment record form that can be used in evaluating second language learning is included in Appendix A. This form is divided into three sections:

I. *Normal Processes of Second Language Acquisition.* This form is used to record specific second language processes (e.g., interference) that the student is manifesting.

Figure 12.3

ASSESSMENT PRE-REFERRAL MODEL

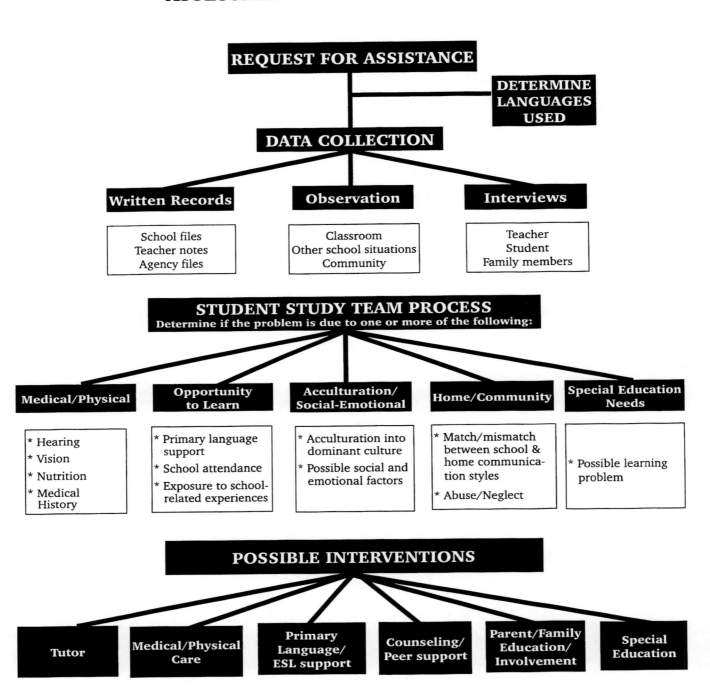

Adapted with permission from Leung (1993)

Table 12.1

Description of the Bilingual Classroom Communication Profile[1]

❑ *Background Information* - The first step in using the BCCP is to collect information about the student's background:

1. Names of individuals residing in the home with the student and their relationship to the student.
2. Countries where student has resided. The time period of residence should be recorded for each country listed.
3. First language or languages learned by the student.
4. Language used most often by the student both at home and at school.
5. Individuals who are responsible for caring for the student. The name, relationship to student, and language(s) spoken by each of these individuals should be recorded.
6. Date and circumstances in which the student was first exposed to English.
7. Previous schools attended, location of these schools, and dates of attendance.

❑ *Health Information* - Specific health concerns and the results of hearing and vision screening tests are recorded.

❑ *Instructional Strategies* - Special programs in the regular classroom that are available to students (e.g.. tutors, ESL, etc.) and classroom modifications made to accomodate the student (e.g., preferential seating, special materials used, etc.) are noted.

❑ *Classroom Language Use* - The student's performance in this section of the BCCP is evaluated by asking the teacher to respond "Yes," "No," or "Don't Know" to each item. Performance is evaluated separately in English and in the home language.

1. *Answers simple questions about everyday activities*
2. *Communicates basic needs to others*
3. *Interacts appropriately and successfully with peers*
4. *Tells a simple story, keeping the sequence and basic facts accurate*
5. *Communicates ideas and directions in an appropriate sequence*
6. *Describes familiar objects and events*
7. *Maintains a conversation appropriately*

❑ *School Social Interaction Problems* - A plus (+) is recorded on the record form for each statement that describes the child accurately, and a minus (–) is recorded for each statement that is false. Responses should be based on observations of the student during interactions with peers from a similar cultural and linguistic background.

1. *Communicates ineffectively with peers in both English and the home language*
2. *Often plays alone*
3. *Is ridiculed or teased by others*
4. *Is often excluded from activities by peers*
5. *Does not get along well with peers*

❑ *Language and Learning Problems* - The teacher indicates areas of concern by responding "Yes, ' "No," or "Don't Know" to each item on the record form.

Items 1-10 in this section provide an "overall performance summary."
1. *Appears to have difficulty communicating in English*
2. *Appears to have difficulty communicating in the primary language*
3. *Has difficulty learning when instruction is provided in English*
4. *Has difficulty learning when instruction is provided in the primary language*

[1]Source: Roseberry-McKibbin, C. (1993). *Bilingual Classroom Communication Profile*. Oceanside, CA: Academic Communication Associates. Items from the BCCI are reprinted in this table with permission from the publisher.

(continuation of Table 12.1)

5. *Acquires new skills in English more slowly than peers*
6. *Acquires new skills in the primary language more slowly than peers*
7. *Shows academic achievement significantly below his/her academic English language proficiency, as assessed by an ESL or bilingual professional*
8. *Is not learning as quickly as peers who have had similar language experiences and opportunities for learning*
9. *Has a family history of learning problems or special education concerns*
10. *Parents state that student learns language more slowly than siblings*

Items 11 through 26 are used to pinpoint specific problems observed.
11. *Rarely initiates verbal interaction with peers*
12. *Uses gestures and other nonverbal communication (on a regular basis) rather than speech to communicate*
13. *Is slow to respond to questions and/or classroom instructions*
14. *Is not able to stay on a topic; conversation appears to wander*
15. *Often gives inappropriate responses*
16. *Appears to have difficulty remembering things*
17. *Does not take others' needs or preferences into account*
18. *Has difficulty conveying thoughts in a clear, organized manner*
19. *Appears disorganized much of the time*
20. *Appears confused much of the time*
21. *Has difficulty paying attention even when material is understandable and presented using a variety of modalities*
22. *Has difficulty following basic classroom directions*
23. *Has difficulty following everyday classroom routines*
24. *Requires more prompts and repetition than peers to learn new information*
25. *Requires a more structured program of instruction than peers*
26. *Has gross and/or fine motor problems*

❑ ***Environmental Influences and Language Development*** - The teacher indicates areas of concern by responding "Yes," "No," or "Don't Know" to each item on the record form.
1. *Has the student had frequent exposure to literacy-related materials (e.g., books) in the primary language?*
2. *Has the student had sufficient exposure to the primary language to acquire a well-developed vocabulary in that language?*
3. *Was the student a fluent speaker of the primary language when he/she was first exposed to English?*
4. *Have the student's parents been encouraged to speak and/or read in the primary language at home?*
5. *Has the student's primary language been maintained in school through bilingual education, tutoring, or other language maintenance activities?*
6. *Does the student show an interest in interacting in his/her primary language?*
7. *Has a loss of proficiency in the primary language occurred because of limited opportunities for continued use of that language?*
8. *Doe the student have frequent opportunities to speak English during interactions with peers at school?*
9. *Has the student had frequent opportunities to visit libraries, museums, and other places in the community where opportunities for language enrichment and learning are available?*
10. *Has the student had frequent, long-term opportunities to interact with fluent English speakers outside of the school environment?*

❑ ***Impressions from Classroom Observations*** - The teacher is asked to respond to questions designed to elicit descriptive information about the child's performance.
I. *To what extent does the student have difficulty learning in school because of limited proficiency in English?*
2. *Do you feel that this student requires a different type of instructional program than other students who have had similar cultural and linguistic experiences? Please explain.*
3. *Briefly summarize the communication and learning problems observed in the school setting.*

2. *Affective Second Language Acquisition Variables.* This form is used to record variables relating to motivation, personality, and socioeconomic status that may influence second language learning.

3. *Second Language Learning Styles and Strategies.* This form is used to record comments relating to learning styles and strategies (e.g., avoidance, use of routines) that are influencing communication in the second language.

Table 12.2 is a reproducible assessment tool that can be used to collect information related to the student's conceptual development.

Ethnographic Interviewing

A challenge that confronts many professionals is that of learning about cultural differences and their impact on performance in the school environment. When a student is being considered for a special education assessment, it is crucial for the assessment team to understand that student's culture. When professionals acquire this understanding, they can make informed decisions about the child's performance abilities and instructional needs. One way to gain this cultural information is through the use of *ethnographic interviewing.*

Ethnographic interviewing, a data collection technique originally used by anthropologists, makes it possible to obtain information from the point of view of a cultural informant. In other words, the purpose of the ethnographic interview is to help the interviewer get the perspective of the particular culture that the student is from. In the ethnographic interview, the interviewer asks a cultural informant questions about such issues as cultural values, traditions, and attitudes. Cultural informants can be the student's parents, family members, or they can be persons from the local community who are indirectly involved with the student. Interviews can be general (e.g., about a certain cultural group), or can pertain to a particular student.

Westby (1990, p. 105) gave several suggestions for conducting and developing rapport in an ethnographic interview:

1. Explain the purpose of the interview so that interviewees understand why they are being interviewed (e.g., "You told me on the phone that you were concerned about Juan's stuttering at home; I'd like to find out more about that so we can help him here at school.").

2. Avoid "why" and "what do you mean" questions because they may have a judgmental tone. Questions of this type give the impression that clients know the cause of various problems observed at school. For example, a professional might say, "Tell me more about what happens when Juan starts stuttering" instead of "Why do you think Juan is stuttering?"

3. Restate what informants say to ensure understanding.

An ethnographic interview, conducted with one or more members of the student's culture, can include but should not be limited to the following questions (adapted from Mattes & Omark, 1991):

1. Why has the student's family left the homeland?

2. Why have they settled in the local community?

3. Did the community members come from the same area in the homeland?

4. What is the typical family size and constellation in the community?

Table 12.2

LINGUISTIC AND CONCEPTUAL DEVELOPMENT CHECKLIST

Student's Name: _____ Date of Birth:_____ Chronological Age:_____

Language Spoken: _____

Questions	Yes	No	Don't Know
❑ Has the child been regularly exposed to L1 literacy-related materials?	___	___	___
❑ Is the child's vocabulary in the first language well-developed?	___	___	___
❑ Was the child's L1 fluent and well-developed when s/he began learning English?	___	___	___
❑ Have the child's parents been encouraged to speak and/or read in L1 at home?	___	___	___
❑ Has the child's' L1 been maintained in school through bilingual education, L1 tutoring, and/or other L1 maintenance activities?	___	___	___
❑ Does the child show interest in L1 maintenance and interaction?	___	___	___
❑ Is the English classroom input comprehensible to the child?	___	___	___
❑ Does the child have frequent opportunities for negotiating meaning and practicing comprehensible output in English?	___	___	___
❑ Has the child had frequent exposure to enriching experiences such as going to museums, libraries, etc.?	___	___	___
❑ Has the child's school attendance been regular?	___	___	___
❑ Has the child had long-term exposure to standard English models?	___	___	___

The more "yes" answers that are checked, the more likely it is that the child has a good conceptual foundation for language and academic learning. The more "no" answers that are checked, the more likely it is that the child has underdeveloped conceptual and linguistic abilities due to limitations within the school and/or home environment, language loss, limited English practice opportunities, inadequate bilingual services, or a combination of these factors.

5. What is the typical family hierarchy of authority?

6. How are children expected to behave with an adult?

7. What behaviors are expected within the culture to show courtesy (e.g., speaking only when spoken to, avoiding eye contact with authority figures)?

8. What are the family/community concerns (e.g., jobs, food, etc.)?

9. Are the members of the student's cultural group experiencing poverty?

10. How does this cultural group view the role of regular education and the role of special education?

11. How does this cultural group view the role of individuals with disabilities?

12. What role does religion play in the cultural group's daily life and decisions?

The Case History

It is crucial to gather a case history for the particular student who is being considered for special education assessment (see Appendix B). Although this can take some time, the information will be helpful in planning for instruction. The parent report has been found to be an excellent and valid way to help the professional distinguish a language difference from a language disorder (Gutierrez-Clellen, 1998; Peña, Iglesias, & Lidz, 2000; Restrepo, 1998).

The case history can be obtained from the student's parents or other available relatives who have some knowledge of the student's background. Uncles, aunts, siblings, and grandparents can provide valuable information, especially if they serve as the student's primary caretakers. Professionals can utilize the services of a trained interviewer who is fluent in English and the student's primary language. Experienced professionals find that when parents can speak with someone from their own cultural background, they often feel more comfortable during the interview/case history gathering process.

If an interpreter is used, the interviewer and interpreter need to prepare carefully for the interview in order to ensure its success. The parents/interviewees must understand the purpose of the interview and the questions that are being asked (Wyatt, 2002). Some parents may feel that the case history questions are personal and, therefore, inappropriate. If parents understand why the questions are being asked, however, they will probably feel more comfortable and will be less likely to be offended by the interview questions.

Educational professionals should attempt to develop rapport with parents, create a comfortable atmosphere, and ask open-ended questions that will encourage parents to express themselves freely. This author has found that parents often become overwhelmed when confronted with a large team of school professionals in a formal meeting. At times, parents speak most freely when they are in a small, informal setting with only one professional and an interpreter present.

Language Proficiency Variables

Before considering a special education assessment, it is important to deal with language proficiency issues. There are several steps involved in determining language proficiency and dominance:

1. Determine the student's primary language.

2. Determine language dominance.

3. Determine oral and written proficiency level in each of the languages spoken by the child.

Terms commonly used in discussions relating to bilingual students' language abilities are defined below:

> - **primary language** - the language the student learned first and used most frequently in the early stages of language development. Information regarding language use in the home is best established through carefully conducted parent interviews and home language surveys.
>
> - **dominant language** - the language spoken most proficiently by the student. The dominant language often changes when there are changes in language usage patterns in the child's environment. Moreover, language dominance can vary depending on what aspect of language is assessed (e.g., syntax vs. vocabulary).
>
> - **language proficiency** - the child's level of skill in the use of a particular language.

Whenever special education assessments are conducted, an important preliminary step is to find out the student's relative proficiency in the languages spoken. Schools often make use of individuals who do not have specialized training in language to administer these tests. Adler (1991) recommended that speech-language pathologists and other special education personnel participate actively in language proficiency testing.

Measurement of a child's language proficiency should consist of three steps:

1. *completion of a language background questionnaire by the parents*. Language background questionnaires provide information about the languages used in the home.

2. *conducting parent or teacher interviews*. Parent and teacher interviews provide information about the child's language use and proficiency in the home and in classroom situations.

3. *using information obtained from direct and indirect language measures*. Direct measures of proficiency in a child's two languages yield scores that can be helpful in identifying strengths and weaknesses in each language.

The focus in language proficiency testing is shifting from assessment of knowledge of grammatical forms to the assessment of communication competence. Proficiency testing should provide information about the students' competence in the functional use of language and their effectiveness in using language in all social domains.

Traditionally, language proficiency has been measured using discrete-point tests that yield a proficiency score in each language. It is common practice in public schools for students to be considered "proficient" in a language when they are able to speak and listen to the language with a basic level of conversational fluency. Most language proficiency tests assess speaking and listening skills only. These measures are often highly structured (e.g., *yes-no* and *fill-in-the-blank* questions) and provide little or no information about the child's effectiveness in using language in natural speaking situations. Few measures assess more than general proficiency in communication.

Researchers have stated that limiting proficiency testing to the assessment of speaking and listening skills is often appropriate (Hernandez-Chavez, Burt, & Dulay, 1978; Ortiz, 1984). Many children attending school in the United States, for example, had no formal education in their first language. These children are likely to perform poorly if tests administered in the first language require reading or writing skills. If proficiency tests that require reading and writing skills are used, they should be used in conjunction with oral communication measures.

The neglect of the academic (reading and writing) side of language competence, however, has negative ramifications. Professionals must keep in mind that the student's level of proficiency in a language can vary depending on the aspect of language being assessed. For example, a student who is proficient in daily conversational English does not necessarily have the cognitive-academic language proficiency skills necessary for success in reading and writing. Children who have learned to answer questions and to share experiences often give the appearance of being fluent in a language. Problems, however, are often observed in situations that require specific and precise responses. These students may also experience difficulty in situations where contextual information is limited. Skill in reading requires students to construct meaning from textual information based on what they know about language and how it is structured. The cognitive demands placed upon the student in reading and writing activities are much greater than those required for success in an informal conversational setting. As mentioned previously, it takes only about two years for a second language learner to acquire basic interpersonal communication skills. The cognitive-academic language skills necessary for success in classroom reading and writing activities generally reach a level commensurate with that of monolingual English speakers in five to seven years (Cummins, 1992b). Thus, a LCD student who is labeled "English proficient" on the basis of a basic conversation skills-oriented language proficiency measure may, in fact, not have the language abilities necessary to function effectively in classroom academic tasks.

This author has encountered numerous situations in the schools in which students identified as "English proficient" on a conversation-based oral proficiency measure were placed in special education because of reading and writing "problems" in English. The cognitive-academic aspects of language proficiency need to be considered in determining a student's need for special education intervention.

✐ *REFLECTION* ✐

Discuss the importance of the pre-evaluation process when LCD students are referred for special education testing. What kinds of problems can be prevented by going through this process?

_____

_____

_____

_____

_____

SUMMARY

When LCD students are struggling in school, professionals must decide if poor school performance can be attributed to language and/or cultural differences or underlying disabilities that affect school performance. Professionals must remember that:

❑ Behaviors commonly observed among second language learners may be inappropriately labeled as "abnormalities."

❑ Testing must conform to legal requirements and must be non-discriminatory.

❏ Formal language tests do not provide a complete picture of the child's communication skills. Standardized tests have many limitations that need to be recognized and accommodated if these tests are used.

❏ It is important to use a pre-evaluation process to obtain information about the student's background to determine if formal special education testing is truly necessary.

❏ This pre-evaluation process should consist of several components including the classroom teacher's evaluation of classroom performance, a case history, and assessment of the student's primary language, dominant language, and proficiency in L1 and English.

❏ Bilingual students are not language-learning disabled if they demonstrate problems in English only; difficulties must be evident in both the primary language and English.

It is appropriate for professionals who assess LCD students to avoid using norms from standardized tests altogether because of the bias inherent in these instruments. Pre-evaluation procedures and nonstandardized, informal assessment methods provide more valid information about the student's level of language proficiency and about factors that may be contributing to problems observed in the school setting. These methods are described in the next chapter.

STUDY QUESTIONS

1. Discuss the types of bias inherent in norm-referenced tests. Why is the use of test scores from these measures so inappropriate for the majority of LCD students?

2. You are going to conduct an ethnographic interview with a family that just arrived from Romania. What are four things you will keep in mind as you prepare for this interview?

3. List five potential indicators of a language-learning disability in a LCD student.

TRUE-FALSE

Circle the number beside each statement that is true.

4. Most of the language proficiency tests currently in use assess all aspects of language (speaking, listening, reading, writing).
5. Quadrant 3 of the Diagnostic Pie includes students who have had an adequate language learning background, show no evidence of a language-learning disability, but need more time to learn English.
6. In *overinterpretation bias*, examiners make judgments about a wide range of the student's abilities based on a small sample of a student's linguistic skills.

7. When collecting case history information, the parents should be the only ones interviewed because other relatives often provide inaccurate information in an effort to appear knowledgeable.
8. A student who has a true language-learning disability has an impairment that will affect the acquisition of any language.
9. Professionals who assess LCD students with standardized tests may be able to obtain less biased assessment results on some measures by using a dual-scoring system in which students' answers in both languages are counted in the total score.
10. The development of nationally-normed standardized tests in the primary languages spoken by students in our nation's schools will solve most problems currently being experienced in assessment.

MULTIPLE CHOICE

Circle all choices that are correct.

11. Which of the following statements are TRUE?
    A. The student's primary language is the language the student learned first and used most frequently in the early stages of language development.
    B. The student's dominant language is the language spoken most fluently by the student.
    C. The term "language proficiency" refers to the child's level of skill in the use of a particular language.

12. Which of the following are TRUE statements about laws governing the assessment of LCD students?
    A. *Lau vs. Nichols* - Testing must be carried out in the student's primary language. Assessment teams must document the appropriateness of special education placement by collecting extensive supportive data.
    B. *Diana vs. State Board of Education* - Schools need to provide language programs in the primary language to ensure equal educational opportunities for LCD students.
    C. *PL 93-380 - Educational Amendments of 1974* - Testing must be conducted in a nondiscriminatory manner.
    D. *The 1975 PL 94-142 - The Education of All Handicapped Children Act (updated in 1990 to the Individuals with Disabilities Education Act, re-updated in 1997)* - All children, regardless of handicap, are entitled to an appropriate and free education.
    E. *The 1975 PL 94-142 - The Education of All Handicapped Children Act (updated in 1990 to the Individuals with Disabilities Education Act, re-updated in 1997)* - Accommodations may include alternative forms of assessment and evaluation.

13. Which question would NOT be part of an ethnographic interview?
    A. How are children expected to behave with an adult?
    B. Why has the student's family left the homeland?
    C. Does the family believe in corporal punishment of children?
    D. What is the typical family size and constellation in the community?
    E. To what extent are members of the student's cultural group living in poverty?

14. When teachers provide information about a student's classroom performance for language assessment purposes, they should include the following:
    A. Information about school social interaction problems
    B. Information about student's classroom language use
    C. Impressions from classroom observations
    D. Information about language and learning problems (in both the primary language and English)
    E. Documentation about the student's personal habits (e.g., eating habits, hygiene, etc.)

15. Indicators of a language-learning disability in an LCD student would include the following:
    A. Family history of special education/learning difficulties
    B. Difficulty in learning language at a normal rate, even with special assistance in both languages
    C. Lack of organization, structure, and sequence in spoken and written language; difficulty conveying thoughts
    D. A low level of proficiency in only one of the languages spoken by the student
    E. A low level of proficiency resulting from limited exposure to English

ANSWERS TO STUDY QUESTIONS

  4. False
  5. False
  6. True
  7. False
  8. True
  9. True
10. False
11. A, B, and C
12. C, D, and E
13. C
14. A, B, C, and D
15. A, B, and C

Chapter 13

ECOLOGICALLY VALID ASSESSMENT: PRACTICAL STRATEGIES

Outline

ALTERNATIVES TO NORM-REFERENCED TESTS

The use of norm-referenced tests poses many difficulties when professionals assess students from diverse cultural and linguistic backgrounds, and these difficulties were described in the previous chapter. The use of nonstandardized, informal procedures and instruments for the assessment of LCD students has become increasingly common. Many experts recommend use of these informal methods of evaluation either alone or in conjunction with use of standardized, formal tests in evaluating language skills (Anderson, 2002; Brice & Roseberry-McKibbin, 1999; Goldstein, 2000; Wyatt, 2002). A major advantage of informal testing is that the data obtained can be evaluated in relation to the demands of the classroom curriculum. This curriculum-based approach is consistent with the widely recognized need for outcome-based assessment (Moore-Brown & Montgomery, 2001). Another major advantage of informal testing is that it allows one to evaluate the student's functioning in real-life contexts. Formal testing seldom taps these students' individualized, functional skills in their own environments. Using informal measures permits ecologically valid assessment, which considers the environment, home, and culture of the child and family (van Keulen, Weddington, & DeBose, 1998). But most important of all, informal assessment measures and methods that are geared toward the individual student circumvent many of the biases inherent in standardized tests.

In the preceding chapter, it was stated that federal law (IDEA, 1997) does not require the use of formal, standardized measures in the special education assessment and placement of students. Kratcoski (1998) stated that

> Evaluations and assessments in school settings have traditionally involved the use of standardized tests...to adhere to state and federal regulations...According to federal regulations, the present level of performance must be presented in terms of objective measurable evaluations 'to the extent possible' (U.S. Department of Education, 1980, p. 20). [But] the provisions of P. L. 94-142 IDEA do not mandate specific assessment tools *or even require that standardized measures are used*...tools must display equity, validity, and nondiscrimination...and they stipulate a team assessment approach that incorporates multi-measure decisions, an evaluation based on specific educational needs, and a look at the whole child...Traditionally, many SLPs have used standardized tests...operating from the belief that *a quantitative standard score is mandated by federal law*...however, *the law does not exclude subjective or qualitative measures...it leaves the choice of measurement tools and criteria to the educator.* (excerpts quoted from pp. 3-10; italics are this author's)

Thus, professionals can be assured that the provisions of P. L. 94-142/IDEA 1997 allow the use of subjective, qualitative measures in the assessment of LCD students—as long as a team approach is used and the measures are equitable, valid, and nondiscriminatory. It is best to use a combination of formal and informal measures in assessment (see Figure 13.1). When formal measures are used, a variety of skills can be assessed in a short period of time. In many school districts, eligibility for assessment is determined based on standardized test scores although the federal law does not require this. Scores on these measures are not always valid measures of the child's abilities. Information obtained from informal measures can be used to document how the child performs in various situations.

Informal measures often rely on observational data. Developing skill in observing students enables professionals to report information that can be compared to information obtained from language samples and other measures. Combining the information from these data sources

Figure 13.1

TEAM APPROACH TO COMPREHENSIVE ASSESSMENT

ASSESSMENT WHEEL FOR MULTICULTURAL STUDENTS

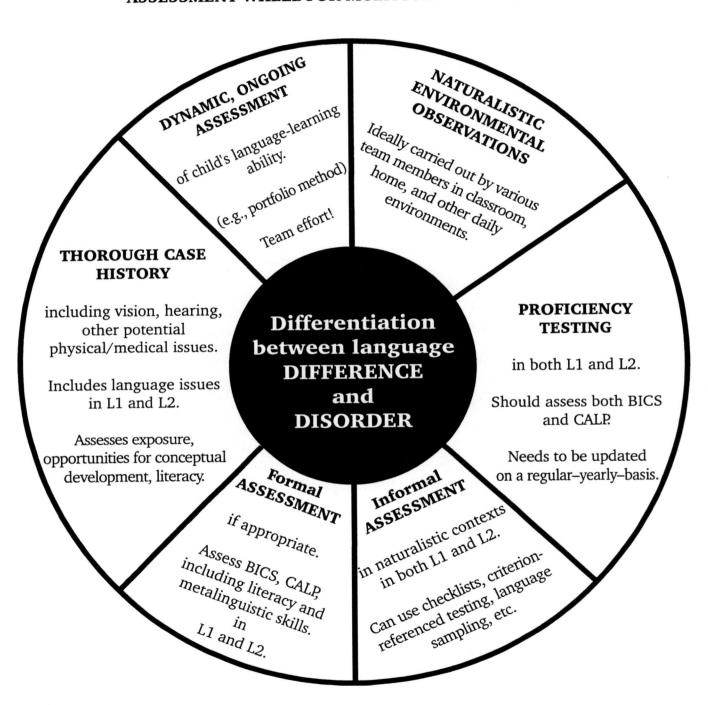

DYNAMIC, ONGOING ASSESSMENT

of child's language-learning ability.

(e.g., portfolio method)

Team effort!

NATURALISTIC ENVIRONMENTAL OBSERVATIONS

Ideally carried out by various team members in classroom, home, and other daily environments.

THOROUGH CASE HISTORY

including vision, hearing, other potential physical/medical issues.

Includes language issues in L1 and L2.

Assesses exposure, opportunities for conceptual development, literacy.

Differentiation between language DIFFERENCE and DISORDER

PROFICIENCY TESTING

in both L1 and L2.

Should assess both BICS and CALP.

Needs to be updated on a regular–yearly–basis.

Formal ASSESSMENT

if appropriate.

Assess BICS, CALP, including literacy and metalinguistic skills. in L1 and L2.

Informal ASSESSMENT

in naturalistic contexts in both L1 and L2.

Can use checklists, criterion-referenced testing, language sampling, etc.

provides a broader base for making instructional decisions than the use of any single strategy. Skill in informal assessment enables individuals who are most familiar with the students to develop meaningful, quantifiable data bases that can be used in developing instructional objectives and in determining the most appropriate educational environment for students.

In this chapter, nonstandardized, informal procedures for assessment are described. It is recommended that professionals use the following strategies to assess students:

❑ Use authentic assessment. Evaluate the child's performance within the classroom setting by evaluating portfolios of work completed, essays, stories, and other materials (Falk-Ross, 2002).

❑ Take advantage of curriculum-based assessment to determine the child's level of functioning and performance in the classroom setting.

❑ Use a dynamic approach to assessment. Evaluate the student's performance over time. This is highly preferable to a static approach in which the student is tested in one or two assessment sessions (Roseberry-McKibbin & Hegde, 2000).

❑ Evaluate the student's ability to learn language. Because so many students come from backgrounds of limited exposure to mainstream school concepts and vocabulary, they do poorly in formal testing situations. Thus, professionals should evaluate ability to learn rather than focusing only on identifying the student's current level of functioning. Students who have normal language-learning ability but limited experiences will generally learn new language rules readily, while students with genuine underlying language-learning disabilities will have difficulty learning language rules (Peña, Iglesias, & Lidz, 2001). Students with disabilities usually require more repetition in their instructional programs than students who are developing language in the typical manner.

❑ Evaluate communication holistically. Focus on the functional aspects of language as the child uses language to communicate meaning and to meet the demands of various communication situations.

❑ Collect observational data in a variety of naturalistic contexts. It is important to evaluate the student's ability to interact in everyday situations. Use of multiple observations in naturalistic settings makes it possible to obtain information about the child's overall communication behavior in multiple contexts (Langdon & Cheng, 2002). Professionals can observe students in the classroom, at recess, at lunch, in the library, in the home, and in a variety of other settings.

❑ Use questionnaires to obtain information from individuals who interact with the student. Use of questionnaires gives a broad picture of the student's communication functioning in daily contexts.

❑ Use narratives. Assess the student's ability to construct narratives and to remember stories that have been heard.

❑ Use natural language samples. These samples can be used to evaluate students' communication skills.

❑ Use school records of students' achievement and performance. A review of the student's cumulative record file may yield helpful information.

✐REFLECTION ✐

You are a new professional in a school district that requires special education personnel to use only standardized measures in the assessment of LCD students. You are told by an administrator in the school district that the law mandates the use of standardized scores, and that other types of assessment methods will not be considered in educational decision-making. Summarize what you will share with this administrator.

_____

_____

_____

_____

_____

_____

DYNAMIC ASSESSMENT OF LANGUAGE-LEARNING ABILITY

Program placement decisions are often made based on static assessment procedures in which test scores are obtained during one or two testing sessions. It was stated earlier that this is a less than optimal approach to testing. It was also stated that a major difficulty with static assessment is that the information obtained represents the child's performance at one point in time. If testing is conducted once a year, the child's instructional objectives for an entire year are usually based on these results.

Dynamic, ongoing assessment of students' learning holds much greater promise for obtaining accurate measures of student abilities. Dynamic assessment determines the child's capacity to learn rather than just assessing the child's knowledge at one point in time. The dynamic assessment model is characterized by a *test-teach-retest* format that focuses on the learning process (Peña et al, 2001). Dynamic assessment allows the examiner to observe how the student learns rather than focusing entirely on what the student already knows.

The Diagnostic Pie was described previously as a graphic representation of the dilemma many professionals face when attempting to determine whether a student manifests a language difference or a language-learning disability. Some students may show typical behavior in acquiring language skills, but limitations of environmental experience and/or linguistic exposure prevent them from developing the skills assessed on standardized tests. Many students come to school with a background that, while adequate for effective functioning within their culture, has not prepared them for demands of the typical classroom in this country. They may be labeled "disabled" because they enter school lacking skills that most of their classmates have already mastered.

Other students have a true, underlying disability that has impeded their learning of language. Differentiating these students from those described above is difficult, as both groups do poorly on standardized tests.

Few researchers have empirically addressed the evaluation of language-learning ability in bilingual student populations (Roseberry & Connell, 1991). Thus, professionals have few tools with which to carry out this type of assessment although some researchers have made specific recommendations about measures that can be used (Jacobs & Coufal, 2001). Professionals who wish to evaluate language-learning ability must first understand the theory underlying language-learning assessment.

Theory Underlying Language-Learning Assessment

Reuven Feuerstein, a Romanian philosopher/practitioner/scholar, developed the Theory of Structural Cognitive Modifiability. This theory was based on many years of experience working with low-functioning children from over 70 cultures. He worked with Holocaust survivors, children from concentration camps, and immigrants from Persia, Morocco, and the former Soviet Union among others. Feuerstein's theory gave birth to the Learning Potential Assessment Device (LPAD) (see Cummins, 1984). The major tenets of Feuerstein's theory and the LPAD are summarized here:

❑ Conventional tests and most other current methods of assessment are static measures that "passively catalog children's current knowledge and measure their...level of functioning" at one point in time (Cummins, 1984, p. 199). These tests accept a student's current level of functioning as a predictor of how well the student will function in the future.

❑ The LPAD attempts to assess the child's "zone of proximal development" (Vygotsky, 1962) which shows what the child can achieve with active help from a more knowledgeable person such as an adult.

❑ The LPAD "stresses trainability, or the ability to profit from learning experiences...the learning potential paradigm provides subjects with training experiences directly relevant to the reasoning task presented; they are given the opportunity to demonstrate that they can apply their problem-solving ability and to show whether they can improve their performance on the task. The improved performance indicates problem-solving capability not evident when training is not provided as part of the test administration" (Budoff, 1987, p. 173).

❑ All children are modifiable.

❑ Adults must engage children in mediated learning or purposeful directed activities.

❑ Adults need to use instrumental enrichment (IE) or specific materials and exercises along with guidance and direction in activities.

The LPAD itself can take several days and up to 25 hours to complete with an individual student. This is a very daunting proposition for professionals who assess many students! However, professionals can utilize the concepts provided by Feuerstein to develop approaches to assessment that examine the student's actual functioning over a period of time.

Practical Implications of Language-Learning Assessment Theory

Cummins (1984) stated that learning potential can be informally assessed in classrooms by observing how rapidly students acquire knowledge and skills when instruction is provided in a manner that is context-embedded and culturally relevant. It has also been suggested that professionals compare students' assisted performance with their unassisted performance in order to evaluate their ability to learn when provided with help in a "guided participation" format. Professionals can also use a *pretest-training-posttest* paradigm that evaluates a student's ability to learn when provided with relevant instruction in the natural environment.

Mattes & Omark (1991, p. 115) presented a helpful list of questions that professionals can ask when assessing a student's underlying language-learning ability. (Professionals should always be sure to compare students with peers who come from similar cultural and linguistic backgrounds):

❑ *How much structure and individual attention is needed for the student to acquire new language skills?* Students with language-learning disabilities usually need more prompts, modeling, and repetition than their peers.

❑ *During instructional activities, to what extent does the student exhibit off-task behaviors or inappropriate responses?* Language-learning disabled students may give responses that are off-topic or inappropriate. Because their problems make learning difficult, they also may show off-task behaviors such as fidgeting, annoying other students, and generally not attending to task.

❑ *To what extent does the student require instructional strategies that differ from those that have been used effectively with peers?* Strategies that have worked very effectively with LCD students may not be effective with students who have language-learning disabilities and, therefore, these students require a more "customized" approach to instruction.

SUMMARY

Language-learning assessment is a dynamic method for evaluating students' ability to learn language over time when provided with instruction. Before referring students for special education services, professionals need to ensure that these students are given instruction in relevant and comprehensible contexts. If students are given these learning opportunities and continue to exhibit problems, the need for special education services should be examined. Placement in a program for children with communication disorders is warranted only in situations where it is determined that a disability is the cause of the problems observed in the school setting. Problems resulting from limited exposure to English are not "disabilities."

ASSESSMENT OF LANGUAGE PROCESSING CAPACITY

Research has documented that children with specific language impairment (or language-learning disability) have difficulty recalling information from stories, repeating orally-presented nonsense words, and repeating orally-presented sentences. Gillam, Cowan, and Day (1995) stated that children with specific language impairment may exhibit a variety of verbal short-term memory deficits and may have difficulty retaining the sequential order of information. Fazio (1998) summarized studies that suggested that children with language impairments have specific difficulty on tasks that require immediate, verbatim ordered recall. For example, children with specific language impairment have difficulty recalling lists of words and also do poorly on tests of auditory digit span (e.g., repeating a number sequence such as "6-3-5-1"). Difficulty repeating a series of nonsense words appears to be a measure that is particularly sensitive to memory problems in children with specific language impairment (Montgomery, 1998).

Recent research has focused on the assessment of students' language processing capacity as a way to circumvent problems associated with the bias in standardized tests that measure acquired knowledge (e.g., knowledge of vocabulary). Dollaghan and Campbell (1998) developed a battery of measures designed to assess language processing capacity. They compared these measures with knowledge-based standardized tests and found that the processing measures were much more valid in assessing LCD children's language ability than the knowledge-based measures. Specifically, the processing-based measures were more accurate in differentiating language delays from language differences in LCD subjects.

Although few research studies have been conducted on the use of language processing tasks with LCD children, there is evidence supporting the use of tasks that do not depend on background knowledge and which tap immediate, verbatim ordered recall. For example, if a Spanish-speaking student knows the numbers 1 through 10 in Spanish, the professional might compare the students' skill in repeating digits with that of peers. Difficulties identified in repeating digits may be an indicator of an underlying language-learning disability.

Auditory memory measures that focus on meaningless sequences of auditory stimuli (e.g., digits, nonsense words), however, need to be used with caution because children who have difficulty on these measures do not necessarily have problems processing meaningful language. More research is needed to assess the efficacy of language-processing tasks in distinguishing language differences from language disorders in LCD students.

Profile

Tran, a Vietnamese 14-year-old high school freshman, was referred for special education assessment. He had a history of learning problems dating back to kindergarten, but school personnel were concerned about mislabeling him. The student spoke Vietnamese as his dominant language and he had limited proficiency in English. Thus, Tran participated in non-special education support programs such as tutoring and ESL small group work, but he was never evaluated for special education. His high school teachers were concerned because Tran had greater difficulty remembering information than his Vietnamese peers. Several teachers confided that "I tell Tran something, and five minutes later he's forgotten it." Tran had few friends and was beginning to show signs of a clinically significant behavior problem. His parents were concerned because he had stated that he wanted to join a gang.

The speech-language pathologist, working with a Vietnamese interpreter, conducted a dynamic assessment screening to evaluate Tran's ability to learn. He found that Tran was slow to learn new information and concepts, even with repeated demonstrations and explanations in both English and Vietnamese. Tran was unable to repeat a sequence of more than four digits (immediate rote memory) in either Vietnamese or English. The interpreter conversed with Tran at length about various topics, and noted that Tran often gave inappropriate responses. Tran also never initiated topics during the conversation. The interpreter said that "When Tran tells me something, I don't know what he's talking about—he makes me confused." The speech-language pathologist scheduled a formal evaluation for Tran because he suspected an underlying language-learning disability.

LANGUAGE SAMPLING

In assessing oral communication, many experts recommend gathering a spontaneous language sample in English and in the child's primary language. Some experts give specific strategies for counting C-units and T-units and utilizing this data (e.g., Goldstein, 2000; Gutierrez-Clellen et al., 2000; Washington, Craig, & Kushmaul, 1998). General suggestions for language sampling are presented below.

❑ *Collect language samples in familiar contexts such as the classroom or home.* When a variety of locations are used, assessment yields a more accurate and representative picture of the student's language.

❑ *Use a variety of conversation partners.* Conversational samples are often obtained in situations in which an adult "interviews" a child. Although these samples can be diagnostically useful, the information obtained may be quite different from that obtained when the student interacts with peers. Student interaction with peers is one of the most important sources of information regarding a student's use of language in social contexts. Samples can also be collected while students interact with siblings or parents. Samples of this type provide information about family interaction patterns, social relationships between peers, and so forth.

❑ *Collect the sample in several different settings over a period of time.* It is recommended that three oral samples be obtained in which the communication partners interact for at least 10 minutes. Each sample should be obtained on a different day.

❑ *Tape-record the language sample for analysis.*

❑ *Ask a bilingual speech-language pathologist to evaluate the primary language sample.* If one is not available, knowledgeable professionals who speak the primary language can listen to the sample and give their impressions. If school professionals who speak the student's language are not available, bilingual community members may need to be used. Ideally, at least two native speakers should transcribe the sample. The information obtained should be discussed in detail with the speech-language pathologist.

❑ *Analyze both content and form.* It is important to examine the student's morphosyntactic (grammatical) usage in both English and the primary language. However, professionals must also evaluate the student's communicative competence in various settings.

❑ Remember that grammatical errors in English are sometimes a result of the influence from the student's primary language. One should not label a student "language-learning disabled" based only on grammatical errors in English! Grammatical errors are to be expected among second language learners who have had limited exposure to the "rules" of English.

❑ Ensure that the student is relaxed when a language sample is collected. The student may verbalize very little if the person conducting the assessment is unfamiliar to him or her. The student may also experience anxiety if the testing is conducted in an unfamiliar environment. It is important to establish rapport with the student and to establish an environment in which the student feels comfortable. Children often verbalize more during interactions with familiar adults.

Suggestions for Eliciting Language

It is important to elicit a large quantity of verbal responses as language is used for various speaking purposes. Recommendations for eliciting language samples include the following:

❑ Use interesting, culturally relevant materials such as toys, puppets, and picture books. Older students might enjoy magazines with articles focusing on specific topics such as sports, motorcycles, etc. Make sure that the materials are culturally relevant for students and that the students have prior experience with the materials.

❑ Ask students to talk about the steps required to complete a task such as playing a favorite game, cooking a certain dish, fixing a bike, etc.

❑ Have students tell a story about something they did, or have them talk about a book they have read.

❑ Ask students to describe television shows or movies that they like to watch.

❑ Ask students to describe objects of different shapes, sizes, and textures.

❑ Present pairs of related picture cards. Ask students to choose pictures that go together and to explain how they are related.

❑ Present the student with a group of pictures from a specific category (e.g., several types of food) and with a picture that doesn't fit in that category (e.g., picture of a car). Ask the student to choose the picture that is unrelated and explain why it is unrelated.

❑ Have the student sequence story picture cards and tell the story.

❑ Present problem situations verbally or in picture form and ask students to resolve the problems. For instance, students might be asked to describe how a child should react in a situation where peers do not want him or her to play on their team.

❑ Ask the students to give directions to a location (e.g., home, local grocery store, etc.).

❑ Play barrier games with identical sets of objects. A student is selected to arrange pictures of objects on a board. The other students cannot see the pictures on this board. After arranging the pictures, the student describes the picture arrangement and another student tries to duplicate it based on the verbal information presented. There are other variations of barrier games that can be used (e.g., building a tower with blocks, drawing a picture, etc.)

❑ Present students with pictures or objects and ask them to explain how these items are similar and how they are different.

❑ Name several members of a category. Ask the student to give the name of the category (e.g., " A chair, desk, and table are all types of _____.")

EVALUATING LANGUAGE USE

It is critical to analyze student interactions in natural communication situations with peers from similar cultural and linguistic backgrounds. Research indicates that mainstream monolingual English-speaking students may not respond readily to students who are not yet fluent speakers of English (Rice, Sell, & Hadley, 1991). In addition, students should be judged by comparing their performance to that of peers from their own culture and language background.

If a communication disorder is suspected, problems in the functional use of language need to be documented based on observations of the student in natural speaking situations. Some of the behaviors commonly observed in students with communication disorders include the following:

❑ Nonverbal aspects of language are culturally inappropriate.

❑ Student does not express basic needs adequately.

❑ Student rarely initiates verbal interaction with peers.

❑ When peers initiate interactions, student responds sporadically.

❑ Student replaces speech with gestures and communicates nonverbally when talking would be more appropriate.

❏ Peers give indications that they have difficulty understanding the student.

❏ Student often gives inappropriate responses.

❏ Student has difficulty conveying thoughts in an organized, sequential manner that is understandable to listeners.

❏ Student shows poor topic maintenance.

❏ Student has word-finding difficulties that are caused by factors other than the child's limited experience in using the language.

❏ Student fails to provide significant information to the listener.

❏ Student has difficulty taking turns appropriately during communicative interactions.

❏ Student perseverates on conversation topics.

❏ Student fails to ask and answer questions appropriately.

❏ Student needs to have information repeated, even when that information is easy to comprehend and expressed clearly.

❏ Student often echoes what is heard.

Summary

In addition to assessing the student's mastery of various language structures, it is important to examine how language is used functionally in various social settings. When a student speaks two languages, language samples should be analyzed in both languages. Performance should always be compared to that of peers from similar backgrounds. Language sampling provides valuable information about students' communication skills that is necessary to differentiate language differences from disorders.

Profile

M. S., a 12-year-old Mien girl, was referred for speech-language testing because she was having academic difficulties. M. S. was born in Thailand, and she and her family came to the United States as refugees from Laos in 1980. M. S. had received a kidney transplant when she was in third grade and missed school frequently due to medical concerns. She had undergone a period of elective mutism during the dialysis. Mr. S. had no concerns about M. S.'s development in Mien. He stated that he and his wife had noticed that M. S. was slower to develop English than her siblings. After the dialysis was completed, however, her English language skills had shown rapid growth.

(continued on following page)

(continued from previous page)

The speech-language pathologist worked with a Mien interpreter, using informal dynamic measures administered in Mien. M. S. performed well on these measures. She, however, had more difficulty when these measures were administered in English.

Members of the school assessment team argued that M. S. should be placed into a class for communicatively disabled students. The speech-language pathologist strongly disagreed with this recommendation, stressing the need for a descriptive analysis of oral communication in natural speaking contexts.

The first time the speech-language pathologist attempted to obtain a spontaneous language sample, M. S. said almost nothing despite repeated attempts to elicit language. M. S. did not know the speech-language pathologist, and the testing room was unfamiliar to her. The speech-language pathologist then talked with M. S. on several different occasions to establish better rapport with her.

Once rapport had been established, a second attempt was made to collect a language sample. In addition to obtaining an informal conversation sample, M. S. was asked to describe pictures.

E = Examiner   M = Student

E: What's the girl doing?

M: Eating breakfast.

E: Can you tell me more about that?

M: The girl is eating breakfast in the morning.

E: What is happening in this picture?

M: Drinking milk.

E: What else is happening?

M: The parent is drinking milk and smiling.

E: What about in this picture?

M: Baking.

E: Can you tell me more?

M: They are having a party and they made turkey and bacon and they had fruits and cake.

(continued on following page)

(continued from previous page)

> *The topic then changed to M. S.'s home life. The speech-language pathologist asked about the child's experiences when living in Seattle.*
>
> M: In Seattle I did [go to a party]. They make egg roll and they bake some corn muffin . . . and we had turkey and bread stuffing and mashed potato and gravies. I make the mashed potato and they make the turkey . . . we all help. They say if they don't help, they don't get some.
>
> *The speech-language pathologist then encouraged M. to talk about her current home life.*
>
> M: Yeah, sometime my mommy go to the clinic. . . my mom's go home. And I had to take care of my little baby brother—it's Lim. Sometime I carried him in my back with . . . I don't know how to call it. Sometime my mom tell my daddy. . . my daddy say tell him what to buy . . . like baby diaper, baby's powder, some bread and butter and plants. . . my daddy like plants. So we buy vegetable like broccoli and fruit like strawberry.

Analysis

It was previously mentioned that this young Mien student did not speak to the examiner during the first attempt to gather a language sample. The examiner had seen this behavior when working with other Asian children—they were often very shy initially and, due to cultural differences (not disorders!) would not speak willingly with an unfamiliar authority figure. During this second session, however, M. S. seemed much more relaxed because she was no longer interacting with a "stranger."

It was interesting to note that M. S.'s initial descriptions of pictures (a standard technique for eliciting verbalization in children) were quite brief. When asked to elaborate, however, M. S. gave longer, more detailed responses. When topics relevant to her experiences were introduced, M. S. talked enthusiastically and gave detailed responses.

M. S. produced frequent grammatical errors. Plural noun endings, for example, were omitted. This grammatical form, however, is not used in Mien and is commonly omitted by second language learners from Southeast Asia. Problems with verb endings were also commonly observed. M. S.'s level of proficiency in English grammar was felt to be adequate, however, considering her limited experience in using the language.

Summary

The following points can be made based upon this brief case study:

❏ Although M. S. did manifest some grammatical errors, the errors produced did not seem to be abnormal considering her Mien language background and her limited experience in using the English language. She gave the examiner clear verbal explanations and manifested very appropriate language usage.

❑ M. S.'s language skills in her primary language, Mien, were superior to her English skills (based on comparisons of assessment measures in Mien and English). Her basic interpersonal communication skills were adequate in English, although she had not yet developed the cognitive-academic language proficiency necessary for success in an academic curriculum in which English was used as the language of instruction.

❑ M. S. did not qualify for speech-language intervention or for placement in a self-contained classroom for children with severe communication disorders. A program for teaching English as a second language, however, was appropriate.

USE OF NARRATIVES AND STORY-RETELLING

Many authors recommend that language evaluations include an assessment of the students' ability to construct narratives and retell stories. There are cultural differences in rules for narrative construction and story-telling that must be taken into account when evaluating students' narrative skills (Bliss, McCabe, & Mahecha, 2001). For example, van Keulen et al. (1998) stated that most standardized tests are scored based on criteria that require use of a *topic-centered style* when telling stories. In this style, there is structured discourse on a single topic, elaboration upon the topic, and lack of presupposed shared knowledge. However, among many working-class African Americans, the *topic-associating style* is typically used. Traditional examiners may view students who use this style as being disorganized because the topic-associating style is characterized by presupposition of shared knowledge, lack of consideration for detail, and structured discourse on several linked topics. Thus, professionals must take students' cultural backgrounds into account during narrative assessment.

During the evaluation, professionals can ask the student to tell a familiar story, to create a story, or to re-tell a story. Mattes & Omark (1991) emphasized the importance of using culturally appropriate stories for story retelling that are within the student's realm of experience. When evaluating students' stories, it is important to consider factors such as story organization, effectiveness in making the sequence of story events comprehensible to the listener, and skill in describing important story events.

Story-telling can be used alone or in the context of a spontaneous language sample. Professionals should ask the following questions when evaluating the student's narrative skills:

❑ Does the student organize the story in such a way that it can be easily understood?

❑ Is the information in the story comprehensible to the listener?

❑ Does the student give elaborated comments, opinions, and explanations that are relevant to the story? Or does the student give minimal or even irrelevant comments?

❑ Does the student include all the major details of the story?

❑ If questioned, can the student remember specific details from the story?

THE PORTFOLIO METHOD OF ASSESSMENT

Definition

A portfolio is a box, folder, notebook, or other container that holds materials by and information about a student. Portfolios are a dynamic assessment tool that can be used to obtain performance data in a variety of areas over a period of time. Portfolios engage teachers and students in a continual process of mediated learning and self-reflection that can be used to develop programs of instruction that are highly individualized (Falk-Ross, 2002).

Characteristics of a Portfolio

❑ A portfolio may contain the following:

1. Student work samples such as writing, art work, science and math projects, social studies reports
2. Video or audiotapes of the student's performance
3. Language samples collected in English and the primary language over time
4. Teacher and parent observation notes
5. Lists of books a student has read
6. Illustrations and pictures drawn by the student
7. Pictures of students' creations (e.g., 3-dimensional art or building projects)

❑ Portfolios are valuable in developing instructional programs for a variety of reasons:

1. They promote student creativity and independence.

2. They help students more fully understand their abilities and strengths so that they can set their own goals.

3. They help students understand learning as a process, not a product.

4. They provide a multidimensional view of students' development.

5. They include information that can be used to track and evaluate students' performance over time.

6. They include information relevant to evaluating the effectiveness of instruction.

7. They can be used to provide parents with samples of the student's achievements.

8. They include examples of what students have achieved.

9. They give professionals a better picture of students' abilities than that revealed by standardized tests.

10. They reflect the student's performance within the classroom curriculum and provide a picture of the types of educational opportunities students have been given.

11. They can be used to generate discussion topics during student-teacher conferences.

12. They help parents understand that the professionals working with their children have specialized knowledge.

13. They engage students in learning and promote an understanding of how learning facilitates the achievement of specific goals.

How to Create and Use Portfolio Assessment

There are many ways that portfolios can be created and used. The following are general suggestions that can be tailored to each student's needs:

1. Teachers and students can make choices together about what goes into the portfolio. Students and teachers can each have separate sections within the portfolio for holding specific items.

2. Portfolios are used to showcase the best examples of students' work.

3. Teachers and students periodically review the portfolio together to assess achievement, effort, etc. Students can also review one another's portfolios in small groups.

4. Students share their portfolios with parents.

5. At the end of the year, students are given their portfolios to take home. Selected portions of the student's work can be maintained by the school as a record of progress.

6. Assessment teams can review students' portfolios to evaluate performance changes over time.

7. Special education personnel can set up portfolios for students at I.E.P. time. They can also use portfolios as part of the pre-referral process.

8. Portfolios are public documents; confidential information should not be included.

✐ REFLECTION ✐

List and briefly describe two reasons why the use of portfolio assessment with LCD students is advantageous in obtaining valid assessment data.

_____

_____

_____

_____

_____

USE OF INTERPRETERS

In addition to using the above-described methods of informal, nonstandardized assessment such as portfolios, schools are often using interpreters for assistance in family conferencing, assessment, and intervention. The term "interpreter" is used in this chapter to refer to a bilingual individual who translates written information or who facilitates communication between speakers who do not speak the same language. The role of the interpreter may include translating forms, administering tests, interviewing parents, translating for parents and teachers, and so forth. Finding interpreters is often not an easy task, especially if there are few people in the community who speak the target language.

Family members can be used effectively as interpreters in some situations. It is often difficult to use family members, however, in situations where test items need to be administered in a predetermined format (Anderson, 2002). Sometimes family members tell the child the answers or show signs of being upset if the child has difficulty performing specific tasks.

Criteria that should be used in selecting and using interpreters have been described (Langdon, 2000; Langdon & Cheng, 2002; Mattes & Omark, 1991) These criteria are explained below, and include (most importantly) the characteristics of interpreters.

Characteristics of Interpreters

1. Interpreters must be trained for their roles.

2. Interpreters must have excellent bilingual communication skills. Interpreters must possess good oral and written proficiency in both English and the primary language.

3. Interpreters must understand their ethical responsibilities. Interpreters must be able to maintain confidentiality at all times. They must also be honest about their abilities and limitations.

4. Interpreters must act in a professional manner. It is important for interpreters to be able to function on professional teams. Interpreters must understand the importance of punctuality, impartiality, responsibility, and professional dress.

5. Interpreters must be able to relate to members of their cultural group (Isaac, 2001). Some interpreters may have grown up in circumstances quite different from those of the students and families with whom they work. Others may speak a different dialect than the students and their families. Interpreters should have the ability to relate to students and families and should be able to establish rapport.

6. Interpreters need good short-term memory skills so that they can record information and report what they learn from contacts with parents and students.

School districts should provide funding so that interpreters can be paid for their services. Interpreters take their jobs more seriously when compensation is provided.

Training Interpreters

When interpreters are being trained, it is optimal for school districts to work together to provide the training. This type of collaboration can reduce costs and promote cooperation between school districts.

The training of interpreters will vary depending on the nature of the interpreters' responsibilities. The following areas are recommended for inclusion in the training of interpreters:

1. Characteristics of speech-language disorders and learning disabilities

2. Information about first and second language acquisition

3. Guidelines for distinguishing language differences from disorders

4. Special education terminology relevant to their roles in working with family members

5. Role of the interpreter on the team

6. Goals of special education testing

7. Procedures for administering tests

8. Cultural differences and their impact on assessment

9. Strategies for interacting with families

10. Use of assessment results in placement decisions

11. Legal requirements and professional ethics

Use of Interpreters in Assessment

The professional who is using the services of an interpreter in assessment has important ethical responsibilities. It is important for the professional to do the following:

1. Recognize the limitations of interpreted tests.

2. Allow the interpreter only to carry out activities for which training has been provided.

3. Involve others in training the interpreter when appropriate.

4. Make sure that the permission for assessment form specifies that the services of an interpreter will be used during the assessment.

5. Be sure to specify in the assessment report that the services of an interpreter were used.

6. Provide the interpreter with background information about the student who is to be tested.

7. Prepare the interpreter for each testing session and debrief the interpreter afterwards.

8. Show the interpreter how to use tests and make sure that the interpreter feels comfortable with the testing. Some interpreters come from cultures where it is not appropriate to admit that something has not been understood. It is imperative that the professional makes certain that the interpreter truly understands the assessment tasks.

9. Allow the interpreter time, before the student arrives, to organize test materials, read instructions, and clarify any areas of concern.

10. Ensure that the interpreter does not protect the student by hiding the extent of the student's limitations/disabilities.

11. Show the interpreter how to use tests.

The professional needs to be sure that the interpreter participates only in activities for which training has been provided. Family members should be informed that an interpreter will be used in assessment. It is important to prepare the interpreter for each testing session and to provide feedback following the assessment. Langdon & Cheng (2002) recommended the process of *B. I. D.*: (1.) *briefing*, (2) *interaction*, and (3) *debriefing*. Interpreters should be observed during the testing sessions to prevent the following problems:

1. Recording the assessment data incorrectly

2. Prompting the student or giving clues

3. Using too many words

4. Giving directions that are too brief or too complicated

5. Over- or under-using reinforcement

It is important to remind the interpreter to write down all behaviors observed during testing, even if the behaviors seem extraneous to the immediate task.

Matsuda & O'Connor, (1993) suggested that professionals watch for the following behaviors in students being tested:

1. Response delays (latencies)

2. Use of gestures to replace words

3. False starts, word repetitions

4. Perseveration

5. Confusion

6. Inattention, distractibility

7. Language and articulation errors

Although interpreters can be useful in data collection, they should not be given the responsibility for educational decision-making. Recommendations for educational placement should be made by a team of professionals.

Use of Interpreters as Interviewers

During meetings, interpreters should be seated as close to family members as possible. It is important to introduce family members to everyone at the meeting. The parents should hear each person's name and understand each person's role as it relates to the student. It is important for family members to understand the purpose of the meeting.

Before the interview, the questions to be asked should be discussed with the interpreter. The interpreter must understand the interview questions completely and know how to record the family's responses.

The educational professional needs to be on hand during the interview to answer questions or resolve problems. It is optimal to tape-record the interview (unless this makes families nervous or uncomfortable).

This author has interviewed interpreters to obtain their viewpoints about common problems encountered in the schools. Interpreters said that translating paperwork (e.g., IEPs and reports) was extremely time-consuming, and they were not given enough time for these tasks. Several interpreters stated that during meetings professionals spoke for too long without pausing, and thus the information was difficult to remember and convey. Interpreters also stated that they were frequently called at the last minute and put into meetings or other situations with no preparation at all. Recommendations for optimal utilization of interpreters in meetings include the following:

1. Speak in short units and avoid slang and professional jargon.

2. Encourage the interpreter to translate the family's words without paraphrasing them.

3. Look at the family rather than the interpreter when speaking.

4. Observe the nonverbal behaviors of the family during the interview.

5. Allow opportunities for family members to ask questions.

6. Provide written information when appropriate.

7. Tape-record the interview if the family is comfortable with the use of a recording device.

It is important that interpreters have the skills necessary to explain the special education process to families. Families who are not familiar with the educational system in the United States may believe that special education is appropriate only for children with severe physical or mental disabilities. As one immigrant put it, "In my country you are either normal, retarded, or crazy. We don't have all these categories like the U.S. does." (E. Rojas, personal communication, December 2001)

The professional should always be present at interviews with family members to ensure that the appropriate information is communicated. The interpreter's responsibility is to facilitate communication between school professionals and family members. If appropriately trained, interpreters can be a valuable resource to school professionals in both assessment and intervention. The material presented in Langdon & Cheng (2002) is excellent for professionals interested in training and using interpreters.

SUMMARY

The traditional assessment practice of relying on the use of standardized, norm-referenced tests to assess LCD students is fraught with bias and difficulties. Professionals in today's schools need to utilize informal, nonstandardized assessment methods and measures that are tailored to the needs and backgrounds of individual students. These methods and measures include dynamic assessment, assessment of language processing capacity, language sampling, use of narratives and story-telling, portfolio assessment, and utilization of interpreters to assist in the assessment process. When professionals assess LCD students in an appropriate, individualized, and non-biased manner, the placement of these students into appropriate educational settings will be much more clear-cut and consistent with students' needs.

STUDY QUESTIONS

1. Many professionals use the services of interpreters in the assessment of LCD students. List and describe four characteristics that you would look for in choosing an interpreter to assist in the assessment process.

2. Summarize the research regarding language information processing as it relates to assessment of specific language impairment. How might professionals apply the results of this research to the assessment of LCD students with language-learning disabilities?

3. Describe three informal procedures that the professional can use to obtain valid, non-biased information about the performance of LCD students with suspected language-learning disabilities.

TRUE-FALSE

Circle the number beside each statement that is true.

4. When an interpreter is used during meetings with parents, it is a good idea for the professional to leave the room for a period of time so that the family can confide in the interpreter.

5. Federal law does not exclude subjective or qualitative measures in assessment, but leaves the choice of measurement tools and criteria to the educator.

6. During language sampling, it is important to remember that grammatical errors in English are sometimes a result of the influence from the student's primary language.

7. The Theory of Structural Cognitive Modifiability was created by Reuven Feuerstein based primarily upon his work with Holocaust survivors.

8. When evaluating LCD students with suspected language disorders, it is important to compare their performance with that of monolingual English-speaking peers.

9. A primary goal of dynamic assessment is to look at a student's ability to learn—or how the student learns—rather than to assess knowledge at one point in time.

10. Although portfolio assessment is used in some school districts, norm-referenced tests are preferred because they reflect a student's performance over time on curriculum-based tasks.

MULTIPLE CHOICE

Unless specified otherwise, circle the number beside each statement that is true.

11. When professionals utilize the services of interpreters during meetings, these professionals should do the following:
    A. Look at the interpreter rather than the family when speaking.
    B. Speak in short units, avoid slang, and refrain from using professional jargon.
    C. Encourage the interpreter to paraphrase the family's words for ease of translation.
    D. Allow opportunities for family members to ask questions.
    E. Provide written information when appropriate.

12. Advantages of informal testing include the following:
    A. This type of assessment is generally ecologically valid and considers the environment, home, and culture of the child and family.
    B. Data obtained can be evaluated in relation to the demands of the classroom curriculum.
    C. This type of assessment allows professionals to evaluate the student's functioning in real-life contexts.
    D. Specific standards are specified for scoring each response.
    E. Specialized training is not needed to interpret the results.

13. Which one of the following questions is NOT critical in evaluating a student's ability to produce narratives?
    A. Can the student respond to questions by recalling specific details from the story?
    B. Does the student organize the story in such a way that it can be easily understood?
    C. Is the information in the story comprehensible to the listener?
    D. Does the student conclude the story with a "moral" or main point?
    E. Does the student include all the major details of the story?

14. In the topic-centered style of story-telling, the following elements are observed:
    A. Structured discourse on a single topic
    B. Elaboration upon the topic
    C. Presupposed shared knowledge
    D. Relational ambiguity
    E. Reduced diadokokinetic rate

15. You are evaluating a student from Argentina who may have a language-learning disability. You are conducting the evaluation in both Spanish and English. Which of the following are indicators that the communication problems observed are caused by a language-learning disability?
    A. The student has difficulty conveying thoughts in an organized, sequential manner that is understandable to listeners.
    B. The student fails to provide significant information to the listener.
    C. The student often echoes what is heard.
    D. The student shows poor topic maintenance.
    E. The student fails to ask and answer questions appropriately.

ANSWERS TO STUDY QUESTIONS

4. False
5. True
6. True
7. False
8. False
9. True
10. False
11. B, D, and E
12. A, B, and C
13. D
14. A and B
15. A, B, C, D, and E

PART 3

Intervention for Students with Special Needs

Chapter 14

FOUNDATIONS OF EFFECTIVE SERVICE DELIVERY

Outline

One of the questions most commonly asked by monolingual professionals is, "What are we supposed to do with all these students who don't speak English?" There is no easy answer to this question. Service to linguistically and culturally diverse (LCD) students is influenced by many factors: (1) availability of various services, (2) current policy and educational trends, (3) needs of students, and (4) legal considerations. Unfortunately, students' needs are often not the primary factor in determining what services they receive. Realistically, service delivery is often driven by the availability of funding; that is, how much money is available to serve the needs of LCD students? The amount of money available is driven in part by policy trends. Prominent current trends include restructuring special education programs, promoting full inclusion, incorporating multiculturalism into curricula, and determining appropriate instructional placements for LCD students.

RESTRUCTURING SPECIAL EDUCATION PROGRAMS

Most people are keenly aware that federal/state policies and the health of the national economy are key factors in determining resource allocation. Policy makers around the United States are attempting to determine ways to restructure education, especially special education. Many people feel that special education has become so expensive that new strategies for serving these students are a high priority.

There is a trend toward streamlining special education in many school programs, although many special educators are opposed to this trend. The number of students with special education needs increases as the population increases, but limited funding is available for special education programs to help these students. When Congress passed IDEA in 1975, it pledged (under IDEA Part B) to fund up to 40% of the average per pupil expenditure for each special education student. However, today the federal government only funds 14.8% of that amount. If this funding continues at the current rate, Congress will not meet its promise to fully fund IDEA before the year 2045. Until then, many school districts will have personnel shortages and professionals with large student caseloads (Annett, 2001).

Policy makers and professional educators have proposed that one way to restructure the educational system is to increase collaboration between regular and special education, thus decreasing the need for a separate special education system. The federal government, in the Individuals with Disabilities Education Act (IDEA, 1997), emphasized that more neutral funding models for school districts would help these districts to allocate funds in any way they wished; money was no longer as specifically earmarked for special education. The goal of this reallocation of monies was to encourage districts to serve special education students within the regular education classroom setting as much as possible, thus decreasing the need for separate, expensive special education services.

It is clear that with limited funding in many parts of the United States, policy makers are looking towards collaborative, full inclusion models where the needs of special learners can be met in the regular classroom rather than in separate special education programs. Reactions to this trend are mixed; however, because it appears that the trend is becoming more and more of a reality, it behooves regular and special educators alike to collaborate, restructure current programs, and truly work together to serve the needs of students (Brice & Roseberry-McKibbin, 1999b; Dodge, 2000; Falk-Ross, 2002). One way to do this is through inclusion. Brice and Miller (2000) summarized the ideal inclusive classroom setting:

1. All children learn together;

2. Educational benefit is maximized;

3. Students are not unduly labeled or identified as special needs learners;

4. The need for a separate curriculum is minimized;

5. The student is served in the least restrictive environment.

EMPHASIS ON MULTICULTURALISM

In addition to streamlining special education and emphasizing inclusion, many schools across the United States are making efforts to include multicultural components within their classrooms. The popular idea of the "salad bowl" embodies the primary concept underlying multiculturalism: ethnic and cultural groups in the United States should preserve and celebrate their diverse identities and backgrounds instead of trying to blend them into a "melting pot." Both regular and special educators can be involved in multiculturalism.

There are two primary "camps" of multicultural education professionals: those who support *particularism* and those who support *pluralism*. Advocates of particularism emphasize separate ethnic studies courses, separate ethnic clubs, etc. In short, some particularists reject assimilation and unintentionally widen ethnic divisions by encouraging separatism. Pluralists, on the other hand, recommend that information about various cultural groups be woven into traditional curricula. Ideally, pluralism emphasizes interconnection between various cultural and ethnic groups.

There are many reasons for incorporating multiculturalism into regular and special education curricula and activities. Children who are centered in and proud of their cultural heritage tend to be more motivated and show greater academic gains than children whose culture is de-emphasized and suppressed. If schools do not show a respect for cultural differences in learners, interactions may be guided by an expectation of inferiority. Wigginton (1992) stated:

> When students are told by a teacher or a text that they should be proud of their culture, the impact is negligible. A guest speaker at an assembly doesn't remedy the situation, nor do ethnic food festivals or once-a-week 'enlightenment' sessions. Rather, it is sustained exposure that is effective in an environment characterized by independent student research and inquiry, where aspects of a culture are discovered...and brought...to a level of consciousness and examined. (p. 224)

Multiculturalism should be infused throughout class curricula, not merely tagged on or added as a once-a-month feature. If students are in supportive environments that promote multiculturalism and multilingualism, they will be empowered to become valuable and contributing members of mainstream society.

Mainstream "majority" students need to be exposed to a multicultural curriculum for a number of reasons. First, such exposure promotes understanding of other groups and potentially reduces race-related conflict. Being exposed to multiculturalism also prepares students for workplaces in which they will be part of a multi-ethnic workforce and interact with colleagues from a variety of cultural and linguistic backgrounds. Regular and special educators need to be able to reach out to children from a variety of cultural and linguistic backgrounds.

INCORPORATING MULTICULTURALISM INTO THE CURRICULUM

By incorporating multicultural components into both regular and special education, professionals can create a climate that is highly motivating for linguistically and culturally diverse students (Roseberry-McKibbin, 2002). Such activities also help mainstream students to develop a better understanding of individuals from other cultural backgrounds. Professionals can reach out to LCD students in the following ways:

❑ Show interest in students' home language, country, and culture.

❑ Use maps of the U.S. and of the world so that all students can see where the families of other students have come from.

❑ Reduce students' anxieties as much as possible. A relaxed learner is an effective learner.

❑ During initial English language instruction, allow a silent period in which students are not required to respond verbally.

❑ Ask parents to come to the classroom in native country dress. Encourage them to talk about their culture and their customs.

❑ Make sure that students know that you are there to help them and that you want them to succeed.

❑ Give students special attention when possible.

❑ If nobody in the classroom speaks the student's language, assign a native-born "peer buddy" to assist the student.

❑ Encourage students to use their primary language in various contexts at school.

❑ Represent languages of the various cultural groups in the school community by having signs in key areas (e.g., front office, auditorium) in these languages.

❑ Display objects and pictures representing various cultures.

❑ Create classroom bulletin boards that display pictures of and information about people from diverse backgrounds and cultures.

❑ Provide books written in a variety of languages.

❑ Invite people from various cultural groups to speak to students and to act as resources.

❑ Give students opportunities to study their primary language and culture in required and elective subjects and in extracurricular activities.

❑ Give all students sustained exposure to multicultural activities. Don't just incorporate sporadic, "token" activities.

❑ Take all students on field trips to places such as Native American reservations, Japan Town, Chinatown, and other local community resources.

❑ Develop thematic units that incorporate information about various cultural groups.

❑ Use comparative study of folktales (Cheng, 1998). For instance, read the story of Cinderella and ask the librarian for books with parallel stories in other cultures. Read, compare, and discuss the similarities and differences in the stories.

❑ Teach the entire class words, phrases, and songs in various languages.

❑ Use biographical sketches in which students read (either silently or aloud) a biographical sketch about a minority leader/role model.

By following the above suggestions, opportunities for LCD students to succeed are maximized. Multicultural activities help mainstream students to experience increased awareness, knowledge, and sensitivity to the needs of others.

This author was working one day with a group of students in the speech-language room in an elementary school setting. She asked individual students to discuss where their ancestors were from, and used a globe to help the students identify their exact countries of origin. One multiracial girl said proudly, "My ancestors are from China, Korea, and Africa." An African American boy said with great pride, "My ancestors are from Africa!" The white boy in the group paused, thought a minute, and said, "And my family is from....Sacramento!" Much can be learned about how students perceive their world and the world of others by engaging them in conversations about their family history and way of life.

AVOIDING TOKENISM IN EDUCATIONAL PROGRAMS

When general and special educators incorporate multicultural education into their work with students, they need to avoid doing the following:

Stereotyping

Examples: People from cultures outside the United States are shown only in "traditional" costumes and in rural settings.

The only non-Anglos shown are those who live in poverty.

The same picture is used over and over to represent a group. The diversity that exists within a population is not depicted.

Trivializing

Examples: Activities are based only on the foods commonly eaten and/or the holidays celebrated by members of a cultural group.

Parents and other family members from multicultural backgrounds are invited to school only on "special days."

The classroom has only one book about a particular ethnic group among 15 books about Anglo European Americans.

There is only one "ethnic" bulletin board in the classroom.

Misrepresentation

Examples: Pictures of people participating in an activity commonly associated with Native Americans are shown when discussing a Native American group that does not practice that particular activity.

Pictures from rural Mexico in the 1900s are used to teach students about modern-day Hispanic life in the United States.

Disconnecting

Examples: Books about specific cultural groups are read only on special occasions (e.g., reading about the Mexican culture only on Cinco de Mayo).

An instructional unit is presented about a cultural group without relating the unit to the regular curriculum.

The goal for all professionals is to incorporate multicultural education into the core curriculum as a natural part of teaching and learning. Professionals also need to reduce cultural conflicts within their classrooms.

REDUCING CULTURAL CONFLICTS IN THE CLASSROOM

There are numerous situations within the classroom that can foster cultural conflicts. The extent to which contextual factors are used to communicate meaning varies from culture to culture. In *high-context* cultures, learning often occurs by observing the actions of others, and the role of the individual as a member of a group is emphasized. Situations in which one individual tries to control the actions of an entire group are viewed as something that should be avoided. In *low-context* cultures an emphasis is placed on the role of the individual, and information is conveyed primarily through verbal interaction. Students from high-context cultures often experience difficulty adjusting to the low-context structure of mainstream American schools (Weiss, 2002). Often, these students do not volunteer information during class, and they may fail to respond when called upon by the teacher (Westby & Rouse, 1985).

The manner in which time is used can also be a source of conflict within the classroom. In mainstream American schools, rigid schedules are often followed. If an activity is not completed during the time allotted for the lesson, the teacher often moves on to the next activity. In many cultures, strict adherence to schedules is less important. Thus, a teacher in that culture may continue with a specific activity until it is completed.

Clearly, there is no single strategy that can work effectively with students from every culture. When students from many different cultural backgrounds receive instruction in the same classroom, conflicts sometimes cannot be avoided. Educational professionals must develop an awareness of cultural differences so that they can adapt their instruction to meet the needs of students. Students must also learn to adapt to cultural differences that they observe in the school environment. When professionals attempt to adapt their instruction to meet students' needs, and students learn to adapt to school expectations, cultural conflicts in the classroom are less likely to occur.

SELECTING INSTRUCTIONAL RESOURCES

It has already been stated that the type of service provided for LCD students depends on a variety of factors. One of those key factors is availability of resources or services. In some school districts, there are few, if any, bilingual education classrooms. There may be no teachers with training in bilingual education or ESL instruction. Legislation eliminating bilingual education in California has resulted in major changes in school programs, although many school districts still offer native language support in their classrooms.

Many teachers are desperately in need of services for the students in their classrooms who do not speak English. Often, they turn to the speech-language pathologist for help. This author has experienced situations wherein the classroom teacher requested special education placement for students because "I need to get these kids that don't speak English out of my class!" In the eyes of many classroom teachers, speech-language pathologists teach language skills and, therefore, should take responsibility for serving limited-English-proficient students in their programs.

Classroom teachers are often overwhelmed by the sheer numbers of students in their classrooms and feel that they are left "holding the bag" when LCD students are their responsibility. Their concerns are valid because the available support for these students is often limited.

In school districts with bilingual education programs, students are often offered native language instruction only for a very short period of time. They struggle academically in English because they have not acquired the level of proficiency necessary for the cognitive tasks required within the classroom curriculum. Often, these students converse well in informal situations and appear to have adequate English language skills for classroom instruction. Where are teachers to turn when these students fail to learn in the classroom?

As mentioned previously, it is illegal for schools to place limited English proficient students into special education if the purpose of the placement is to teach English language skills. Only a select number of these students are truly eligible for special education services—they must have a disability.

✐ REFLECTION ✐

You work as a speech-language pathologist in a school district and speak only English. Approximately 70% of the students on your caseload are from "minority" backgrounds. Describe three strategies you will use to work with these students in a culturally competent manner (either in your therapy room or collaboratively in the students' classrooms).

_____

_____

_____

_____

_____

_____

PROGRAM PLACEMENT ALTERNATIVES

There are various service delivery options available for serving LCD children (see Figure 14.1). Special education professionals need to collaborate with professionals within the regular education curriculum to make such programs work. Increasingly, the perspective supporting newer models of cooperative teaching between general and special education is that there are many advantages to having children with disabilities remain in the classroom as much as possible with consultative help from special education personnel (Falk-Ross, 2002).

Figure 14.1

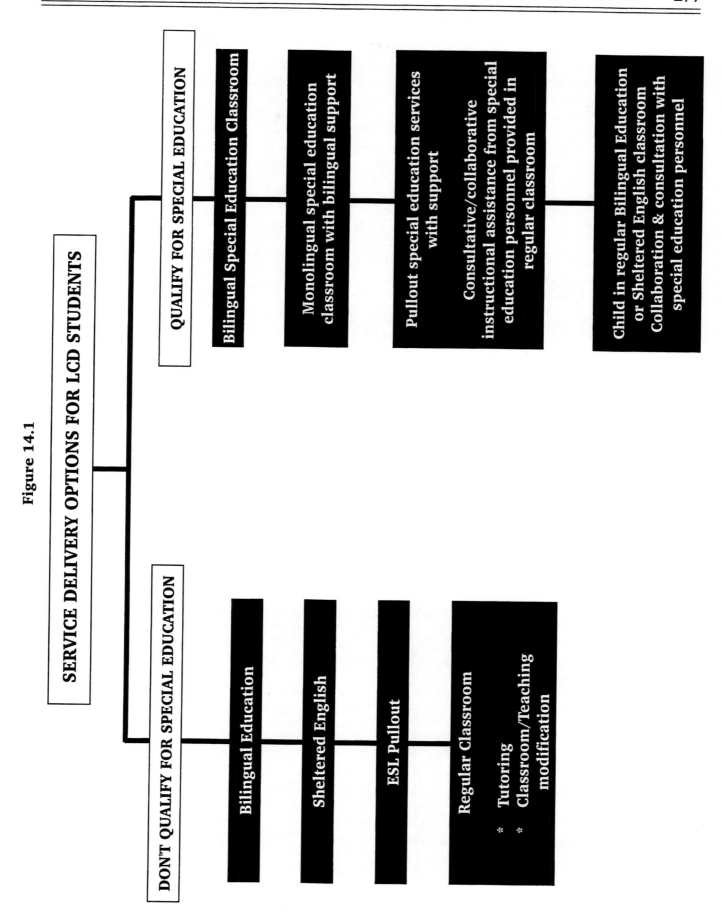

SERVICE DELIVERY OPTIONS FOR LCD STUDENTS

DON'T QUALIFY FOR SPECIAL EDUCATION

- Bilingual Education
- Sheltered English
- ESL Pullout
- Regular Classroom
  - * Tutoring
  - * Classroom/Teaching modification

QUALIFY FOR SPECIAL EDUCATION

- Bilingual Special Education Classroom
- Monolingual special education classroom with bilingual support
- Pullout special education services with support
- Consultative/collaborative instructional assistance from special education personnel provided in regular classroom
- Child in regular Bilingual Education or Sheltered English classroom Collaboration & consultation with special education personnel

Programs for LCD Students Without Special Education Needs

❏ "Sink or swim" all-English classrooms with no additional support (least optimal situation)

❏ All-English classrooms with support (as available). This support might include the following:

1. English and primary language tutors—individually or in small groups

2. ESL pull-out, where students are pulled out of the classroom and brought to a separate room to learn English

3. Multicultural curriculum enhancements within the regular classroom

4. Teacher modification of classroom teaching methods and materials

❏ Bilingual classrooms

1. Instruction in the primary language and English

2. Activities that promote the development of proficiency in both the primary language and English

❏ Sheltered English classrooms

1. Approach to instruction emphasizing the importance of making subject-matter instruction in English comprehensible to limited English speakers

2. Includes curriculum activities to teach academic skills and content, to develop the second language (English), and to promote mastery of academic skills

3. Aims to develop intrinsic motivation and learner autonomy

❏ Participation in additional support programs available through the school (e.g., ESL pullout programs, Chapter I, etc.)

Programs for LCD Students who Qualify for Special Education

1. Consultative, collaborative service provision in which LCD student remains in regular classroom and teacher receives assistance from special education personnel, and/or ESL teachers, or bilingual staff members

2. Pull-out services in English with primary language support

3. Pull-out services (speech-language intervention, learning disability program, or both) in primary language

4. Placement in regular bilingual education or Sheltered English classroom with support from special education

5. Monolingual English special education classroom with primary language support using a bilingual teacher, tutor, etc.

6. Bilingual special education classroom

Many monolingual English-speaking special educators feel inadequately trained to serve LCD children who have limited proficiency in English. If, however, there is collaboration between special and regular education and ESL and bilingual education personnel, the student is far more likely to receive services that will be appropriate.

One way to meet the needs of LCD students is by using tutors. Bilingual tutors can, if properly trained, work with LCD students in their primary language. In the absence of bilingual tutors, monolingual English-speaking tutors can be used to give LCD students extra attention, assistance, and social support. If peer tutors are used, a chart such as that illustrated in Figure 14.2 can be used to help in selecting appropriate materials for peer tutors.

The following suggestions may be implemented, as appropriate, to find both English and primary language tutors to assist LCD students:

❑ Recruit high school and/or college students from various language backgrounds.

❑ Give these students credit/units for tutoring. For example, a high school Vietnamese student might receive independent study credit for tutoring a younger Vietnamese child.

❑ Seek help from local religious and/or community organizations. This author, in one of her workshops, met a speech-language pathologist who said that her district had great success in recruiting members of a local church to tutor children from various language backgrounds. Religious organizations are often looking for ways to reach out to their local communities, and their members will often gladly volunteer to tutor students in school settings. Many communities have churches and religious organizations that represent various cultural/linguistic backgrounds. In some communities, for example, there are Samoan churches in which many members speak both Samoan and English. Churches that offer services in Vietnamese, Spanish, or other languages can offer valuable assistance.

❑ Recruit retired bilingual individuals. Many retired persons are active and have children and grandchildren of their own. Some communities have Foster Grandparents, a group devoted to children who need their support.

❑ Community members may be able to offer helpful suggestions for recruiting tutors.

❑ The Red Cross organization often has multilingual individuals who might be willing to serve as tutors.

❑ The legal system (police, courts) has many bilingual individuals who can be recruited.

❑ Some businesses have a community service requirement for their employees; bilingual employees can serve as tutors to fulfill their community service requirement.

❑ Use peer tutors from the student's classroom or school. Tutors need to be trained. They should observe demonstrations of instructional techniques and should be monitored closely by educational professionals. Professionals should meet with tutors regularly to assess students' progress so that appropriate goals and objectives can be carried out.

Table 14.2

I CAN HELP - YOU CAN HELP

I KNOW

_____Big Letters

_____Small Letters

_____Numbers 1-100

I CAN

_____Write all the Big Letters

_____Write all the Small Letters

_____Write my Name

I CAN

_____Add Numbers to _____

_____Subtract Numbers to _____

I CAN

_____Speak English

_____Read my (Book, Story, etc.)

_____Do my Worksheet

I CAN HELP YOU LEARN

_____Big Letters

_____Small Letters

_____Count to 100

I CAN HELP YOU

_____Write all the Big Letters

_____Write all the Small Letters

_____Write your Name

I CAN HELP YOU

_____Learn to Add

_____Learn to Subtract

I CAN HELP YOU

_____Learn to speak English

_____Read your (Book, Story, etc.)

_____Do your Homework

****

YOU CAN

_____

_____

YOU CAN HELP ME

_____

_____

Source: Hearne, D. (2000). _Teaching Second Language Learners with Learning Disabilities_. Oceanside, CA: Academic Communication Associates, Inc. Reprinted with permission.

DETERMINING THE LANGUAGE OF INSTRUCTION

When a student does qualify for special education assistance, a major consideration is the extent to which the first and second language will be used in the student's instructional program. Many factors need to be considered in making an appropriate decision.

1. ***What is the student's level of proficiency in the primary language and in English?*** These skills can be ascertained by testing language proficiency and observing language usage in functional speaking contexts. If the student is considerably more proficient in the primary language than in English, instruction in the primary language will usually be more effective and efficient (Kayser, 2002; Kiernan & Swisher, 1990; Perozzi & Sanchez, 1992; Goldstein, 2000; Gutierrez-Clellen, 1999). Some professionals are afraid that if students with special needs are given bilingual instruction, they will experience "language confusion." It is recommended that the professional not switch back and forth between languages during intervention sessions. Instruction in the primary language is especially beneficial when new concepts are first introduced. Once a concept has been acquired in the primary language, transfer to a second language will be easier.

2. ***What resources are available for conducting treatment in the primary language?*** If there are no primary language support personnel, and the specialist is a monolingual English speaker, collaboration with the ESL specialist is recommended to develop appropriate goals and strategies for intervention.

3. ***What language is used in the home?*** If the primary language is not developed or reinforced in the school setting, the student may lose the ability to interact with people in the home who speak only that language (Kayser, 2002)

4. ***Do the parents wish for the student's primary language to be maintained?*** Sometimes parents wish for their children to learn English as quickly as possible, and they may feel that intervention should be provided in English only. Other parents wish for the primary language to be maintained and developed.

5. ***Does the student wish to use and maintain the primary language?*** The student's attitudes and motivation are of utmost importance.

6. ***What attitudes do school professionals have about usage of the primary language at school?*** Beaumont (1992, p. 350) stated that ". . . if they ignore or merely tolerate the student's primary language, it will be difficult for the student to sustain the motivation to use that language. On the other hand, if personnel support and develop the primary language, then students will be encouraged to maintain the primary language."

There is no simple formula for determining the language of instruction. Level of proficiency, instructional resources, attitudes of parents and students, and other factors need to be considered. In any instructional situation, it is important to start with the knowledge that the student brings to the learning task. For example, if a student comes to school speaking only Spanish, the use of Spanish in the instructional program can facilitate the learning of basic skills and the acquisition of English (Weiss, 2002). Professionals must always remember that being a proficient bilingual is more advantageous than being a proficient monolingual. Thus, when possible, the development of both English and the primary language should be supported.

WRITING COLLABORATIVE IEP GOALS

Writing goals and objectives for Individual Education Programs (IEPs) is often a challenge, especially if the student speaks two languages. However, there are certain general principles that professionals can follow when writing IEPs for LCD students who need special education services:

❑ The current emphasis on collaboration with the general education curriculum makes it imperative to write IEP goals with a collaborative emphasis.

❑ In writing objectives, an emphasis should be placed on measurable OUTCOMES (also called "benchmarks").

❑ The special educator may be a monolingual English speaker who is unable to provide direct services to the student (if the student's English is very limited). Thus, the professional may need to work with an interpreter to develop and present the instructional activities. This should be stated specifically in the IEP.

❑ The particular type of service delivery model chosen will dictate, in large part, what IEP goals are written for the student.

❑ Programs must be tailored to the individual needs of the student.

❑ The student's primary language must be taken into account.

❑ Goals related to oral communication need to emphasize overall communicative competence rather than isolated skills.

❑ Goals should focus on teaching both content and strategies for learning.

❑ Special educators should collaborate in developing objectives to avoid fragmentation in service delivery.

❑ Special educators can write several joint goals rather than a separate list of goals for each area (e.g., Speech, Resource, etc.).

❑ Teachers and special education personnel can write their own goals, and then use a matrix (see Figure 14.3) to determine who will implement the goals and in which settings these goals will be implemented.

Examples of Collaborative Objectives

The use of collaborative objectives has been described (see Herman, Auchbacher, and Winters, 1992; Montgomery, 1992). Examples of collaborative objectives are presented below:

Sample Objective 1: By December, Susan will demonstrate an understanding of 40 new vocabulary words selected from the classroom curriculum, as measured by data obtained from teacher-made pretests and posttests, classroom assignments, and a review of progress reports obtained from the classroom teacher and the reading specialist.

Sample Objective 2: By October, Jose will count from 1 to 50 and will demonstrate understanding

Figure 14.3

INDIVIDUALIZED EDUCATION PLAN COLLABORATIVE MATRIX

INSTRUCTIONAL GOAL	INSTRUCTIONAL SETTING				
	CLASSROOM	SPECIAL EDUCATION PROGRAM	SPEECH-LANGUAGE PROGRAM	HOME	OTHER
1.					
2.					
3.					
4.					
5.					
6.					
7.					
8.					

of one-to-one correspondence, as measured by a review of classroom assignments and parent observations.

Sample Objective 3: By June, Maria will use oral language to communicate four or more basic needs 80 percent of the time in three situations, as measured by reports from the speech-language pathologist, classroom teacher, and parent.

Sample Objective 4: By December, Jaime will construct a simple, sequenced narrative consisting of 50 or more words when presented with wordless books or picture cards in three or more contexts. Performance will be measured based on reports from the speech-language pathologist, reading specialist, and classroom teacher.

Sample Objective 5: By December, Nadia will write at least three journal entries per week and will discuss the contents of each entry with a group of peers, as measured by observations completed by the teacher and reading specialist over a four-week period.

It is not difficult to write collaborative IEP goals when "the right hand knows what the left hand is doing," so to speak. Speech-language pathologists and other special education professionals should consult with classroom teachers so that they can develop instructional objectives relevant to the goals of classroom instruction (Roseberry-McKibbin, 2001). Professionals should also work with families so that generalization of instructional objectives can occur in the home setting.

WORKING WITH FAMILIES

It is important for professionals to encourage families to participate in their children's educational programs (Tiegerman-Farber, 2002). Families vary greatly in their ability to carry out suggestions from school personnel. Some parents are able to work with their children on a daily basis. Others, however, struggle from day to day to make ends meet and find little time to spend with their children. Families also struggle to adjust to a new country and culture and may have difficulty understanding what the school expects of them. Kelley (2001) summarized four keys to working successfully with parents: *information, encouragement, reassurance,* and *support.* If these are provided by professionals, parents will become more involved in their children's school programs and will be receptive to carrying out the school's recommendations.

Before professionals give suggestions to parents, it is advisable to visit the home to learn about the family and how individual family members interact with the student. If the parents do not speak English, an interpreter may be needed to conduct the interview. In this section, suggestions are provided for enhancing parent and family involvement in students' school experiences.

SUGGESTIONS FOR CONDUCTING HOME VISITS

Professionals can keep the following guidelines in mind when planning and conducting home visits:

❏ Emphasize to parents that being bilingual is a great asset in our society. Many parents, in this author's experience, believe that schools do not support use of the primary language at home. Parents need to be reassured that bilingualism is a desirable goal. Professionals should never suggest that the family needs to speak only English for the student to succeed.

❏ If the student is truly language-learning disabled, it may be appropriate to recommend that adults in the home make language use *person-specific* or *context-specific.* One parent, for example, might speak only Spanish to the child while the other speaks only English. Students with language-learning disabilities may become confused when they observe an adult switching back and forth between two languages.

❏ Bring some of the student's completed assignments to show parents. If the assignments were completed in the primary language, it may be easier for parents to understand the problems that the student is experiencing. Portfolios with examples of children's work over time are especially valuable when discussing the student's progress.

❏ Bring pictures showing students participating in school activities. The classroom situations shown in the pictures can be explained to the parents to help them understand what is being taught at school.

REFLECTION

List four general guidelines for involving multicultural families in the education of their children.

_____

_____

_____

_____

_____

_____

ENCOURAGING COMMUNITY AND SCHOOL SUPPORT

Support groups can be highly effective for multicultural families. Efforts should be made to recruit multicultural individuals or families who are familiar with the nature of school programs. These individuals can form support groups for families from similar backgrounds.

As has been previously stated, multicultural family members often feel more comfortable if they can interact with others from their own culture when the learning needs of their child are being discussed. If support groups are not available, families may benefit from talking to even one other person from their cultural group.

Schools can also sponsor programs to help immigrant parents and their children become accustomed to the "school culture" and its educational practices (Roseberry-McKibbin, 2002). Refreshments can be served, and persons from the parents' cultures can be available to answer questions and provide support for parents and other family members who are new to the U.S. school environment. Evening programs can be quite beneficial because many parents work during the day.

Programs designed to reach out to parents have been described in the literature (see Lindeman, 2001; Manning & Lee, 2001) that can provide an introduction to the U.S school system and curriculum. Topics discussed during these programs might include the following:

❏ School routines for students that are common within U.S. schools (e.g., standing in line and taking turns)

❏ Role of the parent in helping students with homework

❑ Extracurricular activities

❑ Discussion relating to the emphasis on competition and individual achievement in U.S. school programs.

❑ Discussion of the American emphasis on parental involvement (in some cultures, teachers are the authority figures and parents do not "interfere").

The school can also encourage parents to come to the classroom to volunteer for several hours each week. Volunteering helps parents understand how to work with their children at home and increases their overall understanding of what is happening in the classroom.

Profile

Phuong, a Vietnamese kindergarten student, was referred for testing because of a possible stuttering problem. During the evaluation, the student was found to stutter frequently in English.

A meeting was set up with the child's father and a Vietnamese interpreter. The father reported that Phuong stuttered in Vietnamese and English, and that his siblings teased him about the problem. Mr. L. said that when this occurred, Phuong was "sad."

The interpreter explained that services were available in the school to remediate the fluency problem. The father was very relieved, and expressed gratitude that something was going to be done to improve his son's speech. He had been unaware that the school offered services to help his child.

The program placement meeting ended positively with the speech-language pathologist giving suggestions for home carryover. The father indicated that he was interested in participating in a home program.

SUGGESTIONS FOR PARENTS

When professionals interact with and learn about the student's family background, suggestions can be tailor-made for that family. Among the recommendations often made to parents are the following:

❑ Read to the student. If the family members do not read, they can look at books with the children and discuss the stories in the primary language. Wordless books with attractive, relevant pictures are often effective.

❑ Take the student to the local library to check out books.

❑ Visit the student's classroom.

❑ Share folk tales, home recipes, and cultural experiences with the student.

❑ Promote the development of literacy by encouraging functional writing tasks such as making lists, composing letters, and discussing print in the environment.

❏ Continue to develop the student's proficiency in the primary language by presenting a language rich environment in which students are exposed to oral and written language.

❏ Show an interest in seeing the child's homework regularly and offer encouragement and support whenever possible.

❏ Stimulate the language of younger children, even infants and toddlers. Research shows that many families do not believe it is important to talk with very small children. Parents should be made aware of how important it is to provide language stimulation early in infancy (Roseberry-McKibbin, 2000b).

Profile

Ameet S., a kindergarten student from an East Indian family, was first enrolled in a speech and language intervention program in preschool. The family spoke Punjabi at home. Ameet had been placed in a speech and language program because his performance on English language tests was "below the norm for his age." The first speech-language pathologist who worked with Ameet never examined the student's background and, therefore, was unaware that Ameet had spoken only Punjabi until the age of 3 years.

The second speech-language pathologist "inherited" Ameet into her elementary school caseload when the student started kindergarten. After learning about the student's language background, his progress in the classroom was evaluated. The teacher reported that Ameet was making good progress in learning English.

The speech-language pathologist felt that Ameet's progress in English language learning was adequate and that he did not have a language learning disability. The student's mother said that Ameet's use of Punjabi had developed quite well. She never understood why Ameet was in a remedial program and was relieved to learn that these services were being discontinued.

FOSTERING FAMILY LITERACY

It is crucial for professionals to do as much as possible to foster literacy in students' homes. Rather than targeting only the student for literacy development, professionals should include the entire family. It is important to empower both children and parents by fostering literacy for the whole family. Professionals can help foster family literacy by doing the following:

❏ Creating classrooms that are examples of print rich environments with many magazines, books, and posters available to students

❏ Helping parents learn where to find quality reading materials that are inexpensive. Places to find these would include flea markets, used book stores, library sales, garage sales, etc.

❏ Telling parents about the local library and its services, hours of operation, etc. Librarians can be invited to meet parents

❏ Telling parents about local adult literacy services such as literacy volunteer programs and local adult classes

❏ Inviting parents to literacy events such as book fairs

❏ Sending books home so that parents can talk to their children about these books

❏ Encouraging students to read to their parents. In this way, literacy is enhanced for both students and parents.

❏ Teaching literate parents how to use print-referencing behaviors to enhance their children's literacy skills (e.g., "Show me the longest word on this page" or "Which word begins with the letter 'A'?") (Justice & Ezell, 2000)

When parents are actively involved in their children's school experiences, students learn the importance of working hard and learning. By communicating with parents on a regular basis, educational professionals can develop programs of instruction that will be meaningful to students and their families.

Parents may have attitudes and beliefs about educating children that are very different from those of school professionals. It is important to respect their beliefs, to convey an interest in parents' input and suggestions, and to help them understand the goals of the educational program. By making home visits, educational professionals learn about the child's home environment, interests, and way of life.

CONCLUSION

When professionals provide intervention and instruction to linguistically and culturally diverse student populations, they need to keep in mind the following principles:

❏ On the national level, current educational trends are emphasizing multicultural education, full inclusion, and collaboration between general and special education.

❏ As mandated by federal law, the only LCD students who can be placed in special education are those who have been identified as having an underlying language-learning disability or other disabilities based on data obtained from culturally and linguistically appropriate assessment instruments and procedures.

❏ Limited English proficient students who do not qualify for special education can be served using a variety of other options within the regular school program; Ideally, bilingual education programs make it possible to maintain and nurture the primary language while English is being learned.

❏ IEPs need to be collaborative in nature with goals appropriate for the student's cultural and linguistic background.

❏ When students are served in special education programs, instruction should be provided using activities that are culturally relevant—the experiences of the student must be considered.

❏ Professionals must include opportunities for families to participate in planning and implementing programs for students.

Finally, it is always important to view each student as a unique individual. Approaches that have been found to be effective with bilingual student populations as a whole, for example, may not always be appropriate for use with a specific child. Some children require more structure than others, and some can be transitioned into another language more easily than others. When planning special education programs for culturally and linguistically diverse populations, it is important to consider the student's background, interests, and goals, as well as the concerns of the family.

The resources available in the educational environment also need to be considered. The ideal situation is often not possible due to financial constraints, limited materials, and the shortage of appropriately qualified instructional personnel. Through effective collaboration, however, the services currently available for LCD students can be much improved.

STUDY QUESTIONS

1. Discuss the need for collaboration between regular and special education professionals when serving LCD students with special needs. Why do professionals need to collaborate? What policies and principles have driven this need?

2. Describe three ways to help families become involved in their children's education (either regular or special education).

3. List four sources for obtaining tutors who can work with LCD students.

TRUE-FALSE

Circle the number beside each statement that is true.

4. Professionals should emphasize the importance of early language stimulation because many families do not believe it is important to talk with infants and young children.
5. Advocates of multicultural pluralism support separate ethnic studies courses for individuals from specific cultural backgrounds, separate ethnic clubs, etc.
6. The federal government has succeeded in fully funding special education as delineated within the guidelines of the Individuals with Disabilities Education Act.
7. When providing special education services to students with language-learning disabilities who are more proficient in Spanish than English, a program that includes Spanish language instruction may be more effective than a program that focuses only on language development in English.
8. Professionals should emphasize to parents of children with language-learning disabilities that it is best to use only one language when interacting with these children.
9. In low-context cultures, the role of the individual as a member of a group is emphasized, and observation plays a key role in learning.
10. In writing IEP objectives, an emphasis should be placed on writing outcomes or benchmarks.

MULTIPLE CHOICE

Unless otherwise indicated, circle the number before all choices that are true.

11. It is very important to avoid certain activities when working with multicultural students. These activities include the following:
    A. Trivializing by always using pictures from a specific place and time to represent a group. The diversity that exists within a population is not depicted
    B. Misrepresenting by showing pictures from rural Mexico to teach students about modern-day Hispanic life in the United States
    C. Stereotyping by only showing pictures of non-Anglos in conditions that indicate that they live in poverty
    D. Disconnecting by presenting an instructional unit about a cultural group without relating the unit to the regular curriculum

12. Which one of the following is NOT advisable when working with family members?
    A. Inviting them to come to the school to talk about their language and culture
    B. Helping them find where to purchase or borrow books at little or no cost
    C. Emphasizing to parents that they do a disservice to their child if they speak the primary language at home
    D. Encouraging students to read to their parents
    E. Conducting programs that will help parents understand and adapt to the U.S. school system

13. Characteristics of the ideal inclusive classroom include the following:
    A. There is a special, separate curriculum for learners with language-learning disabilities.
    B. Students are not unduly labeled or identified as special needs learners.
    C. The student is served in the least restrictive environment.
    D. Only students with disabilities are included in the setting so that they can receive one-to-one instruction.
    E. Bilingual language services are not available in these programs.

14. When considering which language to use in intervention programs for children with language-learning disabilities, professionals must think about the following question(s):
    A. Does the student wish to maintain his primary language?
    B. Does the student speak a language that is considered prestigious by the community?
    C. Does the student have a high level of intelligence?
    D. Is the classroom teacher a native speaker of the child's primary language?
    E. Does the child have younger siblings who might be affected by recommended changes?

15. Which of the following are possible options for LCD students who qualify for special education?
    A. Placement in a monolingual English special education classroom with primary language support using a bilingual teacher, tutor, etc.
    B. Pull-out services (speech-language intervention, learning disability program, or both) in the primary language
    C. Bilingual special education classroom
    D. Pull-out services in English with primary language support
    E. Consultative, collaborative program implementation

ANSWERS TO STUDY QUESTIONS

4. True
5. False
6. False
7. True
8. False
9. False
10. True
11. B, C, and D
12. C
13. B and C
14. A
15. A, B, C, D, and E

Chapter 15

PRACTICAL STRATEGIES FOR INTERVENTION

Outline

A Holistic Approach to Collaborative Instruction
Whole-Parts-Whole
Suggestions for Intervention and Instruction
Scaffolding
Using Questions During Instructional Activities
Developing Concepts for Language and Literacy
Activities for Developing Vocabulary Skills
Structuring the Environment for Learners with Special Needs
Teaching Compensatory Strategies
Expressive Language Activities for Students with Special Needs
Enhancing Interpersonal Communicative Effectiveness
Developing Academic Literacy
Strategies for Phonological Awareness Training
The Preview-View-Review Technique
Conclusion

Students with language-learning disabilities, memory problems, attention deficits, and other disabilities often require highly individualized programs of instruction developed by professionals with specialized training. Because of the limited availability of bilingual instructional personnel, collaborative approaches to instruction are often necessary. Strategies that have been used effectively in collaborative programs of instruction are described in this chapter. Because of the great diversity that exists among students, it must be stressed that no single "method" of teaching can be used with all students. Flexibility is important if the diverse needs of students are to be met.

If programs for special needs learners are to be effective, the instruction must be comprehensible to the student. In both regular and special education programs, it is important for students to be able to relate new information to what they already know.

In developing programs for students with disabilities, educational professionals should strive to provide the type of instruction that will be most effective for the student rather than trying to "fit" the child into whatever programs are currently available. When the student speaks little or no English, efforts should be made to provide learning experiences in the primary language. Unfortunately, students from bilingual backgrounds often find themselves in situations where the instruction is incomprehensible because support in the primary language is not provided.

A HOLISTIC APPROACH TO COLLABORATIVE INSTRUCTION

When regular and special education professionals work with special needs students, they often treat listening, speaking, reading, and writing as areas of language that should be taught separately. Moreover, each of these areas is often broken down into a series of skills that are taught in isolation. This artificial separation of "sub-skills" or "sub-areas" results in instruction that is often reductionistic and skill-specific. Reading programs, for example, often include structured drills designed to teach reading skills one at a time. Often, these drills require students to perform tasks very different from those used during the actual activity of reading. These tasks may confuse special needs learners, especially those who lack the academic language proficiency necessary to perform these tasks.

Listening, speaking, reading, and writing can be taught simultaneously, using a holistic strategies approach to instruction. The holistic strategies approach was conceived by this author to integrate the best attributes of current approaches into an eclectic model of teaching and learning. In the holistic strategies approach, the various components of language are seen as synergistic in that they develop simultaneously as students learn within meaningful contexts. The holistic strategies approach is a conceptual framework that combines (1) the interactionist theory of language development, (2) constructivist philosophy (see Hearne, 2000; Weiner, 2001), (3) an emphasis on literacy development and academic achievement, (4) the belief that one cannot divorce teaching content from teaching metalinguistic and metacognitive strategies, (5) the experiential/interactive model of pedagogy (see Cummins, 1991), (6) the premise that self-esteem and positive psychosocial adjustment in learners are critical and need to be fostered, (7) Feurstein's Theory of Structural Cognitive Modifiability, and (8) interactive activities to facilitate communicative competence (see Westby & Rouse, 1985).

Basic assumptions of the holistic strategies approach include the following:

❏ Students need to develop a strong conceptual knowledge base in order to be successful in school. Learning relevant vocabulary is especially important.

❑ Students who have difficulty acquiring new information should be explicitly taught strategies for learning and remembering content.

❑ Students need to learn concepts and strategies in naturalistic, authentic communication situations with a focus on MEANING rather than structure.

❑ Students with special education needs require more specific guidance and explicit teaching than other learners.

❑ Children acquire oral language skills most efficiently when they are immersed in a language-rich environment. A language-rich environment is also important for the acquisition of literacy skills.

❑ Students direct their learning to accomplish personal communication goals.

❑ Adults can facilitate the learning process by

1. providing good communication models;

2. listening and responding carefully to children's communication attempts;

3. acting as facilitators rather than imparters of information;

4. mediating learning for students by helping them interpret and make sense of materials, and giving guidance and direction during learning activities;

5. helping students learn by relating new information to what they already know.

WHOLE—PARTS—WHOLE

In the *whole—parts—whole* instructional model, the learner is given the "big picture," and then learns how the component parts relate to the whole. Students are taught within meaningful contexts in which language serves a communicative function.

❑ Students should be encouraged to interact with one another during learning experiences rather than spending the majority of the day listening to an oral presentation of information. Learning requires active participation, not just passive processing.

❑ Students should be allowed to participate in planning the curriculum, choosing activities, and setting goals.

❑ Educators should facilitate the development of cognitive skills that become progressively more difficult rather than emphasizing simple recall (Brice & Montgomery, 1996). Students should be encouraged to:

1. explain new information in their own words;

2. summarize information;

3. apply information to new contexts;

4. relate new information to previously learned information;

    5. analyze new information.

❑ Themes and interest units should be used as often as possible. Topics relevant to the interests of students and the goals of the classroom curriculum should be emphasized (Damico & Hamayan, 1992).

❑ Students should have daily opportunities to ***TALK—LISTEN—WRITE—READ***.

❑ Professionals need to be sensitive to and account for students' cultural characteristics and learning styles because of the influence that these variables will have on responses during intervention. It is also crucial to involve families in the intervention process.

❑ Professionals need to use materials that are culturally appropriate for students.

The holistic strategies approach is illustrated in Figure 15.1.

SUGGESTIONS FOR INTERVENTION AND INSTRUCTION

Strategies that have been shown to be effective with LCD students can be adapted for use in many settings, including settings within both general education and special education programs (e.g., speech and language intervention, self-contained classes, or collaborative regular-special education settings). The following strategies can facilitate learning for LCD students in the general education curriculum or in special education programs (Brice, 2002; Roseberry-McKibbin, 2002).

❑ Review previously learned material daily.

❑ Check frequently for comprehension. Some students may be embarrassed to admit that they do not know specific information. In some cultures, it is inappropriate to admit not knowing something. Thus, if a student indicates that something has been comprehended, it is important to make sure that comprehension has, in fact, occurred.

❑ Use a multimodal instructional approach in which visual and gestural cues are presented frequently. Suggestions for accomplishing this include:

    1. writing assignments on the board;

    2. using pictures, maps, diagrams, and various objects;

    3. accompanying oral presentations with gestures and facial expressions;

    4. using visual organizers, clusters, and mental mapping to help organize information for the student;

❑ Teach beginning students the names for common objects in the classroom.

❑ Make input comprehensible to the student by:

    1. talking slowly enough for them to process the information;

    2. pausing frequently to avoid "overloading" students with information;

Figure 15.1

The Holistic Strategies Tree

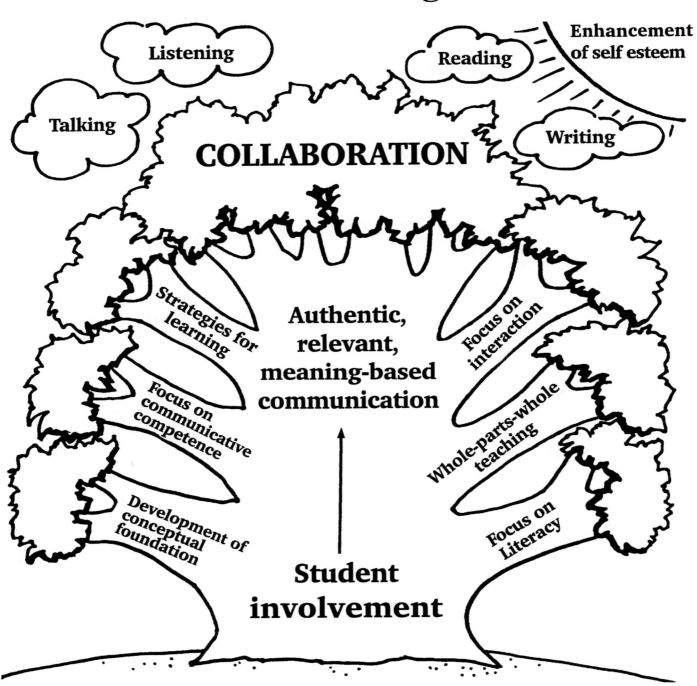

Rooted in constructivism and the interactionist theory

3. using students' names to direct and maintain their attention;

4. using short sentences and phrases;

5. avoiding the frequent use of long words;

6. avoiding use of slang or idiomatic speech;

7. enunciating words clearly (e.g., "Did you eat?" instead of "Jueet?");

8. emphasizing key words through increased volume and slightly exaggerated intonation (Example: "*Now* we will *look* at the *calendar*. The *calendar* shows us the *days* of the *week*.").

❏ Rephrase and restate information to facilitate comprehension. For example, the teacher might say:

"Today we are going to read a chapter in our math books and do the problems on page 10 of the math workbook. We will take our math books and read a chapter. We will then do the problems on page 10 of the math workbook."

❏ Try to seat students who speak the same language together, especially if one student speaks English with enough proficiency to help others. The advanced student can then explain complicated directions and other information in the primary language.

❏ Seat the student close to the front of the classroom to enhance comprehension and minimize distractions.

❏ Focus on the communication of meaning rather than emphasizing the correction of grammatical errors.

❏ When students make grammatical errors, these errors should not be overtly corrected when students are in the early and intermediate stages of learning English (Roseberry-McKibbin, 2001b). Professionals, however, can recast a student's utterance to model the correct form (e.g., Student says, "I having good day." Professional responds, "I'm having a good day, too! I'm glad that I'm having a good day and that you're having a good day.").

❏ For students who make repeated grammatical errors, professionals can use focused stimulation (Roseberry-McKibbin, 2001). For example, if a student always omits articles, the professional can model these articles repeatedly in various situations (e.g., "Look, you have *the* book. You have *a* pencil and *a* piece of paper—and *a* box of crayons!").

❏ Use computers if appropriate, especially if the computer programs have pictures/graphics that will aid in comprehension. (Appendix C includes current websites that have relevant activities for multicultural LCD students.)

❏ Allow students to incorporate their own experiences into learning situations.

❏ Students learn best when they can relate new learning to their own experiences. For example, when students read texts that are congruent with their background and experience, they understand the text more completely. When they write stories, they will perform more effectively if they can write about their own lives and experiences.

❏ Use stories/narratives to enhance learning.

❑ Students can listen to stories, read stories, and write their own stories. The use of stories and narratives is a highly successful teaching tool for students from diverse cultural backgrounds.

❑ Teach literacy to children by using writings from diverse cultures.

❑ Recruit people who can tutor students in their first language.

❑ Allow students to use a dictionary and to make their own dictionaries, using illustrations and pictures to facilitate recall of new vocabulary.

❑ Provide learning experiences in which students work together rather than individually to acquire new information (i.e., cooperative learning). A major goal of cooperative learning is to facilitate and encourage mutual cooperation and interdependence among students. Professionals can use cooperative learning in regular classrooms or in small group settings.

❑ Teach students metacognitive strategies to help them become more efficient learners. Metacognitive strategies include monitoring the success of their current learning efforts, planning ahead so that learning time can be used efficiently, and being aware of one's own learning style and learning strategies.

❑ Match intervention to the student's stage of second language acquisition. Table 15.1 includes information that professionals can use to plan programs for students who are in various stages of acquiring English.

When these intervention strategies are adapted to specific situations and used by all professionals who interact with LCD students, learning will be enhanced. Professionals can also use a variety of other strategies to help LCD students succeed.

⊘ REFLECTION ⊘

You are giving an inservice to teachers in a school where there has been an influx of students from multicultural backgrounds. The teachers have had limited experience working with multicultural student populations and have asked you to give them some ideas. Describe four ideas you will share with these teachers about working successfully in their classrooms with LCD students who have language-learning disabilities.

_____

_____

_____

_____

_____

SCAFFOLDING

Scaffolding is a technique in which the professional (or peer with a high level of skill) gives a student temporary support that is consistent with the student's current ability level (Weiner, 2001). The professional gradually withdraws support until the student can function independently. Suggestions for implementation include the following:

Table 15.1
MATCHING INTERVENTION TO SECOND LANGUAGE (L2) ACQUISITION STAGES

	Stage 1 Preproduction (First 3 months of L2 exposure)	Stage II Early Production (3-6 months)	Stage III Speech Emergence (6 months-2years)	Stage IV Intermediate Fluency (2-3 years)
STUDENT CHARACTERISTICS	• Silent period • Focusing on comprehension	• Focusing on comprehension • Using 1-3 word phrases • May be using routines/ formulas (e.g. "gimme five")	• Increased comprehension • Using simple sentences • Expanding vocabulary • Continued grammatical errors	• Improved comprehension • Adequate face-to-face conversational proficiency • More extensive vocabulary • Few grammatical errors
GOALS: ORAL RESPONSES	• *Yes-no* responses in English • One-word answers	• 1-3 word responses • Naming/labeling items • Choral responses • Answering questions: *either/or; who/what/where, sentence completion*	• Recalling • Telling/retelling • Describing/explaining • Comparing • Sequencing • Carrying on dialogues	• Predicting • Narrating • Describing/explaining • Summarizing • Giving opinions • Debating/defending
GOALS: VISUAL/WRITTEN RESPONSES	• Drawing/painting • Graphic designs • Copying	• Drawing/painting, graphic designs • Copying • Grouping and labeling • Simple Rebus responses	• Written responses • Drawing, painting, graphics	• Creative writing (e.g., stories) • Essays, summaries • Drawing, painting, graphics • Comprehensible written tests
GOALS: PHYSICAL RESPONSES	• Pointing • Circling, underlining • Choosing among items • Matching objects/pictures	• Pointing • Selecting • Matching • Constructing • Mime/acting out responses	• Demonstrating • Creating/constructing • Role-playing/acting • Cooperative group tasks	• Demonstrating • Creating/constructing • Role-playing • Cooperative group work • Videotaped presentations

Source: Hearne, D. (2000). *Teaching Second Language Learners with Learning Disabilities*. Oceanside, CA: Academic Communication Associates. Adapted from Table 10-4 with permission.

❏ Relate the information presented to knowledge that has already been acquired.

Example:
A professional is trying to teach an immigrant Filipino student the concepts *winter, spring, summer,* and *fall.* The professional starts by discussing the rainy season and the dry season that the student experienced in the Philippines. Following this, the teacher discusses how weather changes during the four seasons in the United States.

By teaching the four seasons in this way, the professional scaffolds the task for the student by relating the new information to the student's previously acquired knowledge.

❏ Gradually let the student take control of the task.

Example:
A student is discovering how to use the dictionary. At first, the professional demonstrates the entire task while the student observes. Next, the professional assists the student in finding a particular word. Finally, the professional tells the student to look up a word independently and to request assistance if problems are encountered.

❏ Use a multimodal approach to teaching in which there are repeated exposures to concepts.

Example:
A student is learning verbal opposites. First, opposites are demonstrated with objects, pictures, and activities. The student may color pictures, do physical demonstrations, work with objects, etc. Second, the student is asked to complete paper-and-pencil activities with opposites. Third, the professional shows picture cards and asks the student to point to opposites. Fourth, the professional reads a book and asks questions about opposites. Fifth, the student is asked to create a story about opposites. In this way, multiple exemplars or repeated exposures in different situations help the student learn the concept of opposites.

❏ Help the student to learn from mistakes or from conduct that is viewed as inappropriate.

Example:
An Asian student is reprimanded by the school principal during recess. The student smiles because in her culture it is appropriate to smile when reprimanded by a superior. The principal becomes angry and feels that the student is being disrespectful.

In this case, the professional can explain the situation to the principal and talk with the student about social interaction skills that are consistent with expectations for students in the United States. Thus, the student's inappropriate behavior becomes a positive learning situation.

When professionals use the scaffolding strategy, concentrated initial assistance with tasks is provided. This assistance is faded out as the student becomes more independent in the learning situation.

USING QUESTIONS DURING INSTRUCTIONAL ACTIVITIES

The effective use of questions enhances learning by increasing the student's active participation in classroom learning experiences (Brice & Roseberry-McKibbin, 1999b). It is important to use a variety of questioning strategies, to allow students time to formulate answers, and to include all students in the activities.

Questions are often used to ascertain how much information students comprehend during instructional activities. When asking questions, however, sensitivity to cultural differences is important (Roseberry-McKibbin, 2002). Educational professionals need to remember that students from some cultures may not want to be singled out or to appear different from their classmates. Examples of questions that can be used to assess comprehension are presented below.

❏ Ask for a brief summary of what was just said.

❏ Ask students to express opinions about the material.

> *Example:*
> "Manuel, what do you think of that?"
> "What was your favorite thing about this adventure?"
> "What didn't you like about this story?"

❏ Ask students to speculate about and expand on the information that was presented.

> *Example:*
> "Sergio, can you think of another example of ...?"
> "How would you have done things differently than...?"
> "What do you think might happen in the end?"

❏ Check comprehension frequently throughout the session. Don't wait until the end of the lesson to ask if anyone has questions. Use the above comprehension checks frequently to ensure that students are comprehending the material.

❏ Use clarification requests.

> *Example:*
> "When you said nothing happened, did you mean that...?"
> *or*
> "Can you tell me what you mean by that?"

When making requests, the following types of questions should be avoided:

1. *Rhetorical questions.* Some students who are still learning English may have difficulty distinguishing between rhetorical questions and questions that require a response.

2. *Ambiguous or vague questions.* Be as direct and straightforward as possible. If students don't understand the vocabulary and/or intent of the question, they will be much less likely to respond.

3. *Run-on or "machine gun" questions.* Multiple questions often cause confusion, especially among students who are used to hearing only one question at a time. For example, a teacher may say, "What about the main character in the story? What were his motives? What did he hope to accomplish in the end?" It is important to be specific, especially when students are not completely fluent in the language of instruction.

4. *Questions that may clash with the student's cultural style.* Many American professionals ask questions such as:

> "Did everybody understand that?"

"Are there any questions?"
"Is that clear?"

Students from some cultural groups have been taught that it is a sign of disrespect to tell a teacher that the information presented has not been understood. Some students feel that they will lose face if they indicate a lack of understanding by asking questions.

Profile

Rosario A. immigrated to the U.S. from the Philippines with his family when he was in 4th grade. The teacher referred Rosario to the special education team because, in her words, "Rosario is SO quiet in class, and I can never get him to raise his hand and answer questions. Also, Rosario copies other students' work and can't seem to complete assignments on his own. I wonder if he needs some special education assistance."

The speech-language pathologist, who had grown up in the Philippines, observed Rosario in class. There were 35 students in the somewhat noisy classroom, and Rosario sat quietly in the back, never volunteering any information. In addition, Rosario was observed trying to get other students to help him with a difficult math assignment. The speech-language pathologist shared with the teacher that being quiet and respectful in class was expected in the Philippines, and that corporal punishment was sometimes used there for students who "got out of line." In addition, she shared that Filipino students frequently help one another with assignments rather than working on classroom tasks independently.

Rather than being evaluated for special education, Rosario was placed into the school's Homework Club where he received help from older peer tutors who worked individually and in small groups with younger students. A sixth grade Filipino student was assigned to work with Rosario and three Filipino students from other classrooms in a cooperative, informal, interactive, and friendly situation in the school library. After six months, the teacher reported that Rosario had made excellent gains and that he was even raising his hand occasionally in class to ask questions.

DEVELOPING CONCEPTS FOR LANGUAGE AND LITERACY

The holistic strategies approach emphasizes the importance of building students' content knowledge or conceptual foundation within meaningful contexts. All activities should be accompanied by adult mediation. Students who are learning English as a second language need to develop their knowledge of vocabulary relevant to the content of the classroom curriculum (Wallach & Madding, 2001). Ideally, students with limited proficiency in English should be taught new concepts in the primary language before these concepts are presented in a second language.

This ideal situation, unfortunately, is often not a reality. In order for students to learn words in their primary language, a speaker of that language must be available to work with the students. When speakers of that language are not available, school professionals may need to work with students in English only. If instruction in the primary language is not available, classroom instruction should emphasize basic functional vocabulary in meaningful contexts.

When teaching vocabulary, it is recommended that receptive language activities be presented first. That is, the development of comprehension should be emphasized prior to asking children to produce new concepts verbally. Many students feel uncomfortable in situations that require them to begin speaking immediately. It is ideal for professionals to present receptive vocabulary activities first and follow these by expressive activities that are hierarchically sequenced based on their complexity (Roseberry-McKibbin, 2001b). Indirect language stimulation can be valuable for students who are in the early stages of learning English, and more direct stimulation can follow as students acquire greater proficiency (Paul, 2001).

Formal "drill" activities are often of limited value in developing functional communication skills. It is impossible for a word to have meaning without a context. When students are learning new information, it is ideal if they can have concrete experiences (e.g., going to a zoo to actually see zoo animals). If these concrete experiences are not possible, symbols or representations (e.g., pictures, objects) are the next best choice for teaching new concepts (Wolfe, 2001).

Vocabulary words should be experienced in a variety of meaningful and interesting situations. Students can be asked to describe pictures and to give word definitions; these "classroom skills" have been shown to be predictive of success in literacy and school achievement. Wolfe (2001) emphasized that drawing pictures of recently learned words helps students retain their knowledge of these words much better than activities that target the memorization of dictionary meanings. Rather than teaching individual structures one at a time, and focusing on grammatical form, activities to promote the functional use of language should be emphasized—the primary focus should be the communication of meaning.

As mentioned previously, graphic organizers can be very helpful when students are learning new vocabulary (Damico & Hamayan, 1992; Goldstein, 2000; Hearne, 2000; Roseberry-McKibbin, 2001; Wolfe, 2001). Described as "clustering" by Hearne (2000), the use of graphic organizers is a technique that stimulates divergent thinking as students explore associations relating to a key topic, word, or concept. Graphic organizers help students identify main concepts and assign specific labels to these concepts (Payne, 2001). Professionals and students participate jointly in brainstorming activities and write down all ideas. An example is presented in Figure 15.2.

ACTIVITIES FOR DEVELOPING VOCABULARY SKILLS

Lists of common vocabulary words that schools expect students to know are presented in Appendix D. The professional is encouraged to modify the vocabulary lists and to add additional vocabulary from the classroom curriculum. Thematic units can be developed using vocabulary words from the lists. It is also important to include words that are critical for following directions, completing worksheets, and understanding the content of subject matter emphasized within the classroom. It must be remembered that cultural events that are familiar to most students born in the United States have often not been experienced by children who are recent arrivals from other countries. It is important to incorporate culturally familiar events into classroom learning experiences within the curriculum.

Examples of activities that can be used to build vocabulary skills are presented in Table 15.2.

STRUCTURING THE ENVIRONMENT FOR LEARNERS WITH SPECIAL NEEDS

Most normal learners absorb new information and put that information to use fairly quickly. Special needs learners, however, must often be presented with new information in small "doses." Frequent modeling and repetition may be needed for learning to occur. Thus, each step of a task may need to be presented a number of times before these students are able to grasp the information being taught.

Some special needs learners have difficulty structuring their environments for efficient learning. This difficulty can stem from one or more of the following:

1. limited experience in learning situations

Figure 15.2

BRAINSTORMING WEB SAMPLE[1]

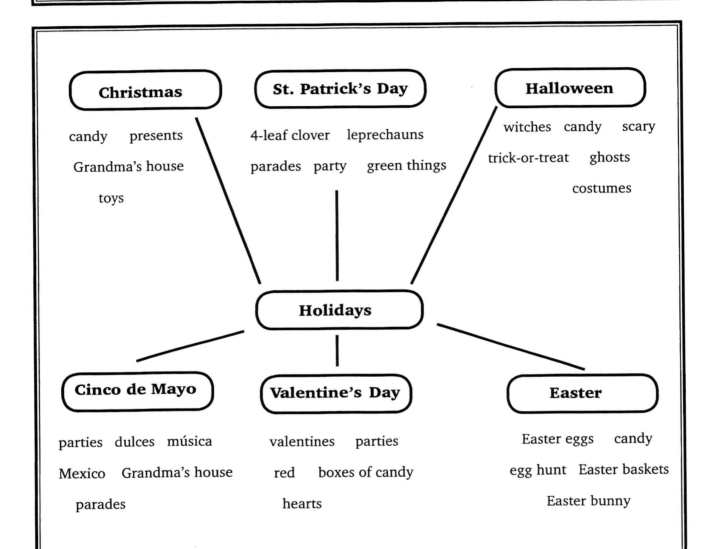

[1]The items listed represent the actual responses of students. Some responses for Cinco de Mayo are in Spanish.

Source: Hearne, D. (2000). *Teaching second language learners with learning disabilities.* Oceanside, CA: Academic Communication Associates. Reprinted with permission.[1]

Table 15.2

ACTIVITIES FOR DEVELOPING VOCABULARY SKILLS

✦ *Create a Story* - Students use books and pictures of vocabulary words to create stories.

✦ *Category Buckets*- Students put pictures in category "buckets." Each bucket is used for a different word category. Pictures of animals, for example, would be placed in the "animal bucket."

✦ *Guess the Picture*- A student is asked to describe a picture. The other students try to guess which of the pictures on the table is being described.

✦ *Which One Doesn't Belong?*- Five pictures are placed on the table. All but one of the pictures are from the same word category. The student's task is to identify the picture that doesn't belong and to explain why it doesn't belong.

✦ *Memory Games* - Auditory memory games can be created, such as Packing the Suitcase, Grocery Shopping, Catalog Orders, etc. Students are asked to listen to and remember the items named.

✦ *Describe it in Detail* - Students are given points for each attribute mentioned when describing an object or picture of an object. When presented with a picture of an apple, for example, four points would be earned if the student said, "it's shiny, red, juicy, and it's a fruit." Each student receives the same number of turns. The student with the most points at the end of the activity wins.

✦ *Follow the Directions* - Students are asked to manipulate the position of various pictures when presented with verbal directions. (e.g., "Put the pencil on the cup before picking up the chair").

✦ *Rhyming Words* - Students think of words that rhyme with vocabulary words presented in pictures. When presented with the word *hat*, for example, the child might say "cat, mat, and fat." Rhyming should only be used with students whose command of English is strong enough for them to complete this activity without experiencing frustration.

✦ *Word Match* - Students match printed words with pictures of these words.

✦ *Construct a Sentence* - Students construct sentences when presented with a group of words.

✦ *Category Stories* - Students create stories using words from specific categories.

✦ *Drawing Pictures* - Students are asked to draw pictures of new words that they have learned.

✦ *Word Wall* - Students generate the wall list, which contains new words they are learning. Each column can start with a letter, and each list begins with a student's name that starts with that particular letter. For example, the "A" column may start with "Arisbel," the "B" column may start with "Bobby," etc.

✦ *Noun Comparisons* - Students are asked to compare two words/concepts and to discuss what is alike and different about them.

2. attention difficulties

3. learning disabilities or language disorders

4. emotional difficulties

5. deficiencies in diet or health care

6. hearing problems

Strategies for Structuring the Environment

Suggested strategies for helping students structure their environment are the following:

☐ *Use preparatory sets.* When preparatory sets are used, learners with special needs will know what to expect because their environment has been structured for them. For example, instead of starting an activity with no explanation, the teacher might say: "Today we will share, read a story, and practice our sounds. What will you do?" . . . That's right - share, read a story, and practice our sounds."

☐ *Limit clutter and excessive visual stimuli in the environment.* Many classrooms and therapy/ resource rooms include beautiful collections of student art projects, work centers, pet cages, etc. While these rooms are colorful and quite attractive, they are often distracting to learners with special needs. These students often respond best in an environment that is attractive but very uncluttered and "plain." Because these students have difficulty screening out extraneous stimuli, they are distracted by items and events that do not distract most students.

☐ *Reduce auditory distractions.* In many rooms, phones ring, people come in and out, and students talk freely. While the casual attitude and freedom in these rooms is often appreciated by many, learners with special needs can be highly distracted in such situations. These students tend to do their best work in quiet, organized environments.

☐ *Use a multimodal approach to teaching.* Special needs learners benefit from learning through various channels—visual, auditory, and tactile. Many professionals in American schools present large amounts of information orally during teaching activities. Students are expected to acquire knowledge by listening to the teacher. Students with special learning needs frequently have auditory processing difficulties that make it hard for them to process and remember information that they hear. Activities that incorporate music and rhythm may facilitate learning and the retention of information (Wolfe, 2001). When an interactive approach involving auditory, visual, and tactile stimuli is used, students will be more likely to learn and remember new information.

☐ *Remember that learners with special needs may become frustrated more easily than normal learners.* Consequently, they may have "shorter fuses" and less tolerance for frustration than the "average" learner. Lessons need to be planned carefully so that these learners experience success with simple tasks before more complex tasks are attempted.

☐ *Provide frequent opportunities for the review of information that has been presented.* In this way students will retain more of what they learn.

☐ *Allow additional time for these students to process information.* Learners with special needs often take longer to process information than students who are learning in the typical manner. Thus, professionals need to give these students time to answer, think, etc.

☐ *Seat learners with special needs in the front of the classroom to minimize distraction.*

❏ *Use the learner's name often during teaching to keep the student focused.*

❏ *Break down assignments into small components.* Students with special learning needs take longer to complete assignments and may become overwhelmed if given work that will take a long time to complete.

❏ *Wait until the room is quiet before presenting important information.* Students who have difficulty concentrating and remembering information will experience even more difficulty if the room is noisy.

When professionals follow the above suggestions, students with special learning needs will function more efficiently and will learn more readily. A self-evaluation checklist that can be used during program implementation with multicultural student populations is presented in Table 15.3.

Profile

Mr. J., a fifth grade teacher, complained that "these bilingual special ed. kids in my class are driving me nuts. I want to put them somewhere else—just not in my classroom!" The only other fifth grade teacher in the school was a recent college graduate with no previous teaching experience. The principal, therefore, told Mr. J. that he needed to adapt to the LCD special education students as best he could.

During lunch one day, Mr. J. asked the speech-language pathologist for suggestions, emphasizing that "these ideas better not take too much time—I'm already busy enough." The speech-language pathologist offered to come and observe Mr. J's class, and did so the following day. She noticed that Mr. J. used no visuals and that he spoke rapidly when presenting instructions to the students. He expected students to respond the first time that an instruction was presented and rarely repeated instructions. The room was noisy and the speech-language pathologist herself found it difficult to focus on what Mr. J. was trying to say.

The speech-language pathologist offered to do a demonstration lesson, and Mr. J. accepted this offer. The speech-language pathologist asked the students to participate in an experiment in being as quiet as possible. She told the students that a lesson would be presented and that a prize would be given to students at the quietest table. During the lesson, the speech-language pathologist used the overhead projector, chalkboard, and other visuals when presenting the lesson. She also repeated key concepts several times in a slow speaking voice. Mr. J. reported at lunch the next day that the students told him they really enjoyed the lesson.

Mr. J. tried implementing the strategies demonstrated by the speech-language pathologist. A few weeks later, he reported to the speech-language pathologist that the LCD special education students had "really turned a corner" academically. Mr. J. realized that changes could be made with little difficulty to meet the needs of these special students.

TEACHING COMPENSATORY STRATEGIES

A major premise of the holistic strategies approach is that special learners need to acquire STRATEGIES to learn. These students often have difficulty absorbing information from the environment and organizing it internally by creating schemata. These students require explicit direction and teaching.

Table 15.3

WORKING WITH LINGUISTICALLY AND CULTURALLY DIVERSE STUDENTS: THE INTERVENTIONIST'S SELF-EVALUATION CHECKLIST

Do I	Almost Always	Some-times	Very Rarely	Never
1. Use a multimodal approach to teaching material?				
2. Review previous material?				
3. Make input comprehensible by slowing down, pausing, and speaking clearly?				
4. Rephrase and restate information?				
5. Check frequently for comprehension?				
6. Focus on teaching meaning rather than focusing on teaching correct grammar?				
7. Avoid putting students on the spot by demanding that they talk immediately?				
8. Give extra time for processing information?				
9. Attempt to reduce students' anxieties and give them extra attention when possible?				
10. Encourage students' use and development of their primary language?				
11. Encourage students to interject their own cultural experiences and backgrounds into learning situations?				
12. Expose all my students to multicultural activities and materials on a regular basis?				
13. Include parents and community members from different cultural backgrounds in my teaching?				

The following strategies can be taught to LCD students who have memory problems, word finding problems, etc. Each student must be assessed individually to ascertain which strategy or combination of strategies produces the best results. A sample instructional objective for the teaching of strategies is presented below:

IEP OBJECTIVE: _____ will use the strategies _____, _____, and _____ to facilitate word retrieval. She will use these strategies in the speech room, resource room, and the classroom, as reported by teachers and specialists in these settings.

Ten compensatory strategies that can benefit special needs learners are described below:

Strategy 1: **Tape-record lectures and then listen to the recording.**

Strategy 2: **Write down information and instructions in a notebook.** This activity facilitates the development of organizational skills and helps the student to recall information presented during class.

Strategy 3: **Focus on key words and write them down**. Many students will need explicit direction to focus attention so that they can write down key words.

Sample instructions:

"Listen. I am going to write a sentence. You tell me what the most important words are. Don't worry about listening to all the little words. Just tell me what the most important words are."

Stimulus sentence: **I went to the store to buy some milk.**

Teacher: Which are the big, important words?

Student: I, store, buy, milk.

Teacher: That's right: *I - store - buy - milk*. These are the important or key words that we need to remember.

The educational professional can also ask the student to name the little words in the sentence. After presenting sentences, short paragraphs can be used for this activity. This procedure is especially helpful for older students who need to take notes during lectures and have difficulty separating content (key) words from function (smaller, less important) words.

Strategy 4: **Use visualization to help students form pictures of information.**

Sample instructions:
"We are going to learn how to make pictures in our mind. Think of watching a TV show or a movie. You see a picture on a screen. Who has seen a movie or TV show lately? Tell me what you saw."

During instructional activities, students should be encouraged to form mental pictures of what they are learning. Visualization helps children remember new information.

Strategy 5: **Use the alphabet to facilitate word retrieval.** If the student cannot retrieve a word, the professional can ask the student to go through the alphabet in an effort to recall the initial letter in the word.

***Strategy 6*: Use categorization or grouping to facilitate memory.** Discuss categories with students, and explain how categories help us to remember information. Students can be taught categories such as *furniture, fruits*, etc.

***Strategy 7*: Use or create acrostic sentences.** For example, to remember the planets, the student can use the sentence, "My very eager mother just served us nine pizzas." (Mercury, Venus, Earth, Mars, Jupiter, Saturn, Uranus, Neptune, Pluto)

***Strategy 8*: Use reauditorization/silent rehearsal.** The students are told that when they hear something (e.g., directions), they are to repeat what they hear quietly to themselves.

> *Example:*
> Do what I say: "Touch your nose, eyes, and ears. I said, *nose - eyes - ears*."
> I want everyone to repeat after me—*nose - eyes - ears* (Wait for students to respond.)
>
> Now, what did I say to touch? That's right—nose-eyes-ears. You remembered the words because you said them quietly to yourself. Let's try another one.

Many students profit from this strategy. The professional should encourage students to repeat items out loud at first to ensure that the strategy is working. Then, move quickly to silent rehearsal.

***Strategy 9*: Create a verbal description.** If a student cannot retrieve a word, encourage the student to describe it. The professional can ask, "What does it look like? Sound like? Feel like? What shape is it?", etc.

***Strategy 10*: Think of words with a similar meaning.** If a student is having difficulty retrieving a word, the professional might say, "Can you think of another word that means the same thing?"

The holistic strategies approach will be most effective when students receive direct and explicit teaching and opportunities for the rehearsal of appropriate strategies. Professionals should monitor carryover of strategy use into the classroom and other settings. Professionals can work collaboratively with parents, teachers, and other school professionals to ensure that students are encouraged to use appropriate strategies for learning and remembering information.

✐ REFLECTION ✐

You are supervising a student teacher who has had not previous experience working with LCD students who have language-learning disabilities. List four strategies that she might use to help these students learn and retain new information.

EXPRESSIVE LANGUAGE ACTIVITIES FOR STUDENTS WITH SPECIAL NEEDS

An LCD student with a language-learning disability will have difficulty learning any language, including the primary language. The term *language-learning disability* implies that the student has a disorder that negatively affects learning language skills, even in situations where high quality language exposure is available.

The activity suggestions that follow can be implemented in classrooms and in small group special education settings. They can also be used in situations where professionals are working individually with students. Collaboration between regular education and special education professionals will give the students continuity and facilitate learning.

❑ Ask students to write stories in their primary language. Stories can be written by hand or using computers. Students with special needs who have difficulty writing by hand may experience less frustration if a computer is used.

❑ Encourage students to create journals in their primary language and English. Some professionals recommend that students write with pens rather than pencils. When students write with pencils, they may spend more time erasing than writing.

❑ Use "bilingual books" and have one student read in the primary language and another student read in English.

❑ Have students create captions (in English or the primary language) for pictures, photos, or comic strips.

❑ Have students write or dictate letters. Students can become pen-pals with individuals from other areas. Encourage students to keep a folder with the letters they receive. Students may use e-mail if computers are available.

❑ Have students create family trees with descriptions and photos.

❑ Use narratives to enhance learning. Students can listen to stories, read stories, and write their own stories.

❑ Narratives can be constructed using the written or spoken word, paintings and drawings, movement, song, and dramatic play. Story maps such as the one in Figure 15.3 can help students organize their stories.

❑ Have students review newspaper advertisements to find items that they would like to buy. They can describe these items orally or in writing.

❑ Have one student hide an object in the room. The student can write or verbally state directions to locate this object. The more precise the directions, the sooner the object will be found.

❑ Have students bring in songs that they like. The songs can be used to help students learn new vocabulary. Students can also play simple instruments and/or use rhythmic objects (e.g., finger cymbals).

❑ Have students prepare a newspaper. They can write stories or poems, draw cartoons with captions, and make illustrations.

Figure 15.3

STORY MAP

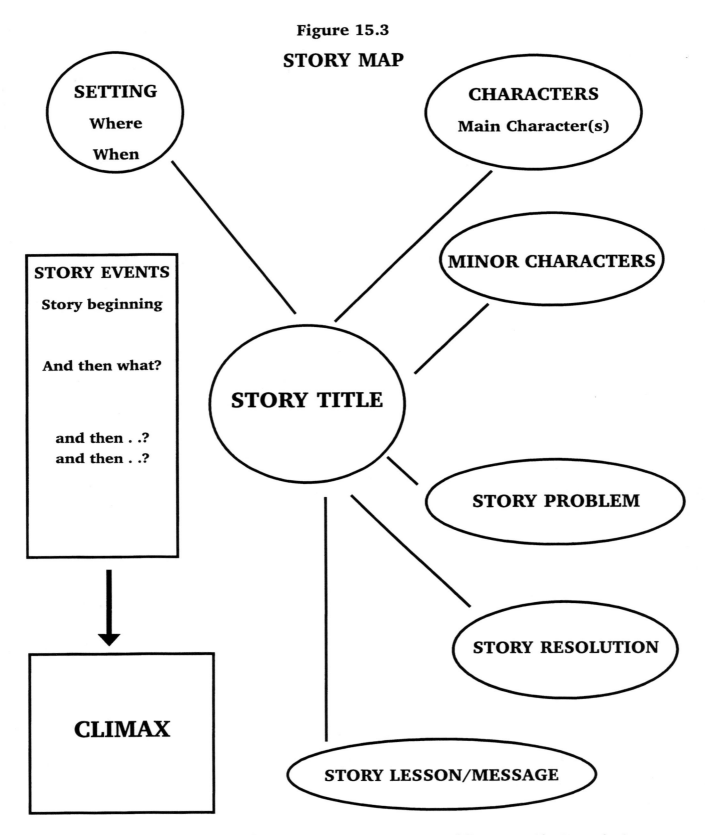

Source: Hearne, D. (2000). *Teaching Second Language Learners with Learning Disabilities*. Oceanside, CA: Academic Communication Associates. Reprinted with permission.

❑ Have students write stories about photographs.

❑ Have students engage in drama and role-playing activities that are relevant to their interests and appropriate for their developmental age.

❑ Prepare a multicultural calendar that includes American holidays and holidays celebrated in other countries throughout the world. Be sure that the holidays shown represent the cultures of students in the classroom. All holidays can be discussed and activities can be planned that incorporate these holidays (see Paul, 2001).

ENHANCING INTERPERSONAL COMMUNICATION EFFECTIVENESS

In the holistic strategies approach to learning, professionals help students become more effective communicators in their daily environments. Many students in special education programs need to enhance their communicative competence in their daily interactions (Brice, 2002; Moore-Brown & Montgomery, 2001). A "Communication Skills Quiz" that students can use to evaluate their own communication is presented in Table 15.4. Students should be asked to respond "yes" or "no" to each question. When presented to a small group, cultural differences can be discussed as they relate to specific items.

The following IEP goals and objectives can be implemented by regular and special educators, tutors, and others who work with the student. It is recommended that professionals work collaboratively to ensure that students practice effective interpersonal communication skills in a variety of communication contexts.

Interpersonal Communication Goals

IEP Goal: The student will demonstrate effective interpersonal communication skills in daily settings as observed by professionals who work with the student on a regular basis.

Objectives/Benchmarks:

1. The student will greet others by smiling and saying "hello" when appropriate.

2. The student will listen to others without interrupting. If an interruption is necessary, the student will say "excuse me."

3. The student will answer questions appropriately and promptly.

4. The student will demonstrate the ability to take turns during conversation.

5. The student will request clarification when something is not understood.

6. If a listener shows confusion, the student will clarify what was said by giving explanations.

7. The student will maintain appropriate eye contact with others during communication.

DEVELOPING ACADEMIC LITERACY

Many speech-language pathologists believe that they should focus only on oral language when working with the students on their caseloads. However, it is crucial for speech-language

Table 15.4

A COMMUNICATION SKILLS QUIZ FOR STUDENTS

Student's Name:_____   Date:_____

____1. I greet people when I see them by smiling and saying "hi."

____2. I listen to people without interrupting.

____3. I apologize when I have to interrupt.

____4. I try to be interested in what people say.

____5. I try to take time to listen when people want to talk to me.

____6. When people ask me questions, I try to answer as best I can.

____7. When I talk, I try to talk as clearly as possible so other people will understand me.

____8. During conversations, I take turns talking.

____9. During conversations, I try to talk about what other people are talking about instead of bringing up new things in the middle of someone else's sentence.

____10. If I don't understand what someone says, I ask the person to please repeat what was said.

____11. If someone doesn't understand me, I repeat myself more clearly.

____12. I try to look at people when I talk to them.

pathologists to work with other educational professionals to facilitate literacy development in LCD students with language-learning disabilities (Montgomery, 1998; Rosa-Lugo & Fradd, 2000). The acquisition of literacy skills is very important for students who are learning English as a second language.

Reading experiences help students develop reading, writing, and speaking skills (Pieretti & Goldsworthy, 2001). As students engage in reading activities, they learn about the world, acquire new vocabulary, and develop a heightened awareness of the structure of language and ways in which words can be used to communicate information. Students with language-learning disabilities often have limited skill in reading and this results in poor academic performance. These students often face five barriers:

1. Academic materials are usually in English.
2. Academic learning is intrinsically difficult for these students.
3. Phonological awareness may be limited.
4. Environmental experiences may be limited.
5. Problems affecting language interfere with learning.

As shown in Figure 15.4, experiences that provide environmental exposure are critical in helping students build the conceptual foundations that they need for success in learning to read. This exposure will lead to better oral language skills, enhanced phonological awareness, and reasoning skills that are critical for success in acquiring literacy. A major problem in many school programs is that professionals begin instruction at the "top of the ladder"—they try to teach literacy without the prerequisites of environmental experience and exposure. The building of oral language skills and phonological awareness is often underemphasized. The importance of enhancing environmental exposure and building strong oral communication skills cannot be overemphasized. Language-learning disabled students, however, may also be in need of activities to stimulate the development of phonological awareness.

Phonological awareness can be defined as the ability to consciously reflect on and manipulate the sound system of a language (Gillam & Van Kleeck, 1998). Phonological awareness is related to spelling, reading, and writing achievement (Goldsworthy, 2002). Thus, when attempting to develop literacy skills in LCD students, it is important to stimulate the development of phonological awareness.

Hadley, Simmerman, Long, and Luna (2000) found that explicit phonological instruction and vocabulary instruction in the classroom helped monolingual and bilingual children make excellent gains in a number of areas including beginning sound awareness, letter-sound association, and overall vocabulary skills. Explicit phonological awareness instruction can be especially valuable for second language learners.

STRATEGIES FOR PHONOLOGICAL AWARENESS TRAINING

The phonological awareness activities and suggestions below are based on information reported by Gillam & Van Kleeck (1998), Goldsworthy (2002), Hadley et al. (2000), and Roseberry-McKibbin (2001, 2002).

❑ Use the following hierarchy to develop phonological awareness. The student will do the following:

   A. Count the number of words in a sentence.

   B. Count the number of syllables in a word.

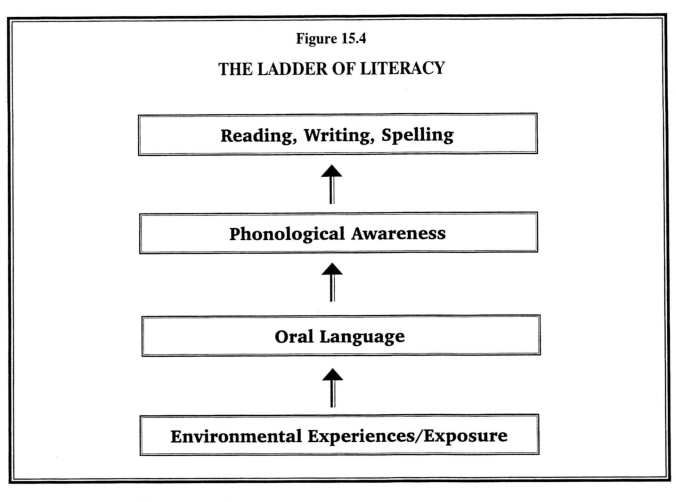

Figure 15.4

THE LADDER OF LITERACY

C. Count the number of sounds in a word.

D. Identify rhyming words.

E. Use sound-blending skills to form words from individual sounds.

F. Identify the first sound in a word.

G. Identify the last sound in a word.

❏ Use rhythm sticks and clapping to emphasize the number of sounds and/or syllables in words.

❏ Ask students to bring items from home than begin or end with target sounds.

❏ Use a grab bag; have students pull out objects, name them, and sort them into piles based on their beginning, middle, or ending sounds.

❏ Use rhymes. Books such as those written by Dr. Seuss work quite well. Children can recite rhymes, act them out, and view pictures that supplement the rhyme. Singing rhymes facilitates the learning of the rhymes.

❑ Use music. For example, the tune to "If you're happy and you know it" may be used by replacing the lyrics with, "If your name begins with **b**, raise your hand."

❑ Use stories with Rebus-style pictures, and ask students to "read" the pictures.

❑ Use word play. For example, the professional might say, "Prinderella and the Cince. What am I really talking about?" The infamous "Pig Latin" is also fun. For example, the professional might say, "I'm so glad that Anuelmay is here today. Who am I really talking about? Right! Manuel!"

❑ Read a familiar story or poem and ask the students to fill in missing words as you read.

❑ As you read a rhyme, have students tap the table for each syllable or use a "shaker" for each syllable.

❑ Ask a student to remove a specific segment from a word. For example, "Say *cowboy* without *boy*."

❑ Tell the student that you are going to play a game that involves making up new words for things. For example, you might say that all things in the room now start with "b." So "desk" becomes "besk," "pencil" becomes "bencil," etc.

Professionals often feel that they have to use special programs to help students who have difficulties with reading, writing, and spelling. If students are to learn to function effectively in the classroom, however, it is important that classroom materials be incorporated into the instructional activities. Specialists can work collaboratively with the classroom teacher to develop individualized reading programs. Specialists can also use classroom materials to work on developing phonological awareness as well as overall literacy skills (Wallach & Madding, 2001).

✐ REFLECTION ✐

You are working in a junior high school where a new group of Hmong students has just arrived from Southeast Asia. These students have not learned to read or write in their primary language, and the teachers are referring them for special education assessment and services. The principal gives you some release time to develop a comprehensive summer program for these students. The program needs to help these students gain pre-literacy skills that will make it easier for them to catch up with their grade-level peers. What components will your summer program need to include? What skills will you emphasize and why?

_____

_____

_____

_____

_____

THE PREVIEW-VIEW-REVIEW TECHNIQUE

Hearne (2000) shared some excellent, practical strategies that professionals can use to enhance the literacy skills of LCD students with learning disabilities. One such strategy is the *Preview-View-Review* technique. The adaptation of the Preview-View-Review (PVR) approach described below can be used effectively to help special needs learners improve their literacy skills. This approach promotes learning within authentic situations in which an emphasis is placed on meaning. Instructional objectives that can be presented when this approach is used are presented below:

IEP Goal: _____ will demonstrate knowledge and use of the preview-view-review technique of reading and studying in school contexts such as the classroom, speech room, and resource room. Performance will be judged by the classroom teacher, Special Education Resource Teacher, and Speech-Language Pathologist during the reading of passages from content area reading materials.

IEP Objectives/Benchmarks:

_____ will summarize and explain the PVR technique verbally upon request.

_____ will demonstrate use of the PVR technique with a chapter from a book used in the classroom.

_____ will demonstrate use of the PVR technique with notes that have been taken in the classroom.

Professionals can help students use the following PVR strategies when reading chapters in books:

Preview

❏ Get an overview of the chapter by:

1. reading the title;

2. reading the introductory paragraph or section;

3. looking at headings, subdivisions, and illustrations;

4. making a table of contents outline from the information, and then using it as a study guide;

5. examining the maps, graphs, charts, pictures, and other visuals;

6. identifying words in boldface or italics.

❏ Read the main idea sentence of key paragraphs to understand the chapter's general concepts.

❏ Highlight key vocabulary words and make a dictionary that includes the meaning of these words.

❏ Read the concluding paragraph or summary.

View

❏ Read the text aloud and have the student follow along.

❏ At natural stopping points, ask the student to explain what has just been read. If the student is working with a primary language tutor, then the tutor and the student can discuss the printed text in the primary language.

❏ Help the student organize and outline class notes and textbook readings.

❏ Review the class notes with the student, and have the student explain them. Make sure the student understands the concepts.

❏ Use the scaffolding technique if the student cannot answer a question. If the student cannot answer the question, "Who was President of the United States during the Civil War?", for example, ask an either/or question such as, "During the Civil War, was Eisenhower or Lincoln the President of the United States?"

❏ Help the student use context to enhance comprehension. For example, if the student fails to understand a word, encourage the use of context to figure out the meaning.

❏ Help the student visualize what is being read, especially if there are no pictures accompanying the text. Remind the student to "make pictures in your mind about what we read." For example, if the student is reading about a village in a particular country, you can say, "Tell me what you think the village looks like" or "Make a picture in your mind about that. What does it look like to you?" Students can even draw pictures to illustrate text.

Review

❏ Look over chapter headings and subdivisions again to keep the big picture in focus.

❏ Ask questions about the content. These questions can be:
   1. general comprehension questions
   2. true-false questions
   3. either/or questions

❏ Help the student answer questions at the end of the chapter. This can be accomplished orally or in writing.

❏ Have the student summarize the chapter orally or in writing. A computer can be helpful. The student can type out the main points of the chapter using the computer. If something was forgotten and omitted, it can be easily inserted in the proper sequence. The final product can be printed out, and the student can keep it for review.

❏ Ask the student for his/her opinions about what was read. For instance, students can be asked:
   1. What were the most important things in the chapter?
   2. What did you think were the most interesting things in the chapter?
   3. Was there anything you disagreed with? Why?

❑ Find out if the student needs questions answered about the chapter.

❑ Help the student create possible test questions and then have that student answer these questions. If there is a small group of students, they can exchange questions for practice.

The preview-view-review technique is illustrated in Figure 15.5. Professionals can use this technique with classroom materials as well as specialized materials. When classroom materials are used, the holistic strategies approach will be applied in that students learn content while they also apply strategies for becoming more effective learners. Ideally, students will learn to use the strategies independently during various learning experiences in the classroom.

When working with students from diverse cultural backgrounds, the use of multisensory approaches to reading instruction is highly recommended. Many students with special learning needs can benefit from the neurological impress method [NIM], a highly successful multisensory approach to reading. The professional sits to the right and slightly behind the student so that she can speak clearly into the student's ear. The student reads the passage aloud with the professional, and follows each word by placing a finger underneath it. This approach and various other multisensory techniques for teaching reading have been reviewed in *Teaching Second Language Learners with Learning Disabilities* (Hearne, 2000), a practical and helpful resource for professionals who are providing instruction to second language learners who have special learning needs. By offering flexible programs of instruction that integrate oral and written language activities into the curriculum, special educators will be better able to meet the needs of students who come from diverse cultural and linguistic backgrounds.

CONCLUSION

To meet the needs of a special education population that is becoming increasingly more diverse, school professionals need to be sensitive to cultural differences and the effects that these differences can have on learning behavior. LCD students with special learning needs often experience difficulty responding appropriately in learning situations that offer instruction in English only. By providing opportunities for instruction in the primary language, the likelihood is increased that these students will experience success.

When developing intervention programs for LCD students, professionals from the general education and special education programs should work as a team to ensure that students are provided with learning experiences that are culturally appropriate and relevant to their experiences. By offering collaborative programs of instruction, the likelihood is increased that LCD students will develop the academic abilities and oral communication skills necessary to reach their full potential.

As professionals use the materials in this book, it is hoped that they will continually examine their beliefs, values, and actions as they relate to the education of LCD students. Diversity helps us to learn new ways of thinking and interacting that can help us to grow as individuals and as a nation.

As we live and work in the 21st century, we must prepare our students, the future leaders of our nation, to understand one another so that they can make use of their diverse experiences to create a better and more peaceful world. LCD students represent a vast gold mine of potential that can be realized only if equal opportunities for educational, social, and economic opportunities are provided. True progress in educating LCD students can be accomplished if educational professionals learn to view diversity as something that helps us all to learn and to grow.

Figure 15.5

SUPER-POWER STRATEGIES FOR BETTER READING

POWER-READING STRATEGIES

Before I read:

LOOK
at title, headings, picture

THINK
about main ideas, vocabulary words

While I read:

PICTURE
things in my head

ASK MYSELF QUESTIONS
about what I just read

USE THE CONTEXT
to understand what it means

(continued from page 323)

After I read:

LOOK
at title, headings, pictures again

ASK AND ANSWER QUESTIONS
about what I just read

SUMMARIZE
what I just read in my own words

STUDY QUESTIONS

1. Summarize key components of the holistic strategies approach.

2. Describe phonological awareness and its relationship to literacy. What are three specific activities professionals can present to enhance phonological awareness in students?

3. Many American teachers use questions to help students become involved in the learning process. Discuss two things that professionals should NOT do when using questions with LCD students who have language-learning disabilities.

TRUE-FALSE

Circle the number beside each statement that is true.

4. The holistic strategies approach emphasizes that professionals should correct students' grammatical errors to help them master English grammar more quickly.
5. Scaffolding is a technique in which the professional (or peer with a high level of skill) gives a student temporary support that is consistent with the student's current ability level. The professional gradually withdraws support until the student can function independently.
6. Phonological awareness can be defined as the ability to consciously reflect on and manipulate the sound system of a language.
7. In the Neurological Impress Technique, the professional uses computer software to help students learn through a multimodal approach.
8. In the strategy of reauditorization/silent rehearsal, students are told to repeat what they hear (e.g., oral directions) quietly to themselves.
9. Rhetorical questions tend to be highly effective with LCD students because questions of this type stimulate critical thinking.
10. Professionals who use the preview-view-review approach need special books with a specific type of focus for use with this strategy.

MULTIPLE CHOICE

Unless specified otherwise, circle the letter beside all choices that are correct.

11. Interpersonal communication goals for language-learning disabled students may include the following:
    A. The student will maintain appropriate eye contact with others during communication.
    B. The student will request clarification when something is not understood.
    C. The student will listen to others without ever interrupting.
    D. If a listener shows confusion, the student will repeat exactly what she said.
    E. The student will greet others by smiling and saying "hello" when appropriate.

12. Which one of the following is NOT included in the hierarchy for teaching phonological awareness skills?
    A. Count the number of words in a paragraph.
    B. Count the number of words in a sentence.
    C. Count the number of syllables in a word.
    D. Count the number of sounds in a word.
    E. Use sound-blending skills to identify words.

13. To help LCD students with language-learning disabilities, professionals should do the following:
    A. Use preparatory sets.
    B. Limit clutter in the environment.
    C. Use few visuals to reduce distractions, and rely primarily on the auditory mode of teaching to help students focus on the information being presented.
    D. Seat the learner in front of the classroom.
    E. Avoid saying the student's name so that he or she does not become self-conscious.

14. Which of the following are TRUE statements about graphic organizers?
    A. They can be very helpful when students are learning new vocabulary.
    B. They are used primarily to teach rules of grammar to LCD students with language-learning disabilities.
    C. They stimulate divergent thinking and help students to explore associations related to a key topic, word, or concept.
    D. They are useful for developing oral but not written language skills.
    E. They are used to integrate students' drawings into various language development activities.

15. Which of the following is not part of the scaffolding technique?
    A. Relating information presented to knowledge that has already been acquired
    B. Helping students learn from mistakes
    C. Using a multimodal approach with repeated exposure to concepts
    D. Helping and assisting the student until the student is able to work independently
    E. Having the student silently observe a model without talking about the activity

ANSWERS TO STUDY QUESTIONS

4. False	11. A, B, and E
5. True	12. A
6. True	13. A, B, and D
7. False	14. A and C
8. True	15. E
9. False	
10. False	

APPENDICES

Appendix A

ASSESSING PROCESSES IN SECOND LANGUAGE ACQUISITION

Student's Name:_____Date of Birth:_____

Chronological Age:_____Assessment Date:_____

Language Background:_____

_____

A. MAJOR SECOND LANGUAGE ACQUISITION PROCESSES

Please put a check mark beside the second language acquisition (SLA) processes you and/or other professionals believe the student is manifesting at this time. Record any comments that are relevant in this situation.

_____**Interference**
    Comments:

_____**Interlanguage**
    Comments:

_____**Silent period**
    Comments:

_____**Code-switching**
    Comments:

_____**Language loss**
    Comments:

B. AFFECTIVE SECOND LANGUAGE ACQUISITION VARIABLES

Please put a check mark beside any variables you and/or other professionals believe are influencing the child's acquisition of English:

_____**Motivation:**

___Acculturation (student and family's ability to adapt to the dominant culture)
___Enclosure with American culture (shared activities with Americans)
___Attitudes of child's ethnic group and dominant group toward one another
___Family plans to stay in/leave this country (circle one)
___Possibility that learning English is a threat to the student's identity
___Student's efforts to learn English are successful/unsuccessful (circle one)
___Student appears enthusiastic/unenthusiastic about learning (circle one)

Comments:

_____**Personality:**

___Self-esteem
___Extroverted/introverted (circle predominant pattern)
___Assertive/non-assertive (circle predominant pattern)

Comments:

_____**Socioeconomic status** (similar to other children in school?):

Comments:

C. SECOND LANGUAGE LEARNING STYLES AND STRATEGIES

Please comment on any second language learning styles and strategies that may characterize or be utilized by this student:

Avoidance (of situation, persons, topics, etc.)

Use of routines and formulas (e.g., "How are you?" or "Have a good day!")

Practice opportunities (quantity and quality; Who does the student interact with in English? In what settings? School? Neighborhood?)

Modeling (Who are the student's primary speech and language models? What languages do these models speak? If they speak English, what is the quality of their English? How much time does the student spend with them?).

Additional Comments/Recommendations:

Appendix B
Sample Background Information Questionnaire

Instructions: We are going to ask you some questions about your child's medical history, educational history, and related areas. Please be as thorough as you can in your remarks. If I am not clear, please stop me and ask me to say it again. If you don't feel comfortable in answering the question, please let me know. All we want to do here is to obtain as much background information as possible, and, since you are the child's parent, we feel that you have much to contribute.

1. When was your child born?

2. Was this a hospital?

3. How was the pregnancy?

4. How was your health during pregnancy?

4. How was the delivery?

5. Were any instruments used?

6. Were there any postnatal complications?

7. How was your child's physical development? Were there any handicapping conditions? If yes, who made the diagnosis? When? How did you feel about it?

8. Was your child ever hospitalized? If yes, where? When? Why? How long? Who was the physician?

9. Were there problems in feeding?

10. Were there any prolonged illnesses? High fever? Accidents?

11. Has his/her hearing been checked?

12. Has his/her vision been checked?

13. Has he/she seen a dentist? What is the condition of his/her teeth?

14. What is his/her diet history?

15. How is his/her diet now?

16. Does he/she have a pediatrician? Who? Has your child seen any other medical specialist? If yes, Who? When? Where? Why?

17. When did you come to the United States? Why did you come?

    For refugees: Was he/she ever in a refugee camp? How long? Tell us about it.

18. Was he/she ever on a boat? How long? Tell us about it.

19. How many brothers and sisters does he/she have? Are they all here?

20. Are there any family members who had or have difficulty in speaking or hearing, or problems such as mental retardation, cerebral palsy, cleft palate, or stuttering? If yes, please explain.

21. Was your child ever in school? Where? How long?

22. How was his/her performance in school? Grade?

23. Do you have a report from the school? Any comments from the teacher?

Source: Cheng., L. L. (1991). *Assessing Asian Language Performance: Guidelines for Evaluating Limited-English Proficient students. (Second edition)* Oceanside, CA. Academic Communication Associates. Reprinted with permission.

24. Was he/she involved in special programs? How did he/she do?

25. Was he/she in a day-care or child care program? If yes, how did he/she do?

26. Did he/she repeat a grade? If yes, why?

27. How was the program similar to his/her program now? How was the program different from his/her program now?

28. How many are living in your home?

29. Who takes care of your child after school?

30. Who makes the decisions at home?

31. Does your child have his/her own room? If no, who does your child share the room with? Where does he/she study?

32. Does your child mostly play inside the house? Outside? By himself/herself? With a sibling?

33. Who does he/she play with? Are they older or younger? How does he/she play?

34. What does he/she like to play? What toys do you have? Does he/she read? What books and magazines do you have?

35. Do you work? If yes, what do you do? When are you home?

36. Does your spouse work? If yes, what does he/she do? When is he/she home?

37. What is your educational background? Your spouse's educational background?

38. What language(s) is used at home?

39. When did your child say his/her first word? How do you feel about his/her speech now?

40. Do you feel that your child understands everything you say? Explain.

41. What language does he/she speak when he/she responds to you?

42. Does your child speak your native language with his siblings? Friends?

43. Do your children speak your native language or English among themselves?

44. Do you help your child with homework?

45. How do you feel about his/her maintenance of your native language? Do you send him/her to language school during the weekend?

46. What do you expect the school to do for your child?

47. Do you attend any social function? Where? With whom? What are your leisure activities?

48. Do you have difficulty disciplining your child? His/her siblings?

49. What responsibilities are placed on your child? On his/her siblings?

50. Does he/she dress himself/herself?

51. Does he/she know your telephone number and address?

52. Do you read to him/her? What are his/her favorite stories? Can he/she tell the story back to you?

53. Does he/she watch TV? What is his/her favorite program?

54. Do you think your child is a hard worker? If so, why? Do you think your child is lazy? Why?

Appendix C

INTERNET SITES

This listing of websites will be helpful in obtaining information relevant to the education of students from multicultural backgrounds. Sources of websites are included in a variety of resources (see Brice & Roseberry-McKibbin, 1999; Goldstein, 2000; Kuster, 2000). These sites may change without notice, and the reader is advised to check each source online.

General Information/Demographic Data

Census Bureau - http://www.census.gov

Center for Immigration Studies - http://www.cis.org

ERIC Clearinghouse on Assessment and Evaluation - http://ericae.net

ERIC Clearinghouse on Early Childhood Education http:/ericeece.org

Multicultural/Bilingual Issues

Bilingual Education Resources on the Internet - http://www.edb.utexas.edu/coe/depts/ci/bilingue/resources.html

Bilingual Families Web Page - http://www.nethelp.no/cindy/biling-fam.html

Center for Multilingual Multicultural Research - http://www-bcf.usc.edu/~cmmr/BEResources.html

Clearinghouse for Multicultural Bilingual Education - http://catsis.weber.edu/MBE/HTMLs/MBE.html

Multicultural Internet Resources - http://www.tr.wosc.osshe.edu/eec/web.htm

Multicultural Pavilion - http://curry.edschool.virginia.edu/go/multicultural

National Association for Bilingual Education - http://www.nabe.org

National Clearinghouse for Bilingual Education - http://www.ncbe.gwu.edu

National Education Association (Information about bilingual education) - http://www.nea.org/issues/bilingual

Office of Bilingual Education and Minority Languages Affairs - http://www.ed.gov/offices/OBEMLA/news.html

U.S. Department of Education - http://www.ed.gov/index.html

Miscellaneous Contacts

http://www.hhs.csus.edu/homepages/SPA/Roseberry (Information from Celeste Roseberry-McKibbin)

http://www.Multicultural Resources Supersite (This site is a valuable source of information and resources.)

http://www.bilingualtherapies.com (Bilingual Therapies recruits bilingual speech-language pathologists and is a source that school districts and other organizations can use to obtain the services of bilingual professionals.

Companies that Publish Bilingual/Multicultural Special Education Learning Resources

American Speech-Language-Hearing Association - http://www.professional.asha.org

Academic Communication Associates, Inc. - http://www.acadcom.com

Pro-Ed, Inc. - www.proedinc.com

Singular/Thompson Learning - http://www.singpub.com

Companies that Publish Bilingual/Multicultural Speech and Language Assessment Instruments

Academic Communication Associates, Inc. - http://www.acadcom.com

Pro-Ed, Inc. - http://www.proedinc.com

African American English Websites

Center for Applied Linguistics - http://www.cal.org/ebonics

Summer Institute of Linguistics - http://www.sil.org

University of Memphis - http://www.ausp.memphis.edu/phonology

Asian Languages

Hmong Language Users Group - http://www.geocities.com/tokyo/4908

SOAS Guide to Asian and African Languages - http://www.soas.ac.uk/languageguide

Native American Cultures/Languages

American Indian Institute - attp://aii.asu.edu

American Indian Studies - http://www.csulb.edu/projects/ais

American Indian Information - http://indiannet.indian.com/americaninfo.html

Spanish

Mexico Web Guide - http://mexico.web.com

Directorio Online de Español - http://donde.uji.es/Donde

CiberCentro - http://www.cibercentro.com

Yahoo! en Español - http://espanol.yahoo.com

Information Regarding Specific Countries

http://www.wtgonline.com/data/(name of country)

http://home.about.com/travel

http://www.iranian.com

Miscellaneous English as a Second Language Websites

http://web1.toefl.org (Teachers of English as a Foreign Language general website)

http://www.comenius.com (free online activities including Fluency Through Fables, short tales created to improve English reading comprehension, and a collection of idioms)

http://www.peakenglish.com/ (Mortal Grammar; activities for middle school students)

http://www.kidsdomain.com (ESL Renegades, other ESL activities)

http://www.wordsmith.org/awad/index.html (mails out various vocabulary words and definitions to its subscribers)

http://www.wordfocus.com/index.html (Focusing on Words site is dedicated to enhancing vocabulary skills through looking at the Latin and Greek elements of words.)

http://www.pacificnet.net/~Sperling/ideas/html (includes ideas for teaching English)

http://www.logos.uoregon.edu (information about linguistics and pragmatic issues of interest to speech-language pathologists who work with adolescent students)

http://www.stonesoup.com (Stone Soup; contains stories by young writers, links, resources, and children's art from around the world)

Appendix D

BASIC VOCABULARY RECORD FORMS

The record forms in this section can be used to assess progress in learning basic vocabulary. Observations of receptive and expressive language performance can be recorded. These forms may be reproduced.

SCHOOL ITEMS

Student's Name:_____ Date:_____

Goal:

The student will demonstrate receptive and expressive knowledge of school items.

Mark a **plus** or **minus** to indicate correct and incorrect responses.

Words	Comp.	Expr.	Words	Comp.	Expr.
1. Desk	____	____	15. Eraser	____	____
2. Chair	____	____	16. Paper	____	____
3. Classroom	____	____	17. Scissors	____	____
4. Rest room	____	____	18. Paste	____	____
5. Library	____	____	19. Book	____	____
6. Office	____	____	20. Notebook	____	____
7. Playground	____	____	21. Ruler	____	____
8. Bus	____	____	22. Crayons	____	____
9. Teacher	____	____	23. Paint	____	____
10. Principal	____	____	24. Computer	____	____
11. Blackboard	____	____	25. Flag	____	____
12. Chalk	____	____	26. Calendar	____	____
13. Pencil	____	____	27. Student	____	____
14. Pen	____	____	28. Map	____	____

SAFETY AND SURVIVAL

Student's Name:_____ Date:_____

Goal:

The student will be able to identify and explain the meaning of safety and survival words when presented with pictures.

Record a **plus** or **minus** to indicate correct and incorrect responses.

Words	Comp.	Expr.	Words	Comp.	Expr.
1. Police	____	____	26. Ambulance	____	____
2. Fire	____	____	27. Open	____	____
3. Poison	____	____	28. Closed	____	____
4. Railroad crossing	____	____	29. Detour	____	____
5. Stop	____	____	30. Gasoline	____	____
6. Emergency	____	____	31. No trespassing	____	____
7. Danger	____	____	32. Condemned	____	____
8. Caution	____	____	33. Wanted	____	____
9. Hot	____	____	34. One way	____	____
10. Out of order	____	____	35. Caution	____	____
11. Entrance	____	____	36. Cigarettes	____	____
12. Exit	____	____	37. Alcohol	____	____
13. Warning	____	____			
14. Men	____	____			
15. Women	____	____			
16. Help	____	____			
17. Doctor	____	____			
18. On	____	____			
19. Off	____	____			
20. Explosives	____	____			
21. Flammable	____	____			
22. Drugs	____	____			
23. Telephone	____	____			
24. Dynamite	____	____			
25. Private	____	____			

BODY PARTS

Student's Name:_____   Date:_____

Goal:

The student will be able to identify and label body parts.

Record a **plus** or **minus** to indicate correct and incorrect responses.

Words	Comp.	Expr.
1. Eyes	____	____
2. Nose	____	____
3. Hair	____	____
4. Ears	____	____
5. Mouth	____	____
6. Legs	____	____
7. Arms	____	____
8. Feet	____	____
9. Hands	____	____
10. Stomach	____	____
11. Back	____	____
12. Knees	____	____
13. Toes	____	____
14. Fingers	____	____

FAMILY RELATIONSHIPS

Student's Name:_____   Date:_____

Goal:

The student will be able to identify and use words relating to family relationships.

Record a **plus** or **minus** to indicate correct and incorrect responses.

Words	Comp.	Expr.
1. Mother	____	____
2. Father	____	____
3. Sister	____	____
4. Brother	____	____
5. Grandmother	____	____
6. Grandfather	____	____
7. Baby	____	____
8. Cousin	____	____
9. Aunt	____	____
10. Uncle	____	____
11. Relative	____	____
12. Niece	____	____
13. Nephew	____	____

COMMUNITY WORKERS/CAREERS

Student's Name:_____   Date:_____

Goal:

The student will be able to identify community workers when presented with pictures and will be able to describe their activities.

Record a **plus** or **minus** to indicate correct and incorrect responses.

Words	Comp.	Expr.	Words	Comp.	Expr.
1. Teacher	____	____	16. Truck driver	____	____
2. Lawyer	____	____	17. Waiter	____	____
3. Nurse	____	____	18. Plumber	____	____
4. Pilot	____	____	19. Librarian	____	____
5. Doctor	____	____	20. Actor	____	____
6. Secretary	____	____	21. Custodian	____	____
7. Dancer	____	____	22. Mail carrier	____	____
8. Beautician	____	____	23. Teacher	____	____
9. Bus driver	____	____	24. Firefighter	____	____
10. Judge	____	____	25. Police officer	____	____
11. Carpenter	____	____	26. Musician	____	____
12. Mechanic	____	____	27. Artist	____	____
13. Cashier	____	____	28. Dancer	____	____
14. Dentist	____	____	29. Soldier	____	____
15. Farmer	____	____	30. Cook	____	____

ANIMALS

Student's Name:_____ Date:_____

Goal:

The student will demonstrate receptive and expressive knowledge of animal names.

Record a **plus** or **minus** to indicate correct and incorrect responses.

Words	Comp.	Expr.	Words	Comp.	Expr.
1. Cat	____	____	16. Sheep	____	____
2. Dog	____	____	17. Rabbit	____	____
3. Bird	____	____	18. Lion	____	____
4. Fish	____	____	19. Zebra	____	____
5. Kitten	____	____	20. Snake	____	____
6. Puppy	____	____	21. Seal	____	____
7. Lamb	____	____	22. Bear	____	____
8. Goat	____	____	23. Elephant	____	____
9. Chicken	____	____	24. Alligator	____	____
10. Rooster	____	____	25. Tiger	____	____
11. Pig	____	____	26. Butterfly	____	____
12. Cow	____	____	27. Frog	____	____
13. Horse	____	____	28. Mouse	____	____
14. Duck	____	____	29. Spider	____	____
15. Goat	____	____	30. Fly	____	____

TIME, SEASONS, AND WEATHER

Student's Name:_____   Date:_____

Goal:

The student will demonstrate receptive and expressive knowledge of concepts relating to time, seasons, and weather.

Record a **plus** or **minus** to indicate correct and incorrect responses.

Words	Comp.	Expr.	Words	Comp.	Expr.
1. Spring	____	____	16. Christmas	____	____
2. Summer	____	____	17. Valentine's Day	____	____
3. Fall	____	____	18. New Year's Day	____	____
4. Winter	____	____	19. Cinco de Mayo	____	____
5. Night	____	____	20. Easter	____	____
6. Day	____	____	21. Independence Day	____	____
7. Month	____	____	22. Halloween	____	____
8. Week	____	____	23. Thanksgiving	____	____
9. Year	____	____	24. Season	____	____
10. Hour	____	____	25. Windy	____	____
11. Minute	____	____	26. Cold	____	____
12. Second	____	____	27. Sunny	____	____
13. Morning	____	____	28. Rainy	____	____
14. Afternoon	____	____	29. Cloudy	____	____
15. Evening	____	____	30. Snowy	____	____

CLOTHING

Student's Name:_____   Date:_____

Goal:

The student will demonstrate receptive and expressive knowledge of articles of clothing.

Record a **plus** or **minus** to indicate correct and incorrect responses.

Words	Comp.	Expr.	Words	Comp.	Expr.
1. Shoes	____	____	16. Bathrobe	____	____
2. Socks	____	____	17. Shorts	____	____
3. Pants	____	____	18. T-shirt	____	____
4. Dress	____	____	19. Cap	____	____
5. Blouse	____	____	20. Mittens	____	____
6. Shirt	____	____	21. Gloves	____	____
7. Skirt	____	____	22. Nightgown	____	____
8. Tie	____	____	23. Belt	____	____
9. Hat	____	____			
10. Boots	____	____			
11. Sweater	____	____			
12. Coat	____	____			
13. Jacket	____	____			
14. Scarf	____	____			
15. Glasses	____	____			

TRANSPORTATION

Student's Name:_____ Date:_____

Goal:

The student will demonstrate receptive and expressive knowledge of transportation items.

Record a **plus** or **minus** to indicate correct and incorrect responses.

Words	Comp.	Expr.
1. Airplane	____	____
2. Helicopter	____	____
3. Parachute	____	____
4. Hot air balloon	____	____
5. Rocket	____	____
6. Bus	____	____
7. Truck	____	____
8. Car	____	____
9. Bicycle	____	____
10. Motorcycle	____	____
11. Wagon	____	____
12. Roller skates	____	____
13. Train	____	____
14. Subway	____	____
15. Boat	____	____

HEALTH AND SELF-CARE

Student's Name:_____ Date:_____

Goal:

The student will demonstrate receptive and expressive knowledge of words relating to health and self-care.

Record a **plus** or **minus** to indicate correct and incorrect responses.

Words	Comp.	Expr.
1. Comb	____	____
2. Brush	____	____
3. Toothbrush	____	____
4. Toothpaste	____	____
5. Soap	____	____
6. Towel	____	____
7. Washcloth	____	____
8. Shampoo	____	____
9. Tissue	____	____
10. Deodorant	____	____
11. Hair dryer	____	____
12. Perfume	____	____
13. Makeup	____	____
14. Thermometer	____	____
15. Medicine	____	____

FOODS AND DRINKS

Student's Name:_____ Date:_____

Goal:

The student will demonstrate receptive and expressive knowledge of labels for foods and drinks.

Record a **plus** or **minus** to indicate correct and incorrect responses.

Words	Comp.	Expr.	Words	Comp.	Expr.
1. Orange	____	____	16. Meal	____	____
2. Apple	____	____	17. Salt	____	____
3. Cherry	____	____	18. Pepper	____	____
4. Grapes	____	____	19. Bread	____	____
5. Banana	____	____	20. Butter	____	____
6. Pear	____	____	21. Cheese	____	____
7. Lemon	____	____	22. Sandwich	____	____
8. Peach	____	____	23. Ice cream	____	____
9. Lettuce	____	____	24. Egg	____	____
10. Tomato	____	____	25. Hamburger	____	____
11. Corn	____	____	26. Hotdog	____	____
12. Carrot	____	____	27. French fries	____	____
13. Potato	____	____	28. Soup	____	____
14. Onion	____	____	29. Milk	____	____
15. Cucumber	____	____	30. Juice	____	____

REFERENCES

Abdrabbah, B. (1984). *Saudi Arabia: Forces of modernization*. Brattleboro, Vermont: Amana Books.

Acevedo, M.A. (1991). Spanish consonant acquisition among two groups of Head Start children. Paper presented at annual convention of the American Speech-Language-Hearing Association, Atlanta, GA.

Adler, S. (1991). Assessment of language proficiency of Limited English Proficient speakers: Implications for the speech-language specialist. *Language, Speech, and Hearing Services in Schools, 22* (2), 12-18.

Anderson, P.P., & Fenichel, E.S. (1989). *Serving culturally diverse families of infants and toddlers with disabilities*. Washington, D.C.: National Center for Clinical Infant Programs.

Anderson, R.T. (1998). The development of grammatical case distinctions in the use of personal pronouns by Spanish-speaking preschoolers. *Journal of Speech-Language-Hearing Research, 41(2)*, 394-406.

Anderson, R. (1999). Impact of first language loss on grammar in a bilingual child. *Communication Disorders Quarterly, 21(1)*, 4-16.

Anderson, R. (2002). Practical assessment strategies with Hispanic students. In A.E. Brice (Ed.), *The Hispanic child: Speech, language, culture and education (pp. 143-184)*. Boston, MA: Allyn & Bacon.

Annett, M.M. (2001). More federal funds could reduce caseloads. *The ASHA Leader*, 6(7), 1.

Argulewicz, E.N. (1983). Effects of ethnic membership, socioeconomic status, and home language on LD, EMR, and EH placements. *Learning Disability Quarterly, 6 (2)*, 195-200.

American Speech-Language Hearing Association (2001). Focused initiative: Culturally/Linguistically diverse populations. *Asha Supplement #21*, 9.

Asian American Handbook (1991). Chicago: National Conference of Christians and Jews, Asian American Journalists Association, & Association of Asian Pacific American Journalists Association.

Barker, A.M. (1999). *Consuming Russia*. London: Duke University Press.

Battle, D.E. (Ed.) (2002a). *Communication disorders in multicultural populations* (3rd ed.). Woburn, MA: Butterworth-Heinemann.

Battle, D.E. (2002b). Middle Eastern and Arab American cultures. In D.E. Battle (Ed.), *Communication disorders in multicultural populations* (3rd ed.) (pp. 113-134). Woburn, MA: Butterworth-Heinemann.

Beardsmore, H.B. (1993). European models of bilingual education: Practice, theory and development. *Journal of Multilingual and Multicultural Development, 14 (1,2)*, 103-120.

Beaumont, C. (1992). Service delivery issues. In H. Langdon and L. Cheng (Eds.), *Hispanic children and adults with communication disorders*. Gaithersburg, MD: Aspen Publishers, Inc.

Bebout, L., & Arthur, B. (1992). Cross-cultural attitudes about speech disorders. *Journal of Speech and Hearing Research, 35(2)*, 45-52.

Bedore, L.M., & Leonard, L.B. (2000). The effects of inflectional variation on fast mapping of verbs in English and Spanish. *Journal of Speech-Language-Hearing Research, 43(1)*, 21-33.

Bell, C. (1987). *The unquiet Pacific*. London: The Centre for Security and Conflict Studies.

Bengston, D., & Baldwin, C. (1993). *The international student: Female circumcision issues. Journal of Multicultural Counseling and Development, 21 (3)*, 168-173.

Berko-Gleason, J. (1982). Insights from child language acquisition for second language loss. In R. Lambert and B. Freed (Eds.), *The loss of language skills* (pp. 13-23.) Rowley, MA: Newbury House.

Bernstein, D.K., & Tiegerman-Farber, E. (2002). *Language and communication disorders in children* (5th ed.). Boston, MA: Allyn & Bacon.

Bliss, L.S. (2002). *Discourse impairments: Assessment and intervention applications*. Boston, MA: Allyn & Bacon.

Bloom, L., & Lahey, M. (1978). *Language development and language disorders*. New York: John Wiley & Sons.

Bozorgmehr, M. (2001). Information available from www.iranian.com/Opinion/2001/May/Iranians.

Brescia, W., & Fortune, J.C. (1988). Standardized testing of American Indian students. *ERIC Digest: American Indian Education [Pub. No. 400-86-0024]*. New Mexico: New Mexico State University.

Brice, A. (1993). *Understanding the Cuban refugee*. San Diego, CA: Los Amigos Research Associates.

Brice, A. (2000a). Code switching and code mixing in the ESL classroom: A study of pragmatic and syntactic features. Advances in speech language pathology. *Journal of the Speech Pathology Association of Australia, 20(1)*, 19-28.

Brice, A. (2000b). Which language for bilingual speakers? Factors to consider. Special Interest Division 14, *Communication Disorders and Sciences in Culturally and Linguistically Diverse Populations, 6(1)*. Rockville Pike, MD: American Speech-Language-Hearing Association.

Brice, A.E. (2002). *The Hispanic child: Speech, language, culture and education*. Boston, MA: Allyn & Bacon.

Brice, A., & Anderson, R. (1999). Code mixing in a young bilingual child. *Communication Disorders Quarterly, 21(1),* 17-22.

Brice, A., & Miller, R.J. (2000). Case studies in inclusion: What works, what doesn't. *Communication Disorders Quarterly, 21(4),* 237-241.

Brice, A., & Montgomery, J. (1996). Adolescent pragmatic skills: A comparison of Latino students in English as a second language and speech and language programs. *Language, Speech, and Hearing Services in Schools, 27(1),* 68-81.

Brice, A., & Roseberry-McKibbin, C. (1999a). *A case example of a bilingual evaluation: A tutorial. Florida Journal of Communication Disorders, 19,* 25-31.

Brice, A., & Roseberry-McKibbin, C. (1999b). Turning frustration into success for English language learners. *Educational Leadership, 56(7),* 53-55.

Bridges, S.J., & Midgette, T.E. (2000). Augmentative/alternative communication and assistive technology. In T. Coleman (Ed.), *Clinical management of communication disorders in culturally diverse children* (pp. 295-333). Needham Heights, MA: Allyn & Bacon.

Brigham Young University (1992). *Culturegrams.* Provo, Utah: David M. Kennedy Center for International Studies.

Brito, L., Perez, X., Bliss, L., & McCabe, A. (1999, November). The narratives of school-aged Spanish speaking children. Paper presented at the annual convention of the American Speech-Language-Hearing Association, San Francisco, CA.

Brown, D. (1980). *Principles of language learning and teaching.* Englewood Cliffs, New Jersey: Prentice-Hall.

Budoff, M. (1987). Measures for assessing learning potential. In C.S. Lidz (Ed.), *Dynamic assessment: An interactional approach to evaluating learning potential* (pp. 52-81). New York: The Guilford Press.

Burnett, B. (2000). *Close-up. The ASHA Leader, 5(10),* 26.

Burt, H., & Dulay, H. (1978). Some guidelines for the assessment of oral language proficiency and dominance. *TESOL Quarterly, 12,* 177-192.

Burt, M., Dulay, H., & Hernandez, E. (1973). Bilingual syntax measure (Restricted edition). New York: Harcourt, Brace, Jovanovich.

California Department of Education (1999). Language census summary statistics, 1998-1999. Sacramento, CA: California Department of Education.

California Education Code (1991). *California Education Code, 1991 Compact Edition.* St. Paul, MN: West Publishing Company.

Campbell, D. (2001). Multicultural competency. *ADVANCE for Speech-Language Pathologists and Audiologists, 11(9),* 7-8.

Campbell, I.C. (1989). A history of the Pacific Islands. Los Angeles: University of California Press.

Campbell, L.R. (1993). Maintaining the integrity of home linguistic varieties: Black English Vernacular. *American Journal of Speech-Language Pathology, 2,* 85.

Campbell, L.R. (1996). Issues in service delivery to African American children. In Kamhi, A.G., Pollock, K.E., & Harris, J.L. (Eds.), *Communication development and disorders in African American children* (pp. 73-94). Baltimore: Paul H. Brookes Publishing Co.

Carney, L.J., & Chermak, G.D. (1991). Performance of American Indian children with fetal alcohol syndrome on the Test of Language Development. *Journal of Communication Disorders, 24 (2),* 123-134.

Center for Immigration Studies (2001). Information available from http://www.cis.org/articles/2001/back101.html.

Chan, S. (1998a). Families with Asian roots. In E.W. Lynch & M.J. Hanson (Eds.), *Developing cross-cultural competence: A guide to working with young children and their families* (2nd ed.) (pp. 251-354). Baltimore: Paul H. Brookes Publishing Co.

Chan, S. (1998b). Families with Pilipino roots. In E.W. Lynch & M.J. Hanson (Eds.), *Developing cross-cultural competence: A guide to working with young children and their families* (2nd ed.) (pp. 355-408). Baltimore, MD: Paul H. Brookes Publishing Co.

Cheng, L.L. (1991). *Assessing Asian language performance* (2nd ed.). Oceanside, CA: Academic Communication Associates.

Cheng, L.L. (1999). Struggling to be heard: The unmet needs of Asian Pacific Americans. *Asha, 41(6),* 10-13.

Cheng, L.L., & Butler, K. (1993). Difficult discourse: Designing connection to deflect language impairment. Paper presented at the annual conference of the California Speech-Language-Hearing Association, Palm Springs, CA.

Cheng, L.L. (2002). Asian and Pacific American cultures. In D.E. Battle (Ed.), *Communication disorders in multicultural populations* (3rd ed.) (pp. 71-112). Woburn, MA: Butterworth-Heinemann.

Cheng, L.L., & Hammer, C.S. (1992). *Cultural perceptions of disabilities.* San Diego: Los Amigos Research Associates.

Cheng, L.L., & Ima, K. (1989). *Understanding the immigrant Pacific Islander.* San Diego: Los Amigos Research Associates.

Cheng, L.L., Nakasato, J., & Wallace, G.J. (1995). The Pacific Islander population and the challenges they face. In L.L. Cheng (Ed.), *Integrating language and learning for inclusion: An Asian-Pacific focus* (pp. 63-106). San Diego: Singular Publishing Group, Inc.

Clark, S., & Kelley, S.D.M. (1992). Traditional Native American values: *Conflict or concordance in rehabilitation? Journal of Rehabilitation, 58 (2),* 23-27.

Cole, L. (1989). E pluribus pluribus: Multicultural imperatives for the 1990s and beyond. *Asha, 31 (9),* 65-70.

Coleman, T.J., & McCabe-Smith, L. (2000). Key terms and concepts. In T.J. Coleman, *Clinical management of communication disorders in culturally diverse children* (pp. 3-12). Needham Heights, MA: Allyn & Bacon.

Craig, H.K., & Washington, J.A. (2000). An assessment battery for identifying language impairments in African American children. *Journal of Speech-Language-Hearing Research, 43(2),* 366-379.

Craig, H.K., Washington, J.A., & Thompson-Porter, C. (1998). Average C-unit lengths in the discourse of African American children from low-income, urban homes. *Journal of Speech-Language-Hearing Research, 41(2),* 433-444.

Cummins, J. (1984). *Bilingualism and special education: Issues in assessment and pedagogy.* Austin: Pro-Ed.

Cummins, J. (1985). Theory and policy in bilingual evaluation. Paper presented at the OECD National Seminar on Education in Multicultural Societies, Ljubljana.

Cummins, J. (1988). Research on bilingualism and language acquisition and development. Presentation in Red Bluff, CA.

Cummins, J. (1989). Language and literacy acquisition in bilingual contexts. *Journal of Multilingual and Multicultural Development, 10 (1),* 17-31.

Cummins, J. (1990, January). *Empowerment and critical pedagogy in bilingual teacher training programs.* San Francisco: California Association of Bilingual Education.

Cummins, J. (1991a). Empowering culturally and linguistically diverse students with learning problems. *ERIC Digest, EDO-EC-91-5,* 9-10.

Cummins, J. (1991b). Interdependence of first- and second-language proficiency in bilingual children. In E. Bialystok (Ed.), *Language processing in bilingual children* (pp. 70-89). New York: Cambridge University Press.

Cummins, J. (1992a). Bilingual education and English immersion: The Ramirez report in theoretical perspective. *Bilingual Research Journal, 16 (1,2),* 91-104.

Cummins, J. (1992b). Empowerment through biliteracy. In J.R. Tinajero & A.F. Ada (Eds.), *The power of two languages: Literacy and biliteracy for Spanish-speaking students.* New York: MacMillan/McGraw Hill.

Cummins, J. (1992c). The role of primary language development in promoting educational success for language minority students. In C. Leyba (Ed.), *Schooling and language minority students: a theoretical framework.* Calif. State University, Los Angeles, CA.

Cummins, J. (1993). Accelerating second language and literacy development. Paper presented at California Elementary Education Association, Sacramento, CA.

Dabars, Z. (1995). *The Russian way.* Chicago: Passport Books.

Damico, J.S., & Hamayan, E.V. (1992). *Multicultural language intervention: Addressing cultural and linguistic diversity.* New York: EDUCOM Associates, Inc.

Dodge, E.S. (1976). *Islands and empires: Western Impact on the Pacific and East Asia.* Minneapolis: University of Minnesota Press.

Dodge, E.P. (2000). Communication and collaboration. In Dodge, E.P. (Ed.), *The survival guide for school-based speech-language pathologists* (pp. 57-97). San Diego, CA: Singular Publishing /Thomson Learning.

Domyancic, L. (2000). Service delivery to Russian immigrants: An ethnographic survey. Unpublished master's thesis, California State University, Sacramento.

Dudden, A.P. (1992). *The American Pacific: From the old China trade to present.* New York: Oxford University Press.

Dulay, H., & Burt, M. (1974). Errors and strategies in children's second language acquisition. *TESOL Quarterly, 8,* 129-136.

Dulay, H., Burt, M., & Krashen, S. (1982). *Language two.* New York: Oxford University Press.

Dunn, S.P., & Dunn, E. (1977). *Slavic studies working paper: The study of the Soviet family in the USSR and in the West.* Columbus, OH: American Institution for the Advancement of Slavic Studies.

Erickson, J. (1979). *Islands of the South Pacific.* Menlo Park, CA: Lane Publishing Co.

Erickson, J.G. (1992). Building blocks: Multicultural considerations. Short course presentation, Annual conference of the California Speech-Language-Hearing Association, San Francisco, CA

Erickson, J.G., & Iglesias, A. (1986). Speech and language disorders in Hispanics. In O. Taylor (Ed.), *Nature of communication disorders in culturally and linguistically diverse populations* (pp. 181-218). San Diego: College-Hill Press.

Erickson, J.G., & Omark, D. (Eds.) (1981). *Communication assessment of the bilingual bicultural child.* Baltimore: University Park Press.

Ervin-Tripp, S. (1974). Is second language learning like the first? *TESOL Quarterly, 8(2),* 111-127.

Fadiman, A. (1997). *The spirit catches you and you fall down: A Hmong child, her American doctors, and the collision of two cultures*. New York: Farrar, Straus, and Giroux.

Falk-Ross, F.C. (2002). *Classroom-based language and literacy intervention: A programs and case studies approach*. Boston, MA: Allyn & Bacon.

Fang, X., & Ping-an, H. (1992). Articulation disorders among speakers of Mandarin Chinese. *American Journal of Speech Language Pathology, 1 (4)*, 15-16.

Fazio, B.B. (1998). Serial memory in children with specific language impairment: Examining specific content areas for assessment and intervention. In R.B. Gillam (Ed.), *Memory and language impairment in children and adults: New perspectives* (pp. 64-82). Gaithersburg, MD: Aspen Publishers, Inc.

Feuerstein, R., Rand, Y., Jensen, M.R., Kaniel, S., & Turzel, D. (1987). Prerequisites for assessment of learning potential: The LPAD model. In C.S. Lidz (Ed.), *Dynamic assessment: An interactional approach to evaluating learning potential* (pp. 35-51). New York: The Guilford Press.

Fixico, D.L. (1986). *Termination and relocation: Federal Indian policy, 1945-1960*. Albuquerque: University of New Mexico Press.

Friedlander, R. (1993). BHSM comes to the Flathead Indian Reservation. *Asha, 35(5)*, 28-29.

Fung, F., & Roseberry-McKibbin, C. (1999). Service delivery considerations in working with clients from Cantonese-speaking backgrounds. *American Journal of Speech-Language Pathology, 8(4)*, 309-318.

Genesee, F. (1988). Bilingual language development in preschool children. In D. Bishop & K. Mogford (Eds.), *Language development in exceptional circumstances* (pp. 62-79). London: Churchill Livingstone.

Ghali, J.K., Cooper, R.S., Kowatly, I., & Liao, Y. (1993). Delay between onset of chest pain and arrival to the coronary care unit among minority and disadvantaged patients. *Journal of the National Medical Association, 85 (3)*, 180-184.

Gillam, R.B., Cowan, N., & Day, L. (1995). Sequential memory in children with and without language impairment. *Journal of Speech and Hearing Research, 38*, 393-402.

Gillam, R.B., & van Kleeck, A. (1998). Phonological awareness training and short-term working memory: Clinical implications. In R.B. Gillam (Ed.), *Memory and language impairment in children and adults: New perspectives* (pp. 83-96). Gaithersburg, MD: Aspen Publishers, Inc.

Gilliland, H. (1988). *Teaching the Native American*. Dubuque, IA: Kendall-Hunt Publishing Co.

Glennen, S., & Masters, M.G. (1999, November). Language development and delay in children adopted internationally. Paper presented at the annual convention of the American Speech-Language-Hearing Association, San Francisco, CA.

Goldstein, B. (2000). *Cultural and linguistic diversity resource guide for speech-language pathologists*. San Diego, CA: Singular Publishing Group/Thomson Learning.

Goldstein, B.A., & Iglesias, A. (1996). Phonological patterns in normally developing Spanish-speaking 3- and 4-year olds. *Language, Speech, and Hearing Services in Schools, 27(1)*, 82-90.

Goldsworthy, C. (2002). *Developmental reading disabilities: A language-based treatment approach* (2nd ed.). San Diego, CA: Singular Publishing/Thomson Learning.

Gonzales, M.D., Ezell, H.K., & Randolph, E. (1999, November). Home literacy environments of migrant Mexican-American families. Paper presented at the annual convention of the American Speech-Language-Hearing Association, San Francisco, CA.

Graham, L.O. (2000). *Our kind of people: Inside America's Black upper middle class*. New York: HarperCollins Publishers.

Grossier, P.L. (1982). *The United States and the Middle East*. Albany: State University of New York Press.

Gutierrez-Clellen, V.F. (1998). Syntactic skills of Spanish-speaking children with low school achievement. *Language, Speech, and Hearing Services in Schools, 29(4)*, 207-315.

Gutierrez-Clellen, V.F. (1999a). Language choice in intervention with bilingual children. *American Journal of Speech-Language Pathology, 8(4)*, 291-302.

Gutierrez-Clellen, V.F. (1999b). Mediating literacy skills in Spanish-speaking children with special needs. *Language, Speech, and Hearing Services in Schools, 30(3)*, 285-292.

Gutierrez-Clellen, V.F., & DeCurtis, L. (1999). Word definition skills in Spanish-speaking children with language impairment. *Communication Disorders Quarterly, 21(1)*, 23-31.

Gutierrez-Clellen, V.F., & Quinn, R. (1993). Assessing narratives of children from diverse cultural/linguistic groups. *Language, Speech, and Hearing Services in Schools, 24 (1)*, 2-9.

Gutierrez-Clellen, V.F., Restrepo, M.A., Bedore, L., Pena, E., & Anderson, R. (2000). Language sample analysis in Spanish-speaking children: Methodological considerations. *Language, Speech, and Hearing Services in Schools, 31(1)*, 88-98.

Hadley, P.A., Simmerman, A., Long, M., & Luna, M. (2000). Facilitating language development for inner city children: Experimental evaluation of a collaborative, classroom-based intervention. *Language, Speech, and Hearing Services in Schools, 31(3)*, 280-295.

Hammer, C.S., & Miccio, A.W. (2001). Bilingual preschoolers. *The ASHA Leader, 6(21)*, 6.

Hammer, C.S., & Weiss, A.L. (1999). Guiding language development: How African American mothers and their infants structure play interactions. *Journal of Speech-Language-Hearing Research, 42(5)*, 1219-1233.

Hammer, C.S., & Weiss, A.L. (2000). African American mothers' views of their infants' language development and language-learning environment. *American Journal of Speech-Language Pathology, 9(2)*, 126-140.

Hanson, M.J. (1998a). Ethnic, cultural, and language diversity in intervention settings. In E.W. Lynch & M.J. Hanson, *Developing cross-cultural competence: A guide for working with young children and their families* (pp. 3-18). Baltimore: Paul H. Brookes Publishing Co.

Hanson, M.J. (1998b). Families with Anglo-European roots. In E.W. Lynch & M.J. Hanson (Eds.), *Developing cross-cultural competence: A guide for working with young children and their families* (2nd ed.) (pp. 93-126). Baltimore: Paul H. Brookes Publishing Co.

Harris, G. (1985). Considerations in assessing English language performance of Native American children. *Topics in Language Disorders, 5(4)*, 42-52.

Harris, G. (1986). Barriers to the delivery of speech, language, and hearing services to Native Americans. In O. Taylor (Ed.), *Nature of communication disorders in culturally and linguistically diverse children*. San Diego: College-Hill Press.

Harris, G. (1998). American Indian cultures: A lesson in diversity. In D. Battle (Ed.), *Communication disorders in multicultural populations* (2nd ed.) (pp. 117-156). Stoneham, MA: Butterworth-Heinemann.

Harry, B. (1992). Making sense of disability: Low-income, Puerto Rican Parents' theories of the problem. *Exceptional Children, 59 (1)*, 27-40.

Hatch, E. (1992). *Discourse and language education*. New York: Cambridge University Press.

Hayes-Bautista, D.E., Hurtado, A., Valdez, R.B., & Hernandez, A.C.R. (1992). *No longer a minority: Latinos and social policy in California*. Los Angeles: University of California, Los Angeles Chicano Studies Research Center.

Hearne, D. (2000). *Teaching second language learners with learning disabilities: Strategies for effective practice*. Oceanside, CA: Academic Communication Associates.

Heath, S. B. (1983). *Ways with words: Language, life, and work in communities and classrooms*. New York: Cambridge University Press.

Heath, S.B. (1986). *Sociocultural contexts of language development*. In Leyba, C.F. (Ed.), *Beyond language: Social and cultural factors in schooling language minority students* (pp. 143-186). Los Angeles: Evaluation, Dissemination, and Assessment Center, Calif. State Univ., Los Angeles.

Helfman, U. (1999). Survey portrays new immigrants as political force: 52% of Russians identify as Jews. *Forward, 1-2*.

Hernandez-Chavez, E., Burt, M., & Dulay, H. (1978). Language dominance and proficiency testing: some general considerations. *NABE Journal, 3*, 41-60.

Holliday, P.A.C. (2001). Demand may exceed supply in future job market. *The ASHA Leader, 6(8)*, 18.

Huer, M.B., Saenz, T.I., & Doan, J.H.D. (2001). Understanding the Vietnamese American community: Implications for training education personnel providing services to children with disabilities. *Communication Disorders Quarterly, 23(1)*, 27-39.

Iglesias, A. (2002). Latino culture. In D.E. Battle (Ed.), *Communication disorders in multicultural populations* (3rd ed.) (pp. 179-202). Woburn, MA: Butterworth-Heinemann.

Individuals with Disabilities Education Act (IDEA; 1997). *Federal Register, Volume 62, No. 204. Part V,* Department of Education, 34 CFR parts 300, 303.

Irujo, S. (1988). An introduction to intercultural differences and similarities in nonverbal communication. In J.S. Wurzel (Ed.), *Toward multiculturalism* (pp. 142-150). Yarmouth, Maine: Intercultural Press.

Isaac, K.M. (2001). What about linguistic diversity? A different look at multicultural health care. *Communication Disorders Quarterly, 22(2)*, 110-113.

Isaacs, G.J. (1996). Persistence of non-standard dialect in school-age children. *Journal of Speech and Hearing Research, 39(2)*, 434-441.

Jackson-Maldonado, D., Batges, E., & Thal, D. (1992). *Fundación MacArthur: Inventario del desarrollo de habilidades comunicativas*. San Diego, CA: San Diego State University.

Jacobs, E.L., & Coufal, K.L. (2001). A computerized screening instrument of language learnability. *Communication Disorders Quarterly, 22(2)*, 67-76.

James, R. (1999). Human rights conference. The Professional, Spring, 1999. *The Elk Grove Education Association Publication* (p. 1).

Jimenez, B. (1987). Acquisition of Spanish consonants in children aged 3-5 years, 7 months. *Language, Speech, and Hearing Services in the Schools, 18*, 357-363.

Joe, J.R., & Malach, R.S. (1998). Families with Native American roots. In E.W. Lynch & M.J. Hanson (Eds.), *Developing cross-cultural competence: A guide to working with young children and their families* (2nd ed.) (pp. 127-164). Baltimore: Paul H. Brookes Publishing Co.

Johnston, R.C. (2001). Who is 'Asian'? Cultural differences defy simple categories. Available from *Education Week* at http://www.edweek.org.

Johnstone, P.J. (1993). *Operation world*. Grand Rapids, MI: Zondervan Publishing House.

Justice, L.M., & Ezell, H.K. (2000). Enhancing children's print and word awareness through home-based parent intervention. *American Journal of Speech-Language Pathology, 9(3),* 257-268.

Kamalipour, Y.R. (2001). Information available from www.iranian.com/Opinion/2001/May/Iranians

Katz-Stone, A. (2000). Russia to the suburbs. *Baltimore Jewish Times,* 58-62.

Kay-Raining Bird, E., & Vetter, R.S. (1994). Storytelling in Chippewa-Cree children. *Journal of Speech and Hearing Research, 37(6),* 1354-1368.

Kayser, H. (1998). *Assessment and intervention resource for Hispanic children.* San Diego: Singular Publishing Group.

Kayser, H. (1989). Speech and language assessment of Spanish-English speaking children. *Language, Speech, and Hearing Services in Schools, 20,* 226-244.

Kayser, H. (1990). Social communicative behaviors of language-disordered Mexican-American students. *Child Language Teaching and Therapy, 6,* 255-269.

Kayser, H. (1995). Assessment of speech and language impairments in bilingual children. In H. Kayser (Ed.), *Bilingual speech-language pathology: An Hispanic focus* (pp. 243-264). San Diego: Singular Publishing Group.

Kayser, H.R. (2002). Bilingual language development and language disorders. In D.E. Battle (Ed.), *Communication disorders in multicultural populations* (3rd ed.) (pp. 205-232). Woburn, MA: Butterworth-Heinemann.

Kayser, H., Cheng, L.L., Gutierrez-Clellen, V., & Anderson, N. (1993). Assessment and intervention in multicultural populations: An update. Paper presented at the annual convention of the American Speech-Language-Hearing Association, Anaheim, CA.

Kayser, H., Montgomery, J.K., Perlmutter, M., Sanford, M., Simon, C., & Westby, C. (1993). Cross-disciplinary language instruction: SLP and ESL. Paper presented at American Speech-Language-Hearing Association, Anaheim, CA.

Kelley, E. (2001). Everything they didn't teach you: *Guide to a successful school year for the caseload-challenged.* Youngtown, AZ: ECL Publications.

Kessler, C. (1984). Language acquisition in bilingual children. In N. Miller (Ed.), *Bilingualism and language disability: Assessment and remediation* (pp. 26-54). San Diego, CA: College Hill Press.

Kiernan, B., & Swisher, L. (1990). The initial learning of novel English words: Two single-subject experiments with minority-language children. *Journal of Speech and Hearing Research , 33,* 707-716.

King, S.H. (1993). The limited presence of African-American teachers. *Review of Educational Research, 63 (2),* 115-149.

Kohnert, K.J., Bates, E., & Hernandez, E. (1999). Balancing bilinguals: Lexical-semantic production and cognitive processing in children. *Journal of Speech-Language-Hearing Research, 42(6),* 1400-1413.

Kornblatt, J.D. (1999) Christianity, antisemitism, nationalism: Russian orthodoxy in a reborn Orthodox Russia. In A.M. Barker (Ed.), *Consuming Russia* (pp. 414-436). London: Duke University Press.

Kozlowski, G.C. (1991). *The concise history of Islam and the origin of its empires.* Acton, MA: Copley Publishing Group.

Krashen, S. D. (1992). Bilingual education and second language acquisition theory. In C. Leyba (Ed.), *Schooling and language minority students: A theoretical framework.* Calif. State University, Los Angeles, CA.

Krashen, S. D. (1993). *Beyond the basics of language education.* Sacramento, CA: California Elementary Education Association.

Kratcoski, A. (1998). Guidelines for using portfolios in assessment and evaluation. *Language, Speech, and Hearing Services in Schools, 29(1),* 3-10.

Kuster, J.M. (2000). English as a second language: Web sites. *ASHA Leader, 5(12),* 6.

Lambert, W., & Tucker, G. (1972). *Bilingual education of children: The St. Lambert experiment.* Rowley, MA: Newbury House.

Langdon, H.W. and Cheng, L. (Eds.) (1992). *Hispanic children and adults with communication disorders: Assessment and intervention.* Gaithersburg, MD: Aspen Publishers, Inc.

Langdon, H.W. (2000). Diversity. In E.P. Dodge (Ed.), *The survival guide for school-based speech-language pathologists* (pp. 367-398). San Diego: Singular Publishing Group/Thomson Learning.

Langdon, H.W., & Cheng, L.L. (2002). *Collaborating with interpreters and translators: A guide for communication disorders professionals.* Eau Claire, WI: Thinking Publications.

Langdon, H.W., & Saenz, T.I. (1996). *Language assessment and intervention with multicultural students: A guide for speech-language-hearing professionals.* Oceanside, CA: Academic Communication Associates.

Latino Legislative Caucus Hearings (1991). Latinos at a Crossroads: Challenges and opportunities into the 21st Century. California: Latino Legislative Caucus Hearings.

Leap, W. (1993). *American Indian English.* Salt Lake City, UT: University of Utah Press.

Leibowitz, A.H. (1971). A history of language policy in American Indian schools. *Curriculum Bulletin #3, Bilingual Education for American Indians.* Washington, D.C.: U.S. Bureau of Indian Affairs.

LeMoine, N. (1993). Serving the language needs of African American students: Strategies for success. Presentation, at the Annual Conference of the California Speech-Language-Hearing Association, Palm Springs, CA.

Leung, B. (1993). Assessment considerations with culturally and linguistically diverse students. Paper presented at National Association for Multicultural Education, Los Angeles.

Li, C.N. (1992). Chinese. *International encyclopedia of linguistics,* 1, 257-263. New York: Oxford University Press.

Liam, C.H.T., & Abdullah (2001). The education and practice of speech-language pathologists in Malaysia. *American Journal of Speech-Language Pathology, 10(1),* 3-9.

Lindeman, B. (2001). Reaching out to immigrant parents. *Educational Leadership, 58(6),* 62-67.

Long, S.O. (1992). *Japan: A country study.* Washington, D.C.: Department of the Army.

Lund, N.J., & Duchan, J.F. (1993). *Assessing children's language in naturalistic contexts (3rd ed.).* Englewood Cliffs, NJ: Prentice Hall.

Lynch, E.W. (1998). Conceptual framework: From culture shock to cultural learning (pp 23-45). In E.W. Lynch & M.J. Hanson (Eds.), *Developing cross-cultural competence: A guide for working with young children and their families* (2nd ed.). Baltimore, MD: Paul H. Brookes Publishing Co.

Lynch, E.W., & Hanson, M.J. (1998). *Developing cross-cultural competence: A guide for working with young children and their families* (2nd ed.). Baltimore, MD: Paul H. Brookes Publishing Co.

Mace-Matluck, B.J. (1971). Order of acquisition: same or different in first- and second-language learning? *Bilingual Resources, 3 (1),* 27-31.

Madding, C.C. (1999, April). Mama e hijo: The Latino mother-infant dyad. Conference proceedings from the fourth annual communicative disorders multicultural conference, California State University, Fullerton. *The Multicultural Electronic Journal of Communication Disorders, 2(1),* 1-4.

Madding, C.C. (2000). Maintaining focus on cultural competence in early intervention services to linguistically and culturally diverse families. *Infant-Toddler Intervention: The Transdisciplinary Journal, 10(1),* 9-18.

Madding, C.C. (2002). Socialization practices of Latinos. In A.E. Brice (Ed.), *The Hispanic child: Speech, language, culture and education (pp. 68-84).* Boston, MA: Allyn & Bacon.

Maestas, A. G., & Erickson, J. G. (1992). Mexican immigrant mothers' beliefs about disabilities. *American Journal of Speech-Language Pathology, 1 (4),* 5-10.

Mahecha, N.R. (1991, November). Perception of pre-switch cues by Spanish-English individuals. Paper presented at the annual convention of the American Speech-Language-Hearing Association, Atlanta, GA.

Mahecha, N.R. (1991, November). Perception of pre-switch cues by Spanish-English individuals. Paper presented at the annual meeting of the American Speech-Language-Hearing Association, Atlanta, GA.

Malach, R.S., Segel, N., & Thomas, T. (1989). *Overcoming obstacles and improving outcomes: Early intervention services for Indian Children with special needs.* Bernalillo, NM: Southwest Communication Resources.

Malakoff, M., & Hakuta, K. (1991). Translation skill and metalinguistic awareness in bilinguals. In E. Bialystok (Ed.), *Language processing in bilingual children* (pp. 141-166). New York: Cambridge University Press.

Mann, D.M., & Hodson, B. (1994). Spanish-speaking children's phonologies: Assessment and remediation of disorders. In H. Kayser (Ed.), *Seminars in speech and language: Communicative impairments and bilingualism* (pp. 137-148). New York: Thieme Medical publishers.

Mannes, M. (1993). Seeking the balance between child protection and family preservation in Indian child welfare. *Child Welfare, 72 (2),* 141-152.

Manning, M.L., & Lee, G.L. (2001). Working with parents—cultural and linguistic considerations. *Kappa Delta Pi Record, 37(4),* 160-163.

Mansuri, S. (1993). Islam in the public school textbooks: Who are Muslims anyway? Paper presented at the National Association for Multicultural Education, Los Angeles, CA.

Markoff, R., & Bond, J. (1980). The Samoans. In J. JcDermott, Jr., W. S. Tseng, & T Maretzki (Eds.), *People and cultures of Hawaii* (pp. 184-189). Honolulu: University of Hawaii, School of Medicine and University Press of Hawaii.

Matluck, J., & Mace-Matluck, B.J. (1977). Bilingualism and language assessment. *Proceedings: Pacific Northwest Council of Foreign Languages. 28 (part 2),* 20-23.

Matluck, J., & Mace-Matluck, B. (1982). *Formal English as a second language. Topics in Language Disorders, 3,* 65-69.

Matsuda, M. (1989). Working with Asian parents: Some communication strategies. *Topics in Language Disorders, 9,* 45-53.

Matsuda, M., & O'Connor, L. (1990, November). Paper presented at the annual convention of the American Speech-Language-Hearing Association, Seattle, WA.

Matsuda, M., & O'Connor, L. (March, 1993). Creating an effective partnership: Training bilingual communication aides. Paper presented at the annual conference of the California Speech-Language-Hearing Association, Palm Springs, CA.

Mattes, L., & Omark, D. (1991). *Speech and language assessment for the bilingual handicapped.* (2nd ed.). Oceanside, CA: Academic Communication Associates.

McAvoy, J., & Sidles, C. (1991). The effects of language preference and multitrial presentation on the free recall of Navajo children. *Journal of American Indian Education, 30 (3),* 33-42.

McGregor, K.K., Williams, D., Hearst, S., & Johnson, A.C. (1997). The use of contrastive analysis in distinguishing difference from disorder: A tutorial. *American Journal of Speech-Language Pathology, 6(3),* 45-56.

McLaughlin, B. (1984). Second language acquisition in childhood. *Volume 1: Preschool children* (2nd ed.). New Jersey: Lawrence Erlbaum and Associates

McNeilly, L., & Coleman, T.J. (2000). Language disorders in culturally diverse populations: Intervention issues and strategies. In T. J. Coleman, *Clinical management of communication disorders in culturally diverse children* (pp. 157-196). Needham Heights, MA: Allyn & Bacon.

McWhirter, J.J., & Ryan, C.A. (1991). Counseling the Navajo: Cultural understanding. *Journal of Multicultural Counseling and Development, 19 (2),* 74-82.

Merino, B., & Spencer, M. (1983). The comparability of English and Spanish versions of oral language proficiency instruments. *NABE Journal, 7,* 1-31.

Merino, B. (1992). Acquisition of syntactic and phonological features in Spanish. In H.W. Langdon & L. Cheng, *Hispanic children and adults with communication disorders: Assessment and intervention.* Gaithersburg, MD: Aspen Publishers, Inc.

Meyerson, M.D. (1983). Genetic counseling for families of Chicano children with birth defects. In D.R. Omark & J.G. Erickson (Eds.), *The bilingual exceptional child.* San Diego, CA: Los Amigos Research Associates.

Micek, T. (1992). Student introductions: A manifold learning opportunity. *TESOL Journal, 1 (4),* 32.

Minochin, S. (1999). Russian immigrants squeezing social services groups. *Forward,* 5-7.

Mohtasham-Nouri, N. (1994). *Iranians in America.* San Francisco: Many Cultures Publishing.

Mokuau, N., & Tauili'ili, P. (1998). Families with Native Hawaiian and Pacific Island roots. In E.W. Lynch & M.J. Hanson (Eds.), *Developing cross-cultural competence: A guide for working with young children and their families* (2nd ed.) (pp. 409-440). Baltimore, MD: Paul H. Brookes Publishing Co.

Montgomery, J.K. (1998). Reading and the SLP: Using discourse, narratives and expository text. *CSHA Magazine, 27(3),* 8-9.

Montgomery, J.W. (1998). Sentence comprehension and working memory in children with specific language impairment. In R.B. Gillam (Ed.), *Memory and language impairment in children and adults: New perspectives (pp. 28-46).* Gaithersburg, MD: Aspen Publishers, Inc.

Moore-Brown, B., & Montgomery, J.K. (2001). *Making a difference for America's children: Speech-language pathologists in public schools.* Eau Claire, WI: Thinking Publications.

Murphy, J. (2001). http://nativeamculture.about.com/culture/nativeamculture/library/weekly/aa052301a.htm

National Center for Education Statistics (1997).*The condition of education, 1997.* Washington, D C: U.S. Department of Education.

National Center for Education Statistics (1999). *Teacher quality: A report on the preparation and qualifications of publilc school teachers.* Washington, DC: U.S. Department of Education.

Nellum-Davis, P., Gentry, B., & Hubbard-Wiley, P. (2002). Clinical practice issues. In D. Battle (Ed.), *Communication disorders in multicultural populations* (3nd ed.) (pp. 461-482). Stoneham, MA: Butterworth-Heinemann.

Ogakaki, L., & Frensch, P.A. (1998). Parenting and children's school achievement: A multiethnic approach. *American Educational Research Journal, 35(1),* 123-144.

Ogbu, J. (1992). Understanding cultural diversity and learning. *Educational Researcher, 21 (8),* 5-14.

Ogbu, J., & Matute-Bianchi, M. (1990). Understanding sociocultural factors: Knowledge, identity, and school adjustment. In Leyba, C.F. (Ed.), *Beyond language: social and cultural factors in schooling language minority students* (pp. 73-142). Los Angeles: Evaluation, Dissemination, and Assessment Center, California State University., Los Angeles.

Omar Nydell, M. (1996). *Understanding Arabs: A guide for Westerners* (revised ed.). Yarmouth, ME: Intercultural Press, Inc.

Omark, D., & Erickson, J.G. (Eds.) (1983). *The bilingual exceptional child.* San Diego: College-Hill Press.

Ortiz, A. (1984). Choosing the language of instruction for exceptional bilingual children. *Teaching Exceptional Children,*

16, 208-212.

Owens, R.E. (2001). *Language development: An introduction* (5th ed.). Needham Heights, MA: Alllyn & Bacon.

Padilla, A.M. (1992). Reflections on testing: Emerging trends and new possibilities. In K.F. Geisinger (Ed.), *Psychological testing of Hispanics* (pp. 271-284). Washington, D.C.: American Psychological Press.

Palcich, W.J. (1992). Native American bilingualism: A hidden challenge for speech-language pathologists. *ADVANCE for Speech-Language Pathologists and Audiologists, 2 (22),* 10-11.

Pang-Ching, G., Robb, M., Heath, R., & Takumi, M. (1995). Middle ear disorders and hearing loss in Native Hawaiian preschoolers. *Language, Speech, and Hearing Services in Schools, 26(1),* 33-38.

Patterson, J.L. (1999). What bilingual toddlers hear and say: Language input and word combinations. *Communication Disorders Quarterly, 21(1),* 32-38.

Patterson, J.L. (2000). Observed and reported expressive vocabulary and word combinations in bilingual toddlers. *Journal of Speech-Language-Hearing Research, 43(1),* 121-128.

Paul, R. (2001). *Language disorders from infancy through adolescence* (2nd ed.). St. Louis, MO: Mosby, Inc.

Payne, K. (1986). Cultural and linguistic groups in the United States. In O. Taylor (Ed.), *Nature of communication disorders in culturally and linguistically diverse populations.* San Diego: College-Hill Press.

Payne, R.K. (2001). *A framework for understanding poverty.* Highland, TX: aha! Process, Inc.

Peal, E., & Lambert, W. (1962). The relation of bilingualism to intelligence. *Psychological Monograph, 72,* 1-23.

Pena, E.D., Iglesias, A., & Lidz, C.S. (2001). Reducing test bias through dynamic assessment of children's word learning ability. *American Journal of Speech-Language Pathology, 10(2),* 138-154.

Pena, E.D., & Quinn, R. (1997). Task familiarity: Effects on the test performance of Puerto Rican and African American children. *Language, Speech, and Hearing Services in Schools, 28(4),* 323-332.

Penfield, J. (1990). Understanding cultural diversity. In M.H. Li & P. Li, *Understanding Asian Americans* (pp. 65-87). New York: Neal-Schuman Publishers, Inc.

Perrozi, J., & Sanchez, M.L.C. (1992). The effect of instruction in L1 on receptive acquisition of L2 for bilingual children with language delay. *Language, Speech, and Hearing Services in the Schools, 23 (4),* 358-352.

Phillips, S. (1982). *The invisible culture: Communication in classroom and community on the Warm Springs Indian reservation.* New York: Longman.

Phillips, S. (1983). *The invisible culture.* New York: Longman.

Pieretti, R.A., & Goldsworthy, C.L. (2001). Language-based reading disorders: A bottom-up perspective. *CSHA Magazine, 31(1),* 8-9.

Politzer, R., & Ramirez, A. (1974). An error analysis of the spoken English of Mexican-American pupils in a bilingual school and a monolingual school. *Language Learning, 23 (1),* 39-51.

Prakash, P. (1984). Second language acquisition and critical period hypothesis. *Psycho-lingua, 14 (1),* 13-17.

Ramirez, J.D., Yuen, S., & Ramey, D. (1991). Executive summary final report: Longitudinal study of structured English immersion strategy, early-exit and late-exit transitional bilingual education programs for language-minority children. Submitted to U.S. Dept. of Education, Washington, D.C.

Randall-David, E. (1989) Strategies for working with culturally diverse communities and clients. Washington, DC: Association for Care of Children's Health.

Restrepo, M.A. (1998). Identifiers of predominantly Spanish-speaking children with language impairment. *Journal of Speech-Language-Hearing Research, 41(6),* 1398-1411.

Restrepo, M.A., & Kruth, K. (2000). Grammatical characteristics of a Spanish-English child with specific language impairment. *Communication Disorders Quarterly, 21(2),* 66-76.

Rice, M., Sell, M.A., & Hadley, P.A. (1991). Social interactions of speech- and language-impaired children. *Journal of Speech and Hearing Research, 34 (6),* 1299-1307.

Richmond, Y. (1995). *From da to yes: Understanding the East Europeans.* Yarmouth, ME: Intercultural Press, Inc.

Richmond, Y. (1996). *From nyet to da: Understanding the Russians.* Yarmouth, ME: Intercultural Press, Inc.

Riquelme, L. (1994, July). Hispanic American cultures. Paper presented at the conference for Competent Assessment and Intervention with Hispanic and Asian/Pacific Islander Populations, Maui, Hawaii.

Roberts, J.E., Medley, L.P., Swartzfager, J.L., & Neebe, E.C. (1997). Assessing the communication of African American one-year-olds using the Communication and Symbolic Behavior Scales. *American Journal of Speech-Language Pathology, 6(2),* 59-65.

Robinson, T.L., & Crowe, T.A. (1998). Culture-based considerations in programming for stuttering intervention with African American clients and their families. *American Journal of Speech-Language Pathology, 29(3),* 172-179.

Robinson-Zanartu, C. (1996). Serving Native American children and families: *Considering cultural variables.* Language, Speech, and Hearing Services in Schools, 27(4), 373-384.

Rosa-Lugo, L.I., & Fradd, S. (2000). Preparing professionals to serve English-language learners with communication disorders. *Communication Disorders Quarterly, 22(1)*, 29-42.

Roseberry, C.A., & Connell, P. J. (1991). The use of an invented language rule in the differentiation of normal and language-impaired Spanish-speaking children. *Journal of Speech and Hearing Research, 34*, 596-603.

Roseberry-McKibbin, C.A. (1993). Bilingual Classroom Communication Profile. Oceanside, CA: Academic Communication Associates.

Roseberry-McKibbin, C.A. (1994). Assessment and intervention for children with limited English proficiency and language disorders. *American Journal of Speech-Language Pathology, 3(3)*, 77-88.

Roseberry-McKibbin, C. (1995). Distinguishing language differences from language disorders in linguistically and culturally diverse students. *The Magazine of the National Association for Multicultural Education, 2(4)*, 12-16.

Roseberry-McKibbin, C. (1997a). Working with culturally and linguistically diverse clients. In K.G. Shipley (Ed.), *Interviewing and counseling in communicative disorders: Principles and procedures* (2nd ed.) (pp. 151-173). Needham Heights, MA: Allyn & Bacon.

Roseberry-McKibbin, C. (1997b). Understanding Filipino families: A foundation for effective service delivery. *American Journal of Speech-Language Pathology, 6(3)*, 5-14.

Roseberry-McKibbin, C. (2000a). Mirror, mirror on the wall: Reflections of a third culture American. *Communication Disorders Quarterly, 21(4)*, 242-245.

Roseberry-McKibbin, C. (2001a). Serving children from the culture of poverty: Practical strategies for speech-language pathologists. *The ASHA Leader, 6(20)*, 4-5, 16.

Roseberry-McKibbin, C. (2000b). Multicultural matters: The culture of poverty. *Communication Disorders Quarterly, 21(4)*, 242-245.

Roseberry-McKibbin, C. (2001b). *The source for bilingual students with language disorders*. East Moline, IL: LinguiSystems, Inc.

Roseberry-McKibbin, C. (2002). Principles and strategies in intervention. In A.E. Brice (Ed.), *The Hispanic child: Speech, language, culture and education* (pp. 199-233). Boston, MA: Allyn & Bacon.

Roseberry-McKibbin, C., & Brice, A. (1999). The perception of vocal cues of emotion by Spanish-speaking limited English proficient children. *Journal of Children's Communication Development, 20(2)*, 19-25.

Roseberry-McKibbin, C.A., & Eicholtz, G.E. (1994). Serving limited English proficient children in schools: A national survey. *Language Speech and Hearing Services in Schools, 25(3)*, 156-164.

Roseberry-McKibbin, C., & Hegde, M.N. (2000). *An advanced review of speech-language pathology: Preparation for NESPA and comprehensive examination*. Austin, TX: Pro-Ed.

Roseberry-McKibbin, C., Pena, A., Hall, M., & Smith-Stubblefield, S. (1996, November). Health care considerations in serving children from migrant Hispanic families. Paper presented at the annual convention of the American Speech-Language-Hearing Association, Seattle, WA.

Saenz, T.I. (1996). An overview of second language acquisition. In H.W. Langdon & T.I. Saenz (Eds.), *Language assessment and intervention with multicultural students: A guide for speech-language-hearing professionals (pp. 51-60)*. Oceanside, CA: Academic Communication Associates.

Samovar, L.A., & Porter, R.E. (1991). *Communication between cultures*. Belmont, CA: Wadsworth Publishing Company.

Samovar, L.A., & Porter, R.E. (1994). *Intercultural communication: A reader* (7th ed.). Belmont, CA: Wadsworth Publishing Company.

Sasson, J. (1992). *Princess*. New York: William Morrow & Co., Inc.

Schiff-Myers, N. (1992). Considering arrested language development and language loss in the assessment of second language learners. *Language, Speech, and Hearing Services in the Schools, 23*, 28-33.

Schumann, J. (1986). Research on the acculturation model for second language acquisition. *Journal of Multilingual and Multicultural Development, 7 (5)*, 379-392.

Scott, D.M. (1998). Multicultural aspects of hearing disorders and audiology. In D.E. Battle (Ed.), *Communication disorders in multicultural populations* (2nd ed.) (pp. 335-354). Newton, MA: Butterworth-Heinemann.

Selinker, L. (1972). Interlanguage. *IRAL, X/3*, 31-53.

Seymour, H.N., Bland-Stewart, L., & Green, L.J. (1998). Difference versus deficit in child African American English. *Language, Speech, and Hearing Services in Schools, 29(2)*, 96-108.

Sharifzadeh, V.S. (1998). Families with Middle Eastern roots. In E.W. Lynch & M.J. Hanson (Eds.), *Developing cross-cultural competence: A guide for working with young children and their families* (2nd ed.) (pp. 441-482). Baltimore, MD: Paul H. Brookes Publishing Company.

Sharabi, H. (1985). The dialectics of patriarchy in Arab society. In S.K. Farsoun (Ed.), *Arab society: Continuity and change* (pp. 83-104). Australia: Croom Helm, Ltd.

Shekar, C., & Hegde, M.N. (1995). India: Its people, culture, and languages. In L.L. Cheng (Ed.), *Integrating language and learning for inclusion: An Asian-Pacific focus* (pp. 125-148). San Diego: Singular Publishing Group, Inc.

Silliman, E.R., & Diehl, S.F. (2002). Assessing children with language learning disabilities. In D.K. Bernstein., & E. Tiegerman-Farber (Eds.), *Language and communication disorders in children* (5th ed.) (pp. 184-255). Boston, MA: Allyn & Bacon.

Singh, S. (2001). Information available from: http://www.aapi.gov/info.aapi_factsheet.htm

Sleeter, C. (1994). White racism. *National Association for Multicultural Education, 1(4)*, 5-8.

Smith, T.T., Lee, E., & McDade, H.L. (2001). An investigation of T-units in African-American English-speaking and Standard American English-speaking fourth-grade children. *Communication Disorders Quarterly, 22(3)*, 148-157.

Sperling, V. (1999). *Organizing women in contemporary Russia: Engendering transition.* New York: Cambridge University Press.

Steckol, K.F., & Cunningham, D.R. (1993). Practitioners speak out. *Asha, 35 (4)*, 40-41.

Steinberg, L. (1996). *Beyond the classroom.* Cited in Johnston, 2001.

Stewart, J.L. (1986). Hearing disorders among the indigenous peoples of North American and the Pacific Basin. In O. Taylor (Ed.), *Nature of communication disorders in culturally and linguistically diverse populations.* San Diego: College-Hill Press.

Stewart, J.L. (1992). Native American populations. *Asha, 34 (5)*, 40-42.

Stockman, I.J. (1996). The promises and pitfalls of language sample analysis as an assessment tool for linguistic minority children. *Language, Speech, and Hearing Services in Schools, 27(4)*, 355-366.

Stockman, I.J. (2000). The new Peabody Picture Vocabulary Test-III: An illusion of unbiased assessment? *Language, Speech, and Hearing Services in Schools, 31(4)*, 340-253.

Swain, M. (1985). Communicative competence: Some roles of comprehensible input and conprehensible output in its development. In S. Gass, & C. Madden (Eds.), *Input in second language acquisition.* Boston: Newbury House.

Swisher, K., & Deyhle, D. (1989). The styles of learning are different, but the teaching is just the same: Suggestions for teachers of American Indian youth. *Journal of American Indian Education, special issue (8/89)*, 1-14.

Tabors, P. O. (1997). *One child, two languages.* Baltimore: MD: Paul H. Brookes Publishing Co.

Tafoya, T. (1989). Coyote's eyes: Native cognition styles. *Journal of American Indian Education, special issue (8/89)*, 29-42.

Terrell, B., & Hale, J. (1992). Serving a multicultural population: different learning styles. *American Journal of Speech-Language Pathology, 1 (2)*, 5-8.

Terrell, S.L., & Jackson, R.S. (2002). African Americans in the Americas. In D.E. Battle (Ed.), *Communication disorders in multicultural populations* (3rd ed.) (pp. 33-70). Woburn, MA: Butterworth-Heinemann.

Terrell, S.L., & Terrell, F. (1996). The importance of psychological and sociocultural factors for providing clinical services to African American children. In A.G. Kamhi, S.E. Pollock, & J.L. Harris (Eds.), *Communication development and disorders in African American children* (pp. 55-72). Baltimore: Paul H. Brookes Publishing Co.

Terrell, S.L., Arensburg, K., & Rosa, R. (1992). Parent-child comparative analysis: A criterion-referenced method for the nondiscriminatory assessment of a child who spoke a relatively uncommon dialect of English. *Language, Speech, and Hearing Services in the Schools, 23 (1)*, 34-42.

Thal, D., Jackson-Maldonado, D., & Acosta, D. (2000). Validity of a parent-report measure of vocabulary and grammar for Spanish-speaking toddlers. *Journal of Speech-Language-Hearing Research, 43(5)*, 1087-1100.

Thomas, W.P., & Collier, V.P. (1998). Two languages are better than one. *Educational Leadership, 12/97-1/98*, 23-26.

Tiegerman-Farber, E. (2002). Interactive teaming: The changing role of the speech-language pathologist. In D.K. Bernstein., & E. Tiegerman-Farber (Ed.), *Language and communication disorders in children* (5th ed.) (pp. 96-125). Boston, MA: Allyn & Bacon.

Tomchak, A.M., & Bain, B.A. (1994, November). Establishing and validating local PPVT-R norms for Native Americans. Poster session presented at the annual meeting of the American Speech-Language-Hearing Association, New Orleans, LA.

Tonemah, S., & Roanhorse Benally, E. (1984). *Trends in American Indian education: A synthesis and bibliography of selected ERIC resources.* Washington, D.C.: The National Institute of Education, U.S. Department of Education.

Uffen, E. (1998). Where the jobs are: Keeping an eye on the future. *Asha, 40(1)*, 24-28.

Ullah, S. (1993). Cultural diversity: Influences and impacts on work environments. Presentation at National Association for Multicultural Education, Los Angeles, CA.

U.S. Bureau of the Census (1986). *Statistical abstract of the United States, 1987* (107th ed.). Washington, D.C.: U.S. Government Printing Office.

U.S. Bureau of the Census (1987). *Statistical abstract of the United States, 1988* (108th ed.). Washington, D.C.: U.S.

Department of Commerce.

U.S. Bureau of the Census (1990). *Statistical abstract of the United States, 1990* (110th ed.). Washington, D.C.: U.S. Department of Commerce.

U.S. Bureau of the Census (1992). *Statistical abstract of the United States, 1992* (112th ed.). Washington, D.C.: U.S. Government Printing Office.

U.S. Bureau of the Census (1999). *Statistical abstract of the United States, 1999* (119th ed.). Washington, D.C.: U.S. Department of Commerce.

U.S. Bureau of the Census (2000). *Statistical abstract of the United States, 2000* (120th ed.). Washington, D.C.: U.S. Department of Commerce.

U.S. Department of Health and Human Services (1985). Health status of minorities and low income groups *(DHHD Publication No. [HRSA] HRS-P-DV 85-1)*. Washington, D.C.: U.S. Government Printing Office.

U.S. Department of Health and Human Services (1986). Report on the Secretary's Task Force on Black and Minority Health Volume IV: Cardiovascular and Cerebrovascular Disease, Part I *[Pub. No. 1986-62038:40716]*. Washington, D.C.: Author.

U.S. Indian Health Service (1986). Chart Series Book, 1986 *[Publ. No. 1986-491-322: 40328]*. Rockville, MD: Public Health Service.

van Keulen, J.E., Weddington, G.T., & DeBose, C.E. (1998). *Speech, language, learning and the African American child.* Needham Heights, MA: Allyn & Bacon.

van Kleeck, A. (1994). Potential cultural bias in training parents as conversational partners with their children who have delays in language development. *American Journal of Speech-Language Pathology, 3(1),* 67-78.

Ventriglia, L. (1982). Conversations of Miguel and Maria. Redding, MA: Addison-Wesley.

Vining, C.B. (1999, November). Navajo perspectives on developmental disabilities. Paper presented at the annual meeting of the American Speech-Language-Hearing Association, San Francisco, CA.

Vygotsky, L.S. (1962). *Thought and language.* Cambridge, MA.: MIT Press.

Wallace, G.L. (1994, July). Asian/Pacific Islander cultures. Paper presented at the Conference on Culturally Competent Assessment and Intervention with Hispanic and Asian/Pacific Islander Populations, Maui, Hawaii.

Wallace, I.F., Roberts, J.E., & Lodder, D.E. (1998). Interactions of African American infants and their mothers: Relations with development at 1 year of age. *Journal of Speech-Language-Hearing Research, 41(4),* 900-912.

Wallach, G.P., & Madding, C.C. (2001, November). *Language-based literacy intervention: From language disorders to language differences.* Short course presented at the annual convention of the American Speech-Language-Hearing Association, New Orleans, Louisiana.

Washington, J.A. (1996). Issues in assessing the language abilities of African American children,. In A.G. Kamhi, K.E. Pollock, & J.L. Harris (Eds.), *Communication development and disorders in African American children: Research and intervention* (pp. 35-54). Baltimore, MD: Paul H. Brookes.

Washington, J.A., & Craig, H.K. (1994). Dialectal forms during discourse of poor, urban, African American preschoolers. *Journal of Speech and Hearing Research, 37(4),* 816-823.

Washington, J.A., Craig, H.K., & Kushmaul, A.J. (1998). Variable use of African American English across two language sampling contexts. *Journal of Speech-language-Hearing Research, 41(5),* 1115-1124.

Weddington, G.T., & Meyerson, M. (November, 1984). Syndrome-related speech and hearing disorders in Black children. Paper presented at the 1984 ASHA convention, San Francisco, CA.

Weiner, C. (2001). *Preparing for success: Meeting the language and learning needs of young children from poverty homes.* Youngtown, AZ: ECL Publications.

Weiss, A.L. (2002). Planning language intervention for young children. In D.K. Bernstein., & E. Tiegerman-Farber (Eds.), *Language and communication disorders in children* (5th ed.) (pp. 256-314). Boston, MA: Allyn & Bacon.

Westby, C.E. (1990). Ethnographic interviewing: Asking the right questions to the right people in the right ways. *Journal of Childhood Communication Disorders, 13 (1),* 101-111.

Westby, C.E. (1997). There's more to passing than knowing the answers. *Language, Speech, and Hearing Services in Schools, 28(3),* 274-287.

Westby, C.E., Dezale, J., Fradd, S.F., & Lee, O. (1999). Learning to do science: Influences of culture and language. *Communication Disorders Quarterly, 21(1),* 50-63.

Westby, C.E., & Rouse, G.R. (1985). Culture in education and the instruction of language-learning disabled students. *Topics in Language Disorders, 5 (4),* 15-28.

Westby, C., & Vining, C.B. (2002). Living in harmony: Providing services to Native American children and families. In D.E. Battle (Ed.), *Communication disorders in multicultural populations* (3rd ed.) (pp. 135-178). Woburn, MA: Butterworth-Heinemann.

Wetherby, A., & Prizant, B. (1993). Communication and Symbolic Behavior Scales. Chicago: Riverside Publishing.

Whitney, A.B., & Friedlander, R. (1994, November). Communication implications of Fetal Alcohol Syndrome across cultures. Paper presented at the annual meeting of the American Speech-Language-Hearing Association, New Orleans, LA.

Wigginton, E. (1992). Culture begins at home. *Educational Leadership, 49 (4)*, 60-64.

Willis, W. (1998). Families with African American roots. In E.W. Lynch and M.J. Hanson (Eds.), *Developing cross-cultural competence: A guide for working with young children and their families* (2nd ed.) (pp. 165-208). Baltimore: Paul H. Brookes Publishing Co.

Wilson, F., Wilson, J.R., & Coleman, T.J. (2000). Culturally appropriate assessment: Issues and strategies. In T.J. Coleman, *Clinical management of communication disorders in culturally diverse children* (pp. 202-238) Needham Heights, MA: Allyn & Bacon.

Wilson, L.C. (1994, November). *Language development as perceived by reservation-based Navajo families.* Paper presented at the annual meeting of the American Speech-Language-Hearing Association, New Orleans, LA.

Wolfe, P. (2001). *Brain matters: Translating research into classroom practice.* Alexandria, VA: Association for Supervision and Curriculum Development.

Wong Fillmore, L. (1976). The second time around: cognitive and social strategies in second language acquisition. Unpublished doctoral dissertation, Stanford University.

Worobee, C.D. (1991). *Peasant Russia: Family and community in the post emancipation period.* Princeton, NJ: Princeton University Press.

Wyatt, T. (1997). Developming a culturally sensitive preschool screening tool. *Asha, 39(2)*, 50-51.

Wyatt, T. (1998). Children's language development. In C.M. Seymour & E. H. Nober, *Introduction to communication disorders: A multicultural approach* (pp. 59-86). Newton, MA: Butterworth-Heinemann.

Yiqiang, W., & Wink, J. (1992). Labels hurt Asian Americans. *Bilingual Basics, Summer/Fall, 1.*

Yoshinaga-Itano, C. (1990). Language difference and language disorder in Asian language populations: Assessment and intervention. In R. Endo, V. Chattergy, S. Chou, & N. Tsuchida (Eds.), *Contemporary perspectives on Asian and Pacific American education* (pp. 11-26). South El Monte, CA: Pacific Asia Press.

Zelensky, E.K. (1999). Popular children's culture in post-perestroika Russia: Songs of innocence and experience revisited. In A.M. Barker (Ed.), *Consuming Russia (pp. 138-160).* London: Duke University Press.

Zuniga, M.E. (1998). Families with Latino roots. In E.W. Lynch & M.J. Hanson (Eds.), *Developing cross-cultural competence: A guide to working with young children and their families* (2nd ed.) (pp. 209-250). Baltimore: Paul H. Brookes Publishing Co.

INDEX